Eagles

BY THE

Numbers

JERSEY NUMBERS AND
THE PLAYERS WHO WORE THEM

John Maxymuk

Camino Books, Inc.
Philadelphia

Manufactured in the United States of America

1 2 3 4 5 08 07 06

Library of Congress Cataloging-in-Publication Data

Maxymuk, John.
 Eagles by the numbers : jersey numbers and the players who wore them / by John Maxymuk.
  p. cm.
 Includes bibliographical references.
 ISBN 0-940159-95-3 (alk. paper)
 1. Philadelphia Eagles (Football team)—History. I. Title.

 GV956.P44M39 2005
 796.332'64'0974811—dc22   2005022919

Cover and interior design: Jan Greenberg
Photo credits: all photos courtesy of Urban Archives, Temple University, Philadelphia,
Pennsylvania.

This book is available at a special discount on bulk purchases for promotional, business, and
educational use.

Publisher
Camino Books, Inc.
P.O. Box 59026
Philadelphia, PA 19102

www.caminobooks.com

This book is for my wife Suzanne, who encouraged me to write it; my daughter Katie, who keeps it all in perspective, and my daughter Juliane, who is the biggest fan in the house.

Contents

Preface

When my older daughter was learning to love football in the early 1990s, she liked Emmitt Smith and rooted for the Cowboys. Oh, the shame and humiliation for a South Jersey guy! Philadelphia fans have a national reputation for their passion toward their team — where had I gone wrong? It was heartbreaking to bear the scar of bad parenting that comes with raising a Dallas fan. How can you turn your back on family and friends? What is so likeable about arrogant frontrunners? And what of the honor of Timmy Brown? Fortunately, good sense eventually prevailed, and she joined the forever-suffering flock of Eagles fans. She needed to know that Philadelphia has a 70-year tradition of quirky characters like Tommy McDonald and Charley Gauer, of punishing hitters like Chuck Bednarik and Bill Bergey, of exciting performers like Steve Van Buren and Wilbert Montgomery, and even the very occasional championship. But where is the whole Eagles story told?

The idea of this book came from my desire to share the knowledge I've accumulated from four decades of reading everything on the sometimes-tarnished local heroes. There have been surprisingly few books and articles written about a team with such a long heritage and such a devoted following, and there has been no full-fledged history of the Eagles published. My starting point in this history is uniform numbers. Uniform numbers conjure vivid memories in sports. If you say "5," most sports fans would remember Joe DiMaggio; Philadelphia Eagles fans would think Donovan McNabb. If you say "12," most football fans would recall Joe Namath or Roger Staubach or Terry Bradshaw, but Eagles fans would remember Randall Cunningham. However, not all players are that memorable, so where to find the number data? The Eagles include an all-time roster with uniform numbers in their Media Guide, but some numbers are missing and a few are wrong. From press accounts and actual game programs, I was able to clear up almost all of these problems. Of the over 1,400 players who have played for Philadelphia in its 70+ years in the NFL, I was able to track down the numbers of all but two Eagles, Herald Frahm and William Holcomb, each of whom appeared in only one game in the 1930s.

The numbers provide the foundation for the book, but I have tried to build an interesting structure on that base. For each number from 1 to 99, I have written a short chapter. Each chapter features one player especially identifiable with that number and usually uses him and his career as a launching point into an essay on a broader Eagle or football topic. Eight of the chapters are decade reviews that present a snapshot of a particular Eagle decade through a range of categories: some are statistical like won-lost records, some are factual like which Hall of Famers played for the team in that period, and many are opinion-based like best and worst trade or best and worst draft of the decade. Each chapter lists all players who have worn the number and provides cross-references to other numbers worn by these players. Other items that are noted in each chapter are the first player to wear the number, the player who wore it for the longest period and players who were "just visiting" — in other words, they played the bulk of their careers elsewhere. In addition, the top section of each chapter profiles notable heroes, goats, head cases and sad stories.

The criteria used to select who represents each number varied from chapter to chapter. I did not always choose the most famous or best player to wear the number. I also have tried to maintain a mix of players from different eras. The history of each number represents a different slice of Eagles history, and this book attempts to serve as a thematic rather than a chronological approach to Philadelphia football's rich cultural legacy. Among those themes are accounts of each year the team has played in the postseason, key rivalries, and a host of idiosyncratic topics like end zone celebrations, religion on the field and shady characters. Ultimately, the selection criterion was to choose the players who best fit into the stories that I felt most needed to be examined and told.

Two examples will provide some illumination on my thought process. Quarterback Tommy Thompson wore 11 from 1945 to 1950 when he took the Eagles to three consecutive NFL championship games. However, 11 was also the number worn by 1960 championship quarterback Norm Van Brocklin. Both players needed to be covered in any Eagles history, so I made Thompson the subject of Chapter 10, the number he wore in 1941 and 1942 for the Birds. I don't know which number he actually preferred. When he arrived in Philly from Pittsburgh, he wore 10 and rookie Lou Ghecas wore 11; when Ghecas went into the service in 1942, Thompson stayed with 10 and rookie Dick Erdlitz wore 11; when Tommy returned from World War II in 1945, 10 was being worn by Allie Sherman, so Thompson switched to 11 for the prime years of his career.

The Antone Davis choice is a bit more complicated. Davis is the subject for 77, although he only wore that number for the first game of his career. After Matt Darwin was cut that week in 1991, Antone switched back to his college number 78 for the rest of his career. Originally, I had penciled in Ray Mansfield and the Steeler rivalry for 77 and had Kevin Allen and the All-Time Draft Bust Team at 72. However, Allen is best summed up in a depressing sentence or two rather than a whole chapter, while local hero Jess Richardson is a more interesting subject for 72. Likewise, Mansfield's connection to Philadelphia was short and not terribly fascinating, while Antone Davis was perfect to drag the Draft Bust mantle from his wide backside. Choosing which players to profile to tell the Eagles story was a constantly shifting balancing act and some worthy individuals were left with brief mentions under the "Highs" category at the top of the chapter. The one missing Eagle who most deserved his own chapter was the always colorful Bucko Kilroy, but he is featured prominently in the text of both 52 and 76.

I think my extensive study of the team has permitted me to make a number of interesting connections and observations. My emphasis in this book has been on thoroughness and accuracy, while I have tried to flavor the narrative with irreverent, intelligent opinions and a sense of humor. I hope that readers find this book fun to read or dip into and a unique resource for research.

How to Use This Book

The text is designed to be approached by uniform numbers; however, if you want to see all the numbers an Eagle wore, the All-Time Roster in the back of the book provides an access point by players' names. In the text *see* references to chapters are provided when appropriate. For those Eagles who are described only in the brief data section at the top of chapters, *see top* references are given. Regarding the player listings both in the chapters and in the All-Time Roster, listings in boldface are Hall of Famers; listings in italics for post-1950 players are men who were selected for the Pro Bowl; listings in italics for pre-1950 players are men who received All-Pro notice; listings with an "r" after the year are for replacement players who took part in the three non-union league games during the 1987 midseason players' strike.

Acknowledgments

I would like to thank several people who have helped me with my research. Chad Reese of the Pro Football Hall of Fame; George Rugg, the Curator of Special Collections at the University of Notre Dame's Hesburgh Library and the staff at Temple University's Urban Archives all helped me gain access to rare, old and essential resources. My colleagues at the Robeson Library of Rutgers University where I work are always supportive and, in particular, InterLibrary Loan ace Mary Anne Nesbit helped me borrow a wealth of material.

Introduction

Preflight Professional Football in Philadelphia

Professional football in Philadelphia predates the Eagles by decades, but it was nothing that today's Eagles fans would recognize. Pro football in the first two decades of the 20th century is roughly analogous to baseball in the middle of the 19th century. Teams generally were sponsored by local athletic clubs that operated independently of each other. The game itself was steadily evolving with equipment, rules and scoring in a state of flux. Unlike baseball, which first took hold in the major cities in the East, football established its strongest roots in smaller towns in Pennsylvania, Ohio and the Midwest. There were some stirrings in Philadelphia, too. The first all-professional team formed as the Philadelphia Football Club in 1901. The team was made up primarily of former Penn players and was called the Stars, All-Stars, Quakers, Phillies and Pros in the papers. They played a short schedule against local athletic clubs and colleges in their first season. The following year the team was sponsored by the Philadelphia Phillies, and in a weak attempt to establish a local league, Connie Mack's Athletics sponsored a football club as well. This attempt at a league failed after one year. Over the next two decades, independent athletic association teams in Frankford, Phoenixville, Holmesburg and Conshohocken all claimed various local championships.

The strongest of these clubs was the Frankford Athletic Association. In 1899, when Frankford was a Philadelphia suburb, the organization was formed and established baseball and soccer teams as well as a football eleven. When that club faded, some of its members formed the Loyola Athletic Club in 1909 and changed the name to the Frankford Athletic Association in 1912. All profits were directed to local charities, including the Frankford Hospital, the Boy Scouts and the American Legion. Most of the players were former stars from the local colleges, and by the early 1920s, Frankford was a top independent team that sometimes took on teams from the NFL and beat them. Frankford's record in 1922 was 13-0-1, and they celebrated their success that year by erecting their own 12,000-seat stadium for $100,000. Frankford Stadium was financed wholly by the club and included a scoreboard, a press box and a grandstand. The Frankford Yellow Jackets christened it with a 9-2-2 season in 1923, and then joined the NFL in 1924.

The main obstacle to success the team faced was the existence of Pennsylvania's Blue Laws, which did not permit games to be played on Sundays. For one thing, that meant competing with the ever-popular college football on Saturday. For another, it put the team out of sync with the rest of the league. The Yellow Jackets worked around this with a couple of different approaches. One was to team with nearby Pottsville in scheduling so that an opponent could play in Frankford on Saturday and then travel to the coal regions to play the Pottsville Maroons on Sunday. Blue Laws generally were ignored in the coal regions where the miners were looking for an outlet on their only day off. A second approach was to play a home-and-away weekend series with an opponent — a Saturday game in Frankford followed the next day by a game in Buffalo or Providence or Canton. Because of this, the Yellow Jackets played more games than the rest of the league; Frankford averaged 16 games a year from 1924 to 1931, while other NFL teams were playing from 10 to 14 games per year. The Yellow Jackets set a league record by playing 20 games in 1925 — and this does not include the non-league exhibitions the team scheduled during the season to make more money. Despite bearing the heaviest workload of any NFL team in the period, Frankford's cumulative record was 69-45-14, an impressive .605 winning percentage.

In their first year in the league, Frankford finished third with an 11-2-1 record and outscored their opponents 326 to 109. They were the first East Coast team to succeed in the NFL, and paved the way for the Giants the following year. In 1925, Frankford signed a proven champion, Guy Chamberlin, as player coach. The 31-year-old Chamberlin had been a two-time All-American at Nebraska as an end and served in World War I before joining Jim Thorpe's Canton Bulldogs in 1919. The next year, Guy joined George Halas' Decatur Staleys in the new American Professional Football Association that later would become the NFL. Chamberlin played on the league's first champion team in 1921, and Halas later called the Hall of Famer the "greatest two-way end in the history of the game." Guy was named player coach of the Canton Bulldogs in 1922, and Canton won the next two NFL titles, moved to Cleveland in 1924 and won the championship again. So Frankford was getting a player who had played on the last four NFL champion teams and had coached the last three. The won-lost record of Chamberlin's teams in his five years in the league was 47-3-7.

With Guy at the helm, the Yellow Jackets got off to a 9-1 start in 1925, but faded badly after injuries to Chamberlin and others to finish 13-7. Guy suspended star lineman Bull Behman for "indifferent play" after a 49-0 loss to Pottsville late in the year, and Frankford got itself involved in the Pottsville title controversy that still reverberates today. Early in the season, a team of Notre Dame All-Stars agreed to play an exhibition game against the best team in Pennsylvania, and both Frankford and Pottsville expressed strong interest in this moneymaker. The week after crushing the Yellow Jackets, the Maroons beat the second-place Cardinals in Chicago and claimed the NFL title even though the season was not over. They agreed to the Notre Dame exhibition the following week in Philadelphia, but football commissioner Joe Carr warned Pottsville that they could not play an exhibition in another team's territory. The league would not guarantee the lost revenue, so Pottsville played and beat the Fighting Irish All-Stars. Frankford filed a protest, and Carr suspended Pottsville. The season continued, and the Cardinals won two more games to give them a higher winning percentage

While Bert Bell was quarterbacking the Penn Quakers to the 1917 Rose Bowl, the Frankford Yellow Jackets were gaining stature as a local independent team. When Bell founded the Eagles' NFL franchise in 1933, he assumed the debts of the defunct team.

than Pottsville — although since the Maroons were suspended from the league, they could not be declared champions no matter what happened. Pottsville players and management and their descendants have continued to lodge periodic protests about this ruling over the years, with the most recent coming in 2003, but do not have the facts on their side.

The Pottsville suspension was short-lived, however. With Red Grange forming his own American Football League in 1926, the NFL welcomed the Maroons back to keep a strong team from jumping to the new AFL. Yellow Jacket star Bull Behman did jump crosstown, though. Leo Conway, who had run the Phoenixville Union Athletic Association's strong independent team in the early 1920s, formed the Philadelphia Quakers that turned out to be the class of the AFL and won the league title. Philadelphia was doubly blessed that year because Frankford won the NFL championship with a 14-

1-1 record. It was the most wins any NFL club would record until the 49ers won 15 games 58 years later in 1984.

There were two key games that clinched the title for the Yellow Jackets. On December 4, the undefeated Bears came to town and took a 6-0 lead with five minutes to play on a 62-yard run by Bill Senn, but Guy Chamberlin blocked the extra point. Frankford countered with a 50-yard run by Tex Hamer and then a fourth and three 27-yard touchdown pass from Houston Stockton to Two Bits Homan in the last two minutes. Hamer booted the extra point for the winning margin. Stockton displayed a family knack for clutch play that would show itself 60 years later in his grandson, basketball great John Stockton. Homan was the 5-foot 5-inch, 145-pound sparkplug of the team known for his unique style of catching punts on the run. That put Frankford ahead of the Bears, but Pottsville still had a chance at the title if they could knock off the Yellow Jackets in the season finale. Two weeks later the two squared off on a bitterly cold day in Frankford and played to a 0-0 tie that clinched the championship for Frankford. The Yellow Jackets' only loss of the year had been in October to the Providence Steamroller, and Chamberlin had his fifth title in six years. For this, each player received a gold watch from the Association. The AFL champion Philadelphia Quakers challenged the NFL leaders to an exhibition, but were rebuffed. The seventh-place Giants agreed to a match, though, and crushed the Quakers 31-0. Both the AFL and the Quakers disbanded.

Chamberlin left for the Cardinals the next season, and the Yellow Jackets dropped to a 6-9-3 record under new coach Charley Moran. Another Nebraska All-American, Ed Weir, took over in 1928, and the team improved to a second-place 11-3-2 record with the year's highlight being a 98-yard kickoff return by Fait Elkins against the Cardinals that set an NFL record for the longest play. Fire damaged Frankford Stadium in 1929, but repairs were made, and the team had a successful third-place 9-4-5 finish under new coach Bull Behman, who had returned to the team as a player in 1927. With the onset of the Depression in 1930, though, the team tried to save costs by bringing in a mostly rookie team, but finished ninth with a 4-13-1 record. 1931 was the end of the road for Frankford. In the summer, the stadium burned down, forcing the team to hop from one field to another in Philadelphia. The team on the field was bad, going 1-6-1, while the club was in financial ruins and disbanded before the end of the year. The Frankford Yellow Jackets were forfeited to the league in 1932, but former Frankford player Lud Wray and his Penn teammate Bert Bell brought professional football back to Philadelphia in 1933 by assuming Frankford's debts and paying the $2,500 new franchise fee. The Frankford Yellow Jackets did not become the Philadelphia Eagles, but they laid the foundation for professional football in the City of Brotherly Love. The Eagles have built a long and dynamic tradition upon that foundation.

1

The Kicking Game

Tony Franklin
K 1979-83

WHO'S WORN THE NUMBER:

Happy Feller (K) 1971, Nick Mike-Mayer (K) 1977-78, Tony Franklin (K) 1979-83, Gary Anderson (K) 1995-96.

Originator: Kicker James "Happy" Feller in 1971.

Longest Tenure: Five years, Tony Franklin.

Number Changes: None.

Just Visiting: None.

Highs: Gary Anderson has scored more points than any player in NFL history.

Lows: Happy Feller's tenure in Philadelphia was not very happy — he made only six of 20 field goal attempts in 1970. The former Texas All-American did little better in parts of two seasons in New Orleans, hitting only 10 of 23 field goals before he was gone from the league.

Tony Franklin

In the old days, kicking was an extra duty handled by one of the regular players. Most were not particularly reliable, but they could make up for a bad kick with a good run, catch pass, tackle, block or interception. They were multi-talented football players, not specialists. The first kicking specialist in the NFL was Ken Strong for the 1944 Giants, but the practice did not catch on fully until the 1960s. And with the advent of the kicking specialist came the stereotype of the kicker as oddball outsider. After all, if a kicker misses a kick, how can he make up for it? More practice kicks into the net on the sideline? Talk it over on the bench with his friend the punter? Strange behavior is a natural reaction to such a tense situation. If that's generally the case for kickers, then how odd should we expect a barefooted kicker to be?

Barefooted Tony Franklin first began to gain notice as a kicker for Arlington Heights High School in Fort Worth, Texas, in 1974 when he set a Fort Worth schoolboy record with a 51-yard field goal during the regular season. In the city championship that year, his record was broken by rival kicker Uwe von Schamann, who booted a 53-yarder in the first quarter. Franklin got in the last word, though, with the 58-yard game winner in the fourth quarter. Von Schamann went on to star at the University of Oklahoma and for the Miami Dolphins. Franklin went to Texas A&M where two years later he set a college record with a 64-yard field goal in the second quarter of a game against Baylor, and then broke that in the third quarter with a 65-yarder. On that same day elsewhere in Texas, though, Ove Johansson topped both with a 69-yard field goal for Abilene Christian. The Swedish Johansson would play briefly for the Eagles the following season, but would make only one of four field goals and one of three extra points before being cut.

The Eagles' kicking situation was dire in Dick Vermeil's first few years. In 1977 and 1978, Johansson and other pretenders made fewer than 50 percent of their field goal tries and missed 10 extra points. Philadelphia squeaked into the playoffs in 1978, but lost 14-13 to Atlanta on a botched extra point and two missed chip-shot field goals. Vermeil addressed the weakness by picking Franklin in the third round of the 1979 draft. Tony responded with a big rookie season that culminated in a *Monday Night Football* clash with Dallas on November 12th. The Eagles beat the Cowboys for the first time in 10 tries that night, winning 31-21. Franklin gave the team a big lift and deflated the Cowboys right before halftime when his 59-yard field goal boosted the Eagles' lead to 17-7. That year, Franklin was successful on 74 percent of his field goal attempts and scored 105 points, both high points of his five-year tenure in Philadelphia.

In the playoffs that year, though, Tony incurred Vermeil's wrath when he ignored the coach's orders to kick the ball deep with the Eagles trailing Tampa 24-17 with three minutes to play, and instead tried an unsuccessful onside kick. Vermeil commented after the game, "I jumped his butt but good…That really showed a lack of discipline on his part. It showed his immaturity, really. Tony's a great talent, but he's going to have to grow up." Franklin also had troubles with his teammates. The week before the playoff game, one of the members of the kickoff team got into a shouting match with Franklin on the field after Tony directed his kickoff to the wrong side of the field. He was a loner with a big head and had few friends on the team. His status was not helped by his lackadaisical work habits, either.

Franklin made only 16 of 31 field goals in his second season and missed six straight field goals in consecutive losses to San Diego and Atlanta by a total of four points, but the Eagles made it to the Super Bowl. During Super Bowl week, Vermeil continued to be unhappy with his kicker, saying that "I don't talk too much about kickers. They are very difficult to coach." When reporters relayed these comments to Franklin, he responded, "He says what he wants. I just go out and kick the football." In the off-season, the Eagles actively shopped Franklin to the Colts, but could not work out a deal. Tony improved a bit in his third and fourth years, but then declined again in 1983, and that would be his last season in Philadelphia. The Eagles traded him to New England for a sixth-round pick in 1984. The trade was good for both sides. Philadelphia drafted barefooted lefty Paul McFadden in the 12th round, and he was successful on more than 80 percent of his field goal attempts in his first two years while being named the Eagles' special teams MVP both years. Franklin never received that honor in Philadelphia, but he did the best kicking of his life over the next three years for the Patriots, making over 78 percent of his field goals and scoring 108, 112 and 140 points. And he played in another Super Bowl — again in a losing cause in 1985.

Tony Franklin had a very strong but inconsistent leg and scored 412 points in five seasons in Philadelphia. His 62.5 percent success rate on field goals does not sound like much today, but at the time it was on par with the league norms. The success rate for both the Eagles and the league has steadily increased over time:

EAGLES FIELD GOAL ACCURACY BY DECADE		
1930s	Incomplete data	
1940s	52/137	38%
1950s	73/170	43%
1960s	132/237	56%
1970s	162/280	58%
1980s	193/294	66%
1990s	211/292	72%
2000s	109/127	86%

Eagles kickers have included the likes of center Hank Reese (who led the team in scoring in 1936 with nine points), guard Cliff Patton, end Bobby Walston, Sam Baker, Happy Feller, Mark Moseley, Tom Dempsey, Horst Muhlmann, Nick Mike-Mayer, Steve Michel, Luis Zendejas, Roger Ruzek, Eddie Murray, Chris Boniol, Gary Anderson, Norm Johnson and the incomparable David Akers.

The steady improvement in efficiency owes itself to several factors: changes in the shape of the ball in the early years, the move to kicking specialists in the 1960s as the roster size expanded, the introduction of soccer-style kicking in the late 1960s, and the increase in special teams coaching in the 1970s and beyond. The life of a kicking specialist is pressure-packed. In their one small job, they are expected to be perfect from the start and then get better; they can't offset a bad kick by excelling in some other phase of offense or defense. That pressure has to contribute to the general flakiness of kickers — that and their often futile efforts to fit in and be respected by regular players. Barefooted Tony Franklin was a case in point.

1930s Decade in Review

Joe Pilconis
E 1934, 1936-37

Joe Pilconis

By a wide margin, the Eagles' .257 winning percentage for the 1930s is the worst record for any decade in team history. The only NFL team with a worse winning percentage for a decade since then has been the expansion Atlanta Falcons when they won at a .223 clip in the last four years of the 1960s. However, one area of strength for the Eagles of the 1930s was the end position where Joe Pilconis was a sometime starter in his three years on the club. Pilconis played football and basketball in addition to being a champion boxer in his four years at Temple, a Philadelphia college that sent 13 players to the Eagles during the decade. As a senior, Pilconis was chosen as the Owls' most valuable lineman.

When he signed with the Birds, though, Pilconis found he was competing at end with former Pottsville Maroon All-Pro George Kennealy and future All-Pro Joe Carter. Carter would lead the NFL in receptions in 1934 and in yards per catch in 1935. Kennealy was replaced in 1935 by All-Pro Ed "Eggs" Manske, who in turn was traded to the Bears in 1937 for Hall of Fame end Bill Hewitt. Pilconis made only 11 receptions in his career and scored two touchdowns. His first touchdown came on an 18-yard pass from fellow Temple alumnus Dave Smukler in a 21-17 loss to the Giants in 1936 that was highlighted by the Eagles physically attacking field judge George Vergara after the game due to a crucial pass interference call that went against the Birds. Joe's second touchdown came on defense when he returned a fumble 22 yards for a score in another loss, 16-7 to Pittsburgh.

Pilconis played with the minor league Patterson (New Jersey) Panthers in 1938 and 1939 before moving on to become a successful high school football coach in Pennsylvania. He was inducted into the Pennsylvania Scholastic Football Coaches Association Hall of Fame in 1988, five years before his death. His last connection to the Eagles was Eagle Alumni Day in training camp on August 8, 1987; he was the oldest former Bird to attend that day. His experience with the fledgling, struggling franchise had to have been frustrating and could be said to be emblematic of the Eagles of the 1930s.

Decade Headline: Learning to Fly.

Where They Played: Baker Bowl, 1933-35; Temple Stadium, 1934-35; Municipal Stadium, 1936-39.

How the Game Was Played: The Single Wing Formation was used by every pro team except the Bears, who generally ran the Tight T Formation. The pro game was noted for more running than passing and more defense than offense. Passing rules were liberalized in 1933 to allow for passing from anywhere behind the line of scrimmage rather than from at least five yards back. On the social justice front, there were no black players on any NFL roster after 1933 by unwritten agreement.

Decade Won-Lost Record: 18-55-3, .257.

Record Against the Giants: 3-11.

Record Against the Redskins: 2-9.

Record Against the Steelers: 6-7.

Playoff Appearances: None.

Championships: None.

Unsung Hero: Bert Bell deserves the bulk of the credit he receives for founding the team in 1933, but he did not do it alone. His old Penn teammate, Lud Wray, was his partner and played a significant role in getting the team established before selling out to Bell in 1936.

Head Coaches: Lud Wray, 1933-35, 9-21-1; Bert Bell, 1936-40, 9-34-2 for the decade.

Best Player: Hall of Famer Bill Hewitt.

Hall of Famers: Bert Bell; Bill Hewitt.

Eagle Honor Roll: Bert Bell; Bill Hewitt.

League Leaders: Davey O'Brien — passing yards, 1939; Joe Carter — yards per catch, 1935.

Award Winners: None.

All-Pros: Swede Hanson, 1933-34; Joe Carter, 1935-36, 1938; Ed Manske, 1935; Bill Hewitt 1937-38; Davey O'Brien, 1939.

All-Star Game Selections: Joe Carter, 1938-39; Davey O'Brien, 1939.

Best Offensive Backfield: 1934 with backs Swede Hanson, Swede Ellstrom, Jim Leonard and Ed Matesic.

Best Draft Choice: Star passer Davey O'Brien, 1939, first round.

Best Overall Draft: 1939. In addition to O'Brien, several other players made the team.

Worst Draft Choice: Jay Berwanger, 1936, first round. The NFL's first-ever draft pick declined the invitation to play pro football.

Worst Overall Draft: 1936. None of the nine picks ever played in the NFL.

Best Free Agent: Dynamite Dave Smukler passed up his senior year at Temple to sign with the Eagles in 1936.

Best Trade: Hall of Famer Bill Hewitt was obtained from the Bears along with Ted Rosequist, Red Pollock and Ookie Miler for Ed Manske, the Eagles' first 1937 draft pick (Sam Francis) and some cash in a series of related deals.

Worst Trade: None of the Eagles' handful of trades in this decade could be said to have worked out badly.

Biggest Off-Field Event: First, the Blue Laws were repealed in Pennsylvania in 1933 and that was instrumental to the Eagles' success, allowing them to play on Sundays when they could draw larger crowds. Second, Bert Bell's idea of an annual collegiate draft helped to level the playing field for NFL teams.

Biggest On-Field Development: The development of a crowd-pleasing passing attack with tailback Davey O'Brien.

Strangest On-Field Event: Bert Bell postponed the opening game in 1939 due to "threatening weather" on a day when the Philadelphia Athletics played a baseball doubleheader at Shibe Park. Most likely, Bell was hesitant to compete with baseball and so rescheduled the game for Thanksgiving.

Worst Failure: The Eagles not only failed to sign the first person ever selected in the NFL draft, but also failed to sign any of their picks that year (1936).

Home Attendance: 492,483 in 36 games for an average gate of 13,680.

Best Game: The postponed 1939 opener against the Steelers that was played on Thanksgiving that year was a 17-14 game that was won in the last minute on a 66-yard touchdown pass to Bill Hewitt.

First Game: October 16, 1933. The Eagles were crushed 56-0 by the New York Giants at the Polo Grounds in their inaugural contest.

Last Game: December 3, 1939. The Eagles lost to the Cleveland Rams 35-13 in a game played in Colorado Springs, Colorado.

Largest Margin of Victory: November 6, 1934. The Eagles stomped the Cincinnati Reds 64-0 with both Swede Hanson and Joe Carter scoring three touchdowns. It was the Reds' last game ever; they were absorbed by the semi-pro St. Louis Gunners, who then replaced them in the NFL for the rest of the season.

Largest Margin of Defeat: 56-0 to the Giants in the Eagles' first game ever in 1933.

Best Offense: In 1938, the Eagles scored 154 points, fourth in the league, en route to their best finish for the sorry decade, five wins and six losses.

Best Defense: In 1934, the Eagles gave up only 85 points, the third best figure in the league, and recorded four shutouts.

Most Games Played: 72, Joe Carter.

Most Points: 133, Joe Carter.

Most Field Goals: 6, Hank Reese.

Most Touchdowns: 22, Joe Carter.

Most Touchdown Passes: 15, Dave Smukler.

Most Passing Yards: 1,357, Dave Smukler.

Most Receiving Yards: 1,609, Joe Carter.

Most Receptions: 102, Joe Carter.

Most Rushing Yards: 1,907, Swede Hanson.

Most Interceptions: NA

Most Sacks: NA

Most Kickoff Return Yards: NA

Most Punt Return Yards: NA

Book Notes: The most detail to be found on the Eagles of the 1930s is in Donald P. Campbell's *Sunday's Warriors.* Campbell provides a brief write-up on every game played by Philadelphia from 1933 to 1993.

Noted Sportswriter: Stan Baumgartner covered the team for the *Philadelphia Inquirer.*

Best Quotation: After the Eagles recorded their first win in their fourth game in 1933, Bert Bell remarked, "Well, I'm glad they finally won a game."

Bubblegum Factoids: On the back of Jim Zyntell's 1935 National Chicle card, Jim is said to be "an example of a fast footed guard, quick to pull out of the line to head the interference." On the back of fellow guard Jim MacMurdo's 1935 National Chicle card, it identifies him as "a giant in size, weighing 210 and standing 6 feet 2."

Accidents of Birth: Max Padlow was born in Russia; Carl Jorgensen was born in Denmark.

Famous Names: Glenn Campbell, not the musician; Jack Dempsey, not the boxer; Glen Frey, not the musician.

Unusual Names: Rankin Britt, Paul Cuba, Bree Cuppoletti, Henry Obst, Lafayette Russell, Dave Smukler and Guy Turnbow.

Nicknames: Herman "Reds" Bassman, "Buckin'" Joe Bukant, "Tom Tom" Bushby, Glenn "Turtle" or "Flash" Campbell, John "King" Cole, Elwood "Rowdy" or "Cub" Dow, Marv "Swede" Ellstrom, John "Fritz" Ferko, Glenn "Wackie" Frey, Thomas "Swede" Hanson, Maurice "Moose" Harper, Bill "Stinky" Hewitt, William "Tex" Holcomb, William "Boss" Hughes, Carl "Bud" Jorgenson, Allen "Rabbit" Keen, George "Gigi" or "Gus" Kenneally, Roger "Red" Kirkman, Joe "Mink" Kresky, Emmet "Sally" Kriel, Charles "Tex" Leyendecker, John "Bull" Lipski, Ed "Eggs" Manske, Ed "Lefty" Matesic, Forrest "Aimee" McPherson, Davey "Slingshot" O'Brien, Edwin "Alabama" Pitts, Joe "Butch" Pivarnick, George "Mousie" Rado, Leo "Fat" Raskowski, John "The Ripper" Roberts, Herbert "Bummie" Roton, Everitt "Deb" Rowan, James "Casey" Russell, Lafayette "Reb" Russell, Mike "The Sharon Express" Sebastian, "Dynamite" Dave Smukler, Ray "Brush" Spillers, Herschel "Mule" Stockton, Clarence "Stumpy" Thomason, Albert "Reds" Weiner, Clyde "Weenie" Williams, Osborne "Diddie" Willson, and James "Iggy" Zyntell.

Fastest Player: An educated guess might be Swede Hanson.

Heaviest Player: Tackle Ray Keeling weighed around 270 pounds in 1938.

Lightest Player: Davey O'Brien was 5 feet 7 inches and 151 pounds, the smallest Eagle ever.

Local Boys: Bill Fielder, Carl Kane, Jim Leonard and Fran Murray all hailed from Philadelphia. From the surrounding area came Jack Dempsey, Rick Lackman, Roy Lechthaler, Pete Stevens and Izzy Weinstock. Among local colleges: Penn — Bill Fielder, Walt Masters, Fran Murray, Stan Sokulis and Osborne Willson; Temple — Chuck Brodnicki, Glenn Frey, Swede Hanson, Tom Graham, Len Gudd, John Konopka, Alex Marcus, John Lipski, Joe Pilconis, James Russell, Hank Reese, Pete Stevens and Dave Smukler; Villanova — Bernie Lee and Vince Zizak; St. Joseph's – John Cole; Ursinus — Herman Bassman; West Chester — John Ferko; and Muhlenberg — Albert Weiner.

Firsts:

Points — on a 35-yard touchdown pass from Roger Kirkman to Swede Hanson on October 29, 1933 against Green Bay.

Safety — By George Kenneally in the same game.

Field Goal — 20 yards by Guy Turnbow in a 3-3 tie with the Bears on November 12, 1933.

Win — November 5, 1933: 6-0 over the Cincinnati Reds in Cincinnati.

.500 All-Time Won-Lost Record — Seventh game in 1933, November 26, 3-3-1. The franchise has not returned to this high point in 72 years.

Shutout — 17-0 over the Pirates in Pittsburgh on September 26, 1934.

Draft Pick — Jay Berwanger in 1936.

100-Yard Rushing Game — Swede Hanson gained 116 yards on 13 carries against Green Bay on October 16, 1934.

100-Yard Receiving Game — Joe Carter.

Kickoff Return for TD — Dave Smukler, 101 yards, versus Brooklyn on November 13, 1938.

First Team All-Pro — Bill Hewitt 1938.

Legal Sunday Athletic Contest in Philadelphia — November 12, 1933. The Eagles wore blue jerseys and tied the Bears in their second home game.

Use of Television — The Eagles demonstrated some of their plays to an audience inside the Franklin Institute in September 1934.

Televised NFL Game — The Eagles lost to Brooklyn on television on October 22, 1939.

Stinkin' Cowboys

Jack Concannon
QB 1964-66

WHO'S WORN THE NUMBER:

Roger Kirkman (B) 1934-35, Jack Concannon (QB) 1964-66, Mark Moseley (K) 1970, Eddie Murray (K) 1994.

Originator: Roger Kirkman in 1934.

Longest Tenure: Three years, Jack Concannon.

Number Changes: Roger Kirkman wore 19 in 1933.

Just Visiting: Mark Moseley and Eddie Murray scored a lot of points for the Redskins and Lions respectively, but passed quickly through Philadelphia.

Highs: None.

Lows: Quarterback Roger Kirkman completed 30 percent of his passes for a lifetime 18.9 passer rating and averaged two yards per carry on the ground.

Jack Concannon

The Eagles surprisingly outbid the Boston Patriots for the services of boy-wonder quarterback Jack Concannon, who grew up in Boston and starred as Boston College's pre-Doug Flutie running quarterback. Concannon did not have a particularly powerful or accurate arm, but knew how to win. With Philadelphia, however, Concannon fell into a three-quarterback competition with Norm Snead and King Hill that he would not win. In three years, he would attempt only 103 passes, completing less than half of them for four touchdowns and eight interceptions.

Jack's one real moment of glory as an Eagle came on December 6, 1964 when he got his first NFL start in the final home game of the year against the Cowboys. Coach Joe Kuharich decided that the rookie's scrambling ability would work well against the Cowboy blitz schemes, and Concannon played a major part in Philadelphia's 24-14 victory over Dallas. He gained 99 yards on eight carries with his scrambles and completed 10 passes for 134 yards and two scores. The first touchdown toss was for 13 yards to Ron Goodwin after Jack scrambled all the way across the field; the winning TD pass went to Pete Retzlaff for 31 yards with seven minutes to go in the final period. Thanks to Kuharich's logic, Concannon would not start again until the end of the 1966 season when he led the Eagles to victories over the Steelers and Browns. The following season he was traded to the Bears for Mike Ditka and spent five mostly unsuccessful seasons in Chicago. He finished a lackluster career with two seasons as a backup in Green Bay and Detroit.

Concannon's exciting game against the Cowboys is mostly forgotten today. The blistering rivalry felt by Philadelphia — the Cowboys usually have been more fired up by the Redskins — did not truly begin for a few more years. As would be expected, the early games in the series against the expansion Cowboys were dominated by Philadelphia winning seven of nine meetings from 1960 through 1964. The teams split the series for the next three years, but on December 10, 1967 in Dallas, things changed. Philadelphia linebacker Mike Morgan broke Don Meredith's nose, knocking him out of the game, and passions heated up quickly in the 38-17 loss. Tom Woodeshick had his eye gouged, and Timmy Brown had his face crushed by a Lee Roy Jordan cheap shot. Timmy suffered a concussion, a broken jaw and lost several teeth, while Jordan received only a 15-yard penalty. Starting with the Tim Brown mugging in 1967, the Cowboys beat the Eagles 11 straight times; Philadelphia's victory drought went from October 29, 1967 to October 28, 1973. All the while, the Cowboys became more and more hateful to Eagle fans. In the 1970s, the Cowboys beat the Eagles 17 out of 20 games. Altogether, the worst stretch was from the Tim Brown game in 1967 through 1978 with the Cowboys winning 21 of 23 games, 15 of them by at least 10 points. It was a biannual humiliation for Philadelphia. During the decade, the Cowboys went to the Super Bowl five times, won twice, and were dubbed by NFL Films "America's Team." From 1966 through 1985, they went to the playoffs in 18 of 20 years. Furthermore, they were coached for 29 years by Hall of Famer Tom Landry, who had all the personality of an emotionless automaton on the sidelines. The players themselves gave off an air of arrogance and privilege that was anathema to Philly fans. They were always on TV, often got the benefit of dubious officiating, and frequently pulled games out at the last minute behind squeaky clean Roger "The Dodger" Staubach.

Meanwhile, the Eagles were going 11 years without a winning record before Dick Vermeil built a competitive team in the late 1970s. Vermeil lost to Dallas the first six times he faced Landry, but by 1979 he had a talented team that would not quit. The Cowboys still had more flashy star power with Tony Dorsett and others, but the Eagles had more heart and were a tougher team. They beat the Cowboys 31-21 in a memorable 1979 *Monday Night Football* game in Dallas and then beat them 17-10 in Philadelphia in 1980. In the NFC Championship that year, the Eagles took apart the Cowboys 20-7 in the most famous and beloved football game ever held at Veterans Stadium.

Marion Campbell succeeded Vermeil, and the 1970s began to reappear. Campbell lost to the declining Cowboys five of six times from 1983 to 1985. However, with Buddy Ryan that all changed, partly because Buddy built a hard-hitting playoff team and partly because the Cowboys sank to the bottom of the league before beginning to resurface. And not only did the Eagles win, they beat up the Cowboys. In 1987, there was a players' strike, but teams hired replacement players and played on. Some of the Cowboy stars crossed the picket line, while Ryan encouraged his team to stick together on the picket line. Buddy became incensed when Landry used his stars to run up the score against the hapless Eagle replacements. When the real players returned, the first Eagle opponent was Dallas. With the Eagles handily beating Dallas 30-20 with seconds remaining, Buddy ordered Randall Cunningham to fake a kneel-down and throw a pass into the end zone for Mike Quick that drew an interference flag. Keith Byars then scored an "in your face" touchdown that only made Buddy more popular in Philadelphia. Buddy also took an instant dislike to Landry's replacement in 1989 — arrogant Jimmy Johnson of the "pretty boy" hairdo. After the Thanksgiving game in which Cowboy kicker Luis Zendejas was laid out by Jessie Small on a kickoff, Johnson accused Ryan, with some justification, of offering a reward to his players for taking out Zendejas and Troy Aikman. The Cowboys visited Philly 17 days later in December, and they and their coach were pelted with snowballs from Philly fans, including, some say, future mayor Ed Rendell. The bottom line is that Buddy beat Dallas eight of 10 times.

After Buddy, the pendulum swung back to Dallas in the Rich Kotite years, as the Cowboys under Johnson became two-time Super Bowl champs while Kotite was running the fearsome Eagles into the ground. This group of Cowboys, led by Michael Irvin, were even more narcissistic and egotistical than those from the 1970s and generated even more hatred from Philly. The chant "Dallas Sucks" took on a life of its own with fathers teaching it to sons too young even to understand the words. Unfortunately, Richie the K could only manage to beat Dallas twice in nine tries and lost to them in the playoffs in 1992. In 1994, Johnson was replaced by loose cannon and strategic moron Barry Switzer. The following season, the Eagles replaced their own strategic moron with Ray Rhodes, who at least understood how to beat the Cowboys. Rhodes'

Eagles played Dallas tough and eked out season splits with them for three straight years before everything fell apart for him in his fourth year. Two games were especially memorable. The first one was the December 1995 game at the Vet when the Cowboys were given two fourth-and-one opportunities due to an officiating miscue, and Switzer called the same running play twice. Both times the Eagles stuffed the play, and this led to Philadelphia's winning field goal. The second was in 1996 in Dallas; Aikman had the Cowboys poised to take the lead inside the Eagles' 10 when James Willis intercepted and lateraled to Troy Vincent, who went the rest of the 104 yards for the clinching touchdown. Andy Reid took over in 1999 and has beaten the Cowboys so regularly and easily, 10 out of 12 tries, that the passions seem to have cooled a bit in this rivalry. However, the regular season series record stands at 39-49, so much work still needs to be done.

Cowboys who became Eagles:

Keith Adams
Sam Baker
Brian Baldinger
Chris Boniol
Louis Cheek
Frank Cornish
Merrill Douglas
Rod Harris
George Hegamin
Steve Hendrickson
Mark Higgs
Lynn Hoyem
Jimmie Jones
Robert Lavette
Kelvin Martin
Dennis McKnight
John Meyers
John Niland
Rodney Peete
John Roper
Oliver Ross
Roger Ruzek
Darrin Smith
Daniel Stubbs
Broderick Thompson
Herschel Walker
Chris Warren

Eagles who became Cowboys:

Dick Bielski
Lee Roy Caffey
Mike Clark
Garry Cobb
Randall Cunningham
Mike Ditka
Walt Kowalczyk
Tommy McDonald
Jerry Norton
Junior Tautalatasi

Those who went there and back:

Fred Whittingham
Luis Zendejas

Disaster

Tommy Hutton
P 1995-98

WHO'S WORN THE NUMBER:

Benjy Dial (QB) 1967, Max Runager (P) 1979-83 and 1989, David Jacobs (K) 1987r, Dale Dawson (K) 1988, Bryan Barker (P) 1994, Tom Hutton (P) 1995-98.

Originator: Quarterback Benjy Dial completed one of three NFL passes for the Eagles; he was said to physically resemble Bart Starr, but that did not carry over to the field.

Longest Tenure: Six years, punter Max Runager.

Number Changes: None.

Just Visiting: Bryan Barker led the NFC in punting in his one season as a Bird. He has spent 15 years punting in the NFL for several teams.

Highs: None.

Lows: In his first game as an Eagle, Dale Dawson missed a fourth quarter 22-yard field goal on September 26, 1988 in a 23-21 loss to Minnesota; Buddy Ryan cut him that week.

Tommy Hutton

Tommy Hutton deserves better. He was a stand-up guy who worked for everything he got, but is remembered solely for his stunning failure at the conclusion of a wild *Monday Night Football* matchup with Dallas in 1997.

Hutton was a walk-on at the University of Tennessee as a freshman, and won a scholarship as a punter by the fifth game of that year. He went undrafted at the conclusion of his college career, and signed on with the Eagles to compete for their vacant punting job. In training camp, he competed against his roommate, another rookie free agent punter, Jeff Beckley from Boston College. Hutton won out not only because of his punting, but also because of his willingness to kick off and to act as holder for placement kicks — neither of which he had ever done before. The Eagles kicker that year was the veteran Gary Anderson, who remarked, "I remember signing the contract and saying to myself, 'Here I am, back in holding school again, teaching someone.' Honestly, my only concern in coming here was who would be my holder."

Anderson spent training camp teaching Hutton the subtleties of holding: spotting the ball, keeping a smooth rhythm, spinning the ball with the laces away and placing it at the proper angle. Anderson noted at the start of the 1995 season that "We've come light-years since those first couple of days at West Chester. Tommy's really come around." Hutton had a strong rookie season punting at a 43.3-yard average. His punting average would decline about a half yard a season for the rest of his five-year career, but his net average would increase about a yard and a half in his second year and stay within a half yard of that figure in his final three years.

Hutton performed ably as a holder until the third game of his third season, the September 15th showdown in Dallas before a national audience on *Monday Night Football*. Both offenses were stymied throughout the game, but the Eagles opened up a 17-3 lead in the first half on a Willie Thomas fumble return touchdown and a Ty Detmer to Chad Lewis scoring pass. The Cowboys fought back with four more field goals and were trailing 20-15 with 51 seconds left when Troy Aikman hit Anthony Miller with a 14-yard TD pass to pull ahead 21-20. In the closing seconds, Detmer led the Eagles back with the big play being a pass to Freddie Solomon from the 50 that Solomon managed to take all the way to the Cowboy four before stepping out of bounds with four seconds left. On the resultant 22-yard chip shot field goal attempt the snap to Hutton was perfect, but when he placed it on the ground, it slipped out of his hands. Hutton was forced to pick up the ball and run and was tackled by Deion Sanders who jokingly said afterwards, "That holder better check his locker. He may have a suitcase full of money."

Instead, Hutton found a swirl of reporters at his locker and answered every one of their questions like a man, "I just dropped it. I take all the blame for it. I should catch every ball. It's my mistake." While Hutton received support for accepting responsibility for the loss, he always will be remembered for failing and driving another dagger in the hearts of Eagle fans. Strangely, the same scenario had been enacted previously against another hated rival, the Redskins, but it is mostly forgotten today. On December 6, 1981, the Eagles trailed the Redskins 15-13 with one minute to play when Ron Jaworski furiously drove the team from his 20 to the Redskins' 7. Tony Franklin came out to attempt the 25-yard chip shot to win the game, but never got the chance because holder John Sciara dropped the snap and was tackled. Why is the game largely forgotten? Why is Sciara not remembered as a goat like Hutton? Primarily because the Hutton bobble was on national TV on Monday night with a much bigger audience. Another factor favoring Sciara is that he was a punt return man and defensive back who had other ways to shine. Punters and place kickers are expected to be perfect because they only have one thing to do, and it's generally a non-contact sidelight to the actual football game.

While coach Ray Rhodes called the Hutton game "the most frustrating loss of my career," if Ray had spent as much time in Philadelphia as lifelong Eagles fans, he would see it as part of a much larger pattern. With pain and loss being regular parts of Philadelphia football history, some games have hurt more than others; they were lost on inexplicably disastrous finishes. Including the two noted above, here, in chronological order, are the Unlucky 13 Top Eagle Disasters:

1. December 2, 1945. The Eagles led the Giants 21-0 when 34-year old backup quarterback Arnie Herber came in and threw three touchdown passes of 38, 41 and 48 yards to Frank Liebel. In the fourth quarter, Herber added a fourth scoring toss to Sam Fox to take the lead. Eagles backup quarterback Tommy Thompson drove the Eagles to the Giants' 4 in the final seconds, but they could not score.

2. October 26, 1975. The Eagles led the Cowboys 17-10 with 1:02 left when Roger Staubach hit Drew Pearson for 21 yards and the tying touchdown. After the Eagles went three-and-out, Staubach again threw to Pearson who raced out of bounds at the 25, and Toni Fritsch kicked the winning 42-yard field goal as time expired.

3. December 7, 1980. In the closing seconds of a 17-17 game with the Falcons, Eagle cornerback Richard Blackmore intercepted Steve Bartkowski and returned the ball deep into Falcon territory. However, Blackmore was flagged for pass interference. The interception was nullified, and Tim Mazzetti kicked the game-winning 37-yard field goal on the next play.

4. December 6, 1981. The Sciara game described above. Interestingly, Sciarra took the blame as manfully as Hutton, saying, "That's what I get paid to do, and I didn't do it."

5. November 11, 1984. Ron Jaworski threw a 38-yard touchdown pass to Melvin Hoover with 1:52 left to draw within 24-23 of the Dolphins. On the extra point attempt, though, 6-foot 7-inch Doug Betters drove past Dean Miraldi to block Paul McFadden's kick. The Eagles dropped to 4-6-1, while Super Bowl-bound Miami went to 11-0 on the season.

6. December 1, 1985. The Eagles led the Vikings 23-0 with eight minutes left in the game. Then backup quarterback Wade Wilson hit Allen Rice for a seven-yard score. With six minutes left, Willie Teal recovered Ron Jaworski's fumble and returned it 65 yards for another touchdown. John Spagnola fumbled next, and with 3:58 left, Wilson hit Anthony Carter for 36 yards to pull the Vikings within two points. With 1:11 left, the Vikings faced a fourth and five at the Eagles' 42 when Wilson found Carter again open for his third TD pass and the lead. Jaworski led Philadelphia down to the Vikings' 29, but could not connect for a winning touchdown as time ran out.

7. September 14, 1986. When Buddy Ryan faced Mike Ditka for the first time, the result was a heartbreaking loss for the new Philadelphia coach. The Eagles tied the game at 10 early in the fourth quarter, but three interceptions by Eagle QBs in the final nine minutes of regulation thwarted Eagle scoring opportunities. In over-time, Eagle Charles Crawford fumbled the opening kickoff and Vestee Jackson recovered for Chicago at the Eagles' 35. The Bears worked the ball inside the Eagles' 10 and won the game on Kevin Butler's 23-yard field goal.

8. November 2, 1986. The Eagles lost a second 13-10 game in Ryan's first year. The Cardinals scored two touchdowns in the final five minutes of the game, having the second extra point blocked to take a 13-10 lead. Ron Jaworski drove Philadelphia to the Cardinal's 36 with nine seconds left. The Cards sent an all-out eight-man rush at Jaws who read the blitz and hit Gregg Garrity at the 30 with six seconds left. Garrity headed up the middle of the field, got past the safety at the 17 with three seconds left, and headed for the end zone with no one in front of him. Cornerback Cedric Mack caught Garrity from behind at the 2 and tackled him as time ran out just short of victory.

9. September 24, 1989. The Eagles sacked the 49ers' Joe Montana eight times and racked up a 21-10 lead at the beginning of the final period. Montana then got red hot, hitting four touchdown passes in the fourth quarter. The first went to John Taylor in a 70-yard catch-and-run, followed by eight yards to Tom Rathman with six minutes left, 24 yards to Brent Jones with three minutes remaining, and final-ly 33 yards to Jerry Rice with two minutes left for a 38-28 victory. Montana com-pleted 25 of 34 passes for 428 yards and five scores for the day.

10. December 24, 1994. Philadelphia finished 1994 by losing the last seven games after having started the year 7-2. This finale in Cincinnati was the most bizarre loss. Leading 30-27 in a wild back-and-forth game, the Eagles allowed the Bengals to drive the length of the field behind quarterback Jeff Blake, who even scrambled to convert a fourth and 16 at one point. At the Eagles' 4 with three seconds left, Doug Pelfrey tied the game with a 22-yard field goal. Lee Johnson squibbed the ensuing kickoff, rookie fullback Brian O'Neal could not handle it, and the Bengals

recovered at the 35. Pelfrey then kicked a game-winning 52-yard field goal as time expired. Two field goals in three seconds.

11. November 24, 1996. The Cardinals defeated the Eagles 36-30 in a game where 37 of the 66 points were scored in the last quarter, including 24 with less than three minutes left. Quarterback Boomer Esiasen threw a two-yard touchdown to Larry Centers with 2:45 remaining to send Arizona up 29-20. Derrick Witherspoon took the ensuing kickoff 95 yards for a touchdown to make it a two-point game. The Eagles then executed a successful onside kick and Gary Anderson kicked a 32-yard field goal to give Philadelphia a 30-29 lead with 1:30 left. That was too much time to leave Esiasen as it turned out. Boomer passed the Cards down the field and threw the game-winning 24-yard touchdown to Marcus Dowdell with 14 seconds left.

12. September 15, 1997. The Hutton games described above.

13. October 31, 1999. It's appropriate to end our Unlucky 13 with a Halloween horror against the Giants and their gap-toothed defensive end, Michael Strahan. Philadelphia led 17-3 in the fourth quarter when LeShon Johnson scored for New York to close the gap and initiate a series of Eagle blunders. First, Doug Pederson drove the Eagles to the Giants' 15 where Norm Johnson missed a 33-yard field goal. Next, Allen Rossum failed to field a punt at the 15, and it was downed by the Giants at the Eagles' 3. On third and 11 from there, Duce Staley got the call and fumbled. The Giants recovered and tied the game on a five-yard TD pass with two minutes left. At the end of regulation, David Akers tried a 59-yard field goal for the Eagles and missed. The Giants got the ball first in overtime, but were forced to punt. The Giants then won the game when Christian Peter deflected Pederson's pass and Strahan intercepted and lugged it 44 yards for the final score.

Handicapping the Draft

Donovan McNabb
QB 1999-04

Donovan McNabb

Andy Reid's reward for taking over the hapless Eagles in 1999 was holding the number two pick in the NFL draft in a year when five highly-rated college quarterbacks figured to go in the first round. His punishment was to have to listen to weeks of campaigning by Angelo Cataldi on the WIP morning radio show for Reid to select Heisman Trophy-winning runner Ricky Williams. As the city's number one fan, Philadelphia Mayor Ed Rendell even got into the act by lobbying for the Williams pick. Reid, however, knew that quarterback was a much more important position, particularly in the West Coast Offense he would be running. On draft day, Cataldi brought a busload of extreme fans to the audience, and this group, known as the "Dirty Thirty," chanted for Williams when the Eagles went on the clock. After the Eagles selected McNabb, they reacted by booing so boorishly that they embarrassed Eagles fans all over the Delaware Valley.

That draft was special in a number of ways. Its five first-round quarterback picks are second only to the fabled 1983 draft when six QBs were selected first — a record three of whom (Marino, Kelly and Elway) have gone into the Hall of Fame. The only other drafts that have included as many as four QBs in the first round are 1959, 1987, 2003 and 2004. The 1999 and 1983 drafts also each produced 10 QBs who played in the league. That total has been equaled in 2002, 2001, 1987, 1980, 1973 and 1971 (an especially good group including Jim Plunkett, Archie Manning, Dan Pastorini, Lynn Dickey and Joe Theismann). In all, 11 QBs made an NFL team in 2000, 1977 and 1964, while 13 generally second-rate signal callers emerged in 1992, the best of the thin bunch being late picks Brad Johnson and Jeff Blake. The 1999 draft also marked the fourth time that the Eagles have picked a passer in the opening round. McNabb followed John Reaves in 1972, Frank Tripucka in 1949 and tailback Davey O'Brien in 1939.

Donovan McNabb reacted to all this fuss with the equanimity that has become his trademark. He would react with the same dignified poise when he became the focus of a media firestorm after Rush Limbaugh on ESPN criticized the media for over-hyping Donovan simply because he is a black quarterback. On the field, fans rarely see McNabb with anything but a smile on his face no matter how tough the situation gets. In some ways, he has the ideal temperament to play in front of the temperamental Philadelphia fans; criticism does not seem to affect him. On the other hand, Eagles don't like to see smiles on the faces of their players. They like to see grit, passion, fire and "atty-tude." Fans could never understand why previous quarterback Rodney Peete was smiling, but Donovan so far has been able to get away with it because he is so good and has been so successful. McNabb did not start at QB until the eighth game of his rookie year, a sloppy but exciting win over the Redskins 35-28, but since 2000, the Eagles have won at least one playoff game each year behind him. He is a leader who has taken the Birds to the playoffs in five consecutive seasons, something no other quarterback has done, and has made the Pro Bowl each year.

While he has weaknesses — he will never be the most accurate passer in the league and has a tendency to throw balls into the ground at times — he has many strengths. He is somewhat reminiscent of Brett Favre with his improvisational talent, positive attitude, control of the team and leadership skills, but he is a better runner than Favre and throws fewer interceptions. McNabb is big and fast and strong and, above all, exciting. He has been the Eagles' best player, and the offense revolves around him.

Each year has produced highlights and disappointments. 2000 featured a special win against the Redskins in which Donovan ran for 125 yards on 11 carries including a juking 21-yard TD dash and a 54-yard fourth-quarter scamper. In the playoffs, the Eagles dominated the Bucs but were beaten by the Giants for the ninth straight time. In 2001, McNabb conquered the New York Giants by beating them twice in the regular season that year in furious comebacks, and the team won the Eastern Division. He then turned in masterful performances in the playoffs against Tampa and Chicago before coming up a little short in the NFC title game against the Rams. In 2002, he had his greatest game in week 10 against the Cardinals, throwing for four touchdown passes on what was later diagnosed as a broken ankle. He missed the last six games of the season and came back rusty in the playoffs, beating Atlanta, but losing the NFC title game to Tampa at home. In 2003, Donovan started off the season terribly. He had an injured hand that did not get better till mid-season at which point the team took off and won another Eastern Division crown. In the playoffs, he managed to bring the team back to defeat the Packers in a game most remembered for McNabb's fourth-and-26 completion to Freddie Mitchell in the fourth quarter. However, the Carolina Panthers physically beat up Donovan and his receivers in another NFC title game home loss. Each year, McNabb carries the team on his back. It wasn't until 2004 that he finally got an offensive weapon to share the load in Terrell Owens.

And 2004 was a special season with Donovan throwing 31 touchdowns against only eight interceptions, the first time an NFL quarterback threw more than 30 touchdowns and fewer than 10 interceptions in a season. Despite missing the injured Owens, McNabb led the Eagles to the Super Bowl for the first time in 24 years with two easy postseason wins over Minnesota and Atlanta. In the Super Bowl, however, Donovan threw often and badly in a loss to New England. Once again the Philly critics came out in force with emotional outbursts that McNabb is a deeply flawed quarterback who would never lead the Eagles to a title. However, a little perspective is needed. Consider Donovan's performance in comparison to the following "bad days at the office" had by nine Hall of Fame quarterbacks in league title games:

YEAR	HALL OF FAMER	A/C	YARDAGE	TDS	INTS	SCORE
1953	Otto Graham	2/15	20	1	3	16-17
1954	Bobby Layne	18/42	177	0	6	10-56
1955	Norm Van Brocklin	11/25	166	1	6	14-38
1963	Y.A. Tittle	11/29	147	1	5	10-14
1964	John Unitas	12/20	95	0	2	0-27
1974	Fran Tarkenton	11/26	102	0	3	6-16
1975	Roger Staubach	15/24	204	2	3	17-21
1984	Dan Marino	29/50	318	1	2	16-38
1987	John Elway	14/38	257	1	3	10-42
1991	Jim Kelly	28/58	275	2	4	24-37
2005	Donovan McNabb	30/51	357	3	3	21-24

Six of these 11 immortals won at least one championship. A bad day, even in the ultimate game, does not make you a bad quarterback. Andy Reid made the right pick in April 1999.

So what became of the Eagles' other options in that 1999 draft? Among the first-round quarterbacks, Cade McNown was out of football in 2002; Akili Smith dropped out in 2003; Tim Couch flopped in 2004, although he may still resurface as a journeyman somewhere. Daunte Culpepper has developed into a star close to the magnitude of McNabb. Actually, fourth-rounder Aaron Brooks has done better than most of the first-rounders. And Ricky Williams, that running back desired so badly by the Dirty Thirty, has had his problems. Despite gaining a lot of yards in New Orleans, he was traded as a head case after three years to Miami. After two fairly successful years with the Dolphins, he abruptly retired when he failed an NFL drug test, giving the impression he would rather smoke marijuana than carry the football. The draft is a series of public choices a team makes that can be evaluated better a few years after the fact. Let's take a look at the history of the Eagles' first-round picks and who they could have chosen instead:

YEAR	EAGLES PICK	ALSO AVAILABLE, SAME POSITION	BEST AVAILABLE TALENT
1936	Jay Berwanger	Riley Smith	Joe Stydahar
1937	Sam Francis	Sammy Baugh; Ace Parker; Johnny Drake	
1938	Jim McDonald	Whizzer White; Cecil Isbell	Alex Wojciechowicz
1939	Davey O'Brien		Bill Osmanski; Pug Manders; Marshall Goldberg
1940	George McAfee		Bulldog Turner
1941	No Selection		
1942	Pete Kmetovic	Spec Sanders	Frankie Albert
1943	Joe Muha		Glenn Dobbs
1944	Steve Van Buren		
1945	John Yonaker		
1946	Leo Riggs	Elmer Angsman; Emil Sitko	
1947	Neill Armstrong	Al Baldwin	Herm Wedemeyer
1948	Clyde Scott	Dan Sandifer	Les Bingaman
1949	Chuck Bednarik	Bill Walsh	Doak Walker
1949	Frank Tripucka	Norm Van Brocklin; George Blanda	Al DeRogatis
1950	Bud Grant	Gordy Soltau	Ernie Stautner; Tobin Rote
1951	Chet Mutryn		Bud McFaddin; Bill George; Dick Stanfel
1951	Ebert Van Buren	Rip Collins	

YEAR	EAGLES PICK	ALSO AVAILABLE, SAME POSITION	BEST AVAILABLE TALENT
1952	Johnny Bright	Hugh McElhenny; Frank Gifford	Gino Marchetti; Bill Howton
1953	No Selection		
1954	Neil Worden	Rick Casares	Max McGee
1955	Dick Bielski	Ron Waller	Dick Szymanski; Rosey Grier; John Unitas
1956	Bob Pellegrini	Sam Huff	Lenny Moore; Forrest Gregg; Bart Starr
1957	Clarence Peaks	Abe Woodson	Jim Parker; Del Shofner; Jack Pardee
1958	Walt Kowalczyk	Jim Taylor; Lenny Lyles	Chuck Howley; Charlie Krueger; Alex Karras; Jerry Kramer
1959	No Selection		
1960	Ron Burton	Bob Jeter	Ron Mix
1961	Art Baker	Bill Brown	Fran Tarkenton
1962	No Selection		
1963	Ed Budde	Bob Vogel	Lee Roy Jordan; Dave Robinson; John Mackey; Bobby Bell
1964	Bob Brown		Charley Taylor; Paul Warfield; Carl Eller
1965	No Selection		
1966	Randy Beisler	Pete Duranko	John Niland; Jim Grabowski; Gale Gillingham
1967	Harry Jones	Bob Grim	Lem Barney; Willie Lanier; Rick Volk
1968	Tim Rossovich	Elvin Bethea; Curley Culp; Bill Staley	
1969	Leroy Keyes	Ron Johnson	Joe Greene; Ted Hendricks; Roger Wehrli; Gene Washington
1970	Steve Zabel	Rich McGeorge; Ray Chester	Mike Reid; Cedric Hardman
1971	Richard Harris	Julius Adams; Lyle Alzado	Jack Ham; Jack Youngblood; Jack Tatum; Isiah Robertson; John Riggins

YEAR	EAGLES PICK	ALSO AVAILABLE, SAME POSITION	BEST AVAILABLE TALENT
1972	John Reaves	Brian Sipe; Joe Gilliam	Lydell Mitchell; Thom Darden
1973	Charles Young	Billy Joe Dupree	Joe DeLamielleure; Chuck Foreman; Greg Pruitt
1973	Jerry Sisemore	John Hannah	
1974	No Selection		
1975	No Selection		
1976	No Selection		
1977	No Selection		
1978	No Selection		
1979	Jerry Robinson	Michael Jackson; Ken Fantetti	Joe Montana; Fred Smerlas; William Andrews
1980	Roynell Young	Leroy Irvin; Dave Waymer; Mark Lee	Dwight Stephenson; Ray Donaldson
1981	Leonard Mitchell	Howie Long; Frank Warren	Mike Singletary; Cris Collinsworth; Ricky Jackson; Eric Wright
1982	Mike Quick	Mark Duper	Andre Tippett; Mike Merriweather; Bubba Paris
1983	Michael Haddix	Roger Craig; Gary Anderson	Dan Marino; Jim Kelly; Darrell Green; Bruce Matthews; Joey Browner
1984	Kenny Jackson	Louie Lipps; Brian Brennan	Wilbur Marshall; Keith Millard; Bill Maas
1985	Kevin Allen	Jim Lachey	Jerry Rice; Al Toon
1986	Keith Byars	Neil Anderson; John L. Williams; Tom Rathman; Ronnie Harmon; Dalton Hilliard	Eric Dorsey; Will Wolford
1987	Jerome Brown	Henry Thomas; Jerry Ball	Rod Woodson; Tim McDonald; Bruce Armstrong
1988	Keith Jackson	Ferrell Edmunds	Thurman Thomas; Michael Dean Perry; Randall McDaniel
1989	No Selection		

YEAR	EAGLES PICK	ALSO AVAILABLE, SAME POSITION	BEST AVAILABLE TALENT
1990	Ben Smith	Leroy Butler; Pat Terrell	Rodney Hampton; Tim Grunhard
1991	Antone Davis	Erik Williams; Pat Harlow	Brett Favre; Herman Moore; Aeneas Williams
1992	No Selection		
1993	Leonard Renfro	Dana Stubblefield; Michael Strahan	Chris Slade
1993	Lester Holmes	Will Shields; Ron Stone	Natrone Means
1994	Bernard Williams	Todd Steusie; Wayne Gandy	Larry Allen; Isaac Bruce; Kevin Mawae
1995	Mike Mamula	Hugh Douglass; Luther Ellis	Warren Sapp; Derrick Brooks; Ty Law
1996	Jermane Mayberry	Roman Oben	Ray Lewis; Tony Brackens
1997	Jon Harris	Trevor Pryce; Mike Vrabel; Marcellus Wiley	Tiki Barber; Corey Dillon; Jamie Sharper; Sam Madison; Jake Plummer
1998	Tra Thomas	Flozell Adams	Randy Moss; Keith Brookings; Takeo Spikes
1999	Donovan McNabb	Daunte Culpepper	Ricky Williams; Edgerin James; Jevon Kearse; Tory Holt; Champ Bailey
2000	Corey Simon	Cornelius Griffin; Chris Hovan	Brian Urlacher; John Abraham; Shawn Ellis; Shaun Alexander
2001	Freddie Mitchell	Reggie Wayne; Chad Johnson; Steve Smith; Chris Chambers; Quincy Morgan	Todd Heap; Travis Henry
2002	Lito Sheppard	Tank Williams	Clinton Portis; DeShaun Foster; Antwaan Randle El
2003	Jerome McDougle		Dan Klecko
2004	Shawn Andrews		

Quarterbacks
from Hell

John Reaves
QB 1972-74

John Reaves

At the University of Florida, John Reaves was used to being the star. He was a candidate for the Heisman Trophy and set the NCAA record for career passing yards in 1971, although controversy surrounded the record. With Florida up 45-8 against the University of Miami, the Florida defenders literally dropped to the ground in what was called the Gator Flop and allowed Miami a cheap touchdown late in the game so Reaves could get the ball back and break the record. The Eagles selected the strong-armed Reaves in the first round of their 1972 draft and had high expectations that they had picked their quarterback of the future.

Unfortunately, Reaves had to be the Eagles quarterback of the very near future because the team was so bad. He was in the starting lineup by October, but was far from ready to play. Press reports noted that in the home loss to the Giants on October 2nd, Reaves received cheers when he started the game, but after fumbling a snap that led to a New York score and throwing an end zone interception, he was booed as he left the field at halftime. Years later he would comment in the *Philadelphia Inquirer* that "In 1972 I didn't know how to read defenses. I didn't throw the ball well. I just wasn't very good." One of his biggest problems was that he did not receive much coaching from Ed Khayat's staff. He had never called his own plays before and needed much more direction than he received. In addition, he tore ligaments in his ankle that year and could not move in the pocket very effectively.

The next season Mike McCormack was hired as coach, and he traded for quarterback Roman Gabriel to replace Reaves. The year after that he traded for Mike Boryla, pushing Reaves even further down the bench. While he had gotten into 11 games as a rookie, Reaves got into only five more games in his last two seasons in Philly, completing 10 of 39 passes. In three years as an Eagle, Reaves threw for seven touchdowns and 15 interceptions, and then was traded to Cincinnati in 1975. In the ensuing years as he went from the Bengals to the Vikings to the Oilers, he developed dependency problems with alcohol, marijuana and cocaine and eventually bounced out of the league in 1982. He landed with the Tampa Bay Bandits of the USFL in 1983 and spent three successful seasons in Tampa under head coach Steve Spurrier, another former Gator QB who struggled in the pros. Reaves threw for over 4,000 yards in 1985. In 1983 he even won his first game at the Vet, beating the Philadelphia Stars in a somewhat triumphal return. Reaves had gone 0-8 at the Vet in games he started for the Eagles in the 1970s. He had one more brief taste of the NFL when he appeared in two games for the Bucs in 1987 at the age of 37 and then went into college coaching.

Reaves was one of two Eagle first-round pick busts at quarterback, but he is part of a much larger community of failed Philadelphia QBs. Since the team switched to the T Formation in 1941, Eagle QBs can be divided into five groups. The first group are those who never threw a pass and may never have even appeared in a game for Philadelphia: Frank Tripucka, Bill Troup, Rob Hertel, Bob Holly, Jeff Christensen, Kyle

Mackey, Don McPherson, Casey Weldon, David Archer, Preston Jones, Jay Fiedler, Ron Powlus and Tim Hasselbeck. These are third quarterbacks who never had to respond to an emergency. Of this group, special attention should be given to Frank Tripucka, a number one pick who was waived later in the year, and Don McPherson, a Syracuse signal caller who was part of the team for three very silent seasons.

The second group are quarterbacks who threw from 1 to 49 passes in the green and silver: John Rauch, Bob Gambold, Al Dorow, Ralph Guglielmi, Benjy Dial, John Huarte, Jim Ward, John Sciarra, Dan Pastorini, Dean May, Marty Horn, Guido Merkens, Pat Ryan, Mark Rypien and Jeff Blake. These are generally third quarterbacks who were called on at moments of desperation. This group includes such has-beens and never-weres as Al Dorow, who had 4 of 36 pass attempts intercepted, Heisman Trophy winner John Huarte, who completed seven of 15 passes; one-time star Dan Pastorini, who went 0 for 5, and former Jet Pat Ryan, who completed 10 of 26 passes with four interceptions for his old boss, Rich Kotite.

The third group features Eagle signal callers who threw from 50 to 199 passes for Philadelphia: Foster Watkins, Len Barnum, Allie Sherman, Fred Enke, Jack Concannon, George Mira, John Walton, Matt Cavanaugh, Scott Tinsley, Brad Goebel, Ken O'Brien, Jeff Kemp and A.J. Feeley. These backups are a mix of second- and third-stringers who received brief chances to shine. Among this group Foster Watkins completed just 34 of 95 passes, Len Barnum completed only 20 of 64 with 11 interceptions, Fred Enke completed merely 22 of 67 with five picks, George Mira completed 25 of 76 with five picks, and Brad Goebel had six of his 56 passes picked off.

The fourth group threw between 200 and 499 passes as Birds: Davey O'Brien, Roy Zimmerman, Bill Mackrides, Rick Arrington, Pete Liske, John Reaves, Joe Pisarcik, Jim McMahon, Bubby Brister, Bobby Hoying, Koy Detmer and Doug Pederson. Now we're getting backup QBs who were given extended trials. Several came up short. Rick Arrington averaged 4.7 yards per pass with three TDs and nine interceptions in three seasons; weak-armed Pete Liske went 214 of 407 for 14 TDs and 22 picks; John Reaves' tortures are described above; Bobby Hoying started out on fire, but quickly regressed to a deer caught in the headlights in 1998 when he threw nine interceptions and no TDs while averaging 4.3 yards per pass; and Doug Pederson kept the seat luke warm for Donovan McNabb in 1999.

The final group are the starters who threw at least 500 passes as an Eagle: Tommy Thompson, Adrian Burk, Bobby Thomason, Sonny Jurgensen, Norm Van Brocklin, King Hill, Norm Snead, Roman Gabriel, Mike Boryla, Ron Jaworski, Randall Cunningham, Rodney Peete, Ty Detmer and Donovan McNabb. Those with few redeeming qualities from this group include King Hill, who completed 325 of 635 passes in the 1960s with 29 TDs and 51 interceptions; the ever-inconsistent Norm Snead, who threw 111 TDs and 124 interceptions while Sonny Jurgensen was in Washington throwing 181 TDs against 116 picks; and Mike Boryla, who somehow got named to a Pro Bowl squad while averaging 5.5 yards per pass and throwing 20 TDs and 29 interceptions in three years.

The following chart shows the 10 lowest NFL quarterback ratings by Eagle starting QBs since World War II:

YEAR	STARTER	COMP.%	YARDS/ATT.	TDS	INTS	QB RATING
1950	Tommy Thompson	44.8	6.73	11	22	44.4
1951	Adrian Burk	42.2	6.10	14	23	44.5
1955	Adrian Burk	48.2	5.96	9	17	49.2
1956	Bob Thomason	50.0	6.82	4	21	40.7
1957	Bob Thomason	50.0	6.85	4	10	47.2
1966	Norm Snead	45.6	5.64	8	11	55.1
1968	Norm Snead	52.2	5.69	11	21	51.8
1972	John Reaves	48.2	6.73	7	12	58.4
1976	Mike Boryla	50.0	5.07	9	14	53.3
1998	Bobby Hoying	50.9	4.29	0	9	45.6

A few of these farcical field generals may have felt some heat from the fans on occasion, but from the perspective of how many weak-winged Birds there have been, is a little booing surprising or undeserved?

1980 – The Super Bowl

Ron Jaworski
QB 1977-86

Ron Jaworski

Ron Jaworski was a tough guy from a mill town, but a tough guy with a ready smile who maintained a cheerful running commentary. Known as Jaws for his talkative nature, he endured 32 concussions over the course of a 15-year NFL career in which he was sacked nearly 400 times. He heard his share of boos in his 10 years in Philadelphia, but had the perfect personality to be able shake it off and not resent the local fans. Instead, he turned the boos into a positive force by using them as a motivation to improve. He won the fans' respect with his toughness, his play and his attitude.

He grew up in Lackawanna, New York, where he spent one summer working in the steel mill — just long enough to appreciate the blue-collar workaday world. He attended Youngstown State on a football scholarship and was drafted in the second round by the Los Angeles Rams in 1974. Los Angeles was not his type of town, and he felt out of place there. Moreover, he was disappointed by his lack of playing time. In 1975, he replaced the injured James Harris for the last two games of the season and led the Rams to two wins. In the playoffs, he then quarterbacked Los Angeles over the Cardinals, but went back to the bench the next week for the NFC title game against Dallas when Harris returned. Some said that owner Carroll Rosenbloom thought Jaws was not the sophisticated sort of star Ram fans wanted, so Ron was handed a clipboard on the sidelines. After one more disappointing season in LA, Jaworski got his wish and was traded to Philadelphia for talented tight end Charlie Young.

Dick Vermeil was embroiled in a massive rebuilding job in Philly and needed a quarterback badly. Installed as a starter in 1977, Jaws immediately showed his potential and upgraded the Eagles' quarterbacking, but clearly had a lot of room for improvement. In his first two years in Philadelphia, Ron completed just 50 percent of his passes and threw 34 touchdowns against 37 interceptions while being sacked 88 times. Jaworski considered Vermeil to be a father figure whom he wanted to kill at times, but also loved and respected nonetheless, because Jaws recognized that Vermeil was just pushing hard to make him better. In 1979, Vermeil brought in retired offensive genius Sid Gillman to redesign the passing offense and to tutor Jaworski. Under Gillman's tutelage, Jaws and the Eagle offense improved tremendously. Jaws threw for 45 touchdowns and only 24 interceptions in 1979-80. In 1980 he threw for a personal high of 3,529 yards and 27 TDs and won the NFL MVP award as he led the Eagles to an NFC Eastern Division crown with a 12-4 record.

In the 1980 playoffs, the Birds first faced the Central Division's 9-7 Vikings at the Vet in a scary game that almost got away from Philadelphia. The undermanned Vikings took a 14-0 lead midway through the second quarter before the Eagles finally got going. The Eagles tied up the game with two scoring drives, one at the end of the half and the other to open the third quarter. By that time, the Eagle defense was firmly in command. In the second half, Viking quarterback Tommy Kramer went 8-22 passing with five interceptions. The interceptions and a fumbled punt by Minnesota led to 17 Eagle points, and Philadelphia won the sloppy game 31-16.

Ron Jaworski, the future president of the Arena League's Philadelphia Soul, was a smart, tough, strong-armed quarterback who led the Eagles to their first Super Bowl appearance in 1981.

The next week brought perhaps the best-remembered game in team history, the NFC title match with the hated Dallas Cowboys. The Eagles, who forced Dallas to wear their "unlucky" blue uniforms, had the home field advantage going for them, including a temperature of 16 degrees and -17 wind chill. The tone for the game was set on its third play when Wilbert Montgomery read his blocks and cut back perfectly on a 42-yard touchdown scamper that put Philadelphia up 7-0. Dallas tied the game before halftime, but in the third quarter the Birds' defense caused two Cowboy fumbles that the Eagles turned into a 17-7 lead. Philadelphia then held the ball for 12 of the 15 minutes of the fourth quarter as their line totally dominated the Dallas defense. The final score was 20-7, and the Eagles ran for 254 yards, 194 of them by Montgomery, to catapult themselves into Super Bowl XV against the AFC Champion Oakland Raiders.

The Raiders were diametrically opposed to the Eagles. They reveled in their image as the bad boys of the league. Soon after the Super Bowl, the team would be deserting their loyal Oakland fan base and moving to Los Angeles in the search for more lucrative finances. They were the first wild card team to get to the Super Bowl and had lost 10-7 to the Eagles in a tough midseason game at the Vet. The Eagles meanwhile were suffering injury problems throughout the playoffs. Montgomery's knee was bothering him, and they had lost starting wide receiver Charlie Smith to a broken jaw and backup receiver Scott Fitzkee to a broken foot. Courageously, Smith returned for the Bowl.

Just as in the Dallas game, the tone was set early against the Raiders, but it was an ominous one. After two running plays achieved a first down, Jaworski tried a quick pass in the flat to tight end John Spagnola. Weakside linebacker Rod Martin jumped in front of the pass and returned it to the Eagles' 30. Seven plays later Jim Plunkett threw a two-yard TD pass to Cliff Branch and the Raiders were on top. They would never trail. Later in the first quarter, the 33-year-old Plunkett rumbled out of the pocket and spotted fullback Kenny King breaking off his pattern and heading upfield. Plunkett hit King on the fly while cornerback Herm Edwards trailed helplessly behind — 14-0 Oakland.

Early in the second quarter, Philadelphia drove 61 yards and Tony Franklin kicked a field goal to get the Birds on the board. Jaworski kept fighting and drove the Eagles back down the field to the Raiders' 11 right before the half. The Raiders held there and Franklin came on to boot the chip shot field goal, but Ted Hendricks blocked the kick and left the Eagles down 14-3 at the half. After the intermission, the Raiders took the kickoff to start the third quarter and went 76 yards in five plays, scoring on a 29-yard pass from Plunkett to Branch, whom Roynell Young lost sight of. It was 21-3 Raiders, but Jaworski kept trying. He had the Eagles in Raider territory again after the kickoff, but once again ended the drive with a pass intended to Spagnola that Martin read perfectly and picked off. That led to an Oakland field goal and a 24-3 lead at the end of three quarters.

Early in the fourth quarter, Jaworski capped off an 88-yard drive with an eight-yard pass to Keith Krepfle for the only Eagle touchdown of the game. This quarter would bring more misery for Jaws and the Eagles. Jaws fumbled a snap and threw a third interception to Martin, this time intended for Montgomery, and the Raiders added a long drive for a field goal. Final score: 27-10, Oakland. Postgame commentators focused on the Eagles' lack of pass rush against Plunkett and on the Raiders' effective blitzes against Jaworski, who still threw for 291 yards. Jaws and other players commented to the effect that they just couldn't seem to get into the flow of the game. Many Eagle fans watching from home remarked on how scared the Eagles looked as they were being introduced; they did not look like a team ready to fight for a championship. Things got out of hand, and the Eagles lost their first Super Bowl badly. They would not return for 24 years.

Jaworski had a frustrating, mistake-laden day and never got the chance to make amends. He was still a quality NFL starter for the next five seasons, but never again had seasons as good as 1979 and 1980. Gillman retired again. The team declined. Carmichael and Montgomery got old and beat-up. Mike Quick emerged in 1982, but the team as a whole had slipped so badly that he and Jaworski are remembered for highlights like the 99-yard touchdown pass against Atlanta, not for championships, or even for very many wins. Buddy Ryan arrived in 1986 and Jaworski's playing time was cut. He was released by the Eagles, but caught on for a couple of seasons as a backup in Miami and Kansas City.

In retirement, Jaws settled in the Philadelphia area and has made a major success of his life in the business world, owning golf courses, sporting goods stores, restaurants and hotels. He maintains his public image on ESPN as an impressively incisive and lively football commentator who studies game film for hours each week at NFL Films in Mount Laurel, New Jersey. Each week on TV he demonstrates that all that training from Sid Gillman clearly paid off.

8
Little Guys

Davey O'Brien
TB 1939-40

Davey O'Brien

Although diminutive for a football player, Davey O'Brien was a mighty mite who produced big things on the gridiron. As a 5-foot 7-inch, 118-pound sophomore tailback, he led Dallas' Woodrow Wilson High School to the Texas state football playoffs in 1932. Three years later, he enrolled at Texas Christian University where he sat on the bench behind All-American Sammy Baugh for two years as the long and lean Slingin' Sammy led the Hornfrogs to 12-1 and 9-2-2 seasons capped off with victories in the Sugar and Cotton Bowls. When Baugh graduated to the pros in 1937, O'Brien succeeded him as a seven-inch-shorter signal caller. Davey had now filled out to a whopping 150 pounds, and he was named All-Southwestern Conference quarterback, although the team slipped to a 4-4-1 record. In his senior season, though, O'Brien outshone Baugh's legacy by completing 55 percent of his passes for 1,733 yards and 19 touchdowns while running for 10 more scores. TCU won the Sugar Bowl and the National Championship with an 11-0 record that year. Dutch Meyer, who coached both TCU stars, considered Baugh the better all-around player, but thought that O'Brien was an unequaled field general and play selector.

For that 1938 season, O'Brien won the Walter Camp Memorial Trophy, the Heisman Trophy and the Maxwell Club Award as the best player in college football. While accepting the Maxwell trophy in Philadelphia, Davey declared that he had no interest in furthering his athletic career and that it was geology, not pro football, that he was thinking of for the future. Bert Bell had already selected O'Brien with the Eagles' first pick in the draft and pursued him fiercely. An offer of $10,000 plus a percentage of the gate persuaded Davey to change his mind. Bell also took out an insurance policy with Lloyd's of London that would pay the team $1,500 for every game that the slightly built O'Brien could not play. Despite playing both offense and defense against players who towered over him, Davey never missed a game for the Eagles.

Philadelphia had finished 5-6 in 1938, so Bell was very optimistic about what O'Brien could do for the club, saying, "The boys think O'Brien can pass them to a championship." Reality set in quickly — the Eagles did not score their first touchdown until the fourth game and finished 1939 1-9-1. Appropriately, the season began with Philadelphia hosting Sammy Baugh and the Redskins, but Sam got the best of his former teammate as Washington won 7-0 on a Baugh TD pass in the fourth quarter. Things would not get better for Davey in Philadelphia. For his two years as an Eagle, the team went 2-19-1 and were outscored 411 points to 216. Although there was an immediate boost to the attendance in the first couple of games, it did not last as soon as the team revealed itself to be the same lousy Eagles. The Philadelphia offense behind O'Brien threw the ball more than any team in the league. They went from passing the ball 36 percent of the time the year before Davey arrived to 45 percent in his first year and 53 percent in his second. O'Brien was a single wing tailback — he did not line up under center — but he did not run the ball by design very much. In effect, the Eagles' single wing with Davey was analogous to a team playing entirely from the shotgun today. It was not successful. Bell had promised to surround Davey with "10 big men to look after him," but Philadelphia had a perennially weak offensive line; their first interior lineman to make All-Pro was guard Dick Bassi in 1940. When a passer was sacked in those years, the loss was counted as a running attempt for the passer. Thus, O'Brien's rushing statistics show him "running" the ball 208 times for minus 194 yards, an average "gain" of -.9 per carry. While he may have run the ball on occasion, most of his "runs" were scrambles and sacks as Davey scampered for his life behind a porous line.

O'Brien broke Baugh's league record for passing yards in his rookie season and earned himself a $2,000 raise, but how good was he? Let's take a look at the passing statistics for his contemporaries, all players who threw at least 125 passes in 1939-40:

	ATT.	COMP.	%	YPP	YARDS	TDS	INTS
Davey O'Brien	478	223	46.7	5.5	2,614	11	34
Parker Hall	391	183	46.8	6.0	2,335	15	29
Sammy Baugh	273	164	60.0	6.9	1,885	18	19
Ace Parker	268	121	45.1	6.9	1,842	14	20
Cecil Isbell	253	111	43.8	7.1	1,786	15	17
Arnie Herber	228	95	41.7	7.3	1,667	13	16
Hugh McCullough	216	75	34.7	4.5	972	6	33
Sid Luckman	156	71	45.5	10.1	1,577	9	13
Dwight Sloan	148	63	42.5	6.2	918	2	11
Billy Patterson	145	48	31.0	4.9	756	6	19
Frank Filchock	143	83	58.0	10.8	1,554	17	16
Bernie Masterson	136	53	38.9	8.3	1,126	10	12

This impressive group of a dozen passers includes four Hall of Famers (Baugh, Herber, Luckman and Parker) and three All-Pros (Filchock, Hall and Isbell) besides O'Brien. From these numbers, we can see that Davey was tops in pass attempts, completions and yards for those two years and his 46.7 completion percentage was the fourth highest rate. On the downside, he was seventh in touchdown passes despite throwing many more passes than anyone else, and he was last in interceptions. His interception rate would be lower than many others because he threw so many passes, but that's still a lot of turnovers. Perhaps of greatest significance is his tenth rank on yards per pass. A 5.5 average gain represents a dink-and-dunk approach that did not lead to a lot of points. While the Eagles had some quality receivers, their backs and linemen were not very good. Furthermore, it is extremely difficult for a passer to overcome such a severe height differential — 5-foot 8-inch Eddie LeBaron and 5-foot 10-inch Doug Flutie would discover this in later eras as players got even bigger. All three deserve acclamation for their accomplishments, but none would ever come close to winning a championship in the NFL.

Davey closed his brief tenure as an Eagle with his most memorable game. The final game of the 1940 season matched O'Brien once again with Sammy Baugh in a

Davey O'Brien (8) was such a straight-arrow that he sued Pabst Beer for using his photo on a 1939 calendar. Despite standing only 5 feet 7 inches, he led a barnstorming basketball team, the Davey O'Brien All-American All-Stars, that same year. He is pictured with team-mate Fran Murray (11), a future Eagle broadcaster.

game Washington needed to win to clinch the Eastern Division. The Redskins spent most of the day running the ball and built a 13-0 lead in the fourth quarter. Meanwhile, O'Brien was passing the ball on almost every down — he would complete a record 33 of 60 passes for 316 yards that day. However, Philadelphia did not mount a scoring drive until the last quarter when Davey completed a 98-yard drive with a 13-yard toss to Frank Emmons for the score. The Eagles got the ball back at their own 31 late and drove to the Redskins' 22 as time ran out. This game was a microcosm of O'Brien's career — lots of short passes but few points, resulting in a loss. After the game, Bert Bell thanked Davey with a plaque inscribed, "To the greatest player of all time. Small in stature with the heart of a lion. A living inspiration to the youth of America."

After two disastrous seasons running for his life and passing constantly to no avail, O'Brien quit the game in 1941 to join the FBI. He spent a decade with the Bureau, as a firearms instructor and a field agent. He left the FBI in 1950 and went into land development and the oil business, but returned to the spotlight by serving as an NFL official in 1952 and being elected to the College Football Hall of Fame in 1955. In 1971, he contracted cancer and fought that disease with his customary fire for six years before passing away in 1977. Most of all, Davey O'Brien should be remembered as a thoroughly decent human being who claimed his most prized accomplishment was winning the Best All-Around Camper award when he was a schoolboy struggling to overcome a bad temper. He attributed much of his success to football. It may be corny and very old school, but he felt the game taught him discipline, cooperation, loyalty and appreciation — qualities that lead to a good life.

While Davey O'Brien was the lightest player ever to play for the Eagles, there have been a few players shorter than he was.

EAGLES UNDER 5'9":

	HGT	POSITION	YEAR
Nick Prisco	5'8"	B	1933
Dick Thornton	5'6"	B	1933
Stumpy Thomason	5'7"	B	1935-36
Davey O'Brien	5'7"	TB	1939-40
Wally Henry	5'8"	KR	1977-82
Nick Mike-Mayer	5'8	K	1977-78
Alan Reid	5'8"	RB	1987
Tom Caterbone	5'8"	DB	1987r
David Jacobs	5'7"	K	1987r
Gizmo Williams	5'6"	KR	1989
Mark Higgs	5'7"	RB	1989
Jeff Sydner	5'6"	WR	1992-94
Mark McMillian	5'7"	CB	1992-95
Vaughn Hebron	5'8"	RB	1993-95
Allen Rossum	5'7"	KR	1998-99
Eric Bieniemy	5'7"	KR	1999
Brian Westbrook	5'8"	RB	2002-04

EAGLES UNDER 180 POUNDS:

	WGT	POSITION	YEAR
Dick Thornton	165	B	1933
Harry O'Boyle	178	B	1933
Alan Keen	170	B	1937-38
Davey O'Brien	150	TB	1939-40
Foster Watkins	163	TB	1940-41
Bosh Pritchard	164	HB	1942, 1946-51
Russ Craft	178	DB	1946-53
Don Stevens	176	HB	1952, 1954
Tommy McDonald	176	WR	1957-63
Wally Henry	175	KR	1977-82
Tom Caterbone	175	DB	1987r
David Jacobs	151	K	1987r
Eric Everett	165	DB	1988-89
Luis Zendejas	175	K	1989-90
Sammy Lilly	178	CB	1989-90
Floyd Dixon	170	WR	1992
Jeff Sydner	170	WR	1992-94
Mark McMillian	162	DB	1992-95
Kelvin Martin	162	KR	1995
Mel Gray	166	KR	1997
Todd Pinkston	174	WR	2000-04

In a Legend's Footsteps

Sonny Jurgensen
QB 1957-63

WHO'S WORN THE NUMBER:

James Zyntell (G) 1934, **Sonny Jurgensen** (QB) 1957-63, Jim Nettles (DB) 1965-68, Billy Walik (WR) 1970-72, Joe Pisarcik (QB) 1980-84, Don McPherson (QB) 1988-90, Jim McMahon (QB) 1990-92, Rodney Peete (QB) 1995-98, Norm Johnson (K) 1999.

Originator: Guard James "Iggy" Zyntell played two years in Philadelphia before jumping to the Boston Shamrocks of the rival AFL in 1936.

Longest Tenure: Seven years, Sonny Jurgensen.

Number Changes: James Zyntell wore 21 in 1933 and 16 in 1935.

Just Visiting: Norm Johnson scored over 1,700 points in the NFL.

Highs: Belligerent, punky former Bear Jim McMahon had a good season replacing the injured Randall Cunningham in 1991.

Lows: Normally reliable veteran kicker Norm Johnson committed a strange gaffe against the Bucs in 1999. With five seconds left in the half, everyone on the field goal unit was lined up on the field except for the kicker. Johnson raced on the field at the last second and then missed the rushed 26-yard attempt.

Sonny Jurgensen

One way to judge the greatness of quarterbacks is by wins — in particular championship wins. By this criterion, the greatest quarterbacks in NFL history are Otto Graham, who won seven titles; Bart Starr, who won five; and Sid Luckman, Terry Bradshaw and Joe Montana, who each won four. The flaw in this way of thinking is obvious. Is Trent Dilfer superior to Dan Marino as a quarterback simply because he won a Super Bowl backed by a terrific defense that Marino never had? The question is absurd. Consider the talented Hall of Fame quarterbacks who never guided their team to a title: Ace Parker, Y.A. Tittle, Sonny Jurgensen, Fran Tarkenton, Dan Fouts, Jim Kelly and Dan Marino, not to mention Warren Moon, who will soon be inducted in Canton as well. Jurgensen at least was a member of a championship club, the 1960 Eagles, but his individual claim to greatness is not dependent on his less-talented teammates.

Sonny was a three-sport star as a schoolboy in Wilmington, North Carolina, and won a football scholarship to Duke. The odd thing was that Duke at that time hardly ever threw the ball, so Sonny's skills were mostly wasted and undeveloped in college. For the Blue Devils, Jurgensen threw the ball only 59 times as a senior and tossed only six touchdown passes as an undergraduate. Former Duke star Ace Parker — one of those Hall of Fame QBs without a title — recommended Sonny to the Eagles. Coach Charley Gauer worked him out, and Philadelphia drafted Jurgensen in the fourth round in 1957.

Gauer took a special interest in tutoring Jurgensen, and Sonny got to start four games as a rookie, winning three of them. The Eagles obtained Norm Van Brocklin the next year, though, so Sonny was relegated to the bench. Rather than resent that, however, he looked on it as a chance to learn the position from a rough-tongued master. Although Van Brocklin frequently berated Sonny, telling him that he could be a good quarterback if he stopped being a clown, Jurgensen always has spoken highly of the knowledge he gained from the one-sided relationship. From 1958 through 1960, Sonny threw only one more pass than he had thrown as a rookie. On the field, Sonny studied Van Brocklin, but off the field he followed a different path along with receiver and fellow fun-seeker Tommy McDonald.

Those Eagles were Van Brocklin's team, and once they won the championship, both Van Brocklin and coach Buck Shaw retired. Instead of giving the coaching job to Van Brocklin as he had expected, the Eagles promoted line coach Nick Skorich. Sonny was now the starting quarterback at last, and his puckish friend McDonald told him, "Don't worry, Sonny. I'll make as great a passer out of you as I did of Van Brocklin." Starting with the 1961 College All-Star Game where Jurgensen showed a flair for the spectacular by completing a pass behind his back to Pete Retzlaff, 1961 was a great year for Sonny and the team. He threw for a team record 3,723 yards and 32 touchdowns with his deadly sidearm delivery while leading the Eagles to a 10-4 record, good for second-place in the East. In the Playoff Bowl that pitted the second-place Eagles against the second-place Lions in a meaningless January exhibition game, disaster struck when Jurgensen suffered a severe shoulder separation.

Between the shoulder problem and other injuries both to Jurgensen and his team-mates, the bottom fell out in 1962 and 1963. The team's 3-10-1 and 2-10-2 records in those years cost Skorich his job, while Sonny's touchdown passes declined to 22 in 1962 and then 11 in 1963. The 1963 season started badly when Sonny and backup quarter-back King Hill walked out of training camp in a contract dispute. Reports that Eagle general manager Vince McNally tore the arm off a chair in his office during these nego-tiations indicate that this ploy left a bad taste for Eagles management. The combination of Sonny's declining production, his reputation as a frivolous playboy, and the bitter relationship with management did not augur well. When new coach/GM Joe Kuharich met with Jurgensen on April 1, 1964, Sonny thought everything went fine. He went to lunch and was shocked when he heard on the radio that he had been traded to the Redskins for Norm Snead. At first he thought it was an April Fool's prank, but it was real. It was reported later that Jurgensen had been offered first to Minnesota for Fran Tarkenton, but coach Van Brocklin nixed that deal.

Sonny lashed out a bit at Eagles management in the press, but saved his worst fury for the field. Over the next 11 seasons in Washington, Jurgensen faced the Eagles 18 times. The Redskins won 12, lost three and tied three as Sonny threw for 33 touchdowns and only 16 interceptions in those games. In their very first meeting in 1964, Sonny threw for 385 yards and five scores in a 35-20 Redskins win. Eleven seasons later, and the last time Jurgensen faced the Eagles, he came off the bench in the second half reliev-ing his friend Billy Kilmer. Sonny was hobbling on a bad leg, but still led Washington back from a 20-7 deficit to win 27-20 on a 30-yard strike to Charley Taylor with two minutes remaining.

Sonny, the pure-passer whose last four years as a Redskin were diminished by injury and coach George Allen's preference for the more ground-oriented Kilmer, twice was a member of a team playing for a championship, but did not play in either the 1960 title game or the 1973 Super Bowl. His last appearance as a pro quarterback was his first appearance in the postseason as he played part of the 1974 playoff game the Skins lost to the Rams. This short-time Eagle hero compiled 255 TD passes and passed for over 32,000 yards in his career. Although he heard the boos in his time in Philadelphia, Sonny Jurgensen is remembered wistfully as an obvious symbol of the inept Eagles management during the 1960s. He has been the Redskins' radio broadcaster for sever-al years.

1947 Playoffs

Tommy Thompson
QB 1941-42

Originator: In 1934, back George Kavel was the first to wear 10. He only played in one game and was replaced in 10 that year by Swede Ellstrom, who had come over from the Redskins.

Longest Tenure: Eight years, long-term backup QBs King Hill and Koy Detmer.

Number Changes: Don Jackson also wore 50 in 1936; Tommy Thompson wore 11 from 1945 to 1950; John Walton wore 11 in 1976 and 1977.

Just Visiting: None.

Highs: Quarterback Adrian Burk was Tommy Thompson's replacement and once threw seven TD passes in a game. He later became an NFL referee. Punter John Teltschik twice was special teams MVP.

Lows: Rich Kotite attempted to bring former Jet Pat Ryan back from the dead in 1991, but he played like a zombie, completing only 10 of 26 passes with four interceptions.

Tommy Thompson

Tossin' Tommy Thompson, the Tulsa Typhoon, took a circuitous route to Philadelphia. As a boy in Arkansas, a stone-throwing incident left him legally blind in one eye. However, with a strong arm developed as a high school athlete throwing the discus, javelin and shot put, he made his way to the University of Tulsa where his passes out of the Single Wing Offense helped the Golden Hurricanes win two straight Missouri Valley Conference titles. Tommy was an All-MVC selection in 1938, but left school in 1939 under very odd circumstances. He was secretly married in February of that year to a dentist's assistant named Ruth, and that marriage made him ineligible to play football because Tulsa had a rule against married athletes. Two weeks later, Ruth swallowed a fatal dose of poison during a party. Some of her friends said that she was despondent because the marriage was costing Thompson his senior season, and this led to her killing herself, although Thompson denied that.

Tulsa declared Tommy eligible for football once again, but he signed with the Chicago Cardinals instead. He still had eligibility problems, though. Tommy could not play in the NFL for another year since his class had not graduated, so he joined the St. Louis Gunners of the minor league AFL for the 1939 season and played with former Eagle Swede Ellstrom. In 1940, the Cardinals released Thompson, but the Steelers signed him 10 days later. He was not much of a runner and floundered as a tailback in Pittsburgh's run-oriented Single Wing. Luckily for Tommy, new Pittsburgh owner Lex Thompson (no relation) swapped franchises with Bert Bell and Art Rooney to get closer to his New York business interests and then hired Greasy Neale to coach the new Eagles.

Neale installed the T Formation that Thompson was much better suited to run. After two losing seasons of learning, the one-eyed Thompson joined the Army in 1943 and won a Purple Heart at Normandy. He mustered out of the service and rejoined the Eagles in October 1945. His old number 10 was now worn by backup quarterback and future Giants coach Allie Sherman, so Thompson switched to 11. Since his greatest years were still to come, he is remembered as number 11 in Philadelphia. When Thompson went in the military, the Eagles obtained Roy Zimmerman from the Redskins as their quarterback. For 1945 and 1946, the two shared the quarterback position and the Eagles finished second in the division both years. Prior to the 1947 season, Neale traded Zimmerman to the Lions for two linemen. Bears Hall of Famer Paddy Driscoll had said in 1943 that "Zimmerman is good, but the other teams are fortunate that Tommy Thompson is gone. They could win the National League title with him." Thompson not only had better touch on his passes, he was a more fiery leader as well. Tommy was popular with both his teammates and his coach. He was not afraid to tell his coach after a questionable play Neale had sent in was successful, "You sure were lucky that time."

By 1947, the Eagles were clearly the best team in the East. However, when they were beaten 45-21 at home by the Chicago Cardinals in the next to last game of the year,

Before joining the Army where he won a Purple Heart on the Normandy beaches, the one-eyed Tommy Thompson wore number 10. Eagles owner Jerry Wolman paid Thompson a $50 personal pension each month in the 1960s.

they found themselves half a game behind the persistent Steelers, who had already completed their schedule with an 8-4 record despite being outscored for the season. The next week, the Eagles easily defeated Green Bay to set up a playoff for the Eastern crown the next week in Pittsburgh. Neale was rewarded with a new three-year contract before the game, but spent three days that week in bed with the flu. The Eagles were favored and did not disappoint their fans. Thompson threw a 15-yard touchdown to Steve Van Buren in the first quarter and a 28-yarder to Jack Ferrante in the second quarter to go up 14-0 in the first half. Bosh Pritchard iced the victory with a 79-yard punt return in the third quarter as the Birds won 21-0. After the game, dour Steeler coach Jock Sutherland stated, "The better team won, but I don't think they're better than us without Van Buren." Apparently he did not notice that Tommy Thompson completed 11 of 18 passes for 255 yards during the game. Neale pointed out, "That Tommy Thompson played a great game. His signal calling was just about perfect."

The championship game the following week was against those same Cardinals that had shellacked Philadelphia three weeks before, but the Eagles were confident. It was 28 degrees on game day, but the problem was that the field was covered with ice. Before the game, the officials approved the cleats the Eagles were going to wear. Then during warm-ups, those same officials told Neale the Eagles could not wear such sharp cleats. Neale's reaction was that it was too late to do anything about it then. The game started and the Cardinals complained to the officials about the shoes of Eagle players. One by one, the officials would eject the offending player until he changed his footwear and penalized Philadelphia five yards each time for illegal equipment. On the second Cardinal possession, Cards star runner Charley Trippi burst up the middle for a 44-yard touchdown run. Early in the second quarter, halfback Elmer Angsman took the same play 70 yards for another Chicago touchdown. Thompson kept the Eagles in the game with a 53-yard touchdown pass before the half. In the third quarter, Trippi caught a punt at his 25 and despite slipping to the icy ground twice, returned it 75 yards for another touchdown. Thompson led the Eagles back and Van Buren went over from the 1 to make the score 21-14 at the start of the fourth quarter. In the final period, though, Angsman again burst up the gut for another 70-yard touchdown jaunt. Thompson, who would complete 27 of 44 passes for 297 yards, led Philadelphia to another score by Russ Craft from the 1, but the game ended 28-21. Neale said afterwards, "We did everything but beat them." He complained about the conditions, "We also had several new plays worked up for this game including cutbacks that we could not use."

The Eagles and Thompson fed on the disappointment from that loss. Tommy had his greatest season in 1948, throwing 25 touchdown passes, and Philadelphia would win the next two NFL titles. Decline set in for Thompson and the Eagles in 1950, and he retired to go into coaching. Severe arthritis sent him to a wheelchair after 1970. In 1988, he was diagnosed with brain cancer and fought that for a year before succumbing in 1989 at the age of 72. The last highlight of his life was traveling to Philadelphia for the 40th reunion of the 1948 champs. It was a joyful occasion where he got to reunite with his old teammates from the greatest years of his life.

11

1960 Championship

Norm Van Brocklin
QB 1958-60

WHO'S WORN THE NUMBER:

Lee Woodruff (B) 1933, Joe Knapper (B) 1934, Ed Manske (E) 1936, John Ferko (G) 1937, Bernie Lee (B) 1938, Francis Murray (B) 1939-40, Lou Ghecas (B) 1941, Richard Erdlitz (B) 1942, *Tommy Thompson* (QB) 1945-50, John Rauch (QB) 1951, *Bobby Thomason* (QB) 1952-57, **Norm Van Brocklin** (QB) 1958-60, Rick Arrington (QB) 1970-73, John Walton (QB) 1976-77, Jeff Christensen (QB) 1984-85, Kyle Mackey (QB) 1986, Scott Tinsley (QB) 1987r, Casey Weldon (QB) 1992, Matt Bahr (K) 1993, Jay Fiedler (QB) 1994-95, Mark Rypien (QB) 1996, Ron Powlus (QB) 2000, Tim Hasselbeck (QB) 2002, Jeff Blake (QB) 2004.

Originator: Cowboy Lee Woodruff played in the backfield for Philadelphia in 1933. He scored one touchdown rushing and another on an interception.

Longest Tenure: Six years, quarterbacks Tommy Thompson and Bobby Thomason.

Number Changes: Joe Knapper also wore 24 in 1934; Ed Manske wore 36 in 1935; John Ferko wore 19 in 1938; Tommy Thompson wore 10 in 1941 and 1942; John Walton wore 10 in 1978 and 1979.

Just Visiting: Matt Bahr scored over 1,400 points with six teams; Mark Rypien led the Redskins to a Super Bowl victory; Jeff Blake had his greatest success as a Bengal throwing bombs to Carl Pickens.

Highs: Eggs Manske was an All-Pro end before being traded to the Bears. He married a former Olympic diver and later coached in the college ranks; Tommy Thompson (see 10); Bobby Thomason was a very inconsistent Pro Bowl quarterback who was the best of four QBs drafted in the first round in 1949 along with John Rauch, Stan Heath and Frank Tripucka.

Lows: Flashy flop backup quarterback Rick Arrington is now better known as the father of sideline reporter Jill Arrington.

Norm Van Brocklin

Acerbic Norm Van Brocklin was known as the Brat by opponents and teammates alike. Hampton Pool, who coached Van Brocklin with the Rams, once said of him, "Soon he'll break every existing record — if some lineman doesn't break his neck first." While examples of the Dutchman's kindness and humanity abound off the field, on it he was a vocal, feared and respected leader. Much of the commentary about the Eagles' 1960 championship concerns Chuck Bednarik's amazing iron man performance in the line, but that largely mediocre squad of overachievers was Van Brocklin's team.

His parents were South Dakota farmers who moved to California when Norm was three. At 17, he forged his mother's signature on his enlistment papers and joined the Navy in 1943. Discharged three years later, Van Brocklin enrolled at the University of Oregon under the G.I. Bill and was named All-American in 1948. Since he was able to complete all his degree requirements in three years — perhaps aided by his wife, who was his former biology lab instructor, Van Brocklin was eligible for the NFL draft and was taken by Los Angeles in the fourth round. His gifts were obvious from the start. While he could not run at all, his arm was strong and accurate. His touch and timing on both long and short passes were second to none. In addition, he was an outstanding punter. He did not play much as a rookie backup for Hall of Famer Bob Waterfield, but new coach Joe Stydahar instituted an unusual platoon system for his quarterbacks in 1950. Waterfield would take the first and third quarters, and Van Brocklin would play the second and fourth periods.

The Rams followed this program for the next three years. Even when Van Brocklin threw for an NFL record 554 yards against the feeble New York Yanks in 1951 on a day when Waterfield was injured, Van was back to half a game the next week. The Rams won the Western Division in 1950 and 1951 and lost a playoff to the Lions in 1952. They won the 1951 title match against the Browns on a 73-yard fourth-quarter touchdown bomb from Van Brocklin to Tom Fears. In an off-year for Van Brocklin, the Rams returned to the title game in 1955, but Cleveland intercepted six of the Dutchman's passes and pummeled Los Angeles. The coach by this time was Sid Gillman, who did not get along with Van Brocklin. After three years, Norm wanted out and went about making life miserable for Rams management. He told Ram general manager Pete Rozelle that he'd be happy to go anywhere but Philadelphia, so Rozelle worked out a deal with the Eagles.

Once the Eagles traded for Van Brocklin, they were able to convince the highly respected Buck Shaw to come out of retirement to coach the team. They still had to convince Van Brocklin not to retire. Commissioner Bert Bell got involved with the negotiations and assured Van Brocklin that once the elderly Shaw retired after three years, he would be named the next Eagles coach. It was a gentleman's agreement; nothing was committed to paper. The Eagles were a bad team under Hugh Devore in 1957, and Shaw made them worse at first by tearing them down completely to build anew. Shaw was following the old saw of having three teams: one going, one here and one

Norm Van Brocklin and Chuck Bednarik were teammates in the 1949 College All-Star Game against the champion Eagles. In the photo, Norm is indicating that they are about to enter their 11th season in 1959.

coming. While Shaw was sorting out the roster, Van Brocklin was building the offense, particularly by working extensively with young receivers Tommy McDonald and Pete Retzlaff to develop their untapped potential. In 1959, the Eagles went from 2-9-1 to 7-5 and second place in the East.

1960 was the beginning of a new decade and a fresh start for Philadelphia, but it did not look that way on opening day when the Eagles were crushed 41-24 at home by the Browns. After the game, Shaw expressed disappointment with everyone including Van Brocklin. Some Philly fans even booed Van that day after three of his first six passes were intercepted. Things began to change the next week with a lackluster 27-25 victory over the expansion Cowboys, won on Bobby Freeman's two blocked extra points. It would be the first of nine straight wins, including five fourth-quarter comebacks. The biggest wins came in the Browns rematch, won on Bobby Walston's 38-yard field goal with 10 seconds left, and the two Giants games played on successive Sundays. The first, at Yankee Stadium, featured Chuck Bednarik's murderous hit on Frank Gifford and was won on Jimmy Carr's fumble recovery in the final period. In the rematch, the Eagles spotted the Giants 17 points before coming back to win 31-23. The Eagles had no running game, and their defense was in the middle of the pack statistically, but they showed throughout the season that they refused to quit.

The Eagles met the Packers for the championship on December 26th, a cold and sunny Monday at Franklin Field, before 67,325 fans, and the young and inexperienced Packers were favored. It was an odd game that could have gone in the opposite direction, but ultimately the more experienced team won. On the game's first offensive play, Packer defensive end Bill Quinlan intercepted a botched pitchout at the Eagles' 14. Three running plays left a fourth and two at the 6. Lombardi decided to go for it with another running play, but Jim Taylor slipped on the slick turf and was unable to hit the hole. The Eagles took over on downs. On a third-down play in the next series, Eagle runner Bill Barnes fumbled at the 22 and linebacker Bill Forester recovered. Once again the Eagles defense rose up, and Paul Hornung kicked a 20-yard field goal. Later in the first quarter, the Packers drove the length of the field only to be forced again to settle for a 23-yard field goal. Meanwhile, Eagle quarterback Norm Van Brocklin led the Eagles to 10 points and the lead via his passing arm. The touchdown came on a 35-yard shot to Tommy McDonald, and Walston's 15-yard field goal was set up by a 41-yard strike to Pete Retzlaff. The Packers drove down the field with time running out, but missed a 12-yard field goal to close the first half.

In the third quarter, the Packers reached the Philadelphia 25, but lost the ball on downs again. The Eagles answered with their own drive to the Packers' 5, but were stopped by an interception. Aided by a 35-yard run for a first down by Max McGee on a fake punt, the Packers finally reached the end zone on a seven-yard pass from Bart Starr to McGee early in the fourth quarter. Assistant coach Charlie Gauer noticed that the left side of the Packers' kickoff team was slower than the right and, on the ensuing kickoff, set up a special return to capitalize on that. Eagle returner Ted Dean took the kick 58 yards to the Packers' 38. The Eagles moved down to the Packers' 5, and Dean scored on a sweep to make the score 17-13. After several exchanges of punts, the Packers got the ball on their own 35 with 1:15 left and quickly moved to the Eagles' 22. On the famous last play of the game, Starr found no one open deep, so he hit Jim Taylor underneath, and Taylor was brought down on the 9 by 60-minute-man Chuck Bednarik as time ran out.

Van Brocklin told reporters after the game that he took advantage of the eager Ray Nitschke's being out of position on several occasions to hit on big plays. In a comparison of quarterbacks, youthful Bart Starr averaged barely over five yards per attempt, while Van Brocklin averaged over 10. The Packers outgained the Eagles 401 yards to 296, but came up short throughout the afternoon. Charlie Gauer crowed afterwards, "This ought to shut those Western Conference people up. I think four or five teams in our division could beat the Packers — the Browns, Giants, Steelers and Cardinals to name them." The Eagles were champions, and each player received $5,116.

Buck Shaw and Norm Van Brocklin capped their triumph by retiring, but the Dutchman had a surprise coming. In a meeting with Eagle management troika Frank McNamee, Joe Donoghue and Vince McNally, Van Brocklin found he was not being offered the coaching job he had been promised. Bert Bell was dead, and there was no written agreement. The Eagles wanted to keep him as a player, but the betrayed

Dutchman would have none of it. Soon after, when accepting the league MVP award at a Philadelphia banquet, Van Brocklin announced that he was going to accept an offer to become the coach of the expansion Minnesota Vikings, since the Eagles had reneged on their promise to him. Eagle management saw him as too much of a headache and not worth the aggravation just as Norman Braman would one day see another brash Eagle leader, Buddy Ryan. Van Brocklin went on to coach for seven years in Minnesota and another seven in Atlanta without great success. Both situations ended badly for the mouthy Dutchman, and he was out of football after 1974. He was elected to the Hall of Fame in 1971 and died in 1983. With what he was able to accomplish in just three seasons in Philadelphia, Norm Van Brocklin is considered by many to be the greatest Eagle quarterback.

12
Fog

Randall Cunningham
QB 1985-95

Randall Cunningham

Philadelphia fans have a more divided reaction to Randall Cunningham than to any other Eagle. One view of him is that he was the greatest quarterback in Eagles history, and that if he only had received better coaching, he would have led the team to multiple championships. The alternate opinion is that Randall was a tremendous though undisciplined athlete who could have been great if he had applied himself to his craft, but instead was a loser who could not read defenses and would never lead any team to a title.

What everyone agrees on is that Cunningham was a human highlight reel. There was the time against the Oilers in 1988 when Randall rolled out to the left, found no one open, and doubled back to the other side of the field. With still no passing options, he took off and juked and sprinted his way for a 33-yard touchdown run. The next week against the Giants, Randall rolled right and found linebacker Carl Banks going for his legs. Randall broke his hurdling fall with his hand, popped up and threw a TD pass to Jimmie Giles. In 1989 he proved his leg was as powerful as his arm when he booted a 91-yard punt against the Giants. Against the Bills in 1990, Cunningham dropped back in his own end zone, eluded the charging Bruce Smith, dashed to his left and launched the ball 60 yards in the air where Fred Barnett leaped to snare it and race the rest of the way on a remarkable 95-yard touchdown pass play. This is not to mention the comeback heroics of last-minute touchdown passes to beat the Cardinals in 1987, the Redskins in 1987 and 1989 and the Cowboys in 1988 and 1990.

Randall was tremendous at improvisation, but less successful when working from a game plan — especially against a playoff-caliber defense. Cunningham's defenders would argue that his problems stemmed from a lack of coaching. Buddy Ryan's attitude toward his offense was to turn Randall loose and hope he would make four or five big plays to win the game. However, trusted quarterback coach Doug Scovil tutored him for his second through fifth seasons in the league. Randall should have been able to carry on himself when his friend Scovil died at that point. When Cunningham was a rookie, Marion Campbell brought in offensive genius Sid Gillman to coach him. In an oft-told story, Gillman would give Randall film to take home to study, but suspected Cunningham was not doing his homework, so he put a piece of paper in the film can one time. The slip was unmoved when Gillman got the film back.

Cunningham clearly was not a devoted student of the game; he had other interests. Each year it seemed he had a new slogan. As a jheri-curled rookie, he showed up at training camp wearing a shirt that read, "Any questions, call my agent." Another year he wore a hat reading "Let me be me." A third year he wore an "I'm still scrambling" hat. His personality was not team-oriented. When he admitted that sometimes he even amazed himself on the field, his teammates were not necessarily amused. Randall was drawn to the entertainment world. He had his own television show in which he took great interest and once got permission to leave an exhibition game early so he could go to Whitney Houston's birthday party. His selfish behavior screamed immaturity, although there were mitigating factors. Both his parents had died when he was young, and he was estranged from his revered big brother Sam, a former Patriot star fullback. He was also a black quarterback before that became a normal occurrence. Finally, he played in front of a bad offensive line, assisted by no true running backs and no great receivers.

The game that epitomizes Cunningham's career is the Fog Bowl, the playoff game between the Eagles and the Bears in 1988. That is not so much because he played well, but inconsistently in trying conditions that day by throwing for 407 yards and three interceptions in a loss. Instead, this was one day when the fog that seemed to engulf Cunningham's mind in the biggest games was visible to everyone. On the television broadcast of the Fog Bowl, Terry Bradshaw summed Randall up as "an athlete, not a quarterback."

After winning two MVP trophies and no playoff games under Buddy Ryan, Cunningham would never really be the same force. He had led the Eagles in rushing four straight years, including gaining 942 yards in 1990 as Ryan's Ultimate Weapon, and four times was the team's offensive MVP. Under new coach Rich Kotite, Randall suffered a knee injury in the 1991 opener. He worked hard and won the Comeback Player award the next season. More importantly, he won his first playoff game against the Saints, but he and the team reverted to form the following week, losing badly to the Cowboys. In 1993, the team started fast by winning its first four games, but Cunningham broke his leg in the fourth game and was lost for another season. He came back again in 1994, but after a fast 7-2 start, Kotite's Birds lost their last seven games, and Randall lost his starting job to Bubby Brister for the last two. He reacted petulantly by packing up his locker and wearing his team jacket inside out on the sidelines.

New coach Ray Rhodes was convinced that boy genius offensive coordinator Jon Gruden was going to teach the West Coast Offense to Randall in 1995, but a struggling Cunningham was benched for journeyman Rodney Peete after the team started 1-3. Randall pouted and withdrew. The Eagles made the playoffs and beat the Lions in the wild card game to earn a trip to Dallas for the divisional playoff. Randall got permission to take off midweek to be with his pregnant wife, but did not bother to bring his playbook. Sure enough, Peete got injured in the first quarter and Cunningham had to replace him. Randall played in a fog, unprepared and confused, as the Eagles got pummeled by the Cowboys.

At that point, the sensitive Cunningham abruptly retired to do masonry in Nevada. The following season, he returned to the league as a Viking, and in his second season in Minnesota he led Randy Moss, Cris Carter and the rest of the Vikings to a 15-1 record. In the NFC championship, though, they were upset by the Falcons, a key play being a costly, boneheaded interception Randall threw right before the half. He spent three more seasons in the league with Minnesota, the Cowboys and the Ravens before retiring for good in 2002, officially as an Eagle and forever an enigma.

Rock Bottom — 1936

Dave Smukler
FB 1936-39

WHO'S WORN THE NUMBER:

George Kenneally (E) 1933-35, Dave Smukler (B) 1936-39, Leonard Barnum (B) 1940-42, Chuck Hughes (WR) 1967-69, Rick Engles (P) 1978.

Originator: Former All-Pro end George Kennealy in 1933. George was a former Pottsville Maroon and was captain and assistant coach for both the first Redskin team in 1932 and the first Eagle team in 1933.

Longest Tenure: Four years, Dave Smukler.

Number Changes: None.

Just Visiting: None.

Highs: None.

Lows: Punter Rick Engles made a name for himself in 1978 when he claimed that Dick Vermeil told him to fake an injury so he could go on injured reserve. The NFL took away an Eagles draft pick to punish them for stashing players.

Dave Smukler

Dynamite Dave Smukler is proof that human nature does not change, that players of the "good old days" could be just as moody and unmanageable as contemporary players often are. His teammate Joe Carter told the story that once against the Redskins, the Eagles had reached the Washington 12-yard line. The play call was for fullback Smukler to fake a run and then pull up short and pass the ball. On the play, though, Dave saw a big hole and ran with the ball. He collided thunderously with the Redskins' enormous Hall of Fame tackle Turk Edwards near the goal line and bulled his way to the 1. After the play, Smukler did not move but lay on the field, apparently unconscious. Carter figured that Dave was faking so that he could be carried off the field on a stretcher as a fallen hero. Carter knelt beside him and whispered that Dave had "almost killed that Edwards elephant." With that, Smukler opened his eyes wide and jumped up, ready to push the ball in the end zone, which he did on the next play.

Smukler was born in upstate New York and graduated high school in Newark, New Jersey, before enrolling at Temple University. At the time, Temple was a football powerhouse under the legendary coach Pop Warner. Dave's talent was undeniable; he was 6 feet 2 inches, 220 pounds and could run the 100 in 10.2 seconds (a fast pace for the time). He was a powerful runner and could pass, punt and kick. Warner was so enamored with Smukler's ability as a sophomore that he compared him to a pair of Hall of Famers Pop had coached in other places: "He is a better fullback now than Ernie Nevers was in Nevers' sophomore year…He may become the greatest fullback I have ever seen, a greater football player than Nevers or Jim Thorpe." In that sophomore season of 1934, Smukler took Temple to an undefeated 7-0-2 season and a berth in the very first Sugar Bowl game where they lost to Tulane, although Dave played well. His junior season was interrupted by injury, and he got angry that Temple would not give him time off from classes for treatment. The next semester he dropped out of college to pursue a business position "too promising to refuse."

Smukler signed with the Eagles as a free agent in 1936. If this was the position he thought too promising to refuse, boy, was he mistaken. For their first three years under owner/coach Lud Wray, the Eagles had compiled a less than stellar 9-21-1 record. His partner Bert Bell bought out Wray in 1936, figuring he could do a better job as head coach, but it did not work out that way. Coming off a 2-9 record in 1935 when the team finished last in the NFL in points with only 60, how could things get worse? A bad line got even worse with the loss of Jim Zyntell to the rival American Football League and Joe Kresky to retirement. Increased playing time for Swede Hanson and the addition of Dave Smukler helped the awful rushing attack move up from eighth to seventh in the nine-team league, but the passing offense went from sixth to last as Philadelphia passers only completed 22 percent of their passes. Joe Carter and Ed Manske were able ends, but no one could get them the ball in 1936. The result was that the Eagles scored only 51 points in 12 games. The team scored just six touchdowns for the entire season; center/kicker Hank Reese led the team in scoring with nine points. Meanwhile, the defense also finished last by giving up 206 points for the year.

Eagle fans may have had their spirits raised by the opening day 10-7 victory over the Giants at home, but the team then went on an 11-game losing streak. They did not score another touchdown until the seventh game of the year. Along the way they were shut out by the Bears, Dodgers, Lions and Pirates. After breaking out for 17 points in a 21-17 loss to the Giants in New York, the Eagles were shut out again by the Pirates and then by the Cardinals. The only games they lost by fewer than 10 points were the afore-mentioned loss in New York, a 6-0 loss to Pittsburgh and a 13-7 loss to Brooklyn. Their 1-11 record with its .083 winning percentage is the worst season in the inconsistent history of the Eagles, a team still carrying a cumulative losing record.

As for Dynamite Dave, he both showed promise and created problems as a rookie. He was second on the team in rushing with 321 yards, but also was suspended for one game due to a rules infraction. In 1937, Dave again finished second on the team in rushing with 247 yards as the team improved slightly to 2-8-1. In Smukler's third season, he led the team in rushing with 313 yards, returned a kickoff 101 yards for a touchdown and had the best passing performance of his career by completing 41 percent of his passes for seven touchdowns and only eight interceptions. The Eagles improved to 5-6.

In 1939, everything fell apart. Dave still led the team in rushing with 218 yards but only played in four games before being suspended for breaking training. At that point, he told Bell that he was through with football. In the off-season, Bell traded Smukler to the Lions for two players, but Dave enlisted in the Army instead. According to the *Washington Post*, he told Detroit coach Potsy Clark: "I got $3,000 a year for playing football professionally. It was great during the season. Everybody shook your hand, slapped you on the back and told you what a swell fellow you were. But the rest of the time I couldn't get a job. Do you know that for four years between football seasons I had difficulty finding a job? It's a good thing I learned something about glove cutting when I was going to high school. But that wasn't steady either. I guess by and large working on piecework and with my football money I made no more than $4,000 a year. It was enough to discourage any man, and I kept thinking about what I was going to do when I couldn't play football anymore. I sat down and figured it out and then decided the best bet was the Army."

Smukler served in the Army for four years before receiving a medical discharge in 1943. The Lions sold his rights to the Boston Yanks, and Smukler appeared in two games for them in 1944 before again being suspended by the team. His rights were transferred to the Steelers and then to the Rams, but he never appeared in the NFL again. He did some college coaching before settling in as a sales executive in the tire industry in California. He died in 1971 at the age of 57.

Family Ties

Ty Detmer
QB 1996-97

WHO'S WORN THE NUMBER:

Swede Hanson (B) 1933-36, Rudy Gollomb (G) 1936, Elwood Dow (B) 1938-40, Bob Gambold (B) 1953, Pete Liske (QB) 1971-72, Marty Horn (QB) 1987r, Rick Tuten (P) 1989, Jeff Wilkins (K) 1994, Ty Detmer (QB) 1996-97, Doug Pederson (QB) 1999, A.J. Feeley (QB) 2001-02.

Originator: Temple Owl Thomas "Swede" Hanson in 1933.

Longest Tenure: Four years, Swede Hanson.

Number Changes: Swede Hanson also wore 42 in 1936 and 1937.

Just Visiting: Jeff Wilkins has scored a lot of points for the Rams.

Highs: Swede Hanson (see 42).

Lows: Weak-armed Doug Pederson kept Donovan McNabb on the bench for half of his rookie season for no apparent reason. His greatest success in Philadelphia came as a Dolphin when he led Miami over the Eagles 19-14 for Don Shula's record 325th victory in 1993.

Ty Detmer

Ty Detmer was Texas Player of the Year for his senior year of high school in San Antonio where his father Sonny was his coach. Ty went on to pass-happy Brigham Young University and starred at quarterback, racking up an NCAA record 15,031 yards passing with 121 TD passes in three and a half years. He threw at least one touchdown pass in 35 consecutive games at BYU and won the Heisman Trophy as a junior and the Davey O'Brien Award for the nation's top college quarterback as both a junior and senior.

However, in the NFL draft, the accomplished Detmer was not taken until the ninth round by Green Bay. The main strike against Ty was his size. At 6 feet and 180 pounds, he was written off by NFL scouts as too small and fragile for the pro game. Precedent was also against him. Few Heisman winners succeed in the pros and the long line of BYU quarterback heroes is filled with names like Robbie Bosco, Marc Wilson, Gifford Nielsen, Gary Sheide and Steve Sarkisian, who did not succeed in the pros. Steve Young and Jim McMahon are obvious exceptions to this string of BYU failures, but Cougar QBs are considered suspect.

In four years backing up Brett Favre in Green Bay, Ty got into only eight games. Eagle coach Ray Rhodes had tried unsuccessfully to obtain Packer backup Mark Brunell in 1995 so when the heady Detmer became free in 1996, Rhodes signed him as someone who was familiar with his coordinator John Gruden's offense. Early in the 1996 season, starter Rodney Peete hurt his knee and Detmer at last got his chance. Things couldn't have gone better at first as the Eagles won Ty's first four starts, but in the second half of the year both Detmer and the Eagles unraveled. The team made the playoffs, but was shut out by San Francisco. In 1997, Detmer just barely won the starting job in training camp. One of Rhodes' major problems as a coach was his constant shuffling of quarterbacks. He lifted Detmer in the third quarter of the opening game, replaced him as starter with Peete in week seven and then gave him his last starting shot two weeks later. At the end of the season, Detmer left Philadelphia and since then has worked as a backup in San Francisco, Cleveland, Detroit and Atlanta. His pro career has not been spectacular, but it has lasted.

Ty and his brother Koy are one of two sets of brothers who played for the Birds at the same time. In Steve Van Buren's last season, 1951, his younger brother Ebert was drafted by Philadelphia. In Ty's second and final year in Philly, Koy Detmer was on the Eagles' practice squad. Several other Eagles have had brothers play in the NFL:

EAGLE	EAGLE YEARS	HIS BROTHER
Matt Bahr K	1993	Chris Bahr K
Brian Baldinger G	1992-93	Gary DE and Rich T Baldinger
Len Barnum B	1941-42	Pete Barnum FB
Tony Brooks RB	1992	Reggie Brooks RB
Al Chesley LB	1979-81	Francis LB and John TE Chesley
Randall Cunningham QB	1985-95	Sam Cunningham FB
Eric Everett DB	1988-89	Thomas Everett DB
Mike Golic DT	1987-92	Bob Golic LB
Don Griffin DB	1996	James Griffin DB
Tim Hasselbeck QB	2002	Matt Hasselbeck QB
Lane Howell T	1965-69	Delles DB and Mike DB Howell
Don Hultz DE	1964-73	George Hultz DE
Turkey Joe Jones DE	1974-75	Charley Taylor WR
Ed Khayat DT	1958-61, 1964-65	Bob Khayat G
Art Malone HB	1975-76	Benny Malone HB
Wes McAfee HB	1941	George McAfee HB
Jerome McDougle DE	2003-04	Stockar McDougle T
Raleigh McKenzie C	1995-96	Reggie McKenzie LB (twins)
Dexter McNabb FB	1995	Eddie Robinson LB
Don McPherson QB	1988-89, 1991	Miles McPherson DB
Nick Mike-Mayer K	1977-78	Steve Mike-Mayer K
Wilbert Montgomery RB	1977-84	Cleo WR and Tyrone RB Montgomery
William Perry DT	1993-94	Michael Dean Perry DT
Art Powell WR	1959	Charley Powell DE
Knox Ramsey G	1952	Buster Ramsey G
Dan Ryzcek C	1987	Paul Ryzcek C
Leo Skladany TE	1949	Joe Skladany DE
Ed Smith TE	1999	Irv Smith TE
Leo Stasica DE	1941	Stan Stasica HB
Terry Tautolo LB	1976-79	John Tautolo G
John Wilcox G	1960	Dave Wilcox LB
Luis Zendejas K	1988-89	Joaquin K and Max K Zendejas

Some Eagles have had their sons play in the league:

EAGLE	EAGLE YEARS	HIS SON
Howard Cassady HB	1962	Craig Cassady DB
Richard Harvey DB	1970	Richard Harvey LB
Don Looney E	1940	Joe Don Looney RB
Ken MacAfee E	1959	Ken MacAfee TE
Wayne Colman LB	1968-69	Doug Colman LB
James McAlister RB	1975-76	Chris McAlister CB
Steve Smith T	1971-74	Brady Smith DE

Other Eagles have had fathers who preceded them in pro football:

EAGLE	EAGLE YEARS	HIS FATHER
Hal Bradley G	1958	Harold Bradley G
Frank Cornish G	1995	Frank Cornish DT
Bill Cronin TE	1965	Bill Cronin B
Bill Dunstan DT	1973-76	Elwyn Dunstan T
Jim Flanigan DT	2003	Jim Flanigan LB
Tim Hasselbeck QB	2002	Don Hasselbeck TE
John Hudson G	1991-95	Dick Hudson T
Jeff Kemp QB	1991	Jack Kemp QB
Scott Kowalkowski LB	1991-92	Bob Kowalkowski G
Pete Lazetich LB	1976-77	Bill Lazetich B
Kyle Mackey QB	1986	Dee Mackey TE
Erik McMillan S	1993	Ernie McMillan T
Jim Pyne C	2001	George Pyne III DT
Antwuan Wyatt WR	1997	Alvin Wyatt DB

A few other Eagle family relationships bear noting. Center Jim Pyne's grandfather George Jr. played tackle for Providence in 1931. Philadelphia wide out Freddie Mitchell was joined on the team by his cousin Rod "He Hate Me" Smart in 2001. Topping that, Dick Vermeil coached his nephew, special teams demon Louie Giammona, from 1978 to 1982.

1949 Championship

Steve Van Buren
HB 1944-51

Originator: Former Northwestern and New York Giant fullback Reb Russell in 1933. Reb appeared in a number of Hollywood westerns in the 1930s.

Longest Tenure: Eight years, Steve Van Buren.

Number Changes: Dick Lackman also wore 24 from 1933 to 1935; Osborne Willson wore 25 in 1933; William Hughes wore 29 from 1938 to 1940; Ted Laux wore 27 in 1944.

Just Visiting: None.

Highs: None.

Lows: St. Joseph's back Ted Laux, the last player to wear 15 before Steve Van Buren, had more success as a baseball umpire in the Eastern League than in five games with the Eagles.

Steve Van Buren

Listening to the plethora of nicknames given to Steve Van Buren during his playing career gives one an idea of not only how good a running back he was, but also his style of play. He was known as "Weavin' Steven the Moving Van," "Wham Bam," "Supersonic Steve," "Blockbuster," "The Flying Dutchman" and the "Barefoot Boy of the Bayou." On the field, he had good speed — he ran the 100 in 9.8 — and was noted for swift, smart cutback ability. He also was celebrated for lowering his shoulder and simply running over defenders. Hard to bring down and hard to catch, he was the best runner in the NFL in his time. Off the field, he was a slow-moving, soft-spoken country boy who didn't wear socks and cared so little about money that he had the Eagles equipment manager Freddie Schubach handle his contract negotiations. Above all, he carried the load for back-to-back Eagle champions in 1948 and 1949. As his teammate Bucko Kilroy put it, "He was our paycheck."

Steve was born in Honduras to an American father, who worked as a fruit inspector, and a Honduran mother. For many years it was said that both his parents died by the time he reached 10. However, later reports indicate that when Steve's mother died, his father abandoned the children. Steve was sent to live with his grandparents in New Orleans and never reconciled with his father. As a 135-pound high school junior, he could not make the football team so he dropped out of school and worked for two years in a steel mill. When he returned for his senior year of high school, he weighed 165 pounds, made the team and won a scholarship to Louisiana State University. In college, he was the blocking back for star runner and future baseball star Alvin Dark. Finally, in Steve's last year as a 200-pound undergraduate, he was given the ball. Van Buren set a new Southeastern Conference rushing record that year and led LSU to victory in the 1944 Orange Bowl by running for a record 160 yards and two touchdowns.

Steve was not picked in the military draft due to vision problems in one eye and that affected his ability to catch passes. On the recommendation of LSU coach Bernie Moore, Greasy Neale made Van Buren the Eagles' first pick in the NFL draft that year without ever having seen him play. At first, Steve asked for a $10,000 contract to sign with Philadelphia, but when he was struck with appendicitis and was forced to miss the College All-Star Game, he took the Eagles' offer of $4,000. The effects of the appendicitis would greatly diminish his playing time as a rookie — he carried the ball only 80 times — but he still made the All-Pro Team for the first of seven straight seasons. In addition to averaging 5.5 yards per carry as a rookie, he also ran back both a punt and a kickoff for a touchdown and intercepted five passes. In his second season, he led the league in rushing for the first of four times. He opened that season suffering from the flu, but still scored on a 47-yard touchdown run the first time he touched the ball. That year he also set a new league record for touchdowns with 18 in 10 games — 15 on the ground, two on receptions and one via a kickoff return. With an offense based on his power running, the Eagles became instant contenders and finished second in the East for the next three years before winning the Eastern crown the next three years after that.

The handoff from Eagles superstar Steve Van Buren on the left to his brother Ebert on the right was unsuccessful as Ebert only lasted three unremarkable years in the NFL.

The durable Van Buren played through injuries and gave out as much punishment as he received. Detroit coach Gus Dorais raved about the time Van Buren ran 69 yards for a score against Detroit in 1945, despite being hit by a half dozen Lions and being knocked down five times.

Onetime Eagles end Jack Ferrante got in Steve's way and Van Buren ran right over him. As Ferrante grimaced in pain, a member of the opposing team laughed at him, saying, "Now you know how it feels." Neale compared Steve to such great runners from the past as Red Grange and Jim Thorpe. Of Grange, Neale said, "Steve is as elusive as Red ever was, and he doesn't need a blocker a lot of the time because he provides his own interference. He's a power runner, which Grange never was." Of Thorpe, with whom he once played, Neale said, "They are alike in the way they ran. Thorpe was shifty with high knee action, and plenty of power." Neale's line coach John Kellison, who also played with Thorpe, saw one difference between them, "When Thorpe hit, he did so with his knees. Steve uses the shoulder."

In 1947, Steve became the second back in league history to gain over 1,000 yards rushing after Beattie Feathers, who attained a very questionable 1,004 yards in 1934. The Eagles also made it to the championship game for the first time that year, losing to Chicago on an icy field that negated Steve's ability to cut back. In the off-season, he was offered $25,000 to jump to the All-America Conference, but chose to stay with Philadelphia for much less money. The Eagles won their first title that year, defeating the Cardinals 7-0 in a Philadelphia snowstorm on the strength of Steve's seven-yard fourth-quarter touchdown run. The following season, 1949, was the culmination of Van Buren's career and of the Eagles' 1940s glory years. Early in the season, Steve surpassed Clarke Hinkle to become the all-time leading rusher in the NFL, and for the year he set a new single-season rushing record with 1,146 yards in 12 games. After losing the fourth game of the year to the Bears, the Eagles won the final eight games of the year, each time by at least two touchdowns.

With an 11-1 record, Philadelphia looked forward to meeting the Los Angeles Rams in the championship game, getting to soak up the sun and reel in a big payday from a large crowd at the massive Los Angeles Coliseum. Instead, a 12-hour rainstorm hit Los Angeles and turned the field into a muddy mess with some puddles six inches deep. Both teams implored NFL commissioner Bert Bell, who was home in Philadelphia, to postpone the game, but Bell wanted the game to go on because he had sold the radio rights for a substantial amount of money. Because only 22,000 hearty fans turned out for the tilt, each victorious Eagle took home a check for a measly $1,090. As for the game itself, it was dominated by Van Buren and the Eagles. Steve ran the ball 31 times for a title game record 196 yards in leading Philadelphia to a 14-0 win, their second consecutive championship via shutout. The Eagles drove the ball 63 yards in six plays early in the second quarter and scored on a 31-yard pass from Tommy Thompson to Pete Pihos. Twice more in the quarter, Philadelphia drove down the field behind Van Buren, but lost the ball first on a Jim Parmer fumble at the Rams' 7 and the second time on an interception at the Rams' 2. After the Rams opened the second half by going three-and-out, Bob Waterfield stepped back into his end zone to punt. A bad snap from center allowed Eagles end Leo Skladany to block the punt and fall on the ball in the end zone for the second touchdown. The Rams only got close to scoring once when Waterfield was intercepted at the Eagles' 2 by Frank Reagan in the fourth quarter. Van Buren would close out the game by running out the clock. With 274 yards on the ground, the Eagles outgained LA 342 yards to 119 in a wet and convincing win.

Neither that Eagles team nor Van Buren would be that good again. In 1950, with Van Buren hobbled by foot and rib injuries, Philadelphia finished 6-6. Van Buren's rushing average dropped over a yard to 3.3 per carry. Steve was joined on the Eagles by his brother Ebert, but was still not healthy in 1951, and his average fell to 2.9 yards per carry. He tried again to come back in 1952, but was tackled awkwardly in a training camp scrimmage. When assistant coach Frank Reagan saw the way Van Buren's knee was twisted at an odd angle, he lost his lunch. It took Van Buren two years to be able to walk normally on that leg again. In retirement, Steve worked for the Eagles in a variety of capacities, primarily scouting, for several seasons. He also did some coaching in minor league football and was inducted into the Pro Football Hall of Fame in 1965. In 1988, he suffered a stroke, but just three months later walked onto the field at the Vet under his own power as part of the 40th anniversary celebration of the Eagles' first title. His spirit remained indomitable.

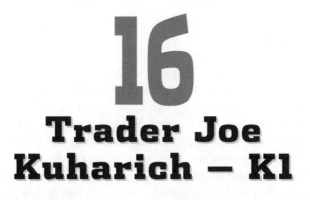

Trader Joe
Kuharich – K1

Norm Snead
QB 1964-70

Norm Snead

Maybe Leo Durocher was right — nice guys do finish last. Norm Snead is a pleasant, low-key, steady Virginian who has been married to his college sweetheart for more than 40 years and is proudest of his five children and 11 grandchildren. However, that personal success did not transfer to the football field in five different cities as a pro.

A three-sport star in Newport News, Snead matriculated at Wake Forest, a school not known for its football program. Norm threw for over 4,000 yards as an undergraduate and the team improved some, but still only went 11-19 in three years. The same pattern followed in the pros. He was drafted by Washington in the first round as the second overall pick in 1961. The Redskins were a terrible club who had not had a winning season in five years. Snead was thrown into the starting lineup immediately as a rookie and displayed a talent for throwing the long ball and for surviving behind a porous offensive line, but not for winning. In three years with the Redskins, he was booed regularly and threw 46 touchdowns and 71 interceptions for a team that finished 9-30-3. Somehow he was named to the Pro Bowl after the 1963 season.

Meanwhile in Philadelphia, things were in turmoil. Injuries and bad management had so depleted the Eagles that colorful star quarterback Sonny Jurgensen had experienced two disappointing seasons in a row with the team losing more than 10 games each year. New coach Joe Kuharich, who had once coached the Redskins, came into Philly with a broom and started making deals. Most notably, Kuharich traded away the Eagles' two biggest stars to division rivals, the popular Tommy McDonald to the Cowboys and the playboy Jurgensen to Washington for Snead, who was four years younger than Sonny. While defensive backs Jimmy Carr and Claude Crabb also changed addresses in the deal, this was a blockbuster quarterback-for-quarterback exchange almost never seen in the NFL. As Trader Joe, Mr. Malaprop, put it, "It's quite rare but not unusual."

Kuharich was the first Eagle head coach whose name began with "K" and as such was an omen for bad things ahead. Joe was a good man who had been a 195-pound All-American at guard for Notre Dame and had played briefly for the Cardinals before spending four years in the service during World War II. He got his first head coaching job with the University of San Francisco in 1948 and led the Dons to a 10-0 record in 1951. He was head coach for the Cardinals in 1952, the Redskins from 1953 to 1957, and Notre Dame from 1958 to 1962. He had a losing record at each stop, the first Fighting Irish coach to do so. Naïve new Eagles owner Jerry Wolman hired his friend Kuharich in 1964 and extended his contract to 15 years in 1965, to the amazement and consternation of the rest of the NFL. Joe was a blustery guy whose true gift was self-expression: "Every coach must view a player with three different eyes"; or "that's a horse of a different fire department"; or "we were three points behind, but that's not the same as being even."

More important than Kuharich's problems with the English language, though, were his problems on the field. He was an incompetent coach and general manager. The

The fans express their "confidence" in coach Joe Kuharich at the end of the 1967 season. "Joe Must Go" banners, chants, and airplane signs became even more popular in 1968.

offensive production of his teams was inconsistent, while the defensive performance was uniformly bad. Although some players like Bob Brown and Ollie Matson thought highly of Joe, many others like Mike Ditka came to despise him. His draft record was poor. His frequent trades were a mixed bag — some worked out and some didn't. Kuharich made a half-dozen major trades in his first year, and the Eagles did improve, but they never became good. As soon as Leonard Tose bought the Eagles from the financially strapped Wolman in 1969, he fired Kuharich. Joe had to battle cancer in the 1970s, but lived long enough to collect his salary for the remaining 10 years of his contract. He died during the Eagles' 1980 Super Bowl appearance and will always be remembered as the man who traded a Hall of Fame quarterback for Norm Snead.

Fans did not have to wait long to see the result of the trade. The Eagles traveled to Washington on October 11 to meet Jurgensen and the Redskins in the fifth game of 1964. In what would be a regular occurrence in these biannual matches, Sonny was magnificent, throwing for five touchdowns and nearly 400 yards in a 35-20 Washington win. In the next seven seasons, Jurgensen's Redskins would go 9-3-2 against Snead's Eagles, and in the 1966 Eagle victory, the slumping Snead didn't even play. Over those seven seasons, the Redskins' lousy record in the rest of their games — 33-48-3 — was almost exactly the same as the Eagles' 32-51-1 record in games outside the series. One would have to conclude that the teams were fairly evenly matched except at quarterback, where the variable Snead was not comparable to Jurgensen.

When the Redskins came into Franklin Field in November 1964, Jurgensen was much less effective, but again led his team to a 21-10 win. Snead could not move the Eagles, tossed two interceptions and was booed heavily before being lifted for King Hill in the third quarter. While Jurgensen threw for close to 3,000 yards in 1964, Snead could only manage 1,906 yards. Norm had a better season in 1965 and made the Pro Bowl for the second time but played very poorly in 1966, throwing only eight TDs against 25 interceptions and being benched for King Hill and Jack Concannon at the end of the season. Despite his performance and the fact that the Eagles were outscored during the year, 1966 was the first winning season of Norm's career, the only one he had in Philadelphia.

After the season, Kuharich tried to trade Snead to the Bears for disgruntled tight end Mike Ditka, but George Halas insisted on Jack Concannon. Snead remained in Philly and for once turned the boos into cheers by having a terrific season throwing bombs to Ben Hawkins and newly acquired Gary Ballman. He threw a career high 29 TD passes that year, although the Eagles slipped back to a losing record. 1968 brought the inevitable decline for Snead, who threw almost twice as many picks as touchdowns. Franklin Field was filled with "Joe Must Go" banners as the team lost its first 11 games en route to a 2-12 record. After being fired, Kuharich no longer had to listen to the boos, but there was no reprieve for Snead. He was not well-suited to the City of Brotherly Love. He was sturdy and had a strong arm, but was not at all mobile and lacked fire as a leader. One of his Eagle teammates once said of him, "He plays like what he is during the off-season: an insurance salesman. Snead dulls you to defeat."

Norm outlasted Kuharich by two mediocre seasons before he was at last traded to a winning team in 1971 when he went to the Vikings for lowly offensive tackle Steve Smith. In Minnesota, however, Snead was part of another three-man tag team at quarterback with Gary Cuozzo and Bob Lee. Despite the weak competition, Norm played the least of the trio for the division-winning Vikings and was sent on to the New York Giants the next year. As a Giant in 1972, he had his finest year by leading the NFL in passing and leading the Giants to an 8-6 record. It was the third and last time he played on a winning team and the third and last time he made the Pro Bowl. Both Snead and the Giants suffered through a terrible season in 1973 and in mid-season 1974, he was traded to the 49ers. After achieving little success in a year and a half in San Francisco, Norm came back to the Giants as a backup in 1976, his 16th and final season in the league.

Overall, Snead threw 196 touchdown passes and 257 interceptions in his long career with the bottom feeders of the NFL. His teams earned a 78-139-10 record. In short, Rarely Stormin' Norman was an ideal neighbor, friend or relative who could be counted on to lead the local PTA, but not a struggling football team in a demanding town. Because of the trade, he will forever be paired with Kuharich in the annals of Philadelphia football.

The Streak

Harold Carmichael
WR 1971-83

WHO'S WORN THE NUMBER:

Joe Carter (E) 1935-40, James Russell (T) 1937, Ebert Van Buren (B) 1951, Fred Enke (B) 1952, Jerry Reichow (E) 1960, Ralph Guglielmi (QB) 1963, Taft Reed (B) 1967, *Harold Carmichael* (WR) 1971-83, Mitch Berger (P) 1994, Freddie Solomon (WR) 1995, Lonny Calicchio (K) 1997.

Originator: Texan end Joe Carter in 1935.

Longest Tenure: 13 years, Harold Carmichael.

Number Changes: Joe Carter wore 31 in 1933 and 1934; James Russell wore 22 in 1936 and 1937; Ebert Van Buren wore 31 in 1952 and 1953; Freddie Solomon wore 84 from 1996 to 1998.

Just Visiting: Jerry Reichow had a few good seasons in Minnesota, as did Mitch Berger decades later.

Highs: Joe Carter was an All-Pro, glue-fingered end who was the first Eagle to gain 100 yards receiving in a game. He captained the team and was the last charter Eagle to leave the team after he fractured his shoulder in 1940. He served as an NFL official in 1952.

Lows: Lonny Calicchio spent two games in Philadelphia as the opposite of a football player — a kickoff specialist, not even a regular kicker.

Harold Carmichael

The 6-foot 8-inch Carmichael did something that many egotistical NFL star wide outs never do. He grew up. Harold was a seventh-round pick out of tiny Southern University in Louisiana and was mostly unrealized potential for his first two seasons as he was shuffled between wide receiver and tight end. New coach Mike McCormack brought in receiver coach Boyd Dowler and veteran quarterback Roman Gabriel in 1973, and the combination developed that potential into star power. Dowler installed Carmichael on the outside, and Gabriel got Harold and the rest of the "Fire High Gang " (6-foot 4-inch receivers Charley Young and Don Zimmerman) the ball. Harold's signature play became the Alley Oop over the head of the defense into the end zone. That season, the Eagles more than doubled their points scored from 1972, and Carmichael led the league in receptions with 67 and yards with 1,116.

On the field, Carmichael celebrated touchdowns with windmill spikes and elaborate setups where he and the other receivers would kneel in the end zone as Harold shook the ball and then spun it as if he were shooting craps. Off the field, he drove a fire-engine-red Coupe deVille with opera windows shaped like footballs and a license plate reading VIRGO 17 — his sign and number. He regularly partied at local clubs till late morning, looking splendorous in his wide-brimmed hats, long coats and platform heels. When his production fell off and he started to drop passes, though, Philly fans let him know they were disappointed by booing him and displaying signs like "Carmichael Couldn't Catch a Cold." Philly fans even booed him when he was carried off the field with an injured leg in 1975.

Carmichael's feelings were hurt and his confidence was shaken, but 1976 brought change. Dick Vermeil took over the Eagles, and Harold settled down, got married and became active in the Fellowship of Christian Athletes. While still the Birds' main scoring threat through the air, he became more of a steady player. He regained his popularity with the fans. His blocking improved, his sure hands returned, and he played every game, catching at least one pass each week. By 1979, he broke Saint receiver Dan Abramowicz's record of catching a pass in 105 consecutive games. The Eagles marked the event by presenting Carmichael with a 22-foot-high trophy after the record-breaking game against the Browns. Harold donated the bizarre trophy to the Hall of Fame, and caught passes in 21 more games before being stopped in a game against the Cowboys when a Dennis Thurman cheap shot knocked him out. Abramowicz at the time claimed that the record would never be broken.

With the wide-open pass offenses of the last quarter century, Abramowicz's statement proved to be ridiculous. Carmichael's 127-game streak was broken by Steve Largent in 1986, and Largent pushed the mark up to 177 games before retiring. Art Monk broke that in 1994, and extended the record to 183 before quitting. Jerry Rice passed Monk in 1998, and was not shut out until 2004 as a Raider after 274 games. Much fuss was made in the media of the end of Rice's streak, but that speaks mainly to the obsession with stats in contemporary sports. In 1964, Cowboy Tommy McDonald

At the beginning of his career, 6-foot 8-inch Harold Carmichael was known for his end zone celebrations. Here's a thunderbolt spike from on high.

had a streak of 93 games when the record was 95 games held by Don Hutson, but Tommy was not even aware of it. He told coach Tom Landry to play Buddy Dial at receiver in his place that day because they were playing Dial's former team, the Steelers. McDonald contented himself with returning punts and kickoffs and did not catch a pass. Incidentally, subsequent research determined that the original mark of Hutson's was bogus; in the middle of his career, Hutson had a game when he did not catch a pass.

The ironic thing is that the once-flamboyant Carmichael became best known for a steadiness record. Along the way, he caught 589 passes in 13 seasons as an Eagle and scored 79 touchdowns. Another irony is that by the time the Eagles obtained another receiver of Carmichael's quality in Mike Quick, Harold was losing his quickness and could not get off the line. As a final irony, he signed on with the Cowboys for two games in 1984 and caught his last pass as a teammate of Dennis Thurman, who ended his streak four years before. After retirement, Carmichael worked in several business ventures in South Jersey before returning to the Eagles in 1998 as director of player and community relations.

18
The Offensive Attack

Ben Hawkins
WR 1966-73

Ben Hawkins

The Hawk was Sixties cool. He had a high tone address at Society Hill Towers, where his bachelor apartment featured a pool table and closets overflowing with trendy clothes. He drove a gray $16,000 Aston Martin sports car and loved to party. He was a skinny, shifty speedster with a knack for big plays and a flair for getting noticed. He never snapped his chin strap, but left it dangling because he found it uncomfortable to wear. While fans saw this as a signature move by a popular player, opposing defensive backs like Mike Gaechter of the Cowboys and Larry Wilson of the Cardinals often felt it was the sign of a hot dog who needed a good whack. Indeed, Ben's helmet popped off on numerous occasions, 10 in one season by one count.

Hawkins was taken in the third round of the 1966 draft out of Arizona State, where he followed Charley Taylor. His rookie season in Philadelphia was essentially a bust in which he had only 14 catches for 143 yards, but in 1967 he caught fire. He finished fifth in the league in receptions with 59 and first in yards with a team record 1,265 yards, an average of 21.4 yards per catch; 10 of those catches went for scores. It was Ben's greatest season by far, and was also strong-armed and inconsistent Norm Snead's best season. Ben was voted the team's offensive MVP, yet strangely, Joe Kuharich almost traded him to the Rams in the off-season. Hawkins would remain a potent deep threat for the Eagles for five more years, but there was no one able to get him the ball consistently, so his numbers declined sharply. He had the moves, the speed and the hands — his career should have been greater. Hawkins broke his leg in 1973 and was traded the following season to the Browns for Turkey Joe Jones. Ben got into only two games in Cleveland before he broke his leg again and caught no passes. He surfaced briefly with the Philadelphia Bell in the World Football League before getting cut in Dick Vermeil's first Eagle training camp. As an Eagle, he averaged 18.3 yards on 261 catches with 32 touchdowns.

The Eagles' offensive production often has been as unrealized as Ben Hawkins' career. In the 1930s, the team ran a Single Wing under Lud Wray and Bert Bell and never finished higher than fourth in points while running the ball from 55 to 74 percent of the time. 1940 was the last season for Bell and the Single Wing. It was also the first year the Eagles threw the ball more often than they ran it. Once Greasy Neale arrived with the T Formation in 1941, the Eagles ran the ball from 64 to 76 percent of the time except for his first year when the run percentage was 59. Three times Philadelphia led the league in points and twice finished second under Neale. The team has never led in scoring since.

After Neale was fired in 1950, the offense became more pass-oriented under four of five different coaches in the 1950s. Twice, Jim Trimble's teams passed the ball slightly more than they ran it and in 1953 they finished second in scoring. However, successor Hugh Devore ran the ball 63 and 68 percent in his two losing seasons. The combination of coach Buck Shaw and quarterback Norm Van Brocklin brought more balance to the offense and more success to the team. Turning the ball over to coach Nick Skorich

There are two characteristic things in this shot: Ben Hawkins' chin strap is flapping freely and he is wide open.

and quarterback Sonny Jurgensen tipped the balance a bit more toward the pass. Not surprisingly, the approach of incoherent and inconsistent Joe Kuharich varied from year to year. In 1966 he ran the ball 56 percent; the next year he passed it 58 percent. The best ranking for points in the decade was third in 1960.

In the first half of the 1970s, Jerry Williams, Ed Khayat and Mike McCormack tended toward balance, with McCormack more willing to pass since he had Roman Gabriel at quarterback, but none of them was terribly successful. Dick Vermeil came in and immediately emphasized the rushing attack, running the ball at least 58 percent in each of his first four years. In 1979, the Eagles finished seventh in points, the best mark for the decade. They followed that by finishing fourth in points in 1980, the best finish for that decade. Vermeil's offense began to slide, though, and by his last year of 1982, he had Ron Jaworski throwing 58 percent of the time. Former defensive coordinator Marion Campbell, Vermeil's unsuccessful successor, ran the ball less than any coach in team history — 45, 39 and 43 percent. The defensive-minded Buddy Ryan gave the quarterback job to Randall Cunningham and brought the team back in balance. In their best year, 1990, Philadelphia finished third in scoring, and that was the best mark for the decade. Hapless Richie Kotite tended toward passing the ball, no matter who played quarterback.

Ray Rhodes brought the West Coast Offense and Rickie Watters east in 1995. The team ran the ball less each year and the offense generally got worse each year. Of course, they were quarterbacked by Rodney Peete, Ty Detmer and Bobby Hoying. Current coach Andy Reid brought in Donovan McNabb to straighten out the offense and did so with his clear propensity toward the pass. Talent plus intelligent design seem to be the keys to a successful offense, whether it focuses on the run, the pass or pure balance. Too often one, or both, of those qualities has been sorely missing in Philadelphia.

Game Winners

Tom Dempsey
K 1971-74

Tom Dempsey

Bootin' Ben Agajanian was the first Eagle kicker without toes, except that he didn't actually get to attempt any field goals or extra points in his one regular season appearance at the start of the 1945 season. Ben, who had lost the toes on his right foot in a freight elevator accident in 1941, went on to score 655 points via his foot with seven teams across three leagues, including three different Los Angeles clubs, and even ran a place-kicking school for many years. Tom Dempsey, the Eagles' second toeless kicker, had more success with the Birds, scoring 282 points in four years in Philly.

Dempsey was born with a deformed right arm and foot, but was encouraged by his parents to participate in sports and not give in to his disability. Tom played defensive end in high school and at Palomar Junior College. He didn't begin placekicking until Palomar, but that took him to the semi-pro Lowell (Massachusetts) Giants in 1967. After his college class graduated, Dempsey was eligible for the NFL, and he hooked on with the expansion New Orleans Saints. He scored 99 points as a rookie, but he is remembered primarily for breaking the NFL field goal distance record of 56 yards with an amazing 63-yard game-winning boot against the Lions on November 16, 1970. His holder for that kick was former Eagle Joe Scarpati. Saints coach J.D. Roberts did not get along with Dempsey, however, and when the hell-raising party boy put on a lot of weight and missed seven of nine field goals in the 1971 preseason, he was cut.

The Eagles had drafted kicker Happy Feller in 1971 to replace Mark Moseley, whom they found disappointing in 1970. Feller was overmatched, making only six of 20 field goal attempts, and Dempsey was signed to the taxi squad. Tom replaced Feller for the last five games of 1971 and converted 12 of 17 field goals, including two over 50 yards, to win the job. Feller was cut and landed in New Orleans the next year. Dempsey would kick for the Eagles for the next three years and score a career-high 106 points in 1973. Along the way, he would convert a number of clutch game-winning field goals. In 1973 he kicked a 12-yard chip shot with 38 seconds left to beat New England 24-23, and he nailed a 45-yarder with 25 seconds left to beat the Cowboys 13-10 in 1974. On the other hand, he also missed a 26-yarder against Buffalo in the final minute, which cost Philadelphia the game, 27-26.

Dempsey seemed to become more inconsistent as the years went on, and he was traded to the Rams in 1975. After two successful seasons in Los Angeles, he drifted on to the Oilers and Bills and finished with a total of 729 points scored for his 11-year career. The onetime New Orleans night owl got married and settled down along the way, going into high school coaching and then the business world. When Denver's Jason Elam tied his distance record in 1998, Dempsey was quick to send along his congratulations. While many looked on Tom as an inspiration, he simply saw himself as a football player. And not just a kicker — he recorded six unassisted special teams tackles in 1974 for Philadelphia. He was a player.

While most last-minute, game-winning plays tend to be field goals, they can be much more exciting than that. Here are a dozen Eagle victories memorable for their game-winning moments:

1. September 25, 1938. The Eagles score both of their touchdowns on fumbles returned 90 yards for touchdowns: the first by Bob Pylman in the second quarter; the winner by Joe Carter in the fourth. Eagles 14, Giants 10.

2. November 23, 1939. Philadelphia wins in the last minute on the hook and lateral, a pass from Davey O'Brien to Bill Hewitt that Hewitt laterals to Jay Arnold, who goes in for the score. The play travels 66 yards. Eagles 17, Steelers 14.

3. November 1, 1959. Trailing by a touchdown in the closing minute, the Redskins have a first and goal at the Eagles' 3. First down takes them to the 1. Washington fullback Don Bosseler is thwarted on three straight line plunges from that point and the game ends on the Eagles' goal line stand. An even greater goal line stand came in 1992 against the Cardinals, which also started with first down at the 3 and second down at the 1. This time the Eagles added three offsides penalties so that the Cards got six shots from the 1 but could not score. That stand came in the first half, though, so it does not qualify here. Eagles 30, Redskins 23.

4. November 20, 1960. In the game in which Chuck Bednarik knocked out Frank Gifford and caused a game-ending fumble, Concrete Charlie prefaced that hit with one on Mel Triplett that also caused a fumble. The first fumble was nabbed in the air by Jimmy Carr and returned 36 yards for the winning score. Eagles 17, Giants 10.

5. October 29, 1961. Trailing by four with a minute to play, Sonny Jurgensen completes three passes to move the ball 80 yards. The game winner comes on a 41-yard crossing pattern to Tommy McDonald with 12 seconds left. Eagles 27, Redskins 24.

6. December 11, 1977. Down by four with a fourth down at the Giants' 1, Ron Jaworski fakes a handoff to Wilbert Montgomery and runs a bootleg to the left to score the winning touchdown with 20 seconds to play. Eagles 17, Giants 14.

7. November 19, 1978. The Miracle of the Meadowlands. Herman Edwards takes Joe Pisarcik's fumble 26 yards for the winner with 20 seconds to go in the game. Eagles 19, Giants 17.

8. September 9, 1984. The Eagles are at the Minnesota 1 with seven seconds left to play after a facemask penalty on third down. Eagle coaches and players think the penalty resulted in a first down, but it is actually fourth down. Jaworski drops back to pass and almost throws the ball away intentionally when no one is open. Tight end John Spagnola breaks free and Jaws hits him with the winning score with two seconds left. Eagles 19, Vikings 17.

9. November 10, 1985. One minute and 49 seconds into overtime, the Eagles are trapped at their own 1 after a great punt by Atlanta's Rick Donnely. On second and 10, Jaworski drops back into his own end zone and finds Mike Quick streaking away from the defender at his own 30. Jaws hits him and Quick races the final 70 yards untouched for a 99-yard walk-off touchdown. Eagles 23, Falcons 17.

10. November 20, 1988. Again in overtime. Luis Zendejas' 31-yard field goal attempt is blocked by Lawrence Taylor, but Clyde Simmons scoops up the free ball and lugs it 15 yards for the winning score. Eagles 23, Giants 17.

11. October 3, 1993. In a wild comeback win over the Jets, the winning score in the fourth quarter comes when Eric Allen intercepts a pass at his own 6 and somehow breaks out of a pack of Jets to juke and streak his way 94 yards for a touchdown. Eagles 35, Jets 30.

12. October 19, 2003. After sleepwalking through the first 58½ minutes of a dull game with the Giants, the Eagles trail 10-7 with no timeouts remaining. Jeff Feagles hurries and dumps a short punt inside the 20. Brian Westbrook grabs the ball on the bounce at the 16, eludes one tackler and breaks free for an 84-yard touchdown. Eagles 14, Giants 10.

Ray Rhodes' Legacy

Brian Dawkins
S 1996-2004

Originator: Center John "Bull" Lipski said after the 56-0 loss to the Giants in the 1933 opener, "When you make less points than the other side, you generally lose."

Longest Tenure: Nine years, Brian Dawkins.

Number Changes: Jim MacMurdo wore 6 from 1934 to 1936; Hank Reese wore 25 in 1935 and 1936; Bibbles Bawell wore 81 in 1952; Vaughn Hebron wore 45 in 1993.

Just Visiting: Vaughn Hebron won two Super Bowl rings in Denver.

Highs: Hank Reese (see 25 top); Bibbles Bawell picked off eight passes one year and nine another; safety Andre Waters was one of the hardest hitters in Philadelphia history.

Lows: Start with the trio of linemen Screeno Bailey, Weenie Williams and Pete Stevens, who appeared in a total of six games in 1935 and 1936. Add failed sprinter Frank Budd whose world-record 9.2 time for the 100 was broken by Bob Hayes, who actually was a football player. Finish with College Football Hall of Famer Leroy Keyes, the consolation prize in the O.J. Simpson sweepstakes that the Eagles lost by winning, who was never better than a mediocre defensive back in the NFL.

Brian Dawkins

The football field brings out a different side of Brian Dawkins. Off the field, he's a quiet family man married to his high school sweetheart. On the field, he is the Eagles' Ray Lewis. He is the last player introduced before games and charges onto the field, prancing from side to side and stopping to flex and pose and preen as he fires up the fans and his teammates. After a hard hit or an interception, Dawkins reacts primally with more flexing and squawks from behind his darkened visor.

Ray Rhodes picked Dawkins out of Clemson in the second round of the 1996 draft to replace the departed free safety Greg Jackson, and Brian was in the starting lineup by game two. Right from the start he made his presence felt physically with the heavy hammer shots he laid on opposing receivers and runners. That alone will make a player a popular legend in scrappy Philadelphia, but Dawkins is a significantly better safety than Philly folk hero Andre Waters, who was simply a pure hitter. As Brian's longtime secondary colleague Troy Vincent once put it, "He can cover like a corner and hit like a linebacker." This makes the four-time Pro Bowler the ideal free safety. Within Jim Johnson's aggressive blitzing defense, having someone of Dawkins' skills at safety is a big advantage. He can come on a blitz, cover for another blitzer or be brought up to line to defense the run.

Dawkins is probably Rhodes' greatest legacy from his tumultuous four-year reign as coach. In 1995, Rhodes replaced Rich Kotite, who had taken Buddy Ryan's talented team and dismantled it. Rhodes went about completely revamping the team by bringing in scores of free agents and aging retreads. In addition to signing big-name Ricky Watters in that first year, Rhodes also signed offensive linemen Guy McIntyre, Raleigh McKenzie and Harry Boatswain; defensive linemen Mark Gunn, Ronnie Dixon, Rhett Hall and Dan Stubbs; linebackers Bill Romanowski, Kurt Gouveia, and James Willis; tight ends Jimmie Johnson, Frank Wainright and Ed West; quarterback Rodney Peete and kicker Gary Anderson. Many more would follow in the ensuing three years, but the most significant free agents were Irving Fryar, Troy Vincent and Kevin Turner in 1996; Steve Everitt, Darrin Smith and Chris Boniol in 1997; and Jeff Graham and Mike Caldwell in 1998. Hugh Douglass was also acquired in 1998 via trade.

This approach was only a short-term solution that would need to be supplemented by the draft. Rhodes' success in the draft was spotty, however. His first-round picks were the disappointing Mike Mamula, the long-term project Jermayne Mayberry, the flop Jon Harris and the blue chipper Tra Thomas. Aside from second-round picks Bobby Taylor in 1995 and Dawkins in 1996, the rest of Rhodes' picks were projects. Some would eventually be successful in Philadelphia, like Duce Staley, Jeremiah Trotter, Brandon Whiting and Ike Reese. Some would develop elsewhere, like James Darling and Allen Rossum. Most would simply languish, like Jason Dunn, Barrett Brooks, Chris T. Jones and Bobby Hoying. It was no way to build a team. After Rhodes' initial success when his fiery leadership was being compared by some to Vince Lombardi, the team declined rapidly. Ray was shown to be a tough-guy fraud who could not develop talent and could not manage quarterbacks. What he left to successor Andy Reid was a fair amount of talent on defense and, in particular, three-fourths of an excellent secondary with corners Troy Vincent and Bobby Taylor and free safety Brian Dawkins.

Andy Reid kept that secondary together through 2003 when he let Vincent and Taylor leave via free agency, having drafted Lito Shepard and Sheldon Brown to replace them in 2002. Teaming with fellow 2002 draftee, hard-hitting safety Michael Lewis, as well as Dawkins, the secondary remains a strength despite the turnover. The most remarkable thing is that the Eagles extended Dawkins' contract in 2003 as he was about to turn 30. Normally when an Eagle reaches that age in the Reid era, the team essentially says to the player, "Go find another sucker to pay for your declining production. We hope you enjoy your pension." The fact that they made an exception for Dawkins shows how highly they think of him and of his immediate future. Here's hoping he bucks the trend and eventually retires as an Eagle.

1992 Playoffs

Eric Allen
CB 1988-94

Originator: Guard Jim "Iggy" Zyntell was purchased from the Giants in 1933.

Longest Tenure: Nine years, Bobby Taylor.

Number Changes: Paul Cuba wore 23 in 1933; John Kusko wore 16 in 1937 and 1938; Jim Zyntell wore 9 in 1934 and 16 in 1935.

Just Visiting: Chuck Cherundolo was a workmanlike center for the Rams and Steelers.

Highs: Gummy Carr was a slow but smart corner and safety who later went into coaching; undrafted free agent Joe Scarpati was an undersized, scrappy safety and the Eagles' defensive MVP in 1966; former Rose Bowl quarterback John Sciarra was a jack-of-all-trades for the Birds and twice was special teams MVP; Bobby Taylor was a rangy cover corner who did not like to tackle.

Lows: Second-round pick Ray Jones experienced a cornerback's worst nightmare in 1970 against the Cowboys when he gave up TD passes of 86 and 56 yards to Lance Rentzel and 40 yards to Bob Hayes in a 21-17 Eagle loss. Ray only lasted one year in Philly.

Eric Allen

Buddy Ryan's aggressive defense was designed to put a lot of pressure on the opposing quarterback, but it also put a lot of pressure on his own cornerbacks. While everyone else was going after the passer, the corners were on their own out on the edge. Ryan's defense demanded skilled man-to-man cover guys, and Eric Allen was one of the best of his time.

Ryan had followed Allen in college at Arizona State and traded up in the second round to draft him in 1988. Buddy named Allen the starter in training camp, and Eric justified that confidence by playing his position boldly and well. He wasn't beaten badly for a score until the seventh game of the year against Cleveland when Don Strock called an audible that took advantage of Allen's eagerness and allowed Webster Slaughter to slip by for an easy score. Ryan dismissed that as "an old quarterback outsmarting a rookie." Allen's teammate Andre Waters said of him at the time, "He's a smart player, he's aggressive, he's a hitter, he's a good cover guy and he has speed. I think Eric Allen is going to be in the Pro Bowl in the next two or three years. He has a knack for the ball."

Waters deserves credit for his perceptiveness and clairvoyance. As a rookie, Allen picked off five passes, four of them deep in the opponents' territory. In his second year, he led the NFC with eight interceptions and knocked down an additional 25 passes. He was named All-Pro that year and went to the Pro Bowl for the first of five trips as an Eagle. By 1991, Eric was complaining of being bored on the field because opponents were throwing to his area so seldom. He covered short and long passes with equal aplomb, and was a willing blitzer and a solid tackler in run defense. Moreover, he was dedicated to improving his skills by spending hours on film study. Highly respected new defensive coach Bud Carson said that year of Allen, "He can do it all, and he's as smart a player as I've coached. He is as fine a pure corner as you will find."

1992 was the last hurrah for the promising team Buddy Ryan had put together, and it was an eventful, tumultuous one full of tension and drama. That year of pride and disappointment was entertainingly described in not one but two boisterous book-length accounts by local sportswriters from competing papers. All-Pro defensive tackle and team leader Jerome Brown died before training camp, and his teammates dedicated the season to his memory. Hall of Famer Reggie White won his lawsuit and would be a free agent likely to fly away at the end of the year. Buddy had been gone for more than a year, and the team still saw his successor, Rich Kotite, as an interloper imposed by the hated owner, Norman Braman.

Like the New Orleans Saints whom the Eagles had drawn as a first-round match-up, this group of players still had not won a playoff game despite an abundance of talent. In the game, the Saints got off to a great start at home, scoring a touchdown on their opening series. The Eagles countered with a 57-yard TD pass from Randall Cunningham to Fred Barnett, but the Saints scored 10 points from two more first half drives to go up 17-7 at the half. The Saints upped their lead with another field goal in the third quarter, but the Eagles scored a three-pointer of their own off an Eric Allen interception. The fourth quarter was all Eagles. Fred Barnett caught a 35-yard jump ball in the end zone to draw within three. Seth Joyner intercepted a Bobby Hebert pass and returned it to the New Orleans 26 to set up the Eagles' go-ahead touchdown. A safety for Reggie White, a field goal for Roger Ruzek and an 18-yard touchdown return on Allen's second interception closed out the Eagles' scoring avalanche 36-20. Philadelphia at last had the playoff win that Buddy Ryan was never able to deliver.

Under Ryan, the Eagles beat Dallas eight of 10 times. In two years under Kotite, the Eagles had split the four games with the improving Cowboys. The immediate future of the series would be demonstrated this day in Dallas. The Eagles scored first with a field goal and last with a touchdown, but in between the Cowboys rang up 34 points in a butt-kicking performance. Dallas outgained Philadelphia 160 yards to 63 on the ground and 186 yards to 115 through the air. Erik Williams controlled Reggie White on the line, and the Aikman/Emmitt/Irvin trio took care of the rest. Dallas would win three of the next four Super Bowls; the Eagles would break apart.

Despite Philadelphia's decline in 1993, Allen had a remarkable year. He picked off six passes and returned four of them for touchdowns, equaling the league record. Two of those touchdown returns came in one game against the Saints, leading to a victory. Another came against the Jets in the fourth game of the season and represented the winning score. On that play, Eric intercepted a Boomer Esiasen pass at the Eagles' 6, surrounded by Jets. He cut right, then juked and jived and crossed the entire field on a diagonal before racing in for the touchdown, a 94-yard return on which he ran at least 150 yards. The following season, Allen made the Pro Bowl again, although it was a bad year for both Eric and the team; he was beaten for scores several times in 1994 and the team went belly up, losing their last seven games.

Allen left bitterly as a free agent and signed inexplicably with the star-crossed Saints despite receiving equivalent offers from the 49ers and Packers. He spent three years in New Orleans before signing with Jon Gruden's Oakland Raiders where he drew more passing action playing opposite young shutdown corner Charles Woodson. Allen responded with more spectacular football. In his 13th season, 2000, Eric returned three interceptions for scores. After one more year, Allen retired with 54 career interceptions, eight of which he returned for scores; 34 of those picks and five of the TDs came as an Eagle. Handsome and articulate, Eric went directly from the playing field to the broadcast booth.

More Stinkin'
Cowboys—The Big Hits

Tim Brown
HB 1960-67

WHO'S WORN THE NUMBER:

Henry Obst (G) 1933, Edward Storm (B) 1934-35, James Russell (T) 1936, Elmer Kolberg (B) 1939, Don Jones (B) 1940, Ralph Goldston (B) 1952 and 1954-55, Lee Riley (DB) 1956 and 1958-59, *Tim Brown* (RB) 1960-67, Cyril Pinder (RB) 1968-70, Larry Marshall (KR) 1974-77, Brenard Wilson (S) 1979-86, Robert Lavette (RB) 1987, Jacque Robinson (FB) 1987r, Mark Higgs (RB) 1989, Vai Sikahema (KR) 1992-93, Marvin Goodwin (S) 1994, James Saxon (FB) 1995, James Fuller (S) 1996, Duce Staley (RB) 1997-03, Eric McCoo (RB) 2004.

Originator:	Guard Henry Obst was an All-American lacrosse player at Syracuse, but only played in one of his three NFL games for Philadelphia.
Longest Tenure:	Eight years, Tim Brown, 1960 to 1967.
Number Changes:	Elmer Kolberg wore 16 in 1940; James Russell wore 17 in 1937.
Just Visiting:	Miniature Mark Higgs gained nearly 1,000 yards twice for the Dolphins.
Highs:	Ralph Goldston was the Eagles' first black player in 1952. Before he reported to training camp, he was stabbed in a fight with a soldier. Vai Sikahema was a spirited return man who celebrated his one Eagle touchdown by punching out the goal post at the Meadowlands. He is now a local sportscaster. Fan favorite and three-time Eagles offensive MVP Duce Staley always got every yard possible whenever he got the ball.
Lows:	Tailback Ed Storm completed 31 percent of his passes for three touchdowns and 16 interceptions over two seasons.

Tim Brown

The Packers picked Tim Brown in the 27th round of the 1959 draft, and against long odds in Vince Lombardi's first year in Green Bay, Brown made the team. Tim only appeared in one game for the Packers, though, before being cut because Lombardi considered him a fumbler. That would turn out to be true; he would fumble 41 times in his career, roughly 3 percent of the time he touched the ball. Brown was familiar with overcoming adversity, having graduated from the Soldier's and Sailor's Childrens Home in Indiana to attend Ball State Teachers College on a basketball scholarship. He hooked on with the Eagles' taxi squad and made the team in 1960, returning kicks and punts for the champions.

In the next season under new coach Nick Skorich, Brown got a bigger chance to show what he could do. He returned the opening kickoff of the season 105 yards for a touchdown against the Browns and led the league in kick returns that year. He also got the opportunity to carry the ball from scrimmage 50 times and averaged 6.8 per carry. The next year, 1962, he was the starting halfback and accumulated a then-record 2,306 total yards — 545 yards rushing, 849 yards on 52 receptions, 831 kick return yards and 81 punt return yards — for 13 touchdowns. In 1963, he topped that with 2,428 total yards for 11 touchdowns. Brown was a shifty, fast runner capable of scoring anytime he touched the ball. He was the best pass-receiving back of his time, twice catching at least 50 passes out of the backfield and averaging an outstanding 14.5 yards per reception for his career. As a return man, he returned five kickoffs, one punt and one missed field goal for touchdowns and averaged 26 yards per kick return.

Despite all this versatility, Tim never averaged as much as 20 touches per game in his career, and his highest rushing total was 861 yards in 1965. For one thing, he was 5 feet 11 inches, 198 pounds and brittle, although muscular and well-sculpted. He missed a full season's worth of 14 games over his eight years in Philadelphia and was particularly susceptible to muscle pulls and hamstring problems. Teammate Jim Ringo called him "Tanker" because he spent so much time in the whirlpool. Second, offense in the 1960s was a two-back attack, and teams liked to split the running load between the fullback and halfback. Finally, he had a critical conflict with Joe Kuharich, who was hired as the Eagles' coach in 1964. Kuharich did not believe in stars (or winning, it seems) and liked to spread the ball around. Trader Joe offered Brown to the Redskins in 1964 for Bobby Mitchell and Lonnie Sanders, but the offer was not taken seriously. Brown's feeling was, "I wish I could carry 20 times every game. I want to be the best halfback in the league. You can't be the best if you don't carry." This difference was not helped by their respective personalities. Kuharich was a hard-liner given to malaprops, while Brown admitted, "I'm a moody, cantankerous guy."

Brown was a handsome man who dated Diana Ross and Dionne Warwick, among many others, and whose goal was to break into the entertainment business. He cut a couple of records that were well-received locally and commuted to New York each Monday for voice and diction lessons. This attention to outside interests was not looked on favorably by Eagles management, but Tim was very popular with the fans because

Timmy Brown somehow maintained his balance making this amazing cutback against the Cardinals' John David Crow during a 99-yard kickoff return for a touchdown on September 16, 1962.

he was a very exciting player to watch. Even in 1966 and 1967, when his rushing average slipped to 3.4 yards per carry due to either injuries or age, he was still capable of delivering a big play, such as when he returned two kickoffs for scores against the Cowboys in 1966. The question of whether his career was mismanaged and he was underutilized will remain unresolved. If he had run the ball from scrimmage 20 times a game, would he have gained over a thousand yards several times, caught even more passes, scored even more touchdowns and gone into the Hall of Fame? Or would he have gotten hurt more quickly and more seriously and had a shorter career, accomplishing much less? Coaches are always looking for the right balance with small, fast scatbacks like Brown, Charlie Garner and Brian Westbrook, to name three Eagles. Timmy Brown may have had the optimum career without realizing it.

Tim's career as an Eagle came to a violent end in the next to last game of the 1967 season, a game that would ignite an explosive rivalry in Philadelphia sports. On December 10, the Eagles met the Cowboys in Dallas. The action quickly turned rough when Philadelphia linebacker Mike Morgan hit quarterback Don Meredith late, broke his nose and knocked him out of the game. The game then got out of hand. Norm Snead was sacked seven times and threw three interceptions in a 38-17 loss. Tom Woodeschick had his eye gouged, and Tim Brown had his face crushed by a Lee Roy Jordan elbow. Tim suffered a concussion and a broken jaw and lost several teeth in his last game for the Eagles. In the off-season, he demanded a trade and was shipped to Baltimore for ace return man Alvin Haymond. Brown's last game as a player was the historic Colts loss to the Jets in Super Bowl III. He went from there to Hollywood where he was a struggling actor, appearing in a few films like *MASH* and *Nashville* and occasionally on television, before becoming a probation officer.

In his role as probation officer, Brown could have served on the sidelines for several other Eagle-Cowboy games where the intensity of the hitting got out of hand. Here are a dirty dozen examples of smackdown action.

1. September 26, 1971. Mel Tom applies a shot to the back of Roger Staubach's head as he's on the ground and knocks him out of the game in the first quarter. Tom is later fined $1,000, a major amount in those days. Cowboys 42, Eagles 7.

2. October 20, 1974. Roman Gabriel of Philadelphia is sacked six times and Roger Staubach of the Cowboys is dropped five. There are frequent fights on the field, and the Eagles score two of their touchdowns after Cowboy personal foul penalties. Cowboys 31, Eagles 24.

3. December 10, 1978. Ron Jaworski is sacked eight times, four alone by Randy White. Harvey Martin is injured on a play and is booed lustily by the Veterans Stadium crowd when he is helped off the field. Cowboys 31, Eagles 13.

4. December 8, 1979. After an incomplete pass, the Cowboys' Dennis Thurman hits an out of bounds Harold Carmichael high and knocks him flat. Carmichael suffers back spasms and can't continue; his streak of 127 consecutive games with a reception comes to an end. Cowboys 24, Eagles 17.

5. December 2, 1984. While Tony Dorsett is in the grasp of linebacker Anthony Griggs, safety Ray Ellis levels him. Dorsett leaves with a concussion, but returns later in the game. Cowboys 26, Eagles 10.

6. November 23, 1989. The Bounty Bowl. Jimmy Johnson later accuses Buddy Ryan of putting cash bounties on the heads of Troy Aikman and Luis Zendejas. Zendejas is laid out on a kickoff by linebacker Jessie Small. Eagle Mike Pitts is

ejected for throwing a punch. Britt Hager throws Aikman to the ground after the whistle blows and a fight erupts between the teams. The league fines 10 Cowboys and seven Eagles for their participation in the fight. The teams meet again at the Vet 17 days later; snowballs rain down from the stands on the Cowboys and their coach, and several fights break out on the field. Eagles 27, Cowboys 0, followed by Eagles 20, Cowboys 10.

7. December 23, 1990. Clyde Simmons slams Aikman in the first quarter and separates his shoulder, knocking him out for the year. Eagles 17, Cowboys 3.

8. September 15, 1991. The next time the teams meet, Aikman is sacked 11 times, one short of the league record. Simmons again leads the way with 4½ sacks. Eagles 24, Cowboys 0.

9. January 7, 1996. In a divisional playoff game, safety Darren Woodson knocks out quarterback Rodney Peete with a helmet-to-helmet shot on the Cowboys' 9 with the score tied in the first quarter. Cowboys 30, Eagles 11.

10. September 30, 1996. Peete is knocked out for the season when Tony Tolbert rolls into his knee. Backup Ty Detmer is knocked woozy by a blind-side whiplash crash from Darren Woodson. Detmer would stay in, but would fumble twice and throw a late interception. Cowboys 23, Eagles 17.

11. October 26, 1997. Aikman is knocked out in the second quarter from a helmet-to-helmet collision with former teammate Jimmie Jones. Eagles 13, Cowboys 12.

12. October 10, 1999. Michael Irvin is buried by a head shot from safety Tim Hauck. As Irvin lies motionless on the turf, fans at the Vet cheer. Irvin recovers, but never plays again. Eagles 13, Cowboys 10.

2001 Playoffs

Troy Vincent
CB 1996-200

Originator: As a member of the undefeated Pittsburgh Panthers, injured tackle Paul Cuba played in the 1933 Rose Bowl that Pitt lost to USC 35-0. This prepared him for his three-year professional career with the fledgling Eagles.

Longest Tenure: Eight years, Troy Vincent.

Number Changes: Paul Cuba wore 21 in 1934 and 1935; Ray George also wore 42 in 1940.

Just Visiting: Carl Taseff was a good defensive back for the Colts.

Highs: None.

Lows: Harry Jones was the Eagles' number one selection in the 1967 draft and racked up a total of 85 yards rushing on 44 carries in four injury-plagued campaigns.

Troy Vincent

Even the best cornerbacks are beaten sometimes. Troy Vincent, who anchored a strong Eagle secondary for eight years, said that when he was beaten, all he wanted was to be left alone on the sidelines so he could get it out of his mind before getting another chance on the next series. That mental resilience and that firmness of purpose are as critical to a successful cornerback as speed, size and cover skills. Troy Vincent had the complete package of tools and was one of the best in the NFL for several years.

His determination to succeed was evident from the start. When Vincent was a junior in Pennsbury High School near Yardley, his mother moved to Trenton for her job. Troy moved in with his best friend's family, the Bodleys, so he would not have to change schools. While he still saw his real family regularly, he formed such a close bond with the Bodleys that they not only helped him choose what college to attend, but also worked as his agent when he became a professional athlete. He starred at the University of Wisconsin and then was selected by Miami as the seventh overall pick in the 1992 draft. He was in the starting lineup by the third week and made the All-Rookie team. In his first playoff game that year, he picked off two passes. He had some knee problems in his second year, but returned at full strength and intercepted five passes in both 1994 and 1995.

Ray Rhodes lured him back home as a free agent in 1996, and Troy took on the role of team leader, especially guiding second-year safety Brian Dawkins and rookie cornerback Bobby Taylor. While Vincent had some off days in that first year in Philly, he also took part in what was then the longest interception return in NFL history, 104 yards. At the end of a close game against the Cowboys, middle linebacker James Willis clinched the Eagle win by intercepting a Troy Aikman pass four yards deep in the end zone. At the Eagles' 10, Willis lateraled the ball to Vincent, and Troy took it the remaining 90 yards for the score.

Even as the Eagles declined under Rhodes, the secondary remained a strength, and Vincent was seen as a top all-around corner. He had the size to lower his shoulder and tackle a ball carrier and was equally good against the pass. He could blitz or lock up in man-to-man coverage down the field. He prided himself on being the most complete, well-rounded corner in the league. When new defensive coordinator Jim Johnson came in with Andy Reid in 1999, the whole defense improved, and Troy began to get more national notice. He was named to his first Pro Bowl after the 1999 season despite the team's 5-11 record. He was named to the team again after the 2000 and 2001 seasons.

By 2001, Andy Reid's team was ready to fly, and Philadelphia won the Eastern division that year. As the division winner with the third-best record in the NFC, the Eagles drew Tampa Bay in the wild card round. Just as in the playoffs the year before, the Eagles dominated the Bucs and won handily 31-9. The Buc defense could not contain Donovan McNabb, and Troy pulled down an end zone interception, one of four picks the Eagles came up with. Then it was on to Donovan's home town, Chicago, to meet the surprising Bears in the divisional round. Once again the Eagles dominated and won going away, but the Bears did take the lead early in the third quarter on a Jerry Azumah interception return for a touchdown. However, McNabb threw a six-yard touchdown pass to an uncovered Duce Staley four minutes later, and the Bears never threatened again. The bad news was that Vincent pulled his groin muscle in the second quarter, and that became the big story in the week leading up to the NFC Championship game against the Rams' aerial circus. He insisted he would play, and he did start.

The game began badly when McNabb fumbled the snap on the second play from scrimmage, and the Rams capitalized with a touchdown to Isaac Bruce for a fast lead. The teams traded field goals to end the first quarter 10-3 Rams. In the second quarter, a 31-yard burst by Correll Buckhalter led to a one-yard touchdown for Duce Staley. After another field goal from the Rams, McNabb hit Todd Pinkston for a 12-yard shot with 46 seconds left to take a 17-13 halftime lead.

Buckhalter was done for the day with an ankle sprain, but Vincent was still playing as the second half began. The Rams came out running and controlled the clock in the third quarter. While the Eagles went three-and-out three times, the Rams drove the ball for a field goal and a Marshall Faulk one-yard run to take a 22-17 lead into the fourth quarter. Vincent aggravated his injury in the third quarter and left when the Eagles were still ahead by a point. From good field position, the Rams pushed down the field again for yet another Faulk one-yard touchdown to take a 29-17 lead. Brian Mitchell's 41-yard kickoff return got the Eagles moving. On the ensuing drive, McNabb converted a fourth-down pass, completed another pass for 17 yards to James Thrash and then scored on a three-yard run to pull within five. Philadelphia did not allow the Rams a first down and forced a punt. N.D. Kalu burst through to block the punt, but the ball went right through his hands. Still, the Eagles had the ball on their own 45 with 2:20 left. A two-yard completion to Freddie Mitchell followed by a one-yard Duce Staley run and an incompletion to Mitchell left the Eagles with fourth and seven from their own 48. Again trying to hit Mitchell, McNabb was picked off by Aeneas Williams, and that was the ball game. A healthy Vincent may have helped against the Rams' second half ground attack, but his presence would not have helped the offense that disappeared in the third quarter and let control of the game slip away. It was an exciting game, but a very tough loss.

Off the field, Vincent has done very well for himself as a businessman involved in many productive ventures and is as competitive in that as he is in football. He also is a religious man who gives generously of his time and money to several charities. He established a foundation to assist at-risk young people and an organization to provide sports opportunities for young women. In 2003, he was named the NFL's Man of the Year in recognition of his excellence as a football player, businessman and member of the community. He was the first Eagle to win the award since Harold Carmichael in 1980. Troy Vincent loved being an Eagle, but the nature of the business of sports is that the clock is always ticking on every athlete's career. The Eagles did not attempt to re-sign Vincent when he became a free agent in 2004, and he signed with Buffalo where he had knee problems and missed most of the year. He intercepted 28 passes and was a stable leader during his eight years in Philadelphia.

Gun Play and Shady Characters

Nate Ramsey
DB 1963-72

Originator: Tackle Joe Carpe played two games for the brand new Eagles in 1933. In the 1920s, he played for the NFL champion Frankford Yellow Jackets as well as the Pottsville Maroons and Boston Bulldogs.

Longest Tenure: 10 years, Nate Ramsey.

Number Changes: Dick Lackman also wore 15 in 1933; Joe Knapper also wore 11 in 1934; Joe Pilconis wore 2 in 1934, 18 from 1936 to 1937 and 28 in 1937; Herm Bassman also wore 19 and 29 in 1936; Russell Gary also wore 38 in 1986; Darnell Autry wore 26 in 1998; Sheldon Brown wore 39 in 2002.

Just Visiting: George Taliaferro was a multitalented back in both the NFL and All-America Conference; Blaine Bishop was a solid hitting safety with Tennessee.

Highs: Although resented by teammates for being overpaid, Ray Ellis was a decent safety for a few years.

Lows: Aspiring actor Darnell Autry was never more than an aspiring running back, averaging only three yards a carry in 2000.

Nate Ramsey

It was no surprise that Nate Ramsey lasted until the 14th round of the 1963 NFL draft. Although he was captain of the Indiana University football team and had scored the very first touchdown in the Hoosiers' new stadium in 1960, the team compiled a 6-21 mark in his three years on the varsity. Nate never led the team in any category and was not named All-American or even All-Big Ten at his halfback position. The surprise is that he not only made the Eagles as a rookie, but stuck with them for a decade, mostly as a starter.

As a rookie in 1963, Ramsey was assigned to the defensive backfield, but did not play much until becoming a starting safety for the last month of the season. In the off-season he returned to Indiana to work on his degree and was arrested along with some former teammates in connection with a prank involving the theft of a pay phone from a laundromat. The solidly built 6-foot 1-inch 200-pounder began the 1964 season as the starting strong safety, but shifted to cornerback later in the year and led the team in interceptions with five. Nate led the Eagles in picks again in 1965 with six, including three in one game against the Cardinals, but also had some tough moments. He was shifted back to strong safety after giving up a game-winning touchdown pass to Bobby Mitchell of the Redskins in November of that year. He settled in at safety for the next six years. While he was never an All-Pro or Pro Bowl player, he was a dependable professional whose strongest suit was his hard-hitting tackling ability.

The week of the last game of the 1970 season, Nate was shot in the chest on a street corner in West Philly. He underwent surgery to have the bullet removed and spent some time recovering in the hospital. The gunman was tracked down and was said to be an acquaintance of Ramsey and his wife. At the trial, the gunman claimed that he was firing at Ramsey in self-defense. The details remain murky, but the gunman was acquitted, and Nate reported to training camp as usual after divorcing his wife. Once again his position was changed in 1971 as he returned to cornerback. For his last two seasons as an Eagle, Ramsey struggled at the corner even though Philadelphia was playing zone coverage for up to 70 percent of the time. It was never his best position, and he had not gained any speed since he turned 30. After 10 years as an Eagle, Nate was cut in 1973 and hooked on briefly with the Saints before leaving the game. He intercepted 21 passes for the Birds and returned one, versus Johnny Unitas, 26 yards for a score in 1969.

Nate Ramsey's post-football life continued to be rocky. He was arrested in 1974 in connection with the shooting death of a man in a barroom quarrel, but was cleared of the murder the following year. In 1978, though, he was convicted of extortion and sentenced to two years probation. While Ramsey survived his problems, other Eagles have not been so lucky. Roy Barni was a fiery defensive back that Philadelphia traded to Washington in 1955. The week before he was to report to training camp in 1957, he intervened in a barroom fight and was shot and killed in the melee. In 1976, Blenda Gay was stabbed fatally in the neck by his wife while the 26-year-old defensive end was sleeping. His wife was found not guilty by reason of insanity and has been institutionalized ever since.

Some Eagles have committed serious crimes. The first prominent example is

Alabama Pitts who gained fame in the 1930s while starring on the baseball team at Sing Sing where he was serving five years for armed robbery. When he was released in 1935, Pitts was signed by Albany of the International League, but the league president disallowed the contract due to the player's background. Eagles owner Bert Bell sensed a publicity opportunity and offered the speedy Pitts an Eagles contract. In the meantime, baseball commissioner Judge Landis overruled the IL president, and Pitts spent a month playing minor league baseball. In September, he took up Bell on his offer and played in three games as a back for the Birds. Small crowds came to check him out, but he only caught two passes for 21 yards and was no great shakes on defense. Pitts disappeared from the sporting world, and turned up six years later, stabbed to death in a bar in a dispute over a woman.

Ironically, soon after that, new Eagles owner Lex Thompson announced that Philadelphia would keep a spot open at training camp each year for one athletic convict, at least 6 feet tall and 200 pounds, to try out for the team. A fellow from Iowa named Don MacGregor, who honed his backfield skills in an Iowa state prison while doing time for auto theft, was given a shot in 1943, but did not make the team. More recently, first-round flop Kevin Allen ended his shaky career after one season when he was convicted of rape at the Jersey shore in 1987. He served nearly three years in jail and unsuccessfully petitioned NFL commissioner Paul Tagliabue for reinstatement in 1990. A former Eagle practice squad player, Chris Buckhalter, was convicted of manslaughter in 1997 for a deadly fight outside a nightclub. He began serving a 20-year prison sentence before his brother Correll joined the Birds in 2001.

Illegal drugs have been a continual issue since the 1970s, and each coach must make his stand. Starter Mike Hogan and teammate James Betterson were cut by Dick Vermeil in 1979 after being arrested on drug charges for which they were later cleared. Cris Carter was cut compassionately in 1990 by Buddy Ryan, who never said why a player who "only catches touchdowns" was not good enough. Andy Reid cut Terrence Carroll, who was arrested for smoking marijuana in a car with Correll Buckhalter and practice squad player Dwayne Crutchfield in 2001. The strangest drug-related story was in 1983 when fullback Leroy Harris testified in family court that he had blown his year-end bonus on cocaine. When this was reported in the paper, Harris issued a statement that he was not actually a drug user, but was trying to avoid giving his estranged wife half of his assets.

Character issues often come to the fore on draft day. The Eagles have passed on stars like Warren Sapp and Randy Moss because of questionable behavior in their pasts. However, they have overlooked the risks in other cases. Sometimes incidents are just youthful indiscretions as with the drug experimentation of Charley Garner, Tra Thomas and Antwuan Wyatt or the fisticuffs of Ike Reese and James Darling. Other incidents turn out to be bright red flags. Bernard Williams tested positive for marijuana and could never get himself clean long enough to play again after his rookie year. Alonzo Johnson, who had tested positive for drugs, was cut by Buddy Ryan as soon as he backslid. Football is a glamorous and violent sport, so it is no surprise that not all Eagles have been eagle scouts.

25

Exuberance

Tommy McDonald
WR 1957-63

Originator: Guard Osborne "Diddy" Willson played for Lud Wray at Penn and then the Eagles in 1933. If he played today, he would be known to the hip-hop community as "O Diddy."

Longest Tenure: Seven years, Tommy McDonald.

Number Changes: Diddy Willson wore 15 in 1934 and 1935; Hank Reese wore 20 from 1937 to 1939; Pete Retzlaff wore 44 from 1957 to 1966; Charlie Garner wore 30 from 1995 to 1998.

Just Visiting: Allen Rossum has had more success as a return man in Green Bay and Atlanta; Dorsey Levens made his name as a runner in Green Bay.

Highs: Temple's Hank Reese was the best lineman and kicker in the Eagle's first decade. He later coached in the All-America Conference and became a real estate developer who started the High Point golf course; Pete Retzlaff (see 44); Tom Sullivan gained 968 yards and caught 50 passes in 1973; Charlie Garner (see 30 top).

Lows: Bob Shann returned his first punt 63 yards for a TD, but was injured and only returned three more in his career for 17 yards; Greg Tremble had an unfortunate name for a defensive back and a short career.

Tommy McDonald

A common response of old-time ball players to touchdown celebrations is "when you reach the end zone, you should act like you've been there before." In Tommy McDonald's day, that's what players did. When a player scored, he generally either handed the ball to the official or just tossed it aside. He made his way to the bench or back to the huddle for the extra point, accepting handshakes and pats on the back from his teammates. Every once in a while, an excited player would toss the ball into the stands, but he would regret that because it would draw a fine. Tommy McDonald started to change all that when he arrived in 1957. On the frequent occasions he scored, he wanted to celebrate. He'd take off toward the closest teammate and hop in his arms or on his back, sometimes knocking the teammate to the ground. One time he even threw the ball into the upper deck at Franklin Field. In Warren Zevon's words, Tommy was "just an excitable boy."

Tommy grew up on a farm in a town so small that they didn't even name the streets until the postal service insisted on it. From Roy, New Mexico, the McDonald family moved to Albuquerque when Tommy was in high school and he starred in football and track. Despite being 5 feet 6 inches and 145 pounds, the speedy scatback received a scholarship to Oklahoma from legendary coach Bud Wilkinson. While filling out to a rather modest 5 feet 9 inches and 170 pounds, McDonald played three seasons for the Sooners, who went 30-0 with two national championships in that time. He scored the winning touchdown in the 1956 Orange Bowl, and as a senior won the Maxwell Award and finished third for the Heisman. To top it off, he married Miss Oklahoma and was drafted in the third round by the Eagles in 1957.

McDonald arrived in Philadelphia in January to accept the Maxwell Award and negotiate his contract with the Eagles. After signing for $12,000, Tommy did some sightseeing before stopping in at a travel agency to buy a return plane ticket. The next thing he knew, he was being arrested because of his close resemblance to the Lonely Hearts Bandit, who was notorious for robbing small businesses in town and tying up the female employees. When tiny Tommy tried to tell the police that he was in town to sign a contract to play for the Eagles, the cops thought that was a joke. Finally he convinced them to check with Birds general manager Vince McNally, and the matter was cleared up.

McDonald's introduction to pro football was not much better than his introduction to Philadelphia. At the College All-Star Game, he sat on the bench with Jim Brown and barely played. As a late arrival to Eagles training camp, Tommy made more of an impression as a clown than as a ball player. He did handstands going back to the huddle, took a flying leap into the laundry basket and pretended to drown in the whirlpool. None of this endeared him to head coach Hugh Devore, but offensive coach Charley Gauer was a strong advocate for both McDonald and fellow rookie Sonny Jurgensen. While Philadelphia was winning just two of its first eight games, McDonald was used primarily as a punt and kickoff returner who occasionally appeared as a halfback on

Hall of Famer Tommy McDonald's autobiography was called *They Pay Me To Catch Footballs*, but at Old Original Bookbinders in December 1960 he asked quarterback Norm Van Brocklin to "pass the lobster."

offense. Finally, in the ninth game against the Redskins, Tommy got his chance to start at flanker, and he caught two touchdown passes from Jurgensen in an Eagle victory. The first score went for 61 yards with McDonald outleaping the defender for the ball. In the last four games of the season, Tommy caught nine passes for three touchdowns, although he knew very little about the receiver position.

McDonald's education began in 1958 with new head coach Buck Shaw and new quarterback Norm Van Brocklin. Van Brocklin, in particular, spent a great deal of time with Tommy and Pete Retzlaff, two former running backs being converted to receivers. McDonald learned how to vary his running pace so he could break away from a defender more easily. He learned what to watch for in film study each week. He improved the crispness of his pass routes, although this would never be his strongest suit. He learned how to fall when being tackled to avoid unnecessary injury. Tommy already had ample natural gifts. He had good speed, sure hands, great balance and surprising strength. His reflexes and quickness were so adept that he could toss three pennies in the air and catch each one separately with his hand flicking out like a frog's tongue catching insects.

Above all, McDonald was tough. He is reputed to be the last NFL player to go without a facemask. Tommy claims that pictures of him wearing a single bar facemask resulted from his wearing a replacement helmet after his own was cracked. He missed only three games in his first 11 years in the league — two in 1958 after he separated his shoulder and one in 1966 with a swollen knee. He once played six games with his jaw wired shut after it was fractured. McDonald was fearless in catching the ball over the middle, and his best pass route was the crossing pattern. And no matter how hard he was tackled, he popped right back up for the next play. It was a point of pride for him.

For both Van Brocklin and Jurgensen, Tommy was a touchdown maker. In his seven years in Philly, he caught 287 passes, and 66 of them were for six points. That's an unsurpassed average of one touchdown for every 4.35 receptions. In comparison, Harold Carmichael caught a touchdown for every 7.45 passes, Pete Pihos caught one for every 6.11 passes, Mike Quick one for every 5.95 passes, Jack Ferrante one for every 5.45 passes, and even Cris Carter — the man who "only catches touchdowns" — caught a TD for every 4.68 passes as an Eagle. There were so many big days and big plays for McDonald: a 91-yard touchdown from Van Brocklin against the Giants in 1958, four touchdowns against the Giants in 1959, 13 touchdowns in 1960 and 1961, 187 yards against the Cardinals in 1961, 237 yards against the Giants the same year, and a 35-yard touchdown in the 1960 title game against Green Bay.

As an Eagle, Tommy was named All-Pro four times and selected for the Pro Bowl five times. Though his numbers slipped a little in 1963 when King Hill was taking half the snaps at quarterback, it was still a shock when new coach Joe Kuharich traded him to the Cowboys in 1964. Kuharich felt he needed bodies to fill the Birds' plentiful gaping holes, so McDonald for Sam Baker, Lynn Hoyem and John Meyers was the first of nearly 10 house-cleaning trades he would make in his first year. Tommy at first considered retirement, but went on to play for the Cowboys, Rams, Falcons and Browns before his career ended five years later. He was a popular figure in Philadelphia sports and settled permanently in the area with his second wife Patty, a Philly girl. Fans loved his enthusiastic personality, the way he popped up after being hit, how he was always having fun, how he talked nonstop to his teammates and opponents alike, how he joyously reacted to scoring.

Tommy's antics predated the first end zone spike in NFL history, said to be by the Giants' Homer Jones in 1965, and the first end zone dance by the Chiefs' Elmo Wright in 1973. Expressive Eagles have followed along in this modern path, though. Harold Carmichael gathered his teammates in the end zone and spun the ball like dice. Byron Evans did his fraternity dance. Vai Sikahema punched out a goal post. Fred Barnett moon-walked, fainted and threw down behind-the-back spikes. Koy Detmer combined a whipping motion with bumps and grinds in something he called the "Whuppin' Stick." Donovan McNabb has dunked the ball, knelt in prayer and moon-walked. Terrell Owens has flapped his arms like Eagle wings, done sit ups, danced like Ray Lewis and ice skated. Even long-snapper Mike Bartrum got into the spirit by following a touchdown pass from McNabb by long-snapping the ball back to Donovan and drawing a penalty for his performance. This is not to mention celebrations of non-scoring plays. These "pointless" celebrations include James Thrash's sky pointing, Freddie Mitchell's championship belt snap, Jeremiah Trotter's ax-chopping motion and Brian Dawkins' muscle flexing.

None of them can match the simple, unalloyed exuberance exuded by Tommy McDonald 40 years ago, and it's unlikely any will get the chance to take "excessive celebration" to the length McDonald did in 1998 during his induction into the Pro Football Hall of Fame. After being introduced by Philadelphia sportswriter Ray Diddinger, 64-year-old Tommy brought a boom box on stage and danced to the Bee Gees. He tossed his 25-pound bronze bust in the air like a football and chest-bumped each of the four other bemused inductees. He bounced uncontrollably around the stage, alternating between thanking people and telling old jokes. It was an unrehearsed quirky, eight-minute festive performance unlike any induction before or since. Some saw it as an undignified mess, while others saw it as an expression of pure joy. Homer Jones may have been the first player to spike the ball in the NFL, but Tommy McDonald was the first to treat Canton like the end zone. His was the ultimate celebration.

Race

Clarence Peaks
FB 1957-63

WHO'S WORN THE NUMBER:

Joe Kresky (G) 1933, Dan Barnhardt (B) 1934, Jack Norby (B) 1934, Forrest McPherson (T) 1935-36, Winford Baze (B) 1937, Herschel Giddens (T) 1938, Lester McDonald (E) 1940, Dave DiFilippo (G) 1941, Clarence Peaks (FB) 1957-63, Al Nelson (DB) 1965-73, Art Malone (RB) 1975-76, John Sanders (DB) 1977-79, Michael Haddix (FB) 1983-88, Ben Smith (DB) 1990-93, Al Jackson (CB) 1994, Jerome Henderson (CB) 1995, Darnell Autry (RB) 1998, *Lito Sheppard* (CB) 2002-04.

Originator: Before guard Joe Kresky came to Philly in 1933, he had some troubles with the law as an undergraduate. He was convicted of beating up a theater electrician because Kresky didn't like the spats on the man's shoes. He was also implicated in the robbery of a furrier.

Longest Tenure: Nine years, Al Nelson.

Number Changes: Joe Kresky wore 5 in 1934 and 1935; Forest McPherson wore 35 in 1937; Winford Baze also wore 37 in 1937; Les McDonald also wore 76 in 1940; Dave DiFilippo also wore 69 in 1941; Darnell Autry wore 24 in 2000.

Just Visiting: Art Malone was a good runner for the Falcons.

Highs: Al Nelson returned two missed field goals for touchdowns in his career; Ben Smith might have been something special at cornerback if he hadn't torn up his knee; Lito Sheppard has the ability to be a top cornerback.

Lows: Michael Haddix was the eighth overall pick in the 1983 draft and never gained more than 276 yards or averaged better than 3.5 yards a carry in six years in Philly. Buddy Ryan said he "looked like a reject guard from the USFL. He's so damn fat."

Clarence Peaks

The 1957 NFL draft was an especially deep one. Of the 13 players taken in the first round, four would go on to the Hall of Fame, including first overall pick Paul Hornung, who was the bonus pick for the Packers. He was followed by Jon Arnett, John Brodie, Ron Kramer, Hall of Famer Len Dawson, Hall of Famer Jim Brown, Clarence Peaks by the Eagles, Hall of Famer Jim Parker, Don Bosseler, Jerry Tubbs, Del Shofner, Bill Glass and Earl Leggett. The only two of these players who would never play in a Pro Bowl were Leggett and Peaks. Clarence was the first black player chosen by the Eagles in the first round who signed with the team. He was part of a complete Eagle backfield selected in 1957 with Billy Barnes, Tommy McDonald and Sonny Jurgensen following in later rounds.

Peaks had a remarkable career as a halfback, defensive back, punter and kicker at Michigan State and starred in the Spartans' 17-14 Rose Bowl victory over UCLA in 1957. In that game he caught one touchdown and precipitated another by being the middle man in a Hook and Lateral play from Earl Morrall to Peaks to John Lewis for a 67-yard score. MSU coach Duffy Daugherty called him the best all-around player he had coached. He was the runner-up for the Heisman Trophy in his senior year.

As an Eagle, Peaks' career never really took off. He was a good outlet receiver and a solid blocker, but of his seven seasons in Philadelphia, he averaged less than four yards per carry in five of them. He never gained more than 471 yards in any season and was a bit of a fumbler. He is most remembered for breaking his leg during the 1960 championship campaign, forcing rookie Ted Dean to step up as his replacement in the starting backfield. Peaks was in the midst of his best year by far when he went down against the Redskins in the seventh game that year; he was averaging 5.4 yards per carry and had accumulated nearly 500 yards rushing at that point.

Peaks was back to averaging 3.5 yards per carry in 1961 and lasted a couple more years in Philadelphia before new coach Joe Kuharich traded him and linebacker Bob Harrison to the Steelers for Red Mack and Glen Glass in 1964. Clarence played pretty well for two years in the Steeler backfield with John Henry Johnson and then retired from the game. It's interesting that when Peaks was a three-sport star at Central High in Flint, Michigan, he was an Honorable Mention All-State quarterback. Blacks, of course, did not play quarterback in the NFL when Clarence was playing. At 6 feet 1 inch and 218 pounds, he had the body of a fullback. If Donovan McNabb had played then, he may have been a fullback, too. Daunte Culpepper probably would have been a defensive end.

Although Peaks was the first black number one draft pick signed by the Eagles, he was not the first black player they selected in the first round. In 1952, Philadelphia selected Drake tailback Johnny Bright with their first pick, but Bright elected to play in Canada. Considering his background, this was not surprising. Bright starred in both football and basketball as a schoolboy in Fort Wayne, Indiana, but no in-state school ever even contacted him, so he enrolled at Drake University in Iowa. At Drake, Bright led the nation in total offense as a sophomore and junior. Midway through his senior year, Johnny was again leading the nation in offense when Drake went to Stillwater, Oklahoma, to play Oklahoma A&M (now Oklahoma State) in a Missouri Valley Conference game. During the game, Bright had his jaw fractured by a vicious blow delivered by Wilbanks Smith well behind where the ball was, and after the play had ended. Bright threw a touchdown pass on the next play before being forced to leave the game.

Two newspaper photographers captured the incident in a sickening sequence of photos that made the cover of *Life* and won them the Pulitzer Prize. Drake pulled out of the conference over the incident, and Bright missed two games before returning for the season finale. Bright decided he did not want to be the Eagles' first black player and did not want to play in the NFL where he felt he might be subject to more incidents like the Oklahoma one. He signed with Calgary and played later with Edmonton as well. When he retired in 1964, he was the Canadian Football League's all-time rushing leader. The 5-foot 10-inch, 225-pound halfback would have been an ideal replacement for the fading Steve Van Buren.

Perhaps coincidentally, the Eagles were one of four NFL teams to employ their first black players in 1952. The Birds signed 10th-round pick Ralph Goldston and 30th-rounder Don Stevens while the Bears added Emerson Cole, Herman Clark and Eddie Macon; the Cardinals signed Ollie Matson, Wally Triplett and Cliff Anderson; and the Steelers took on Jack Spinks. At that point, only the Redskins were still all-white, but they would hold out for 10 more years. Goldston and Stevens had their moments, but neither ever became a starter, although Goldston played and coached in Canada.

For the next 10 seasons, Philadelphia had from one to four blacks on the team in each season. From 1962 through 1965, that total ranged from five to nine blacks, and finally in 1966 the number of black Eagles reached double figures with 11. Since then, as blacks have made strides, the Eagles have been in the mainstream. Randall Cunningham was part of the general acceptance of black quarterbacks in the 1980s, and the Eagles were even trendsetters when they also picked up Don McPherson as one of Cunningham's backups. Ray Rhodes was hired as head coach just as the absence of black head coaches was becoming very embarrassing for the league. The Eagles have strived to create an atmosphere of equality, so it was discouraging to hear Donovan McNabb's agent trying to play the race card during contract negotiations in 1999. Sadly, McNabb became the focus of more racial rhetoric in 2003 when radio talk show host Rush Limbaugh criticized the media for over-hyping McNabb because they want to see black quarterbacks succeed. Limbaugh's criticism was taken to be of McNabb, although it actually was directed at what he saw as a politically correct media. Besides that, if Limbaugh ever listened to local talk radio, he would understand that McNabb is freely criticized for his flaws. Race remains a very tricky proposition. Clarence Peaks probably has the right approach; he says that he spends his time in retirement seeking spiritual knowledge. We could all use more of that.

27

Bad Timing — Arriving for the Aftermath

Irv Cross
CB 1961-65, 1969

WHO'S WORN THE NUMBER:

Milton Leathers (G) 1933, Robert Gonya (T) 1933-34, Jack Dempsey (T) 1934 and 1937, Burle Robinson (E) 1935, George Rado (E) 1937-38, Milt Trost (T) 1940, Sam Bartholomew (B) 1941, Bob Davis (B) 1942, John Butler (B) 1943 and 1945, Ted Laux (B) 1944, Pete Kmetovic (B) 1946, Tom Johnson (B) 1948, Clyde Scott (B) 1949-52, Neil Ferris (B) 1952, Hal Giancanelli (B) 1953-56, Billy Wells (B) 1958, Gene Johnson (B) 1959-60, *Irv Cross* (DB) 1961-65 and 1969, Trent Jackson (WR) 1966, Po James (RB) 1972-74, Richard Blackmore (CB) 1979-82, Topper Clemons (RB) 1987r, Siran Stacy (RB) 1992, Eric Zomalt (S) 1994-96, James Bostic (RB) 1998-99, Julian Jones (S) 2001.

Originator: Guard Milton Leathers was known as the Wild Red Head at Georgia, but appeared in only four games for Philadelphia in 1933.

Longest Tenure: Six years, Irv Cross.

Number Changes: Ted Laux wore 15 in 1942 and 1943; Po James wore 33 in 1975.

Just Visiting: None.

Highs: Clyde "Smackover" Scott ran a 9.6-second 100-yard dash and had his number retired by the University of Arkansas, but his NFL career was shortened by injuries.

Lows: Siran Stacy, with his surgically reconstructed knee, was the Eagles' second-round pick in 1992, despite having had numerous scrapes with the law in high school and college. He washed out in two years. Jack Dempsey fled the country on a grand theft charge 30 years after his playing days and was ultimately sentenced to a year in prison.

Irv Cross

The defending champion Eagles went into the eighth game of the 1961 season against the Bears with a 6-1 record. In the course of defeating Chicago, cornerback Tom Brookshier broke his leg and would never play again. He was replaced by rookie Irv Cross, and the team split its last six games to finish in second place. Philadelphia would not have another winning season until Cross was traded five years later. The Eagles' collapse in the aftermath of their championship must have been all Irv's fault.

Well, not exactly. Cross grew up as one of 15 children and earned a scholarship to Northwestern where he played receiver and defensive back under coach Ara Parseghian. In 1959, he caught the winning touchdown pass in the Wildcats' 30-24 upset of Notre Dame, coached by Joe Kuharich. Irv could run the 100-yard dash in 9.7 seconds and long-jump over 25 feet, but coming from the football backwater of Northwestern, he was not drafted until the seventh round by Philadelphia. He went to Eagles training camp and planned to return to graduate school if he was cut. Cross made the team as a reserve cornerback and was thrust into the starting lineup by Brookie's injury.

The following season, Cross settled in as a starting cornerback and intercepted a career high of five passes. With his speed he could stay with any receiver for 50 yards, even track stars like Bob Hayes. In addition, he was a heavy hitter who relished jamming his helmet into a ball carrier's gut and driving him to the ground. Because of his tackling style, he had four concussions as a rookie and wore a specially padded helmet after that. He was an intelligent guy who relied on extensive film study to fully prepare each week, and was named to the Pro Bowl for both the 1964 and 1965 seasons.

So if it wasn't Cross' fault, why did the Eagles implode after 1960? The first factor is that they were not a great team to start with. The 1960 Eagles are often cited as one of the weakest teams to ever win a title. They had a sub-par offensive line and no running game to speak of. Their defense was iffy and easy to run on. Their defensive backs were slow, although their intelligence and toughness allowed them to be very effective. What they had was great leadership and togetherness. With proven head coach Buck Shaw, fiery veteran quarterback Norm Van Brocklin and indefatigable 60-minute man Chuck Bednarik, the Birds were driven to succeed.

The change in leadership was a second factor. Sonny Jurgensen did a great job replacing Van Brocklin in 1961, but he did not have Van's experience or fire. Rookie head coach Nick Skorich seemed capable with a good background, but proved to be nothing special and was unable to turn things around when things went bad. A third factor is that the team had no depth and were not replenishing as starting players aged. When Brookshier went down, the Eagles were left with an untested rookie who was not quite ready. In 1962, when Jurgensen was injured, he was replaced with King Hill. The defensive line starters were all gone by 1962, and were replaced by a fearsome foursome of Bobby Richards, John Baker, Riley Gunnels and Don Oakes. With no pass rush to speak of, the pass defense sunk to the bottom of the league, while an injured and confused Jurgensen struggled on offense. And then Joe Kuharich arrived with a 15-year contract in 1964 and began the wholesale trading of quality for quantity in his quest for a team without stars while selecting little of value in the draft.

Kuharich traded defensive star and chapel leader Maxie Baughan in 1966, and that was the final straw for fellow chapel leader Cross, who was unhappy with his contract and with the team's defensive style. He issued an ultimatum for the Eagles to trade him, and Trader Joe happily complied two months later. The Rams gave up receiver Willie Brown, whom Kuharich termed "versatile," and Aaron Martin, whom Joe said was "one of the finest defensive backs in the NFL." It was perspicacious talent evaluation like this that led to the Birds having one winning season in 16 years from 1962 to 1978. Willie Brown averaged -0.2 yards as a punt returner and 14.5 yards as a kick returner in one-half season in Philly. Aaron Martin was beaten regularly by opposing wide receivers over two years as an Eagle.

Meanwhile, Cross was reunited with his friend Baughan and with coach George Allen, whom he had met when Irv was at Northwestern and Allen was coaching for the Bears under George Halas. He started for the Rams for the next three years as the team went 29-10-3 and featured a defense among the league's best each year. After Kuharich was fired, the Eagles brought Cross back in another trade in which the Rams got the better deal. Los Angeles received Hall of Fame tackle Bob Brown for Joe Carollo, Don Chuy and Cross. Irv spent one season as a player-coach under Jerry Williams, who had been the Eagles' defensive coach when Cross was a rookie and stayed on for one more season as just a coach before going into broadcasting. He spent 23 years at CBS, most of it as part of the popular *NFL Today* Sunday pregame show. Since then he has served as part-owner of the Baltimore Stallions' CFL franchise and as a college athletic direc-tor — first at Idaho State and then with Macalester College in Minnesota.

Leaders

Bill Bradley
S 1969-76

Originator: Back Richard Thornton, all of 5 feet 8 inches, completed two of 13 passes and gained 14 yards as a ball carrier and 14 as a receiver in 1933.

Longest Tenure: Eight years, Bill Bradley.

Number Changes: Guy Turnbow wore 33 in 1933; Stumpy Thomason wore 29 in 1935; Joe Pilconis wore 2 in 1934, 18 from 1936 to 1937 and 24 in 1937.

Just Visiting: Don Griffin was a starter for the 49ers; Mel Gray returned nine punts and kicks for TDs for the Saints and Lions; Amp Lee was a serviceable third-down back for the Vikings.

Highs: Correll Buckhalter has shown flashes of brilliance in between knee injuries.

Lows: Ray Keeling briefly held the title as the NFL's heaviest player at 271 pounds in 1938, but his girth could not win him a starting job. Don Jonas was too slow to make the Eagles as a defensive back or running back, but as a quarterback was MVP of the Continental League and the Canadian Football League.

Bill Bradley

Free-spirited, free-ranging free safety Bill Bradley was popular both with his teammates and with the fans. Despite playing on a series of flightless Eagle teams that deservedly heard the boos at the Vet, Bradley himself never was booed. With his untamed afro, bushy mustache and wild playing style, Bill was seen as a player who always gave everything he had on the field and made a number of big plays for a disorganized franchise.

Bradley was known as Super Bill for his amazing versatility on the field. He was highly recruited as a schoolboy quarterback and enrolled at the University of Texas. In his sophomore and junior years, Bill was the Longhorn quarterback. As a team captain in his senior year, he lost his starting job, but still helped Texas finish 9-1-1 by lining up as a receiver, a defensive back and as the team's left-footed punter. The Eagles drafted him in the third round and put him to work as a punter, punt returner, kick returner and sometime safety while he studied starters Joe Scarpati and Nate Ramsey. He got his first chance to play safety as a rookie in a game in which the Cowboys were throttling the Birds even worse than usual. After much prodding of the defensive coaches, Bradley was inserted in the fourth quarter and promptly read the pass play that fellow rookie Roger Staubach was running. Bradley jumped the route and returned the interception 56 yards for his only career touchdown to make the final score 49-14 Cowboys.

Scarpati was traded in 1970, but Bradley hurt his left knee and needed surgery in training camp. Unable to play defense all year, he nonetheless was sent out to punt on his injured leg in a bizarre twist that was entirely normal for the dysfunctional organization the Eagles were at the time. Finally, in his third season, Bradley became the starting free safety in 1971 and led the NFL in interceptions with 11. He celebrated his success with a much-ballyhooed 17-day holdout in 1972 that he spent at the Jersey shore, working out on the beach with teammate Tim Rossovich. Rossovich was traded, and Bradley signed. With a league-leading nine picks in 1972, he became the first player in history to lead the league in interceptions in consecutive seasons. He was not big and not fast, but was a hard tackler and had an ex-quarterback's instincts on what the offense was going to do.

Over the next four seasons, Bradley would never nab that many interceptions again, but he did go to his third Pro Bowl and ended his eight-year Eagle career with a team record 34 interceptions that has since been tied by Eric Allen. The difficulty of playing for a recurring loser began to get to Bill and he remarked at the time, "Because there's so much emphasis on winning, as long as you lose, you feel it's all in vain. When you don't win, you don't feel good whether you played good or bad." Bradley welcomed his trade to the Vikings in 1977 as a chance to go to a winner, but he did not make the team. Later, he got into four final games as a Cardinal before quitting football. A few years after, he returned to the game as a coach and has worked in the USFL, CFL and NFL as well as in college where he signed on as defensive coordinator for former teammate Guy Morris at Baylor in 2004.

Bradley is one of only two Eagles to lead the league in interceptions; the other was Roy Zimmerman in 1945. In the other major defensive statistical category, Reggie White led the NFL in sacks twice from 1987 to 1988, and Clyde Simmons led in 1992.

Offensively, the Eagles' receivers have been the most impressive. Reception leaders include Don Looney in 1940, Pete Pihos from 1953 to 1955, Pete Retzlaff in 1958, Harold Jackson in 1972, Harold Carmichael in 1973, and Charlie Young in 1974. Leaders in yards include Pihos in 1953 and 1955, Tommy McDonald in 1961, Ben Hawkins in 1967, Jackson in 1969 and 1972, Carmichael in 1973 and Mike Quick in 1983 and 1985. Four Eagles have led in touchdown receptions: Pihos in 1953, McDonald in 1961, Carmichael in 1979 and Irving Fryar in 1996.

Eagle quarterbacks have led in touchdown passes several times: Tommy Thompson in 1948, Bobby Thomason in 1953, Adrian Burk in 1954, Sonny Jurgensen in 1961, Roman Gabriel in 1973 and Randall Cunningham in 1990. Yardage leaders include Davey O'Brien in 1939, Jurgensen in 1961 and 1962, and Gabriel in 1973. Steve Van Buren is the only Eagle to lead the league in rushing yards, and he did it four times: 1945 and 1947 to 1949. Several Birds have paced the league in highest rushing average including two quarterbacks: Bosh Pritchard in 1949, Tim Brown in 1965, Randall Cunningham in 1989 and 1990, Heath Sherman in 1992, Charlie Garner in 1995 and Donovan McNabb in 2000. Twice the scoring leader has come from Philadelphia, with Steve Van Buren in 1945 and Bobby Walston in 1954. Van Buren also led the league in punt returns in 1944 and kick returns in 1945. Steve is joined here only by Tim Brown who led the NFL in kick returns in 1961 and 1963. Finally, Joe Muha led the league in punting in 1948.

Among awards the Eagles have done best at Coach of the Year. That has been given to Greasy Neale in 1948, Buck Shaw in 1960, Dick Vermeil in 1979, Ray Rhodes in 1995 and Andy Reid in 2000 and 2002. Four Eagles have been named MVP: Norm Van Brocklin in 1960, Pete Retzlaff in 1965, Ron Jaworski in 1980 and Randall Cunningham in 1988 and 1990. Reggie White was named Defensive MVP twice, in 1987 and 1991, and three Bird receivers have been Rookie of the Year: Bobby Walston in 1951, Charlie Young in 1973 and Keith Jackson in 1988. Finally, Comeback Player has been given to quarterbacks Roman Gabriel in 1973, Jim McMahon in 1991 and Randall Cunningham in 1992.

29

Trade Secrets

Harold Jackson
WR 1969-72

WHO'S WORN THE NUMBER:

Ray Smith (C) 1933, Richard Fenci (E) 1933, Stephen Banas (B) 1935, Glenn Campbell (E) 1935, Stumpy Thomason (B) 1935, Herman Bassman (B) 1936, Joe Pivarnick (G) 1936, Charles Knox (T) 1937, William Hughes (C) 1938-40, John Nocera (LB) 1959-62, Israel Lang (FB) 1964-68, *Harold Jackson* (WR) 1969-72, Mark Burke (DB) 1976, Al Latimer (CB) 1979, Jo Jo Heath (DB) 1981, Elbert Foules (CB) 1983-87, Mark McMillian (CB) 1992-95, Adam Walker (FB) 1996, Corey Walker (RB) 1998, Darrel Crutchfield (CB) 2001, Roderick Hood (CB) 2004.

Originator: Ray Smith was a 5-foot 10-inch, 195-pound center who started three games for the Eagles in 1933.

Longest Tenure: Five years, fullback Izzy Lang and cornerback Elbert Foules.

Number Changes: Stumpy Thomason wore 28 in 1936; Herm Bassman also wore 19 and 24 in 1936; Bill Hughes wore 15 in 1937; Corey Walker wore 39 in 1997.

Just Visiting: None.

Highs: Hotdog Mark McMillian made some big plays for a little cornerback.

Lows: Cornerback Jo Jo Heath played in the NFL, USFL and CFL in the 1980s, mostly as a backup. After his playing career he had a record of drug and theft arrests and was stabbed to death in a bad drug transaction at the age of 45.

Harold Jackson

The Jackson State Tigers set an unusual record in 1968. Despite finishing with a respectable 6-3 record in 1967, 11 Tigers were selected in the NFL draft following the season. That was more draftees than any school had ever had up to that point, although it has since been exceeded by the University of Southern California. The coach of that squad was Rod Paige, a former Jackson State quarterback who eventually became the Secretary of Education under President George W. Bush. Of the 11 players drafted, only three would play in the NFL: tackle Tom Funchess, defensive back John Outlaw and wide receiver Harold Jackson. All three would spend time with the Patriots and the latter two would play with the Eagles as well.

Harold Jackson was picked by the Rams in the 12th round and spent most of his rookie year on the practice squad, appearing in only two games. The next year, George Allen traded Jackson and rookie defensive end John Zook to the Eagles for has-been fullback Izzy Lang. It was the best trade that Eagle general manager Pete Retzlaff ever made, and would have been even better had he not then included Zook in a deal with Atlanta for Jim Purnell. Purnell was quickly sent to the Rams for forgettable linebacker Tony Guillory, while Zook was twice selected as a second-team All-Pro and went to one Pro Bowl for the Falcons.

Despite foolishly dumping Zook, the trade was a steal because Harold Jackson was an immediate star, catching 65 passes for a league-leading 1,116 yards and nine touchdowns in 1969. He made the Pro Bowl that year and in 1972 when he led the NFL with 62 receptions for 1,048 yards. Harold was small — 5 feet 10 inches and 175 pounds — but durable; he played in 190 consecutive games from 1969 through 1981 and started all but five of those contests. He was extremely fast, having been clocked at 9.3 in the 100-yard dash at Jackson State, and was a consistent long-ball threat throughout his 16-year career.

After four outstanding years for some very bad Eagle teams, Jackson was sent back to the Rams along with Tony Baker, two number one draft choices and a number three pick, for quarterback Roman Gabriel. New coach Mike McCormack wanted a stud QB, and he overpaid to get one. The Eagles still would not reach the playoffs, but Harold did, starring with the Rams as a three-time Pro Bowler. In 1977, George Allen was rehired to coach the Rams and strangely tried to trade Jackson again (this time to the Redskins), but George was fired after only two exhibition games. Jackson played another year in LA before being traded to the Patriots to replace the paralyzed Daryl Stingley in 1978. For three of his four years in New England, Harold averaged better than 20 yards per catch. For the decade of the 1970s, Harold led the NFL with 432 catches and 7,724 receiving yards, and he averaged 17.9 yards per catch. He finished his career with brief stops in Minnesota and Seattle and a total of 579 receptions for 76 touchdowns. After retiring, he went into coaching at both the pro and college levels.

Below is a register of major Philadelphia Eagle trades, pieced together mostly from newspaper accounts. Most simple money transactions and draft position swaps are not included. Money deals are indicated with a dollar sign and undisclosed draft choices are indicated with "?Draft choice." Deals where the compensation remains a mystery are noted with a question mark. This example demonstrates how to interpret the table:

How to Read this Table:

DATE	GAVE	TO	FOR
1969	Izzy Lang	Rams	Harold Jackson & John Zook
1969	John Zook & Frank Molden & John Mallory & 70-4 (Paul Reed)	Falcons	Jim Purnell
1969	Jim Purnell & 70-2 (49ers - John Isenbarger) & 70-7 (Ted Provost)	Rams	Tony Guillory & 71-6 (Lions - Frank Harris)

In 1969, the Eagles obtained Harold Jackson and John Zook from the Rams in exchange for an Izzy Lang. Also in 1969, the Eagles obtained Jim Purnell from the Falcons in exchange for a John Zook, Frank Molden, John Mallory and a fourth-round pick in the 1970 draft, which Atlanta used to select Paul Reed. Finally in 1969, the Eagles dealt Purnell and second- and seventh-round picks to the Rams for Tony Guillory and a sixth-round pick in 1971. The Rams selected Ted Provost with their seventh-rounder and traded their second-rounder to the 49ers, who used it to grab John Isenbarger. The Eagles traded the sixth-rounder they obtained to the Lions, who selected Frank Harris.

DATE	GAVE	TO	FOR
1933	$	Giants	Jim Zyntell
1935	Bob Gonya	Giants	Glenn Campbell
1935	Swede Elstrom	Giants	Hank Reese
1936	36-1 (Jay Berwanger)	Bears	Art Buss
1937	Swede Hanson	Dodgers	$
1937	37-1 (Sam Francis) & Ed Manske & $	Bears	Bill Hewitt & Ted Rosequist & Red Pollock & Ookie Miller
1937	Izzy Weinstock	Steelers	Marty Kordick
1938	Irv Hall	Giants	Hugh Wolfe
1940	Fred Shirey	Packers	Millard White
1940	40-1 (George McAfee)	Bears	Russell Thompson & Milt Trost
1940	Dave Smukler	Lions`	Ray George & Joe Wendlick
1940	$	Giants	Jerry Ginney
1940	?Draft choice	Rams	Chuck Cherundolo
1940	41-1 (Tom Harmon)	Bears	Dick Bassi & Les McDonald
1941	$	Dodgers	Banks McFadden
1941	Chet Gladchuk	Giants	Len Barnum
1941	Shad Bryant	Lions	Charles Ishmael
1942	John Knolla	Cardinals	Bert Johnson
1942	$	Rams	Bosh Pritchard
1942	$	Steelers	Ernie Steele
1942	Joe Bukant	Cards	Hugh McCullough
1943	Jack Smith & Ken Haydn	Redskins	Leroy Zimmerman
1943	Ted Williams	Redskins	$
1946	$	Bears	Rudy Smeja
1946	$	Lions	Alex Wojciechowicz
1946	Jack Banta	Rams	Walt Zirinsky
1946	Rocco Canale	Yanks	Augie Lio
1947	Roy Zimmerman	Lions	Jim Kekeris & Charles Hoover
1948	49-6 (Sam Tamburro)	Yanks	Mario Giannelli
1948	Jim Kekeris	Packers	Frank Szymanski
1949	50-2 (Thurman McGraw)	Lion	Mike Jarmoluk
1949	Hal Prescott	Lions	?
1949	Frank Tripucka	Lions	Waivers
1949	Lindell Pearson	Lions	51-1 (Chet Mutryn)
1950	51-2 (Jim Staton)	Redskins	Walt Stickel
1951	52-5 (Mel Sinqufield)	Yankees	John Rauch
1951	Cliff Patton	Cards	John Goldsberry

DATE	GAVE	TO	FOR
1951	Jack Dwyer	Redskins	Adrian Burk
1952	Dan Sandifer	Packers	Al Collins
1952	53-1 (Donn Moomaw) & Jack Myers	Rams	Bobby Thomason & Jack Zilly
1952	John Thomas	Lions	Fred Enke
1952	Piggy Barnes & John Rauch	Steelers	Frank Wydo
1952	Chuck Ulrich	Cards	Tom Wham & Knox Ramsey
1953	53-6 (Tom Higgins)	Cards	Roy Barni & 53-7 (Jack Erickson)
1953	54-6 (Charlie Allen)	Rams	Jerry Williams
1953	54-10 (Ed Hughes)	Rams	Tom Scott
1954	Bob Schnelker & Frank Ziegler	Giants	Don Menasco & Chester Lagod
1954	Russ Craft	Steelers	Darrell Hogan
1955	$	Colts	Ed Sharkey
1955	Roy Barni	Redskins	Rob Goode
1956	Waivers	Lions	Pete Retzlaff
1956	57-6 (Bill Rhodes)	49ers	Marion Campbell
1957	Ray Bawel	Packers	Ben Szafaryn
1957	58-3 (Bill Anderson)	Redskins	Al Dorow
1957	58-9 (Mike Henry)	Steelers	Bob Gaona
1958	Menil Mavraidies	Redskins	Volney Peters
1958	Jim Weatherall	Redskins	Don Owens
1958	59-1 (Dick Bass) & Buck Lansford & Jimmy Harris	Rams	Norm Van Brocklin
1958	59-7 (Jim Tucker)	Bears	Ed Meadows
1959	Jerry Norton	Cards	Jerry Wilson & Bob Konovsky
1959	61-3 (Billy Wilson)	Cards	Jim McCusker
1959	Tom Scott	Giants	Gerry Huth & Ken MacAfee
1959	Bill Koman	Cards	Chuck Weber
1959	60-9 (Bob Hall)	Colts	Jimmy Carr
1959	60-10 (Jim O'Brien)	Lions	Stan Campbell
1960	Proverb Jacobs	Giants	61-4 (Dan Ficca)
1960	61-4 (Joe LeSage)	Packers	Bobby Freeman
1960	Jerry Wilson	49ers	John Wittenborn
1960	62-5 (Ben Wilson)	Rams	Don Burroughs
1960	Walt Kowalczyk & 61-5 (Ron Puckett)	Lions	Jerry Reichow

DATE	GAVE	TO	FOR
1960	Lee Riley	Redskins	Will Renfro & Ed Voytek
1961	62-1 (Irv Goode)	Cards	King Hill
1961	Jerry Reichow	Redskins	$
1961	Don Owens	Cards	61-3 (James Wright)
1961	Joe Robb	Cards	Leo Sugar & John Tracy
1961	Bobby Jackson	Bears	62-6 (Gus Gonzales)
1962	63-5 (Rolland Benson)	Rams	Roy Hord
1962	Leo Sugar	Lions	63-3 (Louie Guy)
1962	Ed Khayat	Redskins	63-8 (Gene Sykes)
1962	Bob Pellegrini	Rams	John Baker
1962	Billy Ray Barnes & Bobby Freeman	Redskins	Ben Scotti & Jim Schrader
1962	63-4 (Harrison Rossdahl)	49ers	Bob Harrison
1963	64-4 (Bob Long)	Packers	Ed Blaine
1963	Theron Sapp	Steelers	?Draft choice
1963	John Wittenborn	Cards	Frank Fuller
1963	Waivers	Steelers	George Tarasovic
1963	64-3 (Pat Batten)	Lions	Dave Lloyd & Dick Mills
1963	Buddy Guy	Giants	Paul Dudley
1963	Gene Gossage	Giants	Bill Quinlan
1964	Lee Roy Caffey & 65-1 (Donny Anderson)	Packers	Jim Ringo & Earl Gros
1964	Sonny Jurgenson & Jimmy Carr	Redskins	Norm Snead & Claude Crabb
1964	Ted Dean & Bob Berry	Vikings	Ray Poage & Don Hultz & Chuck Lamson & Terry Kosens
1964	Clarence Peaks & Bob Harrison	Steelers	Red Mack & Glenn Glass
1964	Tommy McDonald	Cowboys	Lynn Hoyem & John Meyers & Sam Baker
1964	J.D. Smith	Lions	Ollie Matson & Floyd Peters
1964	Ray Mansfield	Steelers	$
1964	?Draft choice	Colts	Herm McKee
1964	Mike Clark	Steelers	?Draft choice
1965	Riley Gunnels	Steelers	$
1965	Pete Case	Giants	Lane Howell
1965	John Henderson	Lions	66-6 (Mel Tom)
1966	Maxie Baughan	Rams	Fred Brown & Fred Molden & 67-3 (Harry Wilson)
1966	Irv Cross	Rams	Aaron Martin & Willie Brown
1966	Claude Crabb	Rams	67-7 (John Williams)
1967	Jack Concannon & ?	Bears	Mike Ditka

DATE	GAVE	TO	FOR
1967	Earl Gros & Bruce Van Dyke & 67-3 (Rockne Freitas)	Steelers	Gary Ballman
1967	?Draft choice	Lions	Jim Kearney
1968	Waivers	Falcons	Jim Norton
1968	Tim Brown	Colts	Alvin Haymond
1968	Mike Morgan	Redskins	68-9 (Lynn Buss)
1968	69-3 (Bill Bradley)	Vikings	King Hill
1968	Aaron Martin	Redskins	69-10 (Don Shanklin)
1968	69-3 (Al Jenkins)	Browns	Larry Conjar
1969	Mike Ditka	Cowboys	David McDaniels
1969	Bob Brown & Jim Nettles	Rams	Joe Carollo & Don Chuy & Irv Cross
1969	Alvin Haymond	Rams	Jimmy Raye & Billy Guy Anderson
1969	Randy Beisler	49ers	George Mira
1969	Izzy Lang	Rams	Harold Jackson & John Zook
1969	John Zook & Frank Molden & John Mallory & 70-4 (Paul Reed)	Falcons	Jim Purnell
1969	Jim Purnell & 70-2 (49ers - John Isenbarger) & 70-7 (Ted Provost)	Rams	Tony Guillory & 71-6 (Lions - Frank Harris)
1969	70-3 (Ara Person)	Colts	Ron Porter
1969	Jim Norton	Redskins	Jim Carroll
1970	Chuck Hughes	Lions	Bob Parker
1970	Joe Scarpati & 71-10 (Rocky Pamplin)	Saints	Norman Davis & Bo Burris
1971	Norm Snead	Vikings	Steve Smith & 71-2 (Hank Allison) & 71-6 (Wyck Neely) & 72-3 (Bobby Majors)
1971	71-2 (Dave Thompson) & 72-2 (Falcons - Pat Sullivan) & 72-3 (Ken Sanders)	Lions	Greg Barton
1971	72-5 (Jim Kreig)	Broncos	Pete Liske
1971	Richard Harvey	Saints	Jim Ward
1971	Tony Baker	Saints	?Draft choice
1971	?Draft choice	Bears	Ron Bull
1971	Joe Carollo	Rams	?Draft choice
1971	Bill Cappleman	Lions	72-3 (Tom Lukens)
1971	?Draft choice	Vikings	Bill Cappleman

DATE	GAVE	TO	FOR
1971	Cyrill Pinder	Bears	72-2 (Dan Yochum) & 73-4 (Colts - Gary Palmer)
1972	Tim Rossovich	Chargers	73-1 (Charlie Young)
1972	Bill Hobbs	Patriots	Houston Antwine
1972	?Draft choice	Jets	Pete Lammons
1973	Mike Taylor	Cards	Steve Wright
1973	Leroy Keyes & Ernie Calloway	Chiefs	Gerry Philbin
1973	Harold Jackson & Tony Baker & 74-1 (John Cappaletti) & 75-1 (Dennis Harrah) & 75-3 (Dan Nugent)	Rams	Roman Gabriel
1973	Mel Tom	Bears	74-5 (Jim Cagle)
1973	74-2 (Ed Shuttlesworth)	Colts	Norm Bulaich
1973	Larry Watkins	Bills	Dick Cunningham
1973	Ron Porter & 73-4 (Mike Wells)	Vikings	72-3 (Bobby Majors
1973	74-6 (Chuck Ramsey)	Patriots	Dennis Wirgowski
1973	74-5 (Monroe Ely)	Falcons	Wes Chesson
1974	77-1 (Wilson Whitley) & 78-1 (Ross Browner) & 78-2 (Ray Griffin)	Bengals	Bill Bergey
1974	Ben Hawkins	Browns	Joe Jones
1974	75-2 (Bob Nelson)	Bills	Jerry Patton
1974	Richard Harris	Bears	Charley Ford
1974	75-4 (John Starkebaum)	Saints	Tom Roussel
1974	75-5 (Steve Freeman)	Patriots	John Tarver
1974	76-1 (Billy Brooks) & 75-6 (Tom Shuman)	Bengals	Mike Boryla
1974	Mike Evans	Lions	Willie Germany
1974	75-9 (Dan Natale) & 76-4 (Steve Avery)	49ers	Randy Jackson
1975	76-4 (Oilers - Steve Largent)	Packers	Bill Lueck
1975	Steve Smith	Falcons	Art Malone
1975	Tom Dempsey	Rams	76-4 (Oilers - Steve Largent)
1975	Mark Nordquist	Bears	76-9 (Mike Hogan) & 77-8 (Wilbert Montgomery)
1975	Charley Ford	Oilers	?Draft choice
1975	Norm Bulaich	Dolphins	76-4 (Mike Smith)
1975	John Reaves & 76-2 (Glenn Bujnoch)	Bengals	Stan Walters & Wayne Clark
1975	77-3 (Tony Hill)	Cowboys	John Niland
1975	77-2 (Mike Davis)	Raiders	James McAlister

DATE	GAVE	TO	FOR
1975	Steve Zabel	Patriots	76-4 (Browns - Gene Swick) & 76-8 (Richard Lafargue)
1975	76-3 (Danny Reece)	Bengals	Horst Muhlmann
1976	77-4 (Mark Bailey) & 78-5 (Dwight Carey)	Chiefs	Cliff Frazier
1976	Joe Lavender	Redskins	Manny Sistrunk & 77-6 (Martin Mitchell) & 78-5 (Norris Banks) & 79-4 (Ben Cowins)
1976	78-10 (Ricky Patton)	Falcons	Dave Hampton
1976	76-12 (Dave Buckley)	Jets	76-13 (Terry Tautolo)
1977	Charlie Young	Rams	Ron Jaworski
1977	Bill Bradley	Vikings	78-7 (Greg Marshall)
1977	78-8 (Terry Falcon)	Patriots	Deac Sanders
1977	78-8 (Mike Moch)	Jets	Richard Osborne
1977	78-7 (Art Whittington) & 79-9 (Jim Rourke)	Raiders	Art Thoms
1977	78-6 (Eric Smith)	Bills	Donnie Green
1978	79-6 (Eddie Hicks)	Giants	Asst. Coach Jerry Wampfler
1978	Tom Sullivan	Browns	79-7 (Don Swafford)
1978	Tom Ehlers & Tom Graham	Bills	79-8 (Chuck Correal)
1978	79-10 (Tony Petruccio)	Chargers	Tom Graham
1978	79-12 (Ed Smith)	Steelers	Rick Engles
1979	81-5 (Tommy Vigorito)	Dolphins	Leroy Harris
1979	Waivers	Patriots	John Spagnola
1979	79-4 (Lynn Cain) & 80-4 (I.M. Hipp)	Falcons	Claude Humphrey
1980	81-6 (Edward O'Neal)	Giants	Joe Pisarcik
1980	81-8 (Hosea Taylor)	Colts	Ron Baker
1980	80-10 (Ben Long)	Dolphins	80-11 (Thomas Brown)
1980	Terry Tautolo	49ers	81-7 (Alan Duncan)
1981	82-10 (Robin Fisher)	Dolphins	Steve Howell
1982	Charlie Johnson	Vikings	83-2 (Jody Schulz)
1982	Tom Brown	Browns	83-7 (Jon Schultheis)
1983	85-6 (Jonathan Bostic)	Chiefs	Al Dixon
1983	84-2 (Scott Case)	Falcons	Joel Williams
1983	84-9 (Don Jones)	Browns	Bill Cowher
1984	Carl Hairston	Browns	85-9 (Dave Toub)
1984	85-3 (George Little)	Dolphins	Mark Dennard
1984	85-7 (James Harris)	Redskins	Bob Holly

DATE	GAVE	TO	FOR
1984	Tony Franklin	Patriots	85-6 (Ken Reeves)
1985	Wilbert Montgomery	Lions	Garry Cobb
1985	Dennis Harrison	Rams	86-4 (Matt Darwin) & 87-7 (Chris Crawford)
1985	Jerry Robinson	Raiders	86-2 (Alonzo Johnson)
1985	86-4 (Ty Allert) & 87-8 (Ron Brown)	Chargers	Earnest Jackson
1985	Reggie Wilkes	Falcons	86-7 (Cornelius Redick)
1985	86-8 (Jim Popp)	49ers	Keith Baker
1986	86-3 (Tim McKyer) & 87-2 (Jeff Bragel)	49ers	Matt Cavanaugh
1986	Anthony Griggs	Browns	86-8 (Seth Joyner)
1986	Joel Williams	Falcons	86-5 (Dan McMillin)
1986	Past considerations	Giants	86-12 (Bobby Howard)
1986	Greg Naron	Seahawks	87-6 (Chris Pike)
1986	87-11 (Chris McClemore)	49ers	Joe Conwell
1987	Greg Brown	Falcons	Mike Pitts
1987	88-9 (Todd Irvin)	Lions	Jimmie Giles
1988	89-4 (James Henry)	Seahawks	Ron Heller
1988	89-1 (Andre Rison) & 90-4 (Rick Cunningham)	Colts	Ron Solt
1989	89-5 (Mark Green) & 89-7 (Richard Brothers) & 89-8 (Tony Woody) & 89-9 (LaSalle Harper) & 89-10 (Todd Milliken) & 89-11 (Joe Nelms) & 89-12 (Fred Weygrand)	Bears	89-3 (Britt Hager)
1989	Bobby Morse	Saints	90-11 (John Hudson)
1990	91-6 (Mike Riley)	Jets	Roger Vick
1990	Don McPherson	Oilers	91-6 (Andy Harmon)
1991	91-1 (Vinnie Clark) & 92-1 (Cowboys - Kevin Smith)	Packers	91-1 (Antone Davis)
1992	93-5 (Mike Devlin)	Bills	Leon Seals
1993	93-4 (Horace Copeland)	Chargers	Broderick Thompson
1993	93-1 (Brad Hopkins)	Oilers	93-1 (Lester Holmes) & 93-3 (Derrick Frazier)
1994	Ben Smith	Broncos	95-3 (Chris T. Jones) & 96-5 (Whit Marshall)
1995	Joe Sims	Packers	96-6 (Tony Johnson)

DATE	GAVE	TO	FOR
1995	95-1 (Warren Sapp) & 95-2 (Mel Johnson)	Bucs	95-1 (Mike Mamula) & 95-3 (Greg Jefferson)
1995	Victor Bailey & 95-4 (Dave Wohlabaugh)	Chiefs	95-2 (Bobby Taylor) & 96-6 (Philip Riley)
1995	95-5 (Ryan Christopherson) & 95-7 (Curtis Marsh)	Jaguars	95-6 (Fred McCrary) & 95-7 (Kevin Bouie)
1995	96-7 (Jon Stark)	Browns	Ronnie Dixon
1997	Ronnie Dixon	Jets	97-7 (Koy Detmer)
1997	Past considerations	Jets	Sean Love
1997	?Draft choice	Ravens	Willie Clark
1998	98-2 (Steelers - Jeremy Staat) & 98-5 (Casey Dailey)	Jets	Hugh Douglas
1998	00-7 (49ers Tim Rattay)	Patriots	Dietrich Jells
1998	98-6 (Eric Ogbogu)	Jets	Jeff Graham
1999	Jon Harris	Packers	John Michels
1999	Bobby Hoying	Raiders	00-6 (John Frank)
1999	Rodney Peete	Redskins	00-6 (John Romero)
1999	01-7 (Mike Roberg)	Panthers	Luther Broughton
2000	Allen Rossum	Packers	01-5 (Tony Stewart)
2000	Kaseem Sinceno	Packers	Jeff Thomason
2003	Al Harris & 03-4 (Bills - Sam Aiken)	Packers	03-2 (Chargers - Terence Kiel)
2003	03-6 (Waine Bacon) & 04-6 (Colts - Jason David)	Falcons	Mark Simoneau
2003	?Draft choice	Steelers	Freddie Milons
2004	John Welbourn	Chiefs	04-5 (Thomas Tapeh) & 05-3 (Ryan Moats)
2004	A.J. Feeley	Dolphins	05-2 (Reggie Brown)
2004	James Thrash	Redskins	05-5 (Trent Cole)
2004	04-5 (Dolphins - Tony Bua) & Brandon Whiting	49ers	Terrell Owens

1940s Decade in Review

Bosh Pritchard
HB 1942, 1946-51

Originator: Former Frankford Yellow Jacket center Art Koeninger in 1933.

Longest Tenure: Seven years, Bosh Pritchard, 1942 and 1946-51.

Number Changes: Harry Benson also wore 39 in 1935; Charlie Garner originally wore 25 in 1994; Mike Hogan wore 35 from 1976 to 1978; Ron Lou also wore 51 in 1975; Bob Masters wore 31 in 1943 and 33 in 1942; Milt Smith also wore 82 in 1945.

Just Visiting: Alvin Haymond starred as a return man with the Colts and Rams. Cornerback Joe "Big Bird" Lavender spent most of his career in Washington.

Highs: Don Looney was a league-leading receiver in his only year in Philadelphia when he teamed up with his college passer, Davey O'Brien; much-maligned cornerback Otis Smith was a two-time Eagles special teams MVP; Charlie Garner was a shifty runner and good receiver in Philly and several other cities; spirited Brian Mitchell was one of the greatest return men of all time.

Lows: The Eagles gave up a top return man in Alvin Haymond to obtain cornerback Jimmy Raye in 1969. Raye had injury problems and only appeared in two games for the Eagles, although he has had a long and successful career as an NFL coach.

Bosh Pritchard

The ninth of 10 sons, Abisha Collins Pritchard was named for an uncle who promised to buy him his first pair of long pants when the time came. Pritchard never got the pants, but he became "Bish," which was botched to "Bosh" in the newspapers during his spectacular four-sport high school career. He accepted a football scholarship (as a tail-back) to the Virginia Military Institute, where he established a rivalry and friendship with the University of Virginia's All-American tailback, Bill Dudley. Bullet Bill was the first pick of the 1942 draft by Pittsburgh and would fashion a Hall of Fame career in three cities, but would never win a championship. Bosh's path would be different.

Pritchard went undrafted and signed on with the Cleveland Rams in 1942, but only got into one game in which he lost 27 yards on three carries before being waived. For $100, Greasy Neale's struggling Eagles picked him up and gave him a chance. Bosh showed brilliant flashes in the second half of the season. He returned a kickoff 97 yards for a touchdown against Washington and posted a 100-yard rushing day against the Brooklyn Dodgers. Neale finished his second year in Philadelphia 2-9, and Pritchard joined the Navy as a chief petty officer. For the next three years, he served stateside during World War II. In 1945, while stationed in San Diego, he starred on the field and off for the San Diego Bombers of the Pacific Coast Football League. Bosh was known as the "Crooning Halfback" on his own local radio show, and even sang occasionally at halftime.

Upon his discharge in 1946, Bosh returned to Philadelphia where he found a vast-ly different Eagles team, one that had finished second the past two years and was led by the best runner in the NFL, Steve Van Buren. Pritchard had walked into the perfect sit-uation for someone of his slight (5-foot 11-inch, 165-pound) frame. The speedy and shifty Pritchard became the outside change of pace to Van Buren's speedy and power-ful inside force, and the Eagles' smooth-functioning T-Formation offense thundered to a 32-12-2 record over the next four years, winning two of three title game appearances. Bosh's 4.9 yards per carry average was actually higher than Van Buren's 4.6 during that time, although Van Buren was the workhorse who carried the ball more than twice as much as Pritchard. If he had been used more, Pritchard would have been more likely to break down; his skill was getting into the open field and breaking off big gains. He gained over 500 yards in both 1948 and 1949 and finished in the top 10 for rushing both years. In 1949, he was voted the Eagles' MVP despite hurting his knee in the eighth game of the year. He missed the rest of 1949 and underwent surgery in 1950 when the knee failed to respond to rest. By 1951 neither he nor the Eagles were the same. Neale was gone, and Bosh was released. He was picked up by the Giants, with whom he had one last moment of glory, returning a punt for a score.

After football, Bosh worked as a local sportscaster on television and radio. He was part of the Eagles radio team during the 1960 championship and worked for Tel Ra Productions, which created NFL highlights films for the league in the 1950s, before Ed Sabol came along to create NFL Films. Pritchard stayed active in community theater and was elected to the Virginia and Pennsylvania Sports Halls of Fame. He was the quintessential Eagle scatback and died in 1996 at the age of 77.

Decade Headline: Birds of Paradise.

Where They Played: Shibe Park, 1940-57; Municipal Stadium, 1941 and 1947.

How the Game Was Played: The Bears perfected the Spread T Formation with a man in motion, an offense that would extend to every pro team except the Steelers by the end of the decade. The NFL struggled to stay in business through World War II and then was faced with the new All-America Conference as a strong competitor in the postwar period. Paul Brown, coach of the AAC's Cleveland Browns, introduced the messenger guard to pro football in order to call the plays. Prior to the war, coaches were not permitted to call plays. The two-platoon system was instituted at the end of the decade. In the postwar era, black players returned to NFL rosters.

Decade Won-Lost Record: 58-47-5; .550; 3-1 in the playoffs.

Record Against the Giants: 9-10-1.

Record Against the Redskins: 9-8-1.

Record Against the Steelers: 11-5; 1-0 in the playoffs.

Playoff Appearances: 1947, 1948, 1949.

Championships: 1948, 1949.

Unsung Hero: Art Rooney, for having second thoughts about selling the Steelers to Alex Thompson after the 1940 season and buying half the Eagles from his friend Bert Bell. Bell and Rooney traded franchises with Thompson before the 1941 season, so that Rooney was back in his hometown. Meanwhile, the Eagles were now owned by the young and vibrant Thompson, who was willing to pour large sums of money into the franchise and who hired cunning old Greasy Neale to coach it.

Head Coaches: Bert Bell, 1936-40, 1-10 for the decade; Greasy Neale, 1941-50, 57-37-5 for the decade (3-1 in the playoffs).

Best Player: Hall of Famer Steve Van Buren.

Hall of Famers: Chuck Bednarik, Bert Bell, Bill Hewitt, Greasy Neale, Pete Pihos, Steve Van Buren, Alex Wojciechowicz.

Eagle Honor Roll: Chuck Bednarik, Bert Bell, Bill Hewitt, Greasy Neale, Pete Pihos, Steve Van Buren, Alex Wojciechowicz, plus the 1948 and 1949 championship teams.

League Leaders: Davey O'Brien — pass attempts 1940, completions 1940; Don Looney —catches 1940; Tony Bova — yards per catch 1943; Mel Bleeker — yards per catch 1944; Steve Van Buren — rushing 1945 and 1947-49, rush attempts 1945 and 1947-49, rush TDs 1945 and 1947-49, points 1945, TDs 1945, punt returns 1944, kickoff returns 1945; Leroy Zimmerman — interceptions 1945; Tommy Thompson — completion percentage 1946, TD passes 1948; Joe Muha — punting 1948; Cliff Patton — field goals 1948-49; Bosh Pritchard — rush average 1949.

Award Winners: Greasy Neale, Coach of the Year 1948.

All-Pros: Dick Bassi 1940; Don Looney 1940; Davey O'Brien 1940; Dick Humbert 1941; Phil Ragazzo 1941; Bob Suffridge 1941; Tommy Thompson 1942 and 1948-49; Jack Hinkle 1943; Eberle Schultz 1943; Vic Sears 1943 and 1945; Ernie Steele 1943; Leroy Zimmerman 1943-44; Steve Van Buren 1944-49; Al Wistert 1944-49; Bruno Banducci 1945; Jack Ferrante 1945 and 1949; Augie Lio 1946; Pete Pihos 1947-49; Bucko Kilroy 1948-49; Joe Muha 1948; Cliff Patton 1949.

All-Star Game Selections: Dick Bassi 1940; Don Looney 1940; Dick Humbert 1941; Enio Conti 1942; Tommy Thompson 1942; Bosh Pritchard 1942.

Best Offensive Backfield: 1947-49, with quarterback Tommy Thompson, halfbacks Steve Van Buren and Bosh Pritchard, and fullback Joe Muha.

Best Draft Choice: Hall of Famer Steve Van Buren 1944, in the first round.

Best Overall Draft: 1943. The Eagles picked up All-Pros Joe Muha, Al Wistert, Bruno Banducci, and Russ Craft.

Worst Draft Choice: Leo Riggs in the first round of 1946. He never played in the NFL.

Worst Overall Draft: 1941. Only John Shonk ever played for the Eagles.

Best Free Agents: Two-time All-Pro end Jack Ferrante never played college football; seven-time All-Pro lineman Bucko Kilroy played college ball at Temple in Philadelphia.

Best Trades: Bosh Pritchard and Alex Wojciechowicz were obtained from the Rams and Lions, respectively, for cash. Leroy Zimmerman came over from Washington for Jack Smith and Ken Hayden.

Worst Trade: The Eagles traded the rights to future Hall of Famer George McAfee, their first draft pick in 1940, to the Bears for nonentities Russ Thompson and Milt Trost.

Biggest Off-Field Event: Bert Bell and Art Rooney trading franchises with new Pittsburgh owner Alex Thompson in 1941.

Biggest On-Field Development: When Greasy Neale was hired in 1941, he borrowed films of the 1940 NFL title game when the Bears beat the Redskins 73-0. Neale ran the film back and forth, charted the plays and "stole the whole Bear system. I figured any offense that could score that much was good enough for me." The Eagles were one of the first converts to the Spread T.

Strangest On-Field Event: First, the wartime merger of the Eagle and Steeler franchises in 1943 brought the NFL the Steagles. Second, the Eagles' 1948 opening day loss to the champion Cardinals was further marred by the heart attack death of star Cardinal tackle Stan Mauldin.

Worst Failure: The Eagles were not able to retool on the fly and thus got old and mediocre very quickly once the 1940s passed.

Home Attendance: 1,422,233 in 57 games for an average gate of 24,951.

Best Game: On November 21, 1943, the Steagles won a shootout with the Lions 35-34. On opening day 1947, the Eagles nipped the Redskins 45-42 and set NFL records for points scored (87), touchdowns (12) and TD passes (8). Tommy Thompson threw three TD passes and Steve Van Buren returned a punt 95 yards for another score.

First Game: September 15, 1940. The Eagles lost to the Packers 27-20 at Green Bay although Don Looney scored twice by catching a TD pass and by running back an interception.

Last Game: December 11, 1949. The Eagles beat the Giants at home 17-3. One week later they beat the Rams 14-0 in a Los Angeles rainstorm for the championship.

Largest Margin of Victory: Three times in 1948 the Eagles crushed an opponent 45-0 — October 10 versus the Giants, October 17 at Washington and November 14 versus the Boston Yanks.

Largest Margin of Defeat: 49-14. The Bears showed Greasy Neale how the T worked in person on November 30, 1941.

Best Offense: Tough call. In 1948, the Eagles scored 376 points and finished second in points and yards gained, while in 1949, they scored 364 points but finished first in both points and yards gained.

Best Defense: In 1949, the Eagles gave up only 134 points, finished first in points and yards allowed and recorded two shutouts.

Most Games Played: 83, Vic Sears.

Most Points: 402, Steve Van Buren.

Most Field Goals: 20, Cliff Patton.

Most Touchdowns: 67, Steve Van Buren.

Most Touchdown Passes: 79, Tommy Thompson.

Most Passing Yards: 8,632, Tommy Thompson.

Most Receiving Yards: 2,296, Jack Ferrante.

Most Receptions: 134, Jack Ferrante.

Most Rushing Yards: 4,904, Steve Van Buren.

Most Interceptions: 22, Ernie Steele.

Most Sacks: NA

Most Kickoff Return Yards: 1,920, Steve Van Buren.

Most Punt Return Yards: 925, Bosh Pritchard.

Book Notes: The late-1940s heyday of the Eagles is depicted in David Cohen's *Rugged and Enduring: The Eagles, the Browns and Five Years of Football*, a self-published volume.

Noted Sportswriter: Frank O'Gara covered the team for the *Philadelphia Inquirer*.

Best Quotations: Greasy Neale defended his team in 1947 by saying, "Our team is coached to play hard and aggressive — but always clean — football. There have been few instances all year when we have been called for deliberate roughness, even in retaliations." After winning the first Eagle title in 1948, Tommy Thompson was heard shouting, "We got it!" in the locker room.

Bubblegum Factoids: The 1948 Bowman set includes some surprising facts — Pat McHugh is the "most nervous player on the club," Neill Armstrong "pulled a

Ripley…scored touchdown first play, first game of professional career," Alex Wojciechowicz is "expert with knitting needles," Pete Pihos was married to "a doctor at Philadelphia General Hospital," Bosh Pritchard was "shifty…a good singer…has own television show in off-season," Vic Sears "owns hotel in suburban Philadelphia," and Ernie Steele "operates a tavern in Seattle."

Accidents of Birth: Enio Conti and Bruno Banducci were born in Italy; Steve and Ebert Van Buren were born in Honduras.

Famous Names: Neill Armstrong, not the astronaut; Ted Williams, not the baseball player.

Unusual Names: Bruno Banducci, Enio Conti, Noble Doss, Frank Hrabetin, Pete Kmetovic, Vic Lindskog, Taldon Manton, Baptiste Manzini, Henry Piro, Abisha Pritchard, Eberle Schultz, Busit Warren, Alex Wojciechowicz, and Al Wukits.

Nicknames: "Bootin' Ben" Agajanian the "Toeless Wonder," Neill "Bird" or "Felix" Armstrong, Walter "Piggy" Barnes, Len "Feets" or "Beartracks" Barnum, "Concrete Charlie" Bednarik, "Buckin'" Joe Bukant, Rocco "Walking Billboard" Canale, John "King" Cole, Bob "20 Grand" Davis, Elwood "Rowdy" or "Cub" Dow, Frank "Wild Horse" Emmons, "Black Jack" Ferrante, Mario "Yo Yo" Giannelli, Ray "Parson" Graves, Elmer "One Man Gang" Hackney, Irv "Shine" Hall, Maurice "Moose" Harper, Granville "Rock" Harrison, Bill "Stinky" Hewitt, William "Boss" Hughes, "Big Mike" Jarmoluk, Albert "Man o' War" Johnson, John "Hog Jaw" or "Maggie" Magee, Bob "Chief" Masters, Wes "Rebel" McAfee, Don "Flip" McDonald, Jack "Moose" Myers, Earle "Greasy" Neale, Davey "Slingshot" O'Brien, Elliott "Bus" Ormsbee, Les "Footsie" Palmer, Rupert "Pete" Pate, Pete "Golden Greek" or "Big Dog" Pihos, Henry "Whitey" Piro, Hal "Ace" Prescott, Abisha "Bosh" Pritchard, Herschel "Red" Ramsey, Clyde "Smackover" Scott, Leo "Scoop" Skladaney, Al "Tubby" Thacker, Lou "Babe" Tomasetti, Milt "Bud" Trost, "Flippin'" Foster Watkins, Hodges "Burr" West, Al "Big Ox" Wistert.

Fastest Player: Probably Bosh Pritchard, but Ernie Steele, Russ Craft and Pat McHugh were very fast as well – not to mention Steve Van Buren.

Heaviest Player: Jim Kekeris 275 pounds in 1947.

Lightest Player: Davey O'Brien was 5 feet 7 inches and 151 pounds.

Toughest Injury: Joe Carter broke his collarbone and separated his shoulder in 1940 and never played for the Eagles again. Bosh Pritchard hurt his knee in 1949 and did not return till 1951, nowhere near the player he was.

Local Boys: Dave DiFilippo, Bucko Kilroy, Bert Kuczynski, Bill Mackrides, Mike Mandarino, Fran Murray and Frank Reagan all hailed from Philadelphia. From the surrounding area came Nick Basca, Chuck Bednarik, Jack Ferrante, Bob Friedman, Charley Gauer, Jack Hinkle, Dick Humbert, Ted Laux, Walt Nowak, Steve Sader, George Savitsky, Len Supulski, and Bob Wear. Among local colleges: Penn – Chuck Bednarik, Bert Kuczynski, Fran Murray, Frank Reagan and George Savitsky; Temple – Andrew Brunshi, Mike Jarmoluk, and Bucko Kilroy; Villanova – Nick Basca, Dave DiFilippo, Ed Kasky, Ed Michaels, and Walt Nowak; St. Joseph's

– John Cole and Ted Laux; Ursinus – Dean Steward; LaSalle – Mike Mandarino; Bucknell – Lou Tomasetti; Gettysburg – John Yovicsin; and Scranton – John Rogallen.

Firsts:

Game in Shibe Park – September 28, 1940, a 20-14 loss to the Giants.

Winning Season – 1943, 5-4-1 as the Steagles.

300-Yard Passing Game – Davey O'Brien's last game December 1, 1940. He completed 33 of 60 passes for 316 yards in a 13-7 loss at Washington.

200-Yard Rushing Game – Steve Van Buren carried the ball 27 times for 205 yards on November 27, 1949 in a win over the Steelers.

100 Points Scored – Steve Van Buren scored 110 points in 1945.

20 TD Passes – Tommy Thompson threw 25 TD passes in 1948.

Postseason Game – The Eagles tied with the Steelers for first place in the Eastern Division with 8-4 records in 1947. Philadelphia shut out Pittsburgh 21-0 in a playoff and then lost to the Cardinals 28-21 in the title game.

The Vet

Wilbert Montgomery
RB 1977-84

Wilbert Montgomery

The Montgomery brothers, Wilbert, Cleo and Tyrone, combined for over 7,000 yards rushing in the NFL. Cleo and Tyrone supplied 223 of those yards in eight years as a receiver and returner for the Bengals and Raiders. The remaining 6,789 yards were gained by 5-foot 10-inch, 195-pound big brother Wilbert.

Wilbert was an all-state defensive back from Greenville, Mississippi, when he enrolled at Jackson State in 1972. He transferred to Abilene Christian the next year and set a college record by scoring 37 touchdowns as a freshman tailback. He would go on to rush for over 3,000 yards and score 76 touchdowns in his college career. In addition, he was a sprinter on the track team, running a 9.6-second 100 and a 20.8-second 220. Scouts questioned his size and his susceptibility to injury, and he slipped to the sixth round of the draft where the Eagles grabbed him. When healthy, he was fast and shifty, had great vision for finding a hole and even greater quickness for getting to that hole before it closed.

Wilbert spent his rookie year returning kickoffs, and ran one back for a 99-yard touchdown. He finally got his chance as a running back in the final game of the 1977 season against the Jets, and ran for over 100 yards for the first of 26 times as an Eagle in leading the Birds to a 27-0 victory. In his second season, he broke Steve Van Buren's single-season team rushing record by gaining 1,220 yards despite missing two games to injuries. Actually he was the first Eagle to gain 1,000 yards in a season since Van Buren in 1949, an amazing 28-year gap that says much about the Eagle running game. In his third season, Wilbert pushed his rushing total to 1,512 yards, including a career-high 197 against the Browns. In that 1979 season, he ran the ball 338 times and caught 41 passes for 379 touches. This popular, hard-working, quiet man was the entire Eagles offense. Then-coach Dick Vermeil has always maintained that the key to an offense is getting the ball into your best player's hands as often as possible. As with Vermeil's star runners later in St. Louis and Kansas City (Marshall Faulk and Priest Holmes), Montgomery was a continual threat as a receiver and was stationed out on the flank periodically.

In 1980, Wilbert struggled with a constant string of injuries to his shoulder, hip, knee and ankle and missed four complete games, but still led the team in rushing with a substandard 778 yards. In the opening playoff game against the Vikings, Montgomery gained 74 yards on 26 carries, but did not practice the whole next week to rest up for the NFC Championship against the hated Cowboys at Veterans Stadium. That 20-7 victory on a 15-degree day with a −17 wind chill turned out to be the greatest memory in the 32 years the Eagles spent at the Vet. The game itself can be boiled down to the third Eagles play of the game. From the Cowboys' 42, Wilbert got the ball for an off-tackle play to the left. He saw no hole to the left, but a gaping one to the right, so he quickly cut back right and took off untouched to the end zone. It was the perfect play at the perfect time before 70,000 rabid Eagles fans. It was a moment that was never topped in the oft-disparaged stadium.

Wilbert Montgomery, the all-time Eagles career leading rusher, is caught in full accelera-
tion mode. Like Steve Van Buren in the late 1940s, Wilbert was the Eagles' offense in the
late 1970s. He rushed 26 times for over 100 yards in a game.

The Vet was a multipurpose, circular concrete bowl with artificial turf that was
repeatedly voted the worst in the league by the players. Playing on the Vet turf was said
to be like playing on a parking lot. Cowboy Michael Irvin's career ended after being
banged against that turf. The Bears' Wendell Davis tore the patella tendons in both his
knees in a game there in 1993. On every play, players had to be careful not to trip over
seams and patches in the field. Even when the team replaced the old turf with NeXturf
in 2001, problems continued. An Eagles-Ravens preseason match was the first game
scheduled to be played on the NeXturf in 2001, and it had to be cancelled because there

were too many uneven spots on the field. Far above the frayed field, the fans had their own difficulties with the stadium. It was short on bathrooms and concessions, but long on leaking pipes and the stench of urine. It could be dangerous as well. The 1998 Army-Navy game was marred when a section of the stands collapsed. And the team facilities posed challenges, too. Cats roamed freely in the bowels of the stadium to hold down the population of rats. The cats destroyed materials in coachs' offices and made the place smell of cat urine. Perhaps the strangest situation was with the locker room layout. A lawsuit was filed alleging that there were peepholes in the visitors' locker room that provided a view of the cheerleaders' locker room.

This palace cost $50 million to build and opened in 1971. The first Eagles regular season game was against the Cowboys on September 26th and Dallas won 42-7 by intercepting seven Eagle passes. Eagle fans broke in the stadium by serenading coach Jerry Williams with several choruses of "Goodbye, Jerry," followed by "Goodbye, Leonard" for the owner and finally "Goodbye, Eagles." The Birds would lose again the next week 31-3 to the 49ers, and Jerry Williams was fired. New coach Eddie Khayat's first game turned out to be a 13-0 loss to the Vikings. Finally on a rainy October 25th afternoon, the Eagles beat the Giants for the first victory at the Vet. While the Eagles would boast a 144-111-2 home record at the Vet, plus 7-4 in the playoffs, the team closed the stadium with a dreary, depressing loss in the NFC Championship to an underdog Tampa team on December 30, 2001.

More than anything else the Vet became known for its feisty, rowdy fans, particularly those in the top ring of seats — the 700 level. That area was the scene of countless fights and bizarre incidents and was not a place for a visiting fan to wear any other team's colors. Eventually, the drunken behavior got so bad that the Vet became host to a sad innovation in sports stadium accoutrements, a branch of the municipal court open for business on the premises on game day. Appropriately, the first fan brought before the court threw up on the makeshift judge's bench. The Vet was a dump, but it was the Eagles' dump. It was a place that other teams and their fans did not like to visit and gave the Birds a true home field advantage — never more so than for that NFC Championship victory over Dallas in January 1981.

Wilbert was healthy in 1981 and gained 1,402 yards. He added a team-leading 515 yards in the strike-shortened 1982 season with a 90-yard touchdown against the Oilers as a highlight. Serious knee problems limited him to only five games in 1983, but in 1984 he broke Steve Van Buren's all-time team rushing record while leading the Eagles in rushing for the sixth and last time. The knee problems had robbed him of his quickness to the hole, though, and he averaged less than four yards per carry for the first time. The Eagles traded him to the Lions for Garry Cobb the next season, and Wilbert retired after one year in Detroit. His pinnacle moment will always be the finest memory of a special time in Eagles history.

"For Who? For What?"

Ricky Watters
RB 1995-97

Originator: End Everitt Rowan caught one 12-yard pass in his four-game Eagle career in 1933.

Longest Tenure: Four years, runner James Joseph.

Number Changes: Charlie Gauer wore 85 in 1945.

Just Visiting: None.

Highs: Charlie Gauer (see 85); fullback Jack Myers was the Eagles' MVP in 1950; Michael Lewis has made a name for himself quickly as a heavy-hitting safety in the Philly tradition.

Lows: Some of the shortest Eagle careers were in number 32 jerseys: 1 game — Nip Felber, Rick Duncan and Earl Carr; 2 games — Jim Culbreath; 4 games — Ev Rowan; 5 games — Toimi Jarvi, Jack Smith and Walter Abercrombie.

Ricky Watters

That a dedicated, hard-running tailback from nearby Harrisburg like Ricky Watters was not embraced as an Eagle hero is one of the most surprising things in Philadelphia sports. The high-strung Watters almost always gave everything he had on both the playing and the practice fields. He gained over 1,100 yards and caught at least 48 passes in each of his three seasons as an Eagle. Still throughout his career, Watters was not a popular player with the fans, his teammates or management, and thus became the first player in NFL history to rush for over 1,000 yards in a season for three different teams.

At Notre Dame, Ricky had frequent conflicts with coach Lou Holtz, who wanted to turn him into a wide out, but the Irish won a national championship while he was there. The 49ers drafted him in the second round of the 1991 draft, but he broke his foot in training camp and missed the entire season. He made up for that by rushing for over 1,000 yards in his rookie season and scoring 11 touchdowns in each of his three seasons by the bay. He topped off his 49er tenure by scoring three touchdowns in the 49ers' Super Bowl XXIX win over the Chargers.

The 49ers let Watters go as a free agent, and he was new coach Ray Rhodes' prime signing in 1995. Ricky had openly campaigned for the Eagles to sign him by going on WIP sports talk radio to urge the fans to encourage the team to do so. In interviews he seemed charming in a goofy way, but his honeymoon period lasted less than one full game. In the 1995 season opener against the Bucs at the Vet, the Eagles were losing to Tampa in the fourth quarter when Randall Cunningham tried to hit Watters with a pass over the middle. A frustrated Ricky displayed a bad case of alligator arms on the play, declining to extend himself to catch the pass and take the hit from the closing Buc defenders. Although the play had little to do with the final outcome of the 20-7 loss, it was the play of the day. When asked after the game why he didn't try to catch the ball, Watters achieved Philadelphia sports immortality by responding "For who? For what?" It was not the fact that Ricky had misused "who" as the object of a preposition that upset the fans. It was his perceived indifference to winning.

Philadelphia fans are all about passion, and indifference is unforgivable. Philadelphia is a blue-collar town whose often-confrontational fans admire hard work and hard hitting. They can sense effort, perseverance and intensity, and understand the finer points of the game. They still admire blustering blowhard Buddy Ryan and remember fondly the vicious, violent Body Bag Game against the Redskins. They are rowdy, often inebriated and quick with feedback. That feedback frequently takes the form of booing. Philadelphia has booed Tommy Thompson. They have booed Norm Van Brocklin. They have booed Sonny Jurgensen. They have booed Ron Jaworski. They have booed Randall Cunningham. They booed the selection of Donovan McNabb, and yes, Virginia, they once booed Santa Claus. They have thrown snowballs and cheered when opponents got hurt. They have shot off flares and gotten into more fights than there are names in the Philadelphia phone book.

And yet they continue to support the team through both good and gruesome times. At key points in a game, they raise their voices in a deafening roar to raise the spirits and play of their heroes on the field. Many times they have spurred the defense to make an unyielding stand or the offense to make an improbable comeback. More than the fans of any other team, Eagle fans are the proverbial 12th man on the field, no matter where that field is.

When the Birds moved from the $50 million Vet to the $500 million Linc in 2003, owner Jeff Lurie talked to the *New York Times* about how "We relished the chance to make a statement about urban America. The Eagles are the most popular operating business in Philadelphia and maybe somehow we have set the model for how a city and a team can keep regenerating themselves." What does that blather mean? Has he ever met his fans? Security has increased in the new building, but Eagle fans remain the same belligerent true believers as ever. Management happily encourages fans to sing the Eagles fight song after every score, but I doubt they are pleased that when each opponent is introduced, his name still is answered by the fans with "Sucks!" Or when the fans are upset with anyone, the sing-song chant of "asshole, asshole" still wafts out of the stands. Or that booing still reigns supreme in the City of Brotherly Love. Eagle fans remain gritty Philadelphians, no matter how upscale the surroundings.

Ricky Watters played hard the rest of his time in Philadelphia, but never fully won over the fans. Commonly, he was seen as too selfish and arrogant. Over three years in Philadelphia, there were frequent one-on-one meetings with Ray Rhodes and regular battles with offensive coordinator Jon Gruden — even Watters' girlfriend got in on the act by yelling at Gruden once. Ricky felt he got in trouble because he told the truth, but it was a subjective truth. On every team, he continually complained that he was not getting the ball enough, even though he had over 300 touches a year each year from 1994 through 2000. In San Francisco, he was called the "Forty-Whiner" for his frequent complaints. In his first two years in Philadelphia, he touched the ball 399 and 405 times and still complained. Yes, he played hard and was part of the exciting, productive "Thunder and Lightning" backfield with Charley Garner, but when his contract ran out, Philadelphia did not try to re-sign him. Ricky moved on to Seattle where he gained over 1,200 yards three times before yielding playing time to Shaun Alexander and being phased out. As a free agent again in 2002, Watters received several offers, but none for what he thought he deserved, so he sat out the season. He never played again. In his 10-year career, Ricky gained 10,643 yards, caught 467 passes and scored 91 touchdowns. He was a tremendous talent, but his immaturity prevented him from ever finding a football home.

Browns Showdown

Russ Craft
HB 1946-53

Originator: Tackle Guy Turnbow supplied the Eagles' points in a 3-3 tie of the Bears in the first Sunday football game in Philadelphia history on November 12, 1933.

Longest Tenure: Eight years, Russ Craft.

Number Changes: Guy Turnbow wore 28 in 1934; Bob Masters wore 30 in 1937 and 1938 and 31 in 1943; Po James wore 27 from 1972 to 1974; Kevin Bouie wore 35 in 1995.

Just Visiting: Hall of Famer Ollie Matson had his greatest years for the Cardinals; Eric Bieniemy was a change of pace back for the Chargers and Bengals.

Highs: Billy Ray Barnes was a slow but dependable runner and receiver; William Frizzell twice was the Eagles' special teams MVP.

Lows: Practice squad member Terrence Carroll was cut three days after being arrested for marijuana possession in 2001. Two years after being traded to the Redskins, Roy Barni was shot to death while trying to intercede in a bar fight.

Russ Craft

Out of the University of Alabama and fresh from three years in the Army during World War II, speedy halfback Russ Craft signed first with the Miami Seahawks of the All-America Conference in January 1946. By the 1946 football season, though, Craft fortunately was with the Philadelphia Eagles as a 26-year-old rookie. The Eagles had drafted him in the 15th round three years before. The Seahawks just barely lasted for the full season before disbanding, but they would not be Craft's last disappointing contact with the AAC.

Craft was small (5 feet 9 inches and 175 pounds), but a big hitter who spent most of his career as a defensive back. He annually had the best 40-yard dash time on the team and was a deadly open-field tackler. After experiencing numerous concussions, Russ pioneered the Riddell prototype for the modern padded plastic helmet in 1948. He picked off 19 passes as an Eagle, including seven in 1950. Four of those seven came in one record-setting day against quarterback Jim Hardy of the Cardinals, who was intercepted eight times that day by the Eagles. Russ had a gift for the spectacular play. In 1949 against the Rams, Craft quickly stripped the ball out of the hands of Hall of Fame receiver Elroy Hirsch and raced into the end zone for a touchdown that was later included in an NFL Films video of "The 100 Greatest Touchdowns." In another game against the Rams in 1950, Russ set a record for the longest play in league history with a 103-yard kickoff return for another touchdown. He made the Pro Bowl after both the 1951 and 1952 seasons, was team captain in 1952 and 1953 and team MVP in 1952. He spent one last season with the Steelers before retiring in 1955.

Craft also figured prominently in what some call the first Super Bowl game, the 1950 showdown between the four-time AAC champion Browns and the two-time NFL champion Eagles. The two leagues had battled fiercely for players and fans in a four-year war before finally merging in 1950. The Browns were one of three teams, along with the 49ers and the original Baltimore Colts, to be absorbed into the older league. In setting up the schedule for the season, Commissioner Bert Bell saw an opportunity for optimum exposure for professional football and arranged for the Browns to meet the Eagles in Philadelphia's massive Municipal Stadium on a Saturday night opening game for the NFL season.

Even though Steve Van Buren was recovering from a foot injury, the Eagles were still six-point favorites on game day. The Browns had been scouting Eagle games for the last year and were prepared thoroughly for the game. In addition, they drew motivation from four years of quotes from NFL players, coaches and executives mocking the strength of the AAC. Before they took the field in front of over 71,000 people, Browns coach Paul Brown told his revenge-minded team that "the worst thing you can do to an opponent is beat them."

Cleveland kicked off and quickly forced a punt that Brown Don Phelps returned for a touchdown; however, a clipping penalty nullified the score. On that first series, Brown QB Otto Graham threw three straight incompletions, but those plays laid the groundwork for the Browns' attack. On each play, right halfback Rex Bumgardner went in motion, taking a linebacker with him and clearing out the middle of the field for the Browns' ends, while left halfback Dub Jones ran an out pattern to the sidelines. After receiving the punt, the Eagles put together a drive that led to a 15-yard field goal for the first score. On the kickoff, again Don Phelps returned the ball for a touchdown and again the play was nullified by a clipping call. Toward the end of the first quarter, Russ Craft got tired of Dub Jones running short out patterns in front of him and began to creep up, hoping to jump the route. That's what Jones and Graham were waiting for. Jones faked the out and blew by Craft to catch a 59-yard touchdown from Graham to take the lead they would never relinquish. Graham hit Dante Lavelli for a 26-yard score in the second quarter and Mac Speedie for 12 yards in the third quarter to go up 21-3. Craft later noted that the Eagles had never seen such well-executed timing patterns as the Browns ran. Bill Mackrides briefly replaced Tommy Thompson at quarterback in the third quarter, drove the Birds down the field and hit Pete Pihos with a 17-yard score. Although the Browns had only run the ball 10 times in the first three quarters, they spent the fourth quarter grinding out the clock and scored two more touchdowns on the ground to make the final score a convincing 35-10.

Greasy Neale commented afterwards that the Eagles were lacking their two top runners in Steve Van Buren and Clyde Scott and that the Browns reminded him of a basketball team with their emphasis on passing. In the December rematch between the teams, though, Otto Graham threw only one pass and that did not count because of a penalty on the play. The Browns won that game 13-7 in a rainstorm and went on to the NFL title in 1950. The Eagles' glory days had passed, but they had a new rival. Paul Brown's Browns were a precursor to Tom Landry's Cowboys. There was much for Philadelphia to dislike about them. Brown was a cold, emotionless coach known for producing teams that were almost arrogant in their excellence. Brown wore a sporty dress hat on the sidelines and called all the plays himself. His offense was innovative and was run flawlessly by unsoiled All-American boy Otto Graham. All of this would later be echoed by Landry, the Cowboys and Roger Staubach, so it is not surprising that a rivalry developed.

Unfortunately, it was a one-sided competition. In the 1950s, the Browns beat the Eagles 15 of 20 times, and went 11-5-1 against the Birds in the 1960s. The Browns won seven consecutive games from 1963 to 1966 and won five in a row from 1950 to 1952 and 1958 to 1960. Cleveland swept the series in 1950, 1951, 1956, 1958, 1959, 1963, 1964 and 1965. Philadelphia never won more than two games in a row and never swept the Browns.

Philadelphia finally beat Cleveland for the first time in November 1952 with two fourth-quarter touchdowns by Ralph Goldston to win 28-20. The following year, the Birds ended the Browns' season-long, 11-game winning streak 42-27 in the finale. Many games in the series were marred by fighting, such as the 6-0 Browns victory in November 1954 won on two Lou Groza field goals. Chuck Bednarik carried on a running feud in those years with Browns guard Chuck Noll. A post-game fight between the two clubs erupted in November 1956 and was continued throughout the rematch two weeks later and in the next game the following October. The Eagles lost all three games. In the late 1950s and early 1960s, runners Jim Brown and Bobby Mitchell regularly tormented the Eagles. Mitchell returned two kicks for TDs in 1958. Brown and Mitchell combined for 296 and 309 yards rushing in games in 1959 and 1960. Jim Brown became the NFL's all-time leading rusher in a game against Philadelphia in October 1963. In the midst of all this, it was especially satisfying when Bobby Walston beat the Browns 31-29 with a last-second, 38-yard field goal during the 1960 championship run.

After Paul Brown was fired in 1962, the rivalry began to fade. In 1967 the Browns moved to a different division and in 1970 to a different conference, so the rivalry disappeared altogether. In the meantime, things had heated up with the hated Cowboys. However, before Philly discovered that Dallas sucked, we despised Cleveland for supplanting the Eagles as the power in the league.

34

K3 – Richie the K

Herschel Walker
RB 1992-94

WHO'S WORN THE NUMBER:

Roy Lechthaler (G) 1933, Laurence Steinbach (T) 1933, Mike Sebastian (B) 1935, Jay Arnold (B) 1937-40, Lee Roy Caffey (LB) 1963, Earl Gros (FB) 1964-66, Larry Watkins (B) 1970-72, Dave Hampton (RB) 1976, James Betterson (RB) 1977-78, Hubie Oliver (FB) 1981-85, Terry Hoage (S) 1986-90, Herschel Walker (RB) 1992-94, Kevin Turner (FB) 1995-99, Jamie Reader (FB) 2001, Reno Mahe (RB) 2003-04.

Originator: Guard Roy Lechthaler lost his starting job after the opening 56-0 loss to New York in 1933. He was out of football after three more games.

Longest Tenure: Five years, fullback Hubie Oliver and safety Terry Hoage.

Number Changes: None.

Just Visiting: Lee Roy Caffey was a Pro Bowl linebacker in Green Bay; Dave Hampton was a 1,000-yard rusher in Atlanta; Kevin Turner's better days were in New England.

Highs: None.

Lows: After being arrested on drug charges, backup running back Jim Betterson was cut quickly by Dick Vermeil.

Herschel Walker

Magical realism was a movement in South American literature in which magical events are treated as ordinary occurrences and the mundane is considered amazing. Herschel Walker's career was out of the pages of a magical realist novel. His accomplishments on the football field were truly remarkable, but he is remembered as a disappointing failure who could only run in a straight line and could not make any tackler miss. Part of his problem was that he was an unusual character for his profession. He didn't drink or party hearty, but was very much a homebody devoted to his family life. He slept no more than five hours a night and did as many as 2,000 situps and 1,500 pushups a day. Away from football, he tried out for the Fort Worth Ballet and for the U.S. bobsled team in addition to challenging heavyweight boxing champion Mike Tyson to a match. He was no average guy.

Walker led his high school team to the Georgia state championship in 1979 and followed that by leading the Georgia Bulldogs to the national title in 1980 as a college freshman. He finished third in the Heisman voting that year, second as a sophomore and won the trophy as a junior. At the same time, he was an All-American in track and field as well. With little else to accomplish in college, Walker passed up his senior season and signed with Donald Trump's New Jersey Generals in the USFL. In two of three USFL seasons, he led that league in rushing and also won the league MVP award in 1985. As a General, he gained 5,562 yards rushing and 1,484 yards receiving. When the USFL folded, Herschel signed with the Cowboys, who held his draft rights.

Dallas at this time was in serious decline, and coach Tom Landry was at the end of his long reign. Against the Eagles in 1986, Herschel ran around end for one 84-yard touchdown and followed that by catching a slant pass in the same game and sprinting 84 yards with it as well for another score. In Walker's third year in Texas — Landry's last in charge — Herschel ran for 1,514 yards and caught 53 passes for a 3-13 team. But when Jerry Jones and Jimmy Johnson arrived in 1989, they decided to blow up the whole Cowboy mess. The key to their turning around the team came on October 15th when Walker and four draft picks were sent to Minnesota for five Vikings and eight draft picks. The Cowboys used those picks to turn their fortunes around. The Vikings obtained Walker to get them to the Super Bowl, but coach Jerry Burns had no idea what to do with him, and the team would lose more games than it would win over the next three years.

Philadelphia signed Walker as a free agent in 1992, and he responded with his second 1,000-yard rushing season that year. In 1993, the Eagles became more of a passing team, and Herschel caught 75 balls out of the backfield. During his final year in Philadelphia, he set an unusual record by rushing for a 91-yard touchdown, catching a pass for 93 yards and returning a kickoff for a 94-yard score all in the same year. He finished up his career with a year as a Giant and two more in Dallas. In the NFL, he accumulated 18,168 all-purpose yards. If you add in his 7,000+ yards of offense from the

USFL, Walker gained over 25,000 yards of offense in professional football, better than any other player.

Eagles coach Rich Kotite was not entirely sure what to do with Walker either, but then Kotite often gave the impression that he was not entirely sure what to do about anything on the football field. Richie was the last of the three Eagle coaching strikeouts whose names began with K. Kotite was a lifelong New Yorker who never seemed to fit in with Philadelphia's fans or media. He also seemed out of place at the head of the cocky, talented, undisciplined team he inherited from the revered Buddy Ryan. Kotite had been an unlikely free agent out of Wagner College who played seven years in the NFL as a backup tight end. He worked his way up the coaching ladder to become the Jets' offensive coordinator under Joe Walton, who had first scouted Kotite for the Giants many years before. After Walton was fired, Kotite was out of work until Norman Braman and Harry Gamble hired him as offensive coordinator under Ryan in 1990. The Eagles finished third in the NFL in offense that year, and Kotite was rewarded with the head coaching job after management-irritant Ryan was dumped by Braman.

Randall Cunningham went down in Kotite's first game, but the Eagles managed a 10-6 record in 1991 anyway. Kotite began to reveal his uptight nature that season by closing practices to the media. 1992 was a tumultuous year marked by the death of Jerome Brown, the first benching of Cunningham and a series of outbursts by such outspoken players as Seth Joyner. Still the team went 11-5 and won one playoff game before ultimately losing to Dallas. Things went downhill rapidly from there. Reggie White left as a free agent, and Kotite seemed to make no effort to convince management to try to sign him. Keith Jackson and Keith Byars both headed to Miami. Cunningham went down again, and the team struggled to finish 8-8 by winning its last three games. The team's top picks in Kotite's first three drafts all proved to be disappointments. Somehow the Eagles got off to a 7-2 start under new owner Jeff Lurie in 1994, and Kotite began to make noises about a contract extension. Lurie wisely put that off till the end of the season because the Birds went completely into the tank by losing their last seven games of the year.

Richie the K had a terrible relationship with the media, relying entirely on aggravating coach-speak to respond to real concerns: "Without question, they left nothing in the locker room." He would drone on while trying to explain the latest hapless fiasco, like when he misread a rain-smudged two-point conversion chart in a 1994 loss to Dallas. He let a very skilled team crumble steadily under his direction, but left with a 36-28 record in four years and was almost immediately hired as the head coach of the Jets. Jets owner Leon Hess was quoted as saying that he was an old man who wanted to win now. Why did he hire Kotite then? New Yorkers refused to believe how incompetent one of their own was. They thought it was a case of the Philadelphia media out of control. Glancing through some contemporary headlines from the *New York Times* provides a capsule view of how perceptions change when confronted directly with reality.

1995:

Kotite at Home and In Charge

Kotite Runs a Tight Ship As Jets Are Finding Out

Kotite Doesn't Tiptoe

A Tough Guy Takes Over a Marshmallow Team

Sorry Leon, But It Won't Happen Now

Kotite Aims to Develop a Killer Instinct in Jets

In Assessing Jets, Kotite Sounds Familiar

Kotite's Advice to Jets is Feel More, Think Less

Will the Jets Ever Get This Right?

Jets Morale is Sinking With Season

Kotite's Confidence In the Jets Remains Unbeaten This Season

Kotite Says Front Office Is Sound, But Offense Could Use Shaking Up

1996:

Kotite Has Jets Convinced That All Is Not Lost

At 0-4, It's Open Season on Kotite

Game Film Too Ugly for the Jets to Watch

Jets, Battered in Body and Mind, Are Still Soul-Searching

The Eagles Are Coming, Bringing Bad Memories

Kotite's Long Goodbye Lingers

Kotite Ponders 1-14 Resume

Kotite Fires Himself Before Jets Can Fire Him

Adding Kotite's 4-28 Jets record to his Eagles record leaves Rich with an NFL coaching record of 40-56. But the early 1990s Eagles' potential will remain unfulfilled forever.

All-Pros and Pro Bowls

Pete Pihos
E 1947-55

Originator: Tex Leyendecker was a celebrated tackle at Vanderbilt, but his pro career consisted of two brief appearances for the Eagles in 1933.

Longest Tenure: Nine years, Pete Pihos.

Number Changes: Forest McPherson wore 26 in 1935 and 1936; Mike Hogan wore 30 in 1980; Kevin Bouie wore 33 in 1996.

Just Visiting: Chris Warren starred for several years as a Seahawk runner.

Highs: The Bears traded Santa Clara's Dick Bassi to the Eagles for the rights to Santa Clara center John Schiechl. Dick was an All-Pro guard in Philadelphia before moving on to the 49ers to play under Buck Shaw, his Santa Clara coach; Ted Dean's career was sidelined by injuries, but he played a major role in the 1960 title drive.

Lows: Mark Konecny's 16.2 kickoff return average for 1988 is the second lowest in Eagle history for those who returned at least 10 kicks in a season. His longest return was 25 yards. As a punt return man that year, he fair-caught 25 of 33 punts and returned the rest for a slight 7.1 average.

Pete Pihos

Indiana coach Bo McMillan said of Pete Pihos, "Pete is the most complete football player I've ever coached. He could play any position on the team better than any player we had playing it — in fact, in most cases, better than anyone else in the country." Hoosier fans agreed, and in 1967 voted Pete part of the school's all-time football team as well as their "all-time greatest player." The much-honored Pihos was a two-time All-American who was elected to both the college and professional football Halls of Fame and was named to the NFL's All-Decade Team for the 1940s.

Pete started out as an end for Indiana and led the team in pass receiving in 1942 and 1943. As a junior in 1943, he was tabbed the "best pass receiver of the year" by sportswriting legend Grantland Rice. Pete went into the Army in 1944 and refused an offer to play service ball, preferring to see combat. He enlisted as a private, but won a battlefield commission to second lieutenant, serving in the infantry under General George S. Patton. After fighting in the Battle of the Bulge and winning five battle stars, Pete returned to Indiana. In 1945, Coach McMillan switched the powerfully built, 210-pound Pihos to fullback, where he called signals and led the Hoosiers to a 9-0-1 season. He was Indiana's leading scorer in 1945, and, granted an additional year of eligibility due to his military service, led the team in scoring and rushing in 1946.

The Eagles had drafted Pihos in the third round of the 1945 draft and finally signed him in 1947, in time for their championship run. Coach Greasy Neale switched Pete back to end and made good use of his talents as an early tight end prototype. Greasy designed a middle screen specifically to take advantage of Pihos' skill in gaining yards after the catch. He was a bruising runner with a nose for the goal line and was also a rugged blocker in the Eagles' run-oriented attack. Although he was not particularly fast, he was smart, ran sharp routes, had great hands and was fearless in the face of defenders. Pete was cocky and a star right from the start; in his first NFL game against the Redskins, he caught five passes for 89 yards and two touchdowns. He just missed a third TD when he was tackled at the one-yard line in the 45-42 victory over Washington.

Pihos played both offense and defense in the championship years from 1947 to 1949 and caught a career-high 11 touchdowns in 1948 as well as a 31-yard touchdown pass in the 1949 title game. He walked out of training camp in 1950 in a contract dispute, but signed one week later. With the advent of two-platoon football that year, Pete stuck to offense primarily for the next two seasons, but the Eagles were still running the ball roughly two-thirds of the time. When Steve Van Buren retired, that run percentage moved closer to 50. However, fellow end Bud Grant insisted on playing offense in 1952, so Pihos switched to defensive end for the year. After Grant jumped to Canada in 1953, Pete went back to offense and led the NFL in receptions for the next three years with 63, 60 and 62 catches, scoring 10 touchdowns twice. At the top of his game and third in the NFL in lifetime receptions with 373, Pihos retired after the 1955 season at the age of 32. For his nine-year career, he only missed one game and was named All-Pro every

Hall of Famer Pete Pihos has Lion defender Don Doll beaten in the end zone in 1951. Pihos led the Eagles in receptions in every year except 1952 when he switched to defense to accommodate future Vikings coach Bud Grant who led the team in catches that year.

year but 1951 — even 1952 when he played defense almost exclusively. Moreover, Pete was selected for the first six Pro Bowls from 1950 to 1955.

Only one Eagle, Chuck Bednarik, received more All-Pro recognition than Pete Pihos, and only Bednarik and Reggie White were named to more Pro Bowl squads. In the Eagles' 72-year history, 47 Birds have received All-Pro recognition once and 34 others have received that recognition more than once.

10-time All-Pros — Chuck Bednarik.
8-time All-Pros — Pete Pihos, Al Wistert.
7-time All-Pros — Bucko Kilroy, Steve Van Buren, Reggie White.
5-time All-Pros — Bill Bergey, Bob Brown.
4-time All-Pros — Tommy McDonald, Pete Retzlaff, Vic Sears, Lum Snyder.

3-time All-Pros — Maxie Baughan, Bill Bradley, Jerome Brown, Tim Brown, Don Burroughs, Harold Carmichael, Joe Carter, Randall Cunningham, Brian Dawkins, Keith Jackson, Seth Joyner, Mike Quick, Jerry Robinson, Tommy Thompson, Norm Willey.

2-time All-Pros — David Akers, Eric Allen, Tom Brookshier, Hugh Douglass, Byron Evans, Jack Ferrante, Swede Hanson, Bill Hewitt, Wes Hopkins, Charlie Johnson, Wilbert Montgomery, Joe Muha, Davey O'Brien, Jim Ringo, Tom Scott, Clyde Simmons, Troy Vincent, Tom Woodeshick, Charlie Young, Roy Zimmerman.

In addition, 54 Eagles have been named to a single Pro Bowl, while 33 more have been named multiple times.

8 Pro Bowls — Chuck Bednarik.

7 Pro Bowls — Reggie White.

6 Pro Bowls — Pete Pihos.

5 Pro Bowls — Eric Allen, Maxie Baughan, Tommy McDonald, Donovan McNabb, Mike Quick, Pete Retzlaff, Troy Vincent.

4 Pro Bowls — Bill Bergey, Harold Carmichael, Brian Dawkins.

3 Pro Bowls — David Akers, Billy Ray Barnes, Bill Bradley, Bob Brown, Tim Brown, Randall Cunningham, Hugh Douglass, William Fuller, Keith Jackson, Charlie Johnson, Bucko Kilroy, Chad Lewis, Floyd Peters, Jim Ringo, Bobby Thomason, Tra Thomas, Jeremiah Trotter, Norm Van Brocklin, Charlie Young.

2 Pro Bowls — Sam Baker, Jerome Brown, Adrian Burk, Tom Brookshier, Marion Campbell, Russ Craft, Irv Cross, Irving Fryar, Harold Jackson, Seth Joyner, Randy Logan, Wilbert Montgomery, Jerry Norton, Wayne Robinson, Clyde Simmons, Jerry Sisemore, Lum Snyder, William Thomas, Stan Walters, Ricky Watters, Jim Weatherall, Norm Willey.

In the pro All-Star Game that was the precursor to the Pro Bowl from 1938 to 1942, Joe Carter was selected twice and Davey O'Brien, Dick Bassi, Don Looney, Dick Humbert, Enio Conti, Tommy Thompson and Bosh Pritchard were all selected once.

If we total all of these postseason honors by position, we can get an idea of what have been the strongest and weakest positions for the Eagles through their history. I tabulated each year an Eagle was honored with either an All-Pro selection, a second-team All-Pro notice, a Pro Bowl appointment or an All-Star Game selection. For example, in 1955, Pete Pihos was named All-Pro and selected to the Pro Bowl, so that counts as one honored year for the tight end position in the tabulation, just as 1986 does when Mike Quick was picked for the Pro Bowl, but not for any All-Pro teams. I divided the data into two sections: (1) the 17 years of pre-1950 two-way football and (2) the 55 years of two-platoon football through 2004. I added up all the honored years and divided by the number of starting slots to get a weighted number as a result; i.e., there are two tackle positions, so the total number of honored years is divided by two, but there is only one center position, so that is not divided. Because the Eagles continued with a five-man defensive line for most of the 1950s, that provided a nice balance for the 1970s and 1980s, when the team lined up in a 3-4 defense.

TWO-WAY FOOTBALL, 1933-49

POSITION	HONORED YEARS	WEIGHTED YEARS
End	14	7
Tackle	11	5.5
Guard	7	3.5
Center	0	0
Backs	20	5

TWO-PLATOON FOOTBALL, 1950-2004:

POSITION	HONORED YEARS	WEIGHTED YEARS
Wide Receiver	22	11
Tight End	16	16
Tackle	22	11
Guard	1	0.5
Center	9	9
Quarterback	16	16
Running Back	12	12
Fullback	5	5
Defensive End	22	11
Defensive Tackle/Guard	23	11.5
Linebacker	24	8
Cornerback	17	8.5
Safety	18	9

These tables indicate a number of things. For the two-way era, end was the strongest position, which is not surprising considering the Philadelphia tradition of Joe Carter, Bill Hewitt, Jack Ferrante and Pete Pihos. The weakest slot was center, where an Eagle was never honored among the best in the league. Considering that Vic Lindskog and Hall of Famer Alex Wojciechowicz played there in the 1940s, that was a little surprising.

When we look at the table for the two-platoon era, the strongest positions on offense were Pete Pihos' emerging position of tight end and quarterback. The weakest positions were guard, where only Jermane Mayberry has been honored, and fullback. On defense, the defensive line has a long history of excellence in Eagle green from the rough-and-tumble 1950s to the Buddy Ryan years to the sack specialists of recent years. Honored years are spread fairly evenly over the rest of the defensive positions.

Greasy Neale – Tough Old Bird

Joe Muha
FB 1946-50

Joe Muha

When Greasy Neale took over the Philadelphia franchise in 1941, the only player he inherited who would still be on the team when it reached the title game six years later was Tommy Thompson, a one-eyed, slow-footed Single Wing tailback. What made Neale's task even tougher was that Uncle Sam started drafting all able-bodied men for World War II the next year. Slowly and steadily, Greasy assembled the team he wanted, but the final pieces wouldn't arrive until the war ended and such players as new ace T-Formation quarterback Tommy Thompson, halfback Bosh Pritchard, halfback Russ Craft, end Pete Pihos and fullback Joe Muha came home.

In 1943, Joe Muha was the Eagles' first-round pick and the second overall selection in the NFL draft, but instead he graduated from the Virginia Military Institute and went directly into the U.S. Marines as a second lieutenant. Muha was promoted to first lieutenant, fought with an artillery unit on Iwo Jima and later patrolled occupied Japan during his three years in the Corps. When he was discharged in April 1946, Joe signed a one-year contract with the Eagles.

That year, Muha won the starting fullback job from veteran Ben Kish as a 25-year-old rookie. In Neale's offense, the fullback was similar in function to the fullback position today. Essentially, he was the lead blocker for Steve Van Buren or Bosh Pritchard (his old VMI teammate); Joe never carried the ball more than 27 times in any season as an Eagle. However, Greasy considered him the best blocker in the league. Muha also played linebacker on defense in this era of two-way football. Actually, Joe had more interceptions (five) than receptions (four) in his career, and he scored twice off interceptions, but only once on a reception. When two-platoon football was instituted fully in 1950, Muha concentrated on defense and won second-team All-Pro notice. Greasy called him the NFL's greatest defensive linebacker, while teammates called him "Jolter" for his jolting tackles. Joe was also the team's punter and led the league in punting in 1948 — the only Eagle ever to do so. He still holds the highest career punting average in team history. Finally, Muha handled kickoffs and the occasional extra point conversions and field goal attempts. In Shibe Park with the stands very close to the end zone, Joe was noted for often booting kickoffs into the upper deck.

Above all, Muha was well-respected and trusted by his teammates and coach. For example, after the 1948 championship game, the team awarded a game ball to Joe's brother George, who had played ball at Carnegie Tech and was dying of Hodgkin's disease. When the team owners gave the players Zippo lighters for winning consecutive titles, Joe took it upon himself to design a championship ring that he and his teammates could buy to commemorate their accomplishment. Joe was a reliable, level-headed man who later earned his master's in economics and a doctorate in education. Teammates took advantage of his wise counsel by regularly consulting him on personal and financial matters. Greasy thought so highly of him that Muha was one of only two Eagles (with Van Buren) he selected for his personal all-time team.

Neale's opinion demands respect. He took over a franchise that had never posted a winning record and by the end of the decade, the Eagles had won consecutive championship games by shutout – a feat that has never been duplicated. Until Andy Reid passed him in 2004, Greasy was the all-time team leader in games won with 66. He was the team's greatest coach.

His background was unusual. Alfred Earle Neale grew up in Parkersburg, West Virginia, where he was given the odd nickname of Greasy as a child. A multitalented athlete, he spent eight seasons in the major leagues playing the outfield for the Cincinnati Reds and Philadelphia Phillies and compiled a .259 lifetime batting average. In the tainted 1919 World Series, Neale batted .357 for the victorious Reds. Simultaneously, Greasy played professional football, under an assumed name, with Jim Thorpe for the Canton Bulldogs and coached college football. His career as a college head football coach led him from West Virginia Wesleyan to Washington and Jefferson to the University of Virginia to West Virginia University and finally to an assistant's job with Yale. His greatest achievement was when his Washington and Jefferson team tied the heavily favored California Bears 0-0 in the 1923 Rose Bowl. New Eagle owner Lex Thompson, a Yale man himself, hired Neale on the recommendation of Giants coach Steve Owens as soon as he obtained the team.

Neale had a gruff and crude manner on the football field that shocked some of his players at first. However, he reached out to them and became part of their lives as a friend. Over time the relationship evolved to the point where outsiders were amazed that Eagle players would openly argue with Neale on the field without his losing any control over the direction of the team. Sometimes when Neale would lose his temper, certain players like Piggy Barnes would imitate Greasy's wife and wag their fingers at him, saying, "Now Earle, be careful." His players were continually amazed at Neale's perceptiveness in picking out flaws in their play and relied on him to make them better. He was so close to them that someone like Tommy Thompson could cajole Neale into closing down practice early so they could go play golf together.

As a coach, Neale moved quickly to learn the Bears' T Formation by obtaining a copy of the newsreel footage of Chicago's 73-0 thrashing of the Redskins in the 1940 title match. Greasy ran that film back and forth hours a day for months in Thompson's office to implement what he saw as the offense of the future. Defensively, he was an innovator who devised the Eagle 5-4-2 defense to counter that same T Formation, and the foundation of his championship teams was their defense. Neale was a brutally honest man who was respected throughout the coaching fraternity. The Bears' George Halas, the Steelers' Jock Sutherland and Neale's good friend Steve Owens all spoke of how highly they thought of Greasy. Owens and Neale were strong rivals on the field, but off the field Owens helped Neale with draft advice in the early years, and Greasy repaid Steve by sending him Allie Sherman to teach the Giants the T Formation.

After three consecutive championship game appearances, 1950 was a major letdown for the Eagles right from the start when the Cleveland Browns, the All-America Conference champions, crushed Philadelphia 35-10 on opening day. The team rallied to win their next five games, but without a healthy Steve Van Buren to rely on, they lost five of their last six as the aging, banged-up offense could not get the job done. Things came to a head late in the year after a 7-3 loss to the Giants when James Clark, head of the "100 Brothers" syndicate that had purchased the team in 1949, barged in the locker room to berate Neale in front of his players. Greasy told him off and was let go at the end of the disappointing season. While Greasy probably was loyal to his aging veterans a bit too long, it was a sad end to the greatest era in Eagle football. Greasy's place in the hearts of his players was expressed at the time by tackle Al Wistert who wrote in a letter to the coach that "Greasy is fair, square and honest, he will never let a friend or player down when that person really needs help...My father was killed when I was five years old. For many years I wondered what sort of man my dad would have been. I know now. My dad would have been an awful lot like Greasy Neale. I'm sure — as strong in his convictions as the Rock of Gibraltar, as honest as the day is long, yet tolerant and forgiving...I'll never forget your teachings, Greasy, for I feel that I'm a better man today for having known you." For his part, Joe Muha was grateful to call Neale a close personal friend and continued to depend on his support even after his playing career ended.

In fact, Muha went out the door at the same time as Neale, telling the *Evening Bulletin*, "I want to leave while I can still walk out of Shibe Park." Joe served as an assistant coach at USC and for the Chicago Cardinals, and then did some scouting before becoming an NFL official. He is one of seven former Eagles to serve as referees along with Joe Carter, Davey O'Brien, Don Looney, Adrian Burk, Merrill Douglas and Pete Liske. Muha served as an alternate on the officiating staff for Super Bowl II in 1968, but was fired in 1971, reportedly because he was calling too many holding penalties. It's hard to imagine what he would think of what blockers are allowed to get away with in today's game. After being dumped by the NFL, Muha devoted himself entirely to teaching business at Pasadena City College until his death in 1993.

Not Quite

Tom Woodeshick
FB 1963-71

WHO'S WORN THE NUMBER:

Irv Kupcinet (B) 1935, Robert Rowe (B) 1935, Winford Baze (B) 1937, John Cole (B) 1938 and 1940, Bree Cuppoletti (G) 1939, Fred Gloden (B) 1941, *Ernie Steele* (B) 1942-48, *Tom Woodeshick* (RB) 1963-71, Merritt Kersey (P) 1974-75, Tommy Campbell (DB) 1976, Billy Campfield (RB) 1978-82, Taivale Tautalatasi (RB) 1986-88, Sammy Lilly (DB) 1989-90, Sean Woodson (S) 1998.

Originator: Blocking back Irv Kupcinet's football career was cut short by a shoulder injury as a rookie in 1935. However, his real career was just beginning. He started as a Chicago sportswriter, became a columnist in 1948, and for decades maintained both a syndicated newspaper column and a syndicated interview show on television.

Longest Tenure: Nine years, Tom Woodeshick.

Number Changes: Winford Baze also wore 26 in 1937.

Just Visiting: None.

Highs: Ernie Steele was a blazing fast runner and punt returner who returned a punt 89 yards for a touchdown in his first game and intercepted a fourth-quarter pass in the 1948 championship, his last game.

Lows: Merritt Kersey was an ineffective punter who liked handling snakes. He had two punts blocked and one that traveled only eight yards as a rookie. Kersey went on injured reserve with a fractured finger after the second game of his second season and never made it back to the NFL.

Tom Woodeshick

Local boy Tom Woodeshick was originally scouted for the Eagles by Steve Van Buren, who liked Woody's play at West Virginia University. Woodeshick was a sort of Steve Van Buren Mini-Me: both were big backs with surprising speed who ran the ball in a battering ram style. Of course, Van Buren was a Hall of Fame player on championship teams, while Woodeshick was a little-celebrated fullback on some truly bad Eagle teams in the 1960s.

Born and raised in Wilkes-Barre, Tom was a cousin of baseball relief pitcher Hal Woodeschick. Although drafted in the eighth round of the 1963 draft by Philadelphia, he first signed a contract with the Buffalo Bills of the AFL. Fortunately, that contract was ruled invalid, and Woody joined the Eagles. As a rookie, he was cut in training camp, but was brought back before the 1963 season started when Ron Goodwin went down with appendicitis. Tom played a total of 46½ minutes over 14 games in his first year, mostly as a banger on the kick return teams. Figuring that it would be difficult to compete with Timmy Brown at halfback, Woodeshick bulked up from 205 pounds as a rookie to 220 in his second season under new coach Joe Kuharich.

But when Kuharich obtained fullback Earl Gros by trade in 1964, Woodeshick was left competing for the backup fullback slot with Izzy Lang. After three long years, Woodeshick finally won the starting job when the Eagles gave up on the oft-injured and disappointing Gros and traded him to the Steelers in 1967. Tom responded by gaining 670 yards in 1967, 947 in 1968 and 831 in 1969. He was a physical runner, and attracted punishment. In 1967, Woody had his eye gouged by a Dallas player in a rough game. The following year, he was ejected from the Dallas game after he raced on the field from the sidelines in the defense of a fallen teammate, and he endured another brutal eye injury in the Viking game. But he was more than simply a bruiser. He still had the speed to break away for a 54-yard touchdown against the Giants in 1968 and a 57-yard touchdown against the Cardinals in 1970. After all, Tom outran Tim Brown in the 40-yard dash in 1966.

Tom had another breakaway run of 60 yards against the Bears called back due to a penalty in 1968, and that prevented him from reaching the magical 1,000 yards rushing mark. His 947 yards was the third highest total in the NFL in 1968, and his 831 yards came in fifth in 1969, but 1,000 yards has been the traditional measure of stardom, especially then, and Woody fell short. By that measure, he was not quite a star. He is one of six Eagles who led the team in rushing at least three times, but never gained 1,000 yards:

PLAYER	YEARS	HIGHEST TOTAL
Swede Hanson	1933-36	805
Billy Ray Barnes	1957-59	733
Tim Brown	1962-63, 1965-66	861
Tom Woodeshick	1967-69	947
Tom Sullivan	1973-75	968
Randall Cunningham	1987-90	942

Of course, 1,000 yards isn't everything. Earnest Jackson gained 1,028 yards in 1985, but was cut by new coach Buddy Ryan because he had averaged only 3.6 yards per carry. Unfortunately, since World War II, 10 Eagles have led the team in rushing with even lower averages than that:

RUNNER	YEAR	YARDS	AVG
John Huzvar	1952	349	3.3
Jim Parmer	1954	408	3.4
Billy Ray Barnes	1958	551	3.5
Clarence Peaks	1961	471	3.5
Tim Brown	1966	548	3.4
Po James	1972	565	3.1
Tom Sullivan	1974	760	3.1
Mike Hogan	1977	546	3.5
Keith Byars	1986	577	3.3
James Joseph	1991	440	3.3

James' and Sullivan's 3.1 averages are the lowest in Eagle postwar history, while Huzvar's 349 yards is the lowest leading yardage figure for the same period.

Woodeshick was nothing like most of the names on that second chart. The Eagles' offensive MVP in 1968, he twice received All-Pro recognition and once was selected for the Pro Bowl. He really was a star trapped on a lousy team with a coach who didn't recognize his talents for too long. Unfortunately, he injured his knee at the end of 1969 and broke his ankle in 1970 and was not the same player after that. However, Woody was always a popular player for his obvious Philly attitude and is still remembered fondly today.

Grassy Fields

Sam Baker
K/P 1964-69

Originator: Bill Fiedler was a 5-foot 9-inch guard from the University of Pennsylvania who played in one game for the Eagles in 1938.

Longest Tenure: Six years, Sam Baker.

Number Changes: Bill Olds also wore 39 in 1976; Russell Gary also wore 24 in 1986.

Just Visiting: Rich Miano had his best years with the Jets; Charles Dimry was a 12-year journeyman who played with four other teams.

Highs: None.

Lows: John Huzvar was a 247-pound fullback from Carlisle, Pennsylvania, who incurred multiple head injuries so severe, while playing with the Eagles and Colts, that he developed epilepsy.

Sam Baker

Loris Hoskins Baker was nicknamed "Sam Salt the Sailor" by his grandparents and the moniker stuck. He's been Sam ever since. He was an 11th-round pick of the Redskins as a fullback/punter in 1953. After an uneventful rookie season and two years in the military, Sam took on new duties when he returned to the Skins in 1956. With kicker Vic Janowicz injured, coach Joe Kuharich had his assistant Mike Nixon work with Baker on placekicking. When Sam retired in 1970, he had scored 977 points for four teams over a 15-year career despite never scoring as many as 100 in any one season. At that point, Sam was the fourth leading scorer in NFL history and had punted the ball more than anyone aside from future broadcaster Paul Maguire.

Sam had his problems with some coaches. He told the *New York Times*, "I don't put up with people who have personality conflicts, who are overly demanding, overly dogmatic, overly this, overly that." He spent two uncomfortable years in Cleveland with straitlaced Paul Brown and two in Dallas with Tom Landry. Once Landry told his team that he was willing to go to the roof of the building to pray for his team, and receiver Bill Howton sarcastically mumbled "Hallelujah." When Baker cracked up, Landry glared at him, thinking that Sam was laughing at Tom's faith. Another time, Sam protested having to run the mandatory Landry Mile in training camp by doing so while reading a book. Tom was not amused.

Sam spent eight of his 15 years on Joe Kuharich teams, and thus only played for four winning teams as a professional. He came to Philadelphia in 1964 along with two forgettable linemen for popular All-Pro receiver Tommy McDonald, but at least Sam was good at his job and improved the team's placekicking and punting immediately. He went to four Pro Bowls, including two as an Eagle. For his career, he made 56.6 percent of his field goal attempts, a good record for the straight-ahead kickers of the day, and averaged 42.6 yards per punt.

Baker played in a less successful time in which NFL teams had to make do with what they could for their stadium needs. While Sam played against the Eagles at Connie Mack Stadium, he spent his Eagle years in Franklin Field, a terrific spot to watch a football game. However, the Birds' nests were not always so nice.

In the 1930s, the newly hatched Eagles played their games in three different parks. The first was Baker Bowl, a tiny, dilapidated, deteriorating bandbox in North Philadelphia where the Phillies had played since 1895. Seating capacity was no more than 20,000, and the gridiron just barely fit in between the first base dugout and the left field bleachers. The Eagles never drew more than 18,000 fans to any game and averaged less than 10,000 per game there. However, it was the site of both the Eagles' first home game against the Portsmouth Spartans on October 18, 1933 and the first Sunday football game in Philadelphia on November 12, 1933, against the Bears. The Eagles also tried games at Temple Stadium on the campus of Temple University in both 1934 and 1935, but that field was clearly inadequate. In 1936, Bert Bell moved the team to cavernous Municipal Stadium in South Philly, and they played there for the rest of the decade. Municipal Stadium, later called JFK Stadium, was built in 1926 for the city's Sesquicentennial Exposition celebrating the 150th birthday of the nation. Municipal Stadium was a giant horseshoe that could seat over 100,000 people and did just that for the annual Army-Navy games that were played there. The Eagles, however, never drew more than 33,000 in those years and usually drew 20,000 or less, which made the place a giant echo chamber.

Bell moved the team back to North Philadelphia in 1940 when he signed a lease with the Philadelphia A's to play in Shibe Park (later called Connie Mack Stadium). Aside from an occasional special date played in Municipal Stadium, the Birds spent the next 18 years in Shibe Park, seven blocks away from the old Baker Bowl. Once again the gridiron was stretched from the first base dugout to the left field area. Temporary unprotected bleachers were erected in right field to boost the capacity to 39,000. Generally, during the championship years of the late 1940s, the Eagles drew from 22,000 to 35,000 fans per home game. By 1957, though, they drew less than 130,000 for their six home dates. The team wasn't very good, the neighborhood was declining and the parking facilities were almost nonexistent. Although it was time to move again, Connie Mack Stadium was the first park at which the Eagles attained a winning record: 52-35-6 in 18 years.

The Eagles struck a deal with the University of Pennsylvania to play at Franklin Field. The rent was higher and the team had to help with the maintenance of the field, but the neighborhood was better, there was more parking and the seating capacity was 68,000. Beyond that, Franklin Field was a ballpark with a shape and sightlines designed expressly for football; it was horseshoe-shaped with a brick fieldhouse at the open end. While it was originally constructed from wood in 1895, it was rebuilt with steel and concrete and a brick exterior in 1922. Franklin Field had great atmosphere and history, and attendance jumped an average of 10,000 per game in 1958 despite the fact that fans had to sit on backless benches. Within a few years, the Eagles were drawing 60,000 per game and football started to become a local obsession. The look and feel of the game changed in 1969 when Franklin Field installed an artificial surface, and turf was also installed in the new multipurpose Veterans Stadium that opened in 1971 to be shared by the Phillies and Eagles. The multipurpose stadium was an idea that never really worked very well, but the Vet lasted for 32 tumultuous years. Finally in 2003, the Eagles got a stadium of their very own, Lincoln Financial Field, with real grass, great sightlines and all the modern amenities and conveniences. The Linc is so up-to-date that it even has its own website. Of more importance, it's a place where the Eagles can build a new winning tradition for the 21st century.

1950s Decade
in Review

Bill Mackrides
QB 1947-51

Bill Mackrides

Bill Mackrides, who grew up in Philadelphia, served as the Eagle water boy one year. He graduated from West Philadelphia High in 1942 and received a scholarship to the University of Nevada as a center. His college career was interrupted by World War II, and when he returned to school he made a most unusual position shift to the other end of the center snap — he became a quarterback and led the country in passing. The Eagles drafted their old mascot in the second round in 1947, and Bill spent the next five years as a backup quarterback in Philadelphia, mostly to one-eyed star Tommy Thompson.

Mackrides most notably earned his keep as Thompson's fill-in on October 24, 1948 when he led the Eagles to a 12-7 victory over the always-tough Bears. It was the first time Philadelphia had ever beaten the Bears. Mackrides threw very few passes and was ordered by Greasy Neale to run out the clock himself with three quarterback keepers to end the game while the rugged Bears tore furiously but unsuccessfully at the ball, trying to force a fumble. Interestingly, one creative play that Neale put in for Mackrides in 1950 was an early version of the option play with Bill running down the line with the ball and having the option to turn it upfield or pitch the ball to the trailing back.

When Thompson retired after the 1950 season, the Eagles traded for Adrian Burk, so Mackrides remained a backup, and in midseason they traded for John Rauch, another young quarterback. In 1952, Mackrides headed to Canada for one season as a player coach. His final, unimpressive numbers as an Eagle were 77 of 206 passes, 37.4 percent for 13 TDs and 20 interceptions and a slight average of 5.23 yards per pass. He returned to the NFL with the Giants in 1953 for one final season as a backup. After football, Bill earned his doctorate in psychotherapy and worked at Springfield High School, also coaching the football team.

Decade Headline: The Original Broad Street Bullies.
Where They Played: Shibe Park, 1940-57; Franklin Field, 1958-70.
How the Game Was Played: All NFL teams ran the T in the 1950s as it evolved with the new position of flanker taking the place of one halfback. This led to an explosion of passing and scoring in the decade. National television broadcasts increased the game's popularity and led to rule changes to clean up the violent nature of the game, such as not allowing ball carriers to continue running after they were knocked down and the outlawing of "clothesline" tackling and grabbing the face mask. Paul Brown moved his Browns to the NFL and continued using messenger guards to call the plays.

Decade Won-Lost Record: 51-64-5, .446.
Record Against the Giants: 6-14
Record Against the Redskins: 10-9-1

Record Against the Steelers: 12-8

Playoff Appearances: None.

Championships: None.

Unsung Hero: When 13-year veteran All-Pro lineman Bucko Kilroy suffered a career-ending knee injury in 1955, he moved into the front office as a coach, scout and player personnel guy. The 1957 draft, in which the Eagles picked a full backfield in the first four rounds, was his finest work.

Head Coaches: Greasy Neale 1950, 6-6 for the decade; Bo McMillan 1951, 2-0; Wayne Milner 1951, 2-8; Jim Trimble 1952-55, 25-20-3; Hugh Devore 1956-57, 7-16-1; Buck Shaw 1958-60, 9-14 for the decade.

Best Player: Hall of Famer Chuck Bednarik.

Hall of Famers: Chuck Bednarik, Sonny Jurgensen, Tommy McDonald, Pete Pihos, Norm Van Brocklin, Steve Van Buren, and Alex Wojciechowicz.

Eagle Honor Roll: Chuck Bednarik, Tom Brookshier, Jim Gallagher (executive), Sonny Jurgensen, Tommy McDonald, Pete Pihos, Pete Retzlaff, Norm Van Brocklin, Steve Van Buren, and Alex Wojciechowicz.

League Leaders: Pete Pihos — receptions 1953-55, receiving yards 1953 and 1955, TD catches 1953; Bobby Thomason — TD passes 1953; Adrian Burk — TD passes 1954; Bobby Walston — points 1954; Pete Retzlaff — receptions 1958; Norm Van Brocklin — pass attempts 1958, completions 1958.

Award Winners: Bobby Walston, 1951 Rookie of the Year.

All-Pros: Chuck Bednarik 1950-57; Bucko Kilroy 1950-54; Joe Muha 1950; Pete Pihos 1950 and 1952-55; Vic Sears 1950 and 1952; Steve Van Buren 1950; Al Wistert 1950-51; Vic Lindskog 1951; Bobby Walston 1951; Lum Snyder 1952-55; Bobby Thomason 1953; Norm Willey 1953-55; Frank Wydo 1953; Wayne Robinson 1955; Tom Scott 1955-56; Pete Retzlaff 1958; Tom Brookshier 1959; Tommy McDonald 1959.

Pro Bowl Selections: Walter Barnes 1950; Chuck Bednarik 1950-54, 1956-57; John Green 1950; Pete Pihos 1950-55; Al Wistert 1950; Russ Craft 1951-52; Mike Jarmoluk 1951; Bucko Kilroy 1952-54; Ken Farragut 1953; Lum Snyder 1953-54; Bobby Thomason 1953, 1955-56; Adrian Burk 1954-55; Wayne Robinson 1954-55; Norm Willey 1954-55; Jim Weatherall 1955-56; Buck Lansford 1956; Bill Barnes 1957-59; Jerry Norton 1957-58; Tommy McDonald 1958-59; Pete Retzlaff 1958; Norm Van Brocklin 1958-59; Tom Brookshier 1959; Marion Campbell 1959; Jess Richardson 1959.

Best Offensive Backfield: 1958-59 with quarterback Norm Van Brocklin, halfback Billy Barnes, fullback Clarence Peaks, and flanker Tommy McDonald.

Best Draft Choice: Sonny Jurgensen 1957, fourth round.

Best Overall Draft: In 1957, the first four rounds went to Clarence Peaks, Billy Barnes, Tommy McDonald and Sonny Jurgensen; the Eagles had filled a complete backfield in one draft. In later rounds came John Nocera, John Simerson, Jimmie Harris and Tom Saidock.

Worst Draft Choice: Either Neil Worden in 1954 or Walt Kowalczyk in 1958, both first-round fullbacks who did not last long in town.

Worst Overall Draft: 1958 produced only six players, none who started for more than one year.

Best Free Agent: Halfback Toy Ledbetter or ball-hawking defensive back Bibbles Bawel.

Best Trade: For impact, the trade of Van Brocklin for Buck Lansford and a first-round pick (Dick Bass) in 1958 was the biggest deal, but for one-sidedness either Tom Scott from the Rams for a 10th-round pick in 1953 or Marion Campbell from the 49ers for a sixth-rounder in 1956 would be hard to top.

Worst Trade: Bob Schnelker and Frank Ziegler to the Giants for Don Menasco and Chester Lagod in 1954. Schnelker would be a solid end in New York for several years.

Biggest Off-Field Event: Lineman Bucko Kilroy and linebacker Wayne Robinson were singled out in the October 24, 1955 issue of *Life* for an article about dirty football players called "Savagery on Sunday." Kilroy and Robinson sued *Life* for $250,000. Although both players were long since retired by the time of the trial in 1958, they each won a judgment of $11,600 — more than either had ever earned as salaried NFL players (see 52).

Biggest On-Field Development: The two-time NFL champion Eagles lost their opening game in 1950 to the four-time AAC champion Cleveland Browns, establishing the legitimacy of the merged league and its players (see 33).

Strangest On-Field Event: NFL commissioner Bert Bell dying of a heart attack while watching a game between the Eagles and Steelers on October 11, 1959 at Franklin Field. Bell had owned both the Eagles and Steelers and had played quarterback for Penn at Franklin Field in the early 1900s.

Worst Failure: First, to find a runner to replace Steve Van Buren. Second, to close the deal with Vince Lombardi when they offered him the head coaching job in 1958.

Home Attendance: 1,612,399 in 60 games for an average gate of 26,873.

Best Game: On October 17, 1954, Eagles quarterback Adrian Burk tied an NFL record by throwing seven TD passes in beating the Redskins 49-21. A month later, on November 28th, Burk threw five more TD passes to beat Washington again 41-33.

First Game: September 16, 1950. The Eagles were humiliated by the AAC champion Cleveland Browns in their first NFL game 35-10. After the game, Greasy Neale grumbled that the Browns were too much of a finesse and passing team, so for the rematch on December 3rd in Cleveland, the Browns threw no official passes at all and defeated the Eagles 13-7 this time.

Last Game: December 13, 1959. The Eagles closed the decade as they had started it by losing to Cleveland 28-21, although this was a closely fought battle.

Largest Margin of Victory: On October 25, 1953, the Eagles crushed the Chicago Cardinals 56-17. The Eagles gained 162 yards on the ground and 366 through the air. The Cardinals would finish 1-10-1 that year.

Largest Margin of Defeat: 49-7 again to Cleveland on October 19, 1952, as Otto
   Graham threw four TD passes.

Best Offense: In 1953, the Eagles scored 352 points, and finished second in points and
   first in yards gained.

Best Defense: In 1950, the Eagles gave up only 141 points, the fewest in the league, and
   recorded one shutout.

Most Games Played: 119, Chuck Bednarik.

Most Points: 631, Bobby Walston.

Most Field Goals: 48, Bobby Walston.

Most Touchdowns: 40, Pete Pihos and Bobby Walston.

Most Touchdown Passes: 57, Bobby Thomason.

Most Passing Yards: 8,124, Bobby Thomason.

Most Receiving Yards: 3,987, Pete Pihos.

Most Receptions: 270, Pete Pihos.

Most Rushing Yards: 1,767, Billy Barnes.

Most Interceptions: 18, Chuck Bednarik.

Most Sacks: NA

Most Kickoff Return Yards: 1,155, Al Pollard.

Most Punt Return Yards: 377, Tommy McDonald.

Book Notes: Chuck Bednarik's autobiography, *60 Minute Man,* tells a lot of tales from
   the 1950s.

Noted Sportswriter: Avuncular Hugh Brown covered the team for the Philadelphia
   Evening Bulletin and cowrote *Norm Van Brocklin's Football Book.*

Best Quotation: At the Bucko Kilroy/Wayne Robinson libel trial, former Lion Cloyce
   Box testified that the Eagles were "ornery critters," which he defined as "a domes-
   ticated animal which at periods of time acts without the scope of that domestica-
   tion."

Bubblegum Factoids: The 1957 Topps card for Buck Lansford noted that "Buck's brand
   of football is the old, 'knock 'em down, then knock 'em down again' school. He
   can mangle an enemy defense line with sublime ease and hurl body blocks with
   earthquake force." The Sid Youngelman card from the same set implores, "Hoist
   the storm warnings when Sid goes into a game. Chances are that the field will be
   strewn with enemy ball carriers who thought they could run plays through Sid's
   slot."

Accidents of Birth: Ken Farragut was a direct descendent of Admiral David Farragut,
   famous for saying "Damn the torpedos! Full speed ahead!"

Famous Names: Don King, not the promoter; Tom Scott, not the musician.

Unusual Names: Paige Cothren, Proverb Jacobs, Menil Mavraides, George Mrkonic,
   Maurice Nipp, Volney Peters, Knox Ramsey, Theron Sapp, Ed Sharkey, Len
   Szafaryn, Ebert Van Buren, Frank Wydo.

Nicknames: Neill "Bird" or "Felix" Armstrong, Billy "Bullet" Barnes, Walter "Piggy"
   Barnes, Ed "Bibbles" Bawel, "Concrete Charlie" Bednarik, Adrian "Abe" Burk,

Marion "Swamp Fox" Campbell, Jim "Gummy" Carr, "Black Jack" Ferrante, Neil "Wheel" Ferris, Hal "Skippy" Giancanelli, Mario "Yo Yo" Gianelli, John "Jumbo" Huzvar, Willie "Big Train" Irvin, "Big Mike" Jarmoluk, Christian "Sonny" Jurgensen, Ken "Killer" Keller, Bob "Whitey" Kelley, John "Hog Jaw" or "Maggie" Magee, Ed "Country" Meadows, Brad "Rookie" Myers, Clarence "High" Peaks, Pete "Golden Greek" or "Big Dog" Pihos, Art "King Pin" Powell, Pete "The Baron" Retzlaff, William "Bud" Roffler, John "Rocky" Ryan, Clyde "Smackover" Scott, Lawrence "Buck" Shaw, Ken "Lum" Snyder, Joe "Bud" Sutton, Norm "The Dutchman" Van Brocklin, Ebert "The Red" Van Buren, Bobby "The Sheriff" Walston, Norm "Wild Man" Willey, Al "Big Ox" Wistert, Neil "Bull" Worden.

Fastest Player: Probably Clyde Scott, although Don Stevens was very fast, too.

Heaviest Player: Defensive tackle Jess Richardson weighed 275 pounds in 1956.

Lightest Player: Bosh Pritchard was only 163 pounds.

Toughest Injury: Steve Van Buren spent his last two years (1950-51) continually injuring his toes, ankles and ribs and was unable to perform at anywhere close to his level; Clyde Scott injured his shoulder in 1950 and never developed as a player.

Local Boys: Ed Bell, Gus Cifelli, Ed Cooke, Mike Jarmoluk, Bucko Kilroy, Bill Mackrides, John Michels, Bob Oristaglio, Frank Reagan, Jess Richardson, Walt Stickel, Bud Sutton and Joe Tyrell all hailed from Philadelphia. From the surrounding area came Chuck Bednarik, Frank D'Agostino, Jack Ferrante, John Huzvar, Brad Myers, Andy Nacelli, John Rauch and Chuck Weber. Among local colleges: Penn — Chuck Bednarik, Ed Bell, Bob Oristaglio, Frank Reagan and Walt Stickel; Temple — Mike Jarmoluk, Bucko Kilroy, Bud Sutton, and Joe Tyrell; Villanova — Joe Restic; West Chester — Chuck Weber.

Firsts:

Black Eagles — In 1952, halfbacks Ralph Goldston and Don Stevens joined the team through the draft.

Pro Bowl Players — In 1950, Piggy Barnes, Chuck Bednarik, John Green, Pete Pihos and Al Wistert took part in the first Pro Bowl.

400 Yards Passing — Bobby Thomason completed 22 of 44 passes for 437 yards and four touchdowns on November 8, 1953 in a 30-7 win over the Giants.

200 Yards Receiving — Bud Grant caught 11 passes for 203 yards against the Dallas Texans on December 7, 1952.

1,000-Yard Receiver — Pete Pihos gained 1,049 yards receiving in 1953.

90-Yard Pass Play — Norm Van Brocklin connected with Tommy McDonald for a 91-yard touchdown in a 27-24 win over the Giants.

Game at Franklin Field — On September 28, 1958, the Eagles broke in Franklin Field with a loss 24-14 to the Redskins.

On the Radio

Tom Brookshier
CB 1956-61

Tom Brookshier

Although Tom Brookshier claims to be a shy man, few Philadelphians who have watched or listened to this personable broadcaster over the past 40 years would believe it. Brookie always comes across as knowledgeable, good-natured and at ease, whether he's on the radio or TV. His popularity in the region has remained unchanged over the decades.

Born in Roswell, New Mexico, the son of a service station owner, Tom attended the University of Colorado on a baseball scholarship. A summer of highway construction built up his body from 145 to 175 pounds and led his way to the Buffalos' defensive backfield. The Eagles drafted Tom in the 10th round in 1953 and brought him to training camp where he was surprised at how many players were trying out for the 33 slots on the team. Brookie made a name for himself in camp right away as a savage hitter and tough tackler, and he made the starting lineup. As a rookie, He intercepted a career high eight passes and established a reputation in the league as a tough defender. For the next two years, Brookshier fulfilled his military commitment by serving as an assistant to the Air Force Academy's first football coach, Buck Shaw, who would end up in Philadelphia himself in 1958.

Brookie returned to the Eagles in 1956 and took up where he left off. With his tight coverage, opponents hesitated to throw in his direction. Although he was not blazing fast, he was very smart and had a great feel for playing cornerback. By 1959, Brookshier was rated at the top of his profession and received All-Pro and Pro Bowl recognition for the first time. Those honors were repeated in 1960 when he was one of the veteran leaders in the Eagles' improbable championship run. Off the field, Brookie was a prankster who helped keep the team a loose band of brothers.

Despite losing quarterback Norm Van Brocklin to retirement, the 1961 Eagles continued on by winning seven of their first eight games — that was a two-year streak of 17 wins in 19 games. However, everything went bad in the ninth game of the season against the Bears. Brookshier was hit by two Bears from opposite directions, and his lower leg was shattered by the impact. His shin bone ripped through the skin, and its jagged edge poked out of his leg. The gruesome description of the hit is reminiscent of the horrific leg break suffered by Joe Theisman many years later on *Monday Night Football*. For Brookshier, it was a case of "when you live by the big hit, then you die by the big hit." Over the next two years, doctors performed three surgeries on the leg to make it functional again. Brookshier maintained hope of resurrecting his football career even into training camp in 1963, when he still was hobbling in a cast, but finally faced reality and retired at that point.

Tom had already begun his second career in broadcasting. He had done an Eagles pregame show on radio in 1958 and 1959, and he joined the Eagles radio broadcasts in 1962 with familiar local broadcaster Bill Campbell and former Eagle Bobby Thomason. Several former Eagles have served as color analysts on the team's games, including Fran Murray in 1950, Clarence Peaks in 1969 and 1970, Bill Bergey in 1982 and 1983, Stan

Tom Brookshier "cleans out his desk" as GM Vince McNally ceremoniously removes his name from the team's 1963 depth chart. The helmet, football and jersey were lovely parting gifts.

Walters from 1984 to 1997 and Mike Quick since 1998. Some local celebrities have done Eagles games over the years as well, such as former Packer Herb Adderley, columnist Stan Hochman, city councilman Thatcher Longstreth and broadcaster Taylor Grant. Play-by-play has been done most prominently by Phillies and A's announcer Byrum Saam for 15 years, Bill Campbell for nine, Charley Swift for another nine and Merrill Reese for almost 30 years.

    Brookshier moved into local TV in 1964 when he became the sports director for WCAU. At the time, the local news broadcasts for three television stations in town featured former Eagles as sportscasters with Pete Retzlaff and Chuck Bednarik on two other channels. They were part of a tradition of Philadelphia players doing the local sports, including Bosh Pritchard, Irv Cross, Mike Golic, Vaughn Hebron, Garry Cobb and Vai Sikahema. Brookie would hold his position at WCAU for 17 years. In the meantime, he began broadcasting Eagles games for CBS and, from 1965 to 1974, doing a syndicated weekly highlights show with former Giant Pat Summerall. In playoffs and Super Bowls, he got postgame locker room duty — most memorably in 1973 when he nervously asked sullen, silent Cowboy Duane Thomas, "Are you really that fast?" to which Thomas succinctly replied, "Evidently." When Sumerall moved into play-by-play, his close friend Brookie joined him as the color man on CBS' top NFL broadcast team. They worked together for seven hard-partying years before Tom left the team in 1982 for his own health. He still worked regional NFL games, but also covered boxing and college bowl games for CBS. Basketball, though, was almost Brookshier's undoing in 1983 when he made a thoughtless joke during a football game about the all-black Louisville basketball starters having a "collective IQ of about 40." The offhand remark was so out of character that the effusively apologetic Brookshier weathered the outcry and, after being suspended, remained with the network for another five years.

Tom moved in a new direction in 1991 when he became part-owner of radio station WIP, which had converted to an all-sports format. He worked on the morning show, breaking in former *Inquirer* beat writer Angelo Cataldi, and helped establish the viability of the sports talk format so that it could grow to the massive popularity it enjoys today. With his successful business interests and real estate investments, Brookshier stopped doing a regular show on WIP after a few years. He remains a beloved, respected figure in Philadelphia, able to move freely in many social circles. As a Philadelphia Eagle, Brookie's place is secure; he's a member of the team's Honor Roll and one of only six Eagles to have had their numbers retired.

College Honors

Keith Byars
RB 1987-92

Originator: Pittsburgh Panther center Ted Schmitt in 1938. Ted coached the line for Harvard and the University of Massachusetts for several years.

Longest Tenure: 11 years, Randy Logan.

Number Changes: Forest Watkins wore 39 in 1940; Keith Byars wore 42 in 1986.

Just Visiting: Howard "Hopalong" Cassady starred in the Lions' backfield.

Highs: Frank Ziegler led the Birds in rushing in 1950, but fumbled 10 times; Jerry Norton was a ball-hawking safety and big-legged punter; Randy Logan was the team's defensive MVP in 1973 and a smart safety for Dick Vermeil's defense; Earnest Jackson ran for over 1,000 yards in 1985, although it took him almost 300 carries to do it.

Lows: Harry Wilson from Nebraska got into only six games in three injury-riddled years, gaining seven yards on four carries. He was later arrested on burglary charges in Downingtown.

Keith Byars

As a junior at Ohio State, Keith Byars was a consensus All-American who gained 1,764 yards rushing and scored 24 TDs to finish second in the balloting for the Heisman Trophy. A 6-foot 1-inch, 240-pound tailback, Keith was known as a "tank with speed" and had an unusual running style in which the Buckeye took short, choppy steps and always maintained his balance while finding daylight. Unfortunately, Keith injured his foot three times during his senior season and managed only 213 yards rushing that year before needing surgery.

In Philadelphia, new coach Buddy Ryan was getting ready for his first draft and thought highly of Byars, but questioned whether Keith could be ready to play in 1986. On the day before the draft, Ryan memorably called Byars a "medical reject," indicating the Eagles were not interested. But when Byars was still available at the 10th slot in the first round, the Eagles grabbed him. Ryan now referred to Byars as a "franchise football player" and envisioned him as a perennial 1,000-yard rusher, but bumpy times were ahead.

In 1986, Byars set an Eagles rookie rushing record with 577 yards, but on 177 carries for a disappointing 3.3 average. He was hampered by continuing foot injuries and was benched as a rookie and benched in 1987 as well. While Ryan was not happy with Byars' running, he was effusive in his praise of Keith's blocking and pass-catching skills. As the years passed, it became clear that Byars would never be a great ball carrier, but he was a uniquely versatile back who could help a team win. His best position was as an "H" back — essentially a second tight end who lines up in the backfield. From 1988 through 1991, Byars never caught fewer than 62 passes and was a ferocious blocker as well. He ran the ball on occasion and even threw four touchdown passes in 1990 off the option play. Perhaps behind a better offensive line his career would have been different, but he was most effective for the Eagles catching passes in the open spaces and taking off with a full head of steam.

Keith did not think much of Ryan's replacement, Rich Kotite, but for the good of the team he agreed to move to tight end to replace the departed free agent Keith Jackson in 1992. The next year Byars left for Miami as a free agent, too. As a fullback under Don Shula, Byars made the Pro Bowl in 1993, but when Jimmy Johnson replaced Shula in 1996, he began cleaning house. Byars ended up in New England under Bill Parcells and finally went to a Super Bowl that year when he and Otis Smith faced off against fellow former Eagles Reggie White and Keith Jackson of the Packers. The Patriots lost, and Byars spent another season in New England before going to the Jets in 1998 for his final season. In 2000, Byars and old teammate Seth Joyner signed special contracts with Philadelphia so they could come home and retire officially as Eagles. Byars said on the occasion, "My heart stayed in Philadelphia. It was just my body that left." While he did not have the career that many expected for the consensus All-American, Keith Byars was a steady player who gave an honest effort at all times.

Several Eagles have won honors in college over the years.

Consensus All-Americans

1930	Reb Russell		1980-2	Herschel Walker
1936-37	Alex Wojciechowicz		1981	Jim McMahon
1938	Davey O'Brien		1981-82	Dave Rimington
1940	Bob Suffridge		1982-83	Terry Hoage
1942	Al Wistert		1983	Irving Fryar
1945	George Savitsky		1983	Luis Zendejas
1947-48	Chuck Bednarik		1983	Reggie White
1950-51	Jim Weatherall		1983	William Fuller
1954	Ralph Guglielmi		1984	Keith Byars
1954-55	Howard Cassady		1984	William Perry
1955	Bob Pellegrini		1986	Cris Carter
1956	Tommy McDonald		1986	Jerome Brown
1957	Bob Kowalczyk		1986	Ben Tamburello
1959	Maxie Baughan		1986-87	Keith Jackson
1960	Mike Ditka		1990	Antone Davis
1963	Bob Brown		1990	Eric Bieniemy
1964	John Huarte		1990-91	Ty Detmer
1967	Adrian Young		1991	Casey Weldon
1967	Tim Rossovich		1991	Amp Lee
1967-68	Leroy Keyes		1993	Jim Pyne
1971	Rich Glover		1994	Bobby Taylor
1971-72	Jerry Sisemore		1998	Jevon Kearse
1973	Artimus Parker		1998-99	Corey Simon
1975	John Sciarra		1999	Mark Simoneau
1976	Tony Franklin		2000	Fred Mitchell
1976-78	Jerry Robinson		2000	Keith Adams
1977	Zac Henderson		2000	Sheldon Brown
1978	Matt Bahr		2002-03	Shawn Andrews

Division I-AA Consensus All-Americans

1984	Bruce Collie
1985	Clyde Simmons
1988	Jessie Small
1989	Darion Conner
1989	Tim Hauck
1996-97	Brian Finneran
1996-97	Jeremiah Trotter
1997	Shawn Barber
2001	Brian Westbrook
2003	Andy Hall

Heisman Trophy Winners

1938	Davey O'Brien
1955	Howard Cassady
1964	John Huarte
1982	Herschel Walker
1990	Ty Detmer

Maxwell Award Winners

1938	Davey O'Brien
1948	Chuck Bednarik
1955	Howard Cassady
1956	Tommy McDonald
1982	Herschel Walker
1987	Don McPherson
1990	Ty Detmer

Outland Trophy for nation's best lineman

1951	Jim Weatherall
1972	Rich Glover
1981-82	Dave Rimington

Lombardi Award for nation's best lineman

| 1972 | Rich Glover |
| 1982 | Dave Rimington |

Davey O'Brien Award for best quarterback

1981	Jim McMahon
1987	Don McPherson
1990-1	Ty Detmer

Johnny Unitas Golden Arm Award for best quarterback

1987	Don McPherson
1988	Rodney Peete
1991	Casey Weldon

Walter Payton Award for best I-AA offensive player

| 1997 | Brian Finneran |
| 2001 | Brian Westbrook |

Bert Bell - Signal Caller

Swede Hanson
HB 1936-37

Swede Hanson

Right from the Eagles' very first game against the Giants in 1933, their very first star was Thomas "Swede" Hanson. Despite losing the game 56-0, Philadelphia was heartened by Hanson's 35-yard run as part of his over 70 yards gained in the initial contest. Three days later in the second game against the Portsmouth Spartans, Swede gained 85 yards rushing and 75 yards on punt returns. In the third game against Green Bay, he scored the Birds' first-ever touchdown on a 35-yard reception from Red Kirkman, and in Philadelphia's first win, 6-0 over Cincinnati, he scored the only touchdown of the game on a two-yard run after setting it up with a 35-yard punt return. In the Philly papers, Hanson was being called the "Red Grange of the locals."

Local he was, having grown up in Long Branch, New Jersey, and attended Temple University. At Temple, Swede starred on the football team, of course, but also pitched for the baseball team and boxed as a heavyweight. He was 6 feet 1 inch and 192 pounds — lean, lank, lantern-jawed and limber. After graduating from Temple, he joined the NFL's Brooklyn Dodgers in 1931 before moving on to the Staten Island Stapletons the following year. He also had two tryouts as a pitcher for the Boston Red Sox. After signing with Philadelphia for the Eagles' first season in 1933, he led the team in rushing with 475 yards, the fifth best total in the league.

1934 would prove to be Swede's greatest year. He finished second in the NFL with 805 yards rushing; the Bears' Beattie Feathers led the league with 1,004. Those numbers are so out of whack that there is something suspicious about them. This was the first season that anyone ever gained 1,000 yards, and it was 200 yards greater than the leading total the previous year. The 1,000-yard barrier would not be broken again for 13 years when Steve Van Buren gained 1,008 in 1947. Moreover, in a time of "three yards and a cloud of dust," Feathers, a rookie, averaged 8.4 yards per carry, while Hanson averaged 5.5 yards per carry. Hanson never averaged better than 3.6 yards in any other season he would play. Some have speculated that punt return yards were added in to rushing totals in 1934, since they were not kept separately.

Hanson held out until he received a $5 per game raise in 1935, but when the team lost its first three games, he and his teammates were docked $25. He only gained 207 yards rushing for the year and would never accumulate more than 359 in any other season. In 1936, Swede was in the news again in a game against the Giants when a late interference call against him led to New York's winning score. The official who made the call, George Vergara, had to be escorted from the field by police after members of the Eagles surrounded him, throwing punches and tearing his clothes. Swede was traded to Pittsburgh after the 1937 season, but only lasted one more year in the league. After retiring, Hanson worked for 28 years as a mechanic at the Navy Yard in Philly.

Hanson's backfield coach at Temple was the man who employed him for the Eagles: Bert Bell. De Benneville "Bert" Bell was born into privilege. His maternal grandfather was a U.S. congressman. His father was District Attorney of Philadelphia and then Attorney General of Pennsylvania. His brother John was elected

Pennsylvania's lieutenant governor, served briefly as governor and was named as a justice to the state's Supreme Court. Bert followed a different path. He went from prep school in Haverford to playing quarterback for the University of Pennsylvania in 1916, when the Quakers lost the Rose Bowl to Oregon. Bell took a year off to serve with a hospital unit in World War I before returning to Penn, first as a player and then as backfield coach under head coach John Heisman. He coached there for eight years and then moved on to Temple in 1928.

Bell at this time was a wastrel, a personable rogue who loved to drink and have a good time. In 1929, he found himself $50,000 in debt from gambling, lavish spending and the stock market decline. His father bailed him out, and Bert gave up the gambling vice. After he fell in love with musical comedy star Frances Upton, he gave up drinking in 1932 and they got married in 1934. In this period, Bert tried the hotel business before following his football dream. Bell and former Penn teammate Lud Wray, along with some investors, paid off the debts of the dissolved, bankrupt Frankford Yellow Jackets and paid the NFL franchise fee to form the Philadelphia Eagles in 1933. It was a good thing that

The Not-Quite-Million-Dollar Backfield of, from left to right, John Kusko, Dave Smukler and Swede Hanson in 1936 when the Eagles finished 1-11. All three backs first starred at Temple. Smukler is in the Philadelphia Jewish Sports Hall of Fame, and Hanson was the first Eagle to rush for 100 yards in a game. Hanson also wore 42 in 1936.

Bell had cut down on his vices because the Eagles franchise soon would drain his finances pretty steadily. From the start, the Eagles were a low-budget operation: for their first road trip to Green Bay, the team traveled by bus and would stop at empty fields along the way to practice. To avoid a small gate, Bert once postponed a game due to "inclement weather" on a day that the Philadelphia Athletics played a doubleheader in town. By 1936, the franchise had lost $80,000, and Bell bought out the other investors for $4,500. For the Eagles' first three years, he had served as general manager, ticket seller and public relations agent. In 1936, he added head coach to his responsibilities. His strengths were in ticket sales, promotions and innovations. Bell was the owner who proposed and sold the idea of an NFL draft, and he indefatigably kept the team going. His weaknesses were in selecting and coaching players. Seeing no other way to improve their teams in 1941, Bell and Art Rooney ended up owning the Pittsburgh franchise together in a complicated transaction that brought Lex Thompson to Philly as the owner of the new Eagles.

In Pittsburgh, Bell wasn't much more successful than in Philadelphia. However, when he was named commissioner in 1946, Bert Bell had finally found his niche. The gravel-voiced Bell worked 18-hour days enthusiastically selling pro football and the notion that the success of the league as a whole came first. He ran the NFL from a small office in suburban Bala Cynwood so that for the first 15 years of the postwar period, Philadelphia was league headquarters. He did almost everything over the telephone and would rack up $10,000 annual phone bills. The press loved Bert since he was always available and always good for a comment. As with the Eagles, he tended to do everything himself. For example, each year he would spend weeks working laboriously by hand on the league schedule. In all league matters, he maintained a firm hand in guiding the NFL through difficult times. In his first year in charge, Bell faced a serious challenge from the fledgling All-America Conference and had to deal with a gambling scandal in that year's championship game. Throughout the fifties there were court proceedings, competitive balance concerns and dealings with Congress over antitrust issues. Bell presided over these affairs and the development of league-wide television policies, including the local blackout rules, in a way that enabled the league to grow significantly during the decade. He laid the groundwork for Pete Rozelle's amazing successes in the 1960s and 1970s.

Bell was thinking of retiring as the fifties drew to a close. One thought he had was to rejoin the brotherhood of NFL owners by buying back the Eagles and letting his sons run the team. His older son John worked in the league office and as business manager for the Colts, while his younger son Upton would go on to serve as director of player personnel for the Colts and general manager of the Patriots. However, Bert Bell did not get to live out that dream because he suffered a fatal heart attack at Franklin Field in 1959 while watching a game between his two former teams, the Eagles and Steelers, on the field where he had played quarterback 40 years before. He was like a character out of a Frank Capra film — a rich smoothie to the manor born, but ultimately a man of the people. To put it in Philadelphia terms, he lived on the Main Line, but was at ease on the streets of South Philly. Bert Bell may not have been the most successful Eagles owner, but he worked tirelessly to establish the rabid football tradition that took hold in this town.

Giant Rivals

Jack Hinkle
HB 1941-47

WHO'S WORN THE NUMBER:

Jack Hinkle (HB) 1941 and 1943-47, William Jefferson (B) 1942, James Lankas (B) 1942, Jim Parmer (B) 1948-56, Robert Smith (B) 1956, Walt Kowalczyk (B) 1958-59, Ralph Heck (LB) 1963-65, Al Davis (B) 1971-72, James McAlister (RB) 1975-76, *Roynell Young* (CB) 1980-88, Roger Vick (RB) 1990, Erik McMillan (S) 1993, Randy Kinder (CB) 1997, Damon Moore (S) 1999-01.

Originator: Halfback Jack Hinkle in 1941.

Longest Tenure: Nine years, Roynell Young.

Number Changes: None.

Just Visiting: Roger Vick and Erik McMillan were former Jets that Rich Kotite brought into town for old time's sake.

Highs: Roynell Young played a key role as a rookie shut-down corner during the 1980 Super Bowl run and was defensive MVP in 1986.

Lows: Damon Moore turned down a contract extension in 2001, and then tore knee ligaments in the playoffs and was released. Earlier that year, he was in the news for abandoning his Rottweiler puppy by tying it to a tree next to a soccer field after his girlfriend told him the dog had to go. The Bears signed Moore, but he failed a drug test, was suspended and then released again. The next year, he washed out of the Arena League.

Jack Hinkle

When the Seahawks' Shaun Alexander lost the rushing title by one yard to the Jets' Curtis Martin in 2004, it brought Jack Hinkle back into the news because in 1943 he lost the rushing title to the Giants' Bill Paschal by that same 36 inches. Alexander was upset because he didn't get the ball enough in Seattle's final game; Hinkle was upset because he says the league didn't give him credit for a long run he had against the Giants. Hinkle claimed that the longest run listed in the newspaper for that October 24th game in the Polo Grounds was 20 yards, but that he ripped off one alternately said to be 33, 34, 37, 45 or 47 yards. He did have a 37-yard run that was noted in the *New York Times* account of the October 9th home game against the Giants in which the Steagles fumbled a record 10 times. After an Eagle protest, the league's official scorer ruled that nothing was missing from Hinkle's totals. Whether it's faulty memory or faulty stat-keeping, no one will ever know. But the controversy keeps Jack's name alive 60 years later.

Hinkle was a cousin of Green Bay Hall of Fame fullback Clark Hinkle and attended Syracuse University where he called signals as the blocking back in a backfield that included Olympic sprinter Marty Glickman. Jack could run, catch and kick the ball, but mostly what he did was block. In 1940, he signed with the Giants and competed for a backfield spot with George Muha, the brother of future Eagle Joe Muha. Neither one made the team, but Hinkle was sent to the Giants' farm team in Jersey City. When injuries struck the big boys in November, he was recalled. In 1941, Jack signed with the New York Americans of the third American Football League and was a blocking back for former All-Americans Tommy Harmon and John Kimbrough.

The Eagles signed Hinkle the next year, and the story goes that as compensation to the Americans, Eagles playboy owner Lex Thompson arranged a date with starlet Lana Turner for one of the Americans' executives. Hinkle joined the Army Air Corps, but was given an honorable discharge due to ulcers and joined the Steagles in 1943. He led the Giants' Bill Paschal 571 yards to 480 going into New York's last game of the season, but Paschal gained 92 in the mud against Detroit and took the rushing title. Finally given a chance to carry the ball, the 6-foot 1-inch, 215-pound Hinkle was a precursor to Steve Van Buren as a speedy big back. Unfortunately for Jack, Van Buren arrived in Philly the next year. Hinkle was the team's second leading ball carrier in 1944 and then suffered a serious shoulder separation in 1945 and was never the same player again. He was released during the 1947 season and later coached at Drexel for over a decade before entering the business world.

Jack Hinkle was one of the most prominent Eagles to also play for the Giants. Some other notables who looked funny in blue were Len Barnum, Pete Case, Enio Conti, Jeff Feagles, Brian Mitchell, Gary Pettigrew, Bosh Pritchard, Hank Reese, Tom Scott and Norm Snead. Giants who looked funny in green included Ben Agajanian, Matt Bahr, Mark Bavaro, Greg Jackson, Mark Ingram, Ken McAfee and Bob Schnelker. The first trades the Eagles ever made were with New York, picking up linemen Jim

Zyntell and Hank Reese in separate deals, and the Eagles' first-ever game was a horrendous 56-0 pasting by the Giants. The Eagles lost to the Giants 11 of 14 times in the 1930s and 13 of 16 times in the Bert Bell/Lud Wray era, including nine losses in a row from 1938 to 1942.

When Greasy Neale arrived in 1941, the series became competitive despite Neale and Giants coach Steve Owens being great friends. Neale would go 10-9-1 against New York with many hard-fought battles on the field. In 1948, the Eagles beat the Giants by the widest margin ever in a 45-0 win. Off the field, the two coaches helped one another. Owens assisted Neale with his early drafts, and Greasy returned the favor later in the decade by sending Steve the Eagles' backup quarterback Allie Sherman as an assistant coach to teach the Giants the T Formation.

Neale could peg his downfall to a confrontation with owner James Clark after a tough 7-3 loss to New York in 1950. With Neale's firing, the Eagles declined and won only six of 20 games in the Giants series in the 1950s. However, those games were closely contested with fights, injuries and ejections being frequent occurrences. Chuck Bednarik cracked a rib against New York in 1953, and Bucko Kilroy tore up his knee against them in 1955. Steve Owens was gone from New York after posting a 26-15-1 record against the Birds, but turned up as an Eagle assistant in 1956 and 1957. And there were heroics as well. Norm Willey is said to have sacked Giants quarterbacks 17 times in a game in 1952. Bobby Thomason passed for 437 yards while beating New York 30-7 in 1953. Tommy McDonald arrived and began to regularly scorch the Giants' secondary — a 91-yard TD reception in 1958, four touchdowns in 1959, and more scores each year from 1960 to 1963.

The Eagles won the championship in 1960 largely due to their two fierce, exciting, come-from-behind victories over the Giants, highlighted by Chuck Bednarik's near beheading of Frank Gifford in Yankee Stadium. However, Greasy Neale's protégé Allie Sherman took over the Giants in 1961 and beat the Eagles 11 of 15 times in the decade. The highlights for the Eagles were big days by receivers Tommy McDonald and Ben Hawkins who caught a 92-yard TD in 1968 and was a fourth-and-two game winner in 1969.

Cumulatively, the series stood at 27-46-1 as the 1970s began. The most forgettable game occurred in 1972 and sealed Eddie Khayat's fate as coach when the Eagles quite clearly quit in a 62-10 loss to New York. Under Mike McCormack and Dick Vermeil, though, the Eagles won 12 games in a row from 1975 to 1981, and Vermeil posted an 11-4 record against New York. The highlight of all time was the Miracle of the Meadowlands in 1978, when Herman Edwards scooped up a fumble in the closing seconds and raced for the decisive TD in a 19-17 win. The cumulative series record had closed to 42-50-2 by the end of the decade. In the 25 years since then, the two teams are 25-25 in the regular season, although the Birds have dropped both playoff games between the two. Buddy Ryan was 5-5, Rich Kotite 4-4, Ray Rhodes 4-4 and Andy Reid 7-6 while Bill Parcells went 9-7 against Philadelphia and Jim Fassell went 10-6.

The 1980s belonged to spectacular plays like Randall Cunningham hurdling over Carl Banks to throw a touchdown pass and Clyde Simmons picking up a blocked field goal in overtime and rumbling for the winning score. The 1990s frequently meant gap-toothed Michael Strahan destroying the Eagles with plays like his 44-yard interception return in 1999 for the winning score in overtime. Donovan McNabb has taken over the series in the new millennium. After 62 years, the series stands at 67-75-2 in the regular season and 0-2 in the playoffs. The Eagles have swept the Giants 23 times, while the Giants have swept the Eagles 27 times. If the Eagles can even the number of season sweeps by the end of the decade, the series will be all tied up for the first time ever. There's a challenge for Andy Reid.

The Rinky Dink Bowl

Pete Retzlaff
TE 1957-66

WHO'S WORN THE NUMBER:

Franklin Emmons (B) 1940, Albert Johnson (B) 1942, Ben Kish (B) 1943-49, *Norm Willey* (DE) 1950-51, Bob Stringer (B) 1952-53, Harry Dowda (B) 1954-55, *Pete Retzlaff* (TE) 1957-66. **RETIRED**

Originator: Forgotten back Frank "Wild Horse" Emmons from Oregon caught Davey O'Brien's last TD pass in 1940.

Longest Tenure: 10 years, Pete Retzlaff.

Number Changes: Norm Willey wore 63 in 1952 and 86 from 1953 to 1957; Pete Retzlaff wore 25 in 1956.

Just Visiting: None.

Highs: Ben Kish was a dependable two-way back for Greasy Neale, excelling at blocking and defense; Norm Willey (see 86).

Lows: Bert Johnson finished a thoroughly mediocre NFL career with one season in Philadelphia in which he carried the ball 27 times for 54 yards.

Pete Retzlaff

Comparing Palmer "Pete" Retzlaff to the six tight ends enshrined in the Hall of Fame shows him to be right in his element. He is fourth in the group in receptions, third in total yards and touchdowns and second in yards per catch. If we compare Pete just to the three who played in his era — Mike Ditka, John Mackey and Jackie Smith, he finishes first in touchdowns and second in the other three categories to Smith, who played five more seasons than Retzlaff. While his 452 catches and 47 touchdowns may seem like paltry totals in the contemporary game that is oriented relentlessly to high percentage short passes, Pete was among the league's best in his time and well-fitted for his nickname of the Baron.

Retzlaff was a self-made athlete in many ways. He was a dedicated, tireless workout warrior who had once been a candidate for the Olympics in the decathlon. At South Dakota State, he played fullback and was picked in the 22nd round of the 1953 draft by the NFL champion Lions. Pete was the last player cut in training camp and then fulfilled his military service commitment during the 1954 and 1955 seasons. In 1956, he was back in the Lions' training camp, but they still did not have a place for him and waived him to the Eagles for $100. During the next two seasons, coach Hugh Devore tried Pete at fullback, end, defensive back and special teams, and Retzlaff managed only 22 catches during that time.

Buck Shaw and Norm Van Brocklin arrived in 1958, and Pete's future was finally here. Van Brocklin likened the precise way that Retzlaff ran his pass routes to that of Ram Hall of Famer Elroy Hirsch, and Van made a special effort to turn former running backs Retzlaff and Tommy McDonald into receivers. For his part, Pete would grab anyone he could to throw him passes in practice. Once he caught the ball, he knew what to do with it. In that first year with Van Brocklin, Retzlaff led the league in receptions with 58 and was named to his first All-Pro and Pro Bowl teams. The following year, a broken leg delayed the start of the season for Pete, but he upped his average by almost four yards per catch as he started to catch the deep ball. He further upped his average to 18 yards per catch in the championship season of 1960 as he played a big role in the Eagle offense and went to another Pro Bowl.

The Eagles made a nearly seamless transition from the retired Van Brocklin to Sonny Jurgensen at quarterback in 1961, but finished in second place a half game behind the Giants. However, their season was not over; for the decade of the 1960s, the NFL instituted a meaningless postseason game in Miami between the runners up in the Eastern and Western Conferences. It was called the Playoff Bowl. Coach Nick Skorich tried to feign interest in the match by commenting, "We're approaching the game on the basis that third place means a lot more to us than fourth." Right. In the game itself, though, Detroit came out hitting fiercely, while the Eagles seemed mostly disinterested. The Lions raced to a 24-0 halftime lead on the way to a 38-10 victory in which Retzlaff scored the only Philadelphia touchdown on a pass from King Hill. In the second quarter, Jurgensen threw an interception and was driven into the ground by linebacker

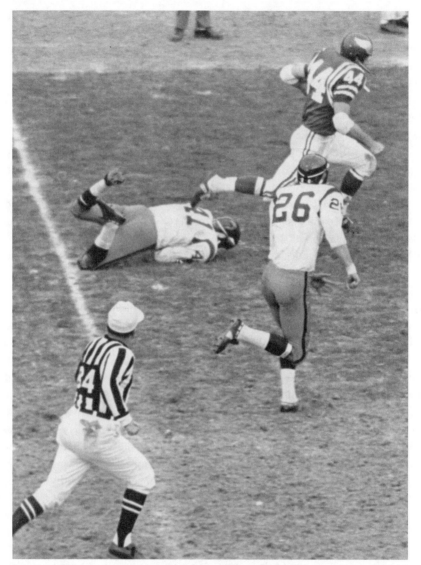

Pete Retzlaff breaks free of the Redskins' Jim Steffen with Paul Krause in pursuit during Pete's MVP year of 1965. That season, Retzlaff caught 66 passes for 1,190 yards and 10 TDs.

Wayne Walker during the return. Sonny suffered what team doctor Mike Mandarino called the "worst shoulder separation I've ever seen." He would not return to form for over a year because of this rinky dink game in which the Lions earned $600 per man for winning, while the Birds received $400.

That injury to Jurgensen signaled a downturn for the franchise, partly due to age and partly to injuries. Retzlaff broke his wrist in the fourth game of 1962, but came back to play six weeks later with a cast on his arm. Pete had played split end until this point, but moved into the tight end slot that year because Bobby Walston broke his arm. Over the last five years of his career, Retzlaff received All-Pro recognition three times and went to three Pro Bowls as he proved himself as one of the best tight ends in the NFL. In 1965, he even received the Bert Bell Award from the Maxwell Club as the NFL's player of the year, an honor never received by another tight end before or since. Pete did have his greatest season that year with 66 catches for 1,190 yards and 10 touchdowns, but he was an odd choice for the award. The team finished 5-9 and Retzlaff finished third in receptions and second in yards and TDs. Meanwhile, the first-place Browns featured Jim Brown's league-leading 1,544 yards and 21 TDs. The second-place Colts were led by Johnny Unitas' 2,530 yards and 23 touchdowns. John Brodie on the 49ers threw for 3,112 yards and 30 TDs, while Bears rookie runner Gale Sayers accumulated 2,272 all-purpose yards and a league-leading 22 touchdowns. A big reason Retzlaff was selected was because the Maxwell Club is based in Philadelphia. Warranted or not, the award still shows that Pete was held in the highest regard at the time.

Pete played only one more year. At age 35, his totals were beginning to slip and he did not get along with coach Joe Kuharich so he retired. His last game was the Eagles' second experience in the Playoff Bowl. This time they faced the Baltimore Colts and actually led the game 14-13 until scrambling quarterback Jack Concannon tried to force a pass to Retzlaff with 3:25 left in the game but did not see safety Jerry Logan who intercepted the ball. That led to Tom Matte scoring the winning touchdown for the Colts with 14 seconds left and earned each Colt $1,200, while the Eagles received $500 apiece. At least no one was injured. Retzlaff, Tim Brown and King Hill are the only three Birds who played in both of these humpty dumpty games. The following year, the NFL would institute an actual playoff system, but the Playoff Bowl would hang around for three more years until the NFL-AFL merger was fully enacted.

Pete worked as a sportscaster in retirement, but had shown an aptitude for executive work by serving two terms as President of the NFL Players' Union. When Leonard Tose gained control of the Eagles in 1969, he first offered Retzlaff the head coaching job and then hired him as general manager. Pete did not work well with Tose, and his record is poor on all accounts. His drafts were weak, his trades were almost uniformly bad and his coaches were overmatched. He resigned after the 1972 season and dropped out of football entirely, which is one reason that he is nearly as forgotten today as those ill-fated Playoff Bowls. While he had problems with some teammates — notably Chuck Bednarik and Bob Brown — he was a respected team leader and popular with the fans. Pete is deservedly a member of the Eagle Honor Roll and is one of six Eagles to have their numbers retired.

1960s Decade in Review

Don Burroughs
S 1960-64

Originator: Former Buckeye tackle and team captain Leo "Fat" Raskowski played two games in 1935 and then went into college coaching.

Longest Tenure: Five years, Don Burroughs and Ron Medved.

Number Changes: Art Buss wore 12 in 1936 and 1937; Tom Brookshier wore 40 from 1956 to 1961; Vaughn Hebron wore 20 in 1994 and 1995.

Just Visiting: Paige Cothren kicked first for the Rams; Buddy Ryan brought Thomas Sanders over from the Bears; Vaughn Hebron won two Super Bowl rings in Denver.

Highs: Tom Brookshier (see 40).

Lows: Number two pick Rocky Ryan spent three years as a combination receiver and defensive back and accumulated five catches and two interceptions.

Don Burroughs

Faced with a situation not covered by the official playing rules in 1955, Bert Bell made an unusual edict that in the future it would be considered an unsportsmanlike conduct penalty if defensive players formed a pyramid to try to block a field goal attempt. Bell's ruling was prompted when the Rams' 6-foot 4-inch Don Burroughs perched on the shoulders of 6-foot 6-inch Big Daddy Lipscomb in an unsuccessful attempt to block a field goal by George Blanda of the Bears.

Burroughs was a rookie free agent with the Rams that year, having played as a quarterback at Colorado State in the same backfield with Detroit defensive backs Jim David and Jack Christiansen. Don was then 170 pounds and known as "the Stick" for his physique; that nickname would evolve into "the Blade" and Burroughs would eventually put on about 15 pounds, but he would still look wholly unsuited to be a professional football player. However, he was a battler who once got into a fight with 230-pound Eagle Buck Lansford during an exhibition game. The Rams converted him to a safety, and he picked off nine passes in his first year. He intercepted another 12 in the next three seasons, but then was shut out during the 1959 season and was traded to Philadelphia for a fifth-round pick.

Don arrived in Philadelphia for the championship run of 1960 and grabbed nine interceptions again. He led the Eagles in picks in each of his first four years with the team, and received some All-Pro recognition from 1960 to 1962. In the crucial second game against the Giants in 1960, Don picked off two passes, and as the final seconds ticked off in the title game against Green Bay, the Blade walked off the field carrying the ball he grabbed from the tackled Jim Taylor. Colts coach Weeb Ewbank complimented Eagles coach Buck Shaw after the game by using Burroughs as an example of the job Shaw did: "The Rams traded [Burroughs] to the Eagles because he was the worst tackler in the league. Now he's a deadly tackler." He was indeed a tough competitor who earned a one-game suspension from the league in 1963 when he grabbed and shoved field judge Dan Tehan, who Don felt had a quick whistle during an exhibition game.

Generally, Burroughs played centerfield for the Birds and had a real nose for the ball. New coach Joe Kuharich employed the Blade on the safety blitz in the 1964 season, most memorably against the Giants when Don knocked down Y.A. Tittle several times. The next July, Kuharich cut Burroughs as part of a youth movement, and he retired. He ended up with 50 career interceptions, the highest total of any player who never scored a touchdown on a return. His 29 picks as an Eagle set a team record that has since been exceeded, but his play was a highlight of the 1960s.

Decade Headline: Birds on the Wing.
Where They Played: Franklin Field, 1958-70.
How the Game Was Played: The success of Vince Lombardi's Green Bay Packers augured in an emphasis on running the ball and defense in the NFL, while the new American Football League followed a more wide-open aerial approach. Rosters

were expanded and specialization began to take hold as placekickers and punters started claiming a seat on the bench. Tom Landry followed Paul Brown's example and called all the plays for the expansion Dallas Cowboys.

Decade Won-Lost Record: 57-76-5, .431; 1-0 in the postseason; 0-2 in the runner-up bowl.

Record Against the Cowboys: 10-9.

Record Against the Giants: 7-11.

Record Against the Redskins: 9-9-2.

Record Against the Steelers: 10-7.

Playoff Appearances: 1960. Runner-up bowl appearances in 1961 and 1966.

Championships: 1960.

Unsung Hero: In the 1960 title game, Charlie Gauer noticed a weakness in Green Bay's kickoff coverage that led to a long return by Ted Dean and a short drive to the winning touchdown. It was also Charlie Gauer who helped develop Sonny Jurgensen into a winning quarterback. And it was Charlie Gauer who served the Eagles in other years as a scout and a broadcaster.

Head Coaches: Buck Shaw 1958-60, 10-2 for the decade plus 1-0 in the postseason; Nick Skorich 1961-63, 15-24-3; Joe Kuharich 1964-68, 28-41-1; Jerry Williams 1969-71, 4-9-1 for the decade.

Best Player: Hall of Famer Tommy McDonald with honorable mention to Timmy Brown.

Hall of Famers: Chuck Bednarik, Sonny Jurgensen, Ollie Matson, Tommy McDonald, Jim Ringo, Norm Van Brocklin.

Eagle Honor Roll: Chuck Bednarik, Bill Bradley, Tom Brookshier, Timmy Brown, Jim Gallagher (executive), Sonny Jurgensen, Tommy McDonald, Pete Retzlaff, Norm Van Brocklin.

League Leaders: Sonny Jurgensen — completions 1961, passing yards 1961, TD passes 1961, passing yards 1962; Tommy McDonald — receiving yards 1961, TD catches 1961; Timmy Brown – rush average 1965, kickoff returns 1961, 1963, kickoff return TDs 1961, 1962, 1966; Gary Ballman — yards per catch 1966; Ben Hawkins — receiving yards 1967; Harold Jackson — receiving yards 1969.

Award Winners: Norm Van Brocklin, MVP 1960; Buck Shaw, Coach of the Year 1960; Pete Retzlaff, MVP 1965.

All-Pros: Chuck Bednarik 1960-61; Tom Brookshier 1960; Don Burroughs 1960-62; Tommy McDonald 1960-62; Jess Richardson 1960; Norm Van Brocklin 1960; Maxie Baughan 1961, 1964-65; Sonny Jurgensen 1961; Leo Sugar 1961; Tim Brown 1963, 1965-66; Bob Brown 1964-68; Pete Retzlaff 1964-66; Jim Ringo 1964, 1966; Tom Woodeschick 1968-69.

Pro Bowl Selections: Maxie Baughan 1960-61, 1963-65; Chuck Bednarik 1960; Tom Brookshier 1960; Marion Campbell 1960; Tommy McDonald 1960-62; Pete Retzlaff 1960, 1963-65; Norm Van Brocklin 1960; Ted Dean 1961; Bobby Walston 1961; Sonny Jurgensen 1961; J.D. Smith 1961; Tim Brown 1962-63, 1965; Sam

Baker 1964, 1968; Irv Cross 1964-65; Floyd Peters 1964-67; Jim Ringo 1964-65, 1967; Bob Brown 1965-66, 1968; Norm Snead 1965; Tom Woodeschick 1968; Harold Jackson 1969; Dave Lloyd 1969; Tim Rossovich 1969.

Best Offensive Backfield: 1962, with quarterback Sonny Jurgensen, halfback Tim Brown, fullback Clarence Peaks and flanker Tommy McDonald.

Best Draft Choice: Among first-rounders, Hall of Famer Bob Brown 1964; for long shots, Pro Bowler Tom Woodeshick, an eight-round pick in 1963.

Best Overall Draft: 1966, when 10 draft picks made the team, including Ben Hawkins, Mel Tom and Gary Pettigrew.

Worst Draft Choice: Harry Jones, a running back from Arkansas taken first in 1967, was a complete bust who carried the ball 22 times for 24 yards in 1968; Leroy Keyes was the consolation prize in 1969 after the Eagles missed out on the O.J. Simpson sweepstakes. He was a great college player on offense and defense, but was never more than an adequate defensive back in the pros.

Worst Overall Draft: 1967. Only four selections made the team and none of them ever was a starter.

Best Free Agent: Joe Scarpatti was an undrafted free agent who was cut by the Packers and played decently as a free safety for several years.

Best Trade: In 1964, the Eagles sent tackle J.D. Smith to the Lions for Ollie Matson and defensive tackle Floyd Peters. Smith would get hurt and Matson was old, but Peters put in several Pro Bowl years in Philadelphia; in 1969, the Eagles obtained Harold Jackson from the Rams for Izzy Lang.

Worst Trade: Obviously, the trade of Sonny Jurgensen and Jimmy Carr to the Redskins for Norm Snead and Claude Crabb was an unmitigated disaster, but Joe Kuharich traded away Tommy McDonald, Lee Roy Caffey, Maxie Baughan and Irv Cross, too.

Biggest Off-Field Event: The collapse of Jerry Wolman's finances, forcing him to sell the team to Leonard Tose in 1969.

Biggest On-Field Development: Joe Kuharich's "no stars" approach to team-building.

Strangest On-Field Event: Santa Claus getting booed and being pelted with snowballs at the Christmas halftime show on December 15, 1968. Philadelphia will never live that down.

Worst Failure: A stunning failure of judgment on the part of new owner Jerry Wolman in not only hiring perpetual failure Joe Kuharich to coach the team, but then giving him an unheard-of 15-year contract.

Home Attendance: 4,029,266 in 69 games for an average gate of 58,395.

Best Game: On October 23, 1960, the Eagles pulled out a last-minute 31-29 victory over Cleveland on Bobby Walston's 38-yard field goal in the final 10 seconds. It was one of six fourth-quarter comebacks in that championship season.

First Game: September 25, 1960. The Eagles opened a second decade being soundly beaten by the Browns at home and giving no indication of how they would finish three months and one day later.

Last Game: December 21, 1969. The Eagles lost a close one 14-13 to the 49ers in San Francisco, because Sam Baker could not convert an extra point after a bad snap and missed a 19-yard field goal with 1:24 left.

Largest Margin of Victory: October 22, 1961. The Eagles destroyed the Cowboys 43-7, including five touchdowns on the ground.

Largest Margin of Defeat: The Cowboys got revenge five years later on October 9, 1966, when they pounded the Eagles 56-7 with Don Meredith throwing five TD passes.

Best Offense: Norm Van Brocklin led the Eagles to 321 points in 12 games in 1960; the following year, Sonny Jurgensen put up 361 points in 14 games. The 1960 team scored slightly more points per game, but the 1961 team finished first in yards gained. Both finished third in points scored.

Best Defense: In 1960, Philadelphia gave up 246 points, only seventh in the league, but they could tighten up when they needed to, as evinced by their championship.

Most Games Played: 96, Tim Brown.

Most Points: 475, Sam Baker.

Most Field Goals: 90, Sam Baker.

Most Touchdowns: 62, Tim Brown.

Most Touchdown Passes: 96, Norm Snead.

Most Passing Yards: 13,349, Norm Snead.

Most Receiving Yards: 5,782, Pete Retzlaff.

Most Receptions: 340, Pete Retzlaff.

Most Rushing Yards: 3,703, Tim Brown.

Most Interceptions: 29, Don Burroughs.

Most Sacks: NA

Most Kickoff Return Yards: 4,483, Tim Brown.

Most Punt Return Yards: 514, Tim Brown.

Book Notes: Robert Gordon's definitive history, *The 1960 Philadelphia Eagles: The Team That They Said Had Nothing But a Championship*, is packed with interviews and details. An obscure but interesting autobiography, nearly impossible to find, is Tommy McDonald's *They Pay Me to Catch Footballs*, which was locally published in 1962.

Noted Sportswriter: The *Philadelphia Daily News* employed a murderer's row of reporters and columnists in the early 1960s, including Jack McKinney, Larry Merchant and Stan Hochman.

Best Quotations: After making the fumble-inducing tackle on Frank Gifford that clinched a game over the Giants in 1960, and after making the game-ending tackle on Jim Taylor in the 1960 title game, Chuck Bednarik made the same exclamation, "This f...ing game is over!" In 1966, Joe Kuharich explained his approach: "The Eagles don't need stars. We need players whose level of performance doesn't rise and fall like the stock market." The fans responded to this in 1968 by filling the stadium with banners reading, "Joe Must Go."

Bubblegum Factoids: Tommy McDonald's 1963 Topps card reported that Tommy's wife was Miss Oklahoma 1955. Irv Cross' 1966 Philadelphia Gum card opined that "Two skull fractures would stop most any man, but not Irv."

Accidents of Birth: Bill Bradley was related to World War II General Omar Bradley; Gene Ceppetelli was born in Canada; Arunas Vasys was born in Lithuania.

Famous Names: Bill Bradley, not the basketball player/politician; Joe Lewis, not the comedian.

Unusual Names: Don Brumm, Don Chuy, Larry Conjar, Claude Crabb, Earl Gros, Riley Gunnels, Ralph Heck, Lane Howell, Wade Key, Israel Lang, Theron Sapp, Ben Scotti, Leo Sugar, Mel Tom, Arunas Vasys, Dean Wink.

Nicknames: Billy "Bullet" Barnes, "Concrete Charlie" Bednarik, Ron "Bye Bye" Blye, "Dollar" or "Super" Bill Bradley, Bob "Boomer" Brown, Don "Blade" Burroughs, Marion "Swamp Fox" Campbell, Jim "Gummy" Carr, Howard "Hopalong" Cassady, Mike "Onside" Clark, "Iron Mike" Ditka, Bob "Goose" Freeman, Glenn "Red" Glass, Alvin "Juggie" Haymond, Stuart "King" Hill, Christian "Sonny" Jurgensen, Howard "Sonny" Keys, Bill "Red" Mack, Ray "The Old Ranger" Mansfield, Ollie "Messiah" Matson, John "Golden Greek" Mellekas, Frank "Bruno" Molden, Al "Pete" Nelson, Don "Tree" Oakes, Clarence "High" Peaks, Pete "The Baron" Retzlaff, Lawrence "Buck" Shaw, "Stormin'" Norman Snead, Norm "The Dutchman" Van Brocklin, Bobby "The Sheriff" Walston.

Fastest Player: Frank Budd was an Olympic sprinter. Another Olympic sprinter, John Carlos, had a tryout with the team, but did not stick. Timmy Brown was also fast.

Heaviest Player: Defensive lineman John Baker hit 290 pounds in 1962, but Bob Brown got up to 295 in 1967.

Lightest Player: Tommy McDonald was 176 pounds and fearless across the middle of the field.

Toughest Injury: Bob Pellegrini's injury in 1960 allowed Chuck Bednarik to become the legendary 60-minute man. Much more problematic was Tommy Brookshier's broken leg in the eighth game of 1961. At that point the Eagles were 7-1. Without Brookie, they went 3-3 the rest of the way and finished second. The injury finished his career.

Local Boys: Jess Richardson and John Tracy hailed from Philadelphia. From the surrounding area came Chuck Bednarik, Frank Budd, Wayne Colman, Ted Dean, Mike Evans, Dick Hart, Ray Rissmiller, Chuck Weber and Tom Woodeshick. Among local colleges: Penn — Chuck Bednarik; Temple — Wayne Colman; Villanova — Frank Budd and Geno Ceppetelli; West Chester – Chuck Weber.

Firsts:

Hall of Fame Inductee — Bert Bell, a charter member in 1963.

3,000-Yard Passer — Sonny Jurgensen, 3,723 yards in 1961.

30 TD Passes — Sonny Jurgensen, 32 in 1961.

2 Kickoff Returns for TDs in One Game — Tim Brown took two kicks back 93 and 90 yards on November 6, 1966, in a 24-23 win over Dallas. Aaron Martin added a 67-yard punt return touchdown for the Eagles.

46

1978 — Miracle of the Meadowlands

Herman Edwards
CB 1977-85

WHO'S WORN THE NUMBER:

Don Miller (B) 1954, Ted Wegert (B) 1955-56, Brad Myers (B) 1958, Glen Amerson (B) 1961, Lee Bouggess (RB) 1970-73, Herman Edwards (CB) 1977-85, Chris Gerhard (S) 1987r, Izel Jenkins (CB) 1988-92, Markus Thomas (RB) 1993, Fredric Ford (CB) 1997, Quintin Mikell (S) 2003-04.

Originator: Southern Methodist University halfback Don Miller played in two games in 1954 before dislocating a finger and disappearing from the NFL.

Longest Tenure: Nine years, Herman Edwards.

Number Changes: None.

Just Visiting: None.

Highs: None.

Lows: Izell Jenkins — what can you say about a cornerback whose nickname was "Toast"? He was no Herman Edwards.

Herman Edwards

The author of the most stunning play in Eagle history, the Miracle of the Meadowlands, was second-year cornerback Herman Edwards. The young, up-and-down Eagles came into the contest 6-5 and found themselves trailing the Giants 17-12 with two minutes left in the game when Ron Jaworski threw an interception at the New York 10. The Giants gained a first down while the Eagles used up their timeouts. With 31 seconds left, all New York had to do was to take a knee and the game would be over. Instead, they tried a running play, but Bill Bergey and Frank Lemaster knocked center Jim Clack backwards which caused quarterback Joe Pisarcik to bobble the ball and miss the handoff to fullback Larry Csonka. Edwards swooped in, grabbed the ball on one bounce and sprinted 26 yards for the winning touchdown. In the aftermath, Edwards became an Eagle hero forever, while Giants offensive coordinator Bob Gibson was fired the next day.

Herman Edwards was recruited out of high school by Dick Vermeil for UCLA, but chose to enroll at Berkeley instead. Despite setting a California record with four interceptions in one game, Edwards eventually transferred to San Diego State to finish his college eligibility. Vermeil signed him as an undrafted free agent in 1977, and Herman led the team with six interceptions as a rookie. By 1978, the Eagles had not been to the postseason since they had won the title in 1960 and had posted only two winning seasons in those 17 years. Had the Birds lost that game at the Meadowlands, they would have dropped to 6-6 and probably finished at 8-8 and out of the playoffs again. Because of Edwards' opportunistic play, however, Philadelphia reached the playoffs with a 9-7 record and headed to Atlanta to face the 9-7 Falcons.

Something else of great significance happened in the game at the Meadowlands and would lead to one of Vermeil's biggest coaching blunders. There was a bad snap on the first Eagles extra point try in the second quarter, and kicker Nick Mike-Mayer was hurt attempting to pass the ball. Rather than signing a new kicker, Vermeil decided to go with his punter Mike Michel, who missed the Eagles' second extra point try in that game as well as two more in the last four games of the year. He did not attempt any field goals in the remaining games. This puzzling decision would cost Philadelphia the game against the Falcons. The Eagles built a 13-0 lead through three quarters in rainy Atlanta that day, but Michel had already missed an extra point and a 42-yard field goal attempt. Trailing by two scores, Falcon quarterback Steve Bartkowski tried the long ball. His 49-yard pass to Wallace Francis was ruled a completion at the Eagles' 23, even though Herm Edwards insisted that he actually intercepted the ball and Dick Vermeil claimed it was clearly offensive pass interference. Four plays later, Bartkowski hit Jim Mitchell for a 19-yard score. On their next possession, Bartkowski hit Francis for a 37-yard touchdown with 1:39 remaining. Both Falcon extra points were converted by Tim Mazzetti, a former Philadelphia bartender and Penn grad who had been cut by the Eagles in training camp. Jaworski led the Birds down to the Falcons' 17 with an unlucky 13 seconds left, and

Michel's 34-yard attempt sailed wide right to finish the Eagles' season and his NFL career. It was another devastating moment for Philadelphia sports fans.

Edwards was moved to safety in 1979, but slid back to the corner for the Eagles' Super Bowl run in 1980. Philadelphia lost that Super Bowl to the Raiders, and one of the images that haunt Eagle fans is the scrambling Jim Plunkett dropping a pass just over the outstretched fingertips of Edwards and into the hands of Kenny King, who went 80 yards for the score. Over the years, Edwards was an all-around cornerback who played both the pass and the run well. He was not blazing fast, but was smart, disciplined and tough. He was not afraid to make a tackle and was a durable player who started all 135 games over his nine-year Eagle career. When Buddy Ryan was hired in 1986, Herm was the second leading interceptor in team history with 33 and had five more in seven playoff games. Ryan was never one for sentiment, but went out of his way to praise Edwards when he cut him in August. Ryan told the *Inquirer*, "He had all the things I look for in a player. I told him this morning, 'I've been trying to find a way to make it work where you can stay.' He was a positive leader; he enjoyed practice and the games. But he just got old and can't do it anymore. I had to make that decision. That's all. I hated to do it."

Herm hooked on briefly with the Rams and Falcons during the 1986 season, and then went into coaching — first at San Jose State from 1987 to 1989. By 1990, he was in Kansas City, coaching under Marty Schottenheimer, and then moved on to Tampa in 1996. There, Tony Dungy promoted him to assistant head coach, and in 2001 the Jets brought him back to the Meadowlands as their real head coach. Edwards has been successful as the Jets' coach, getting to the playoffs three times in four years, but his conservatism on offense and weak clock management skills have done him in so far. His strengths as a coach are the same as his strengths as an Eagle: a tireless work ethic and an all-consuming passion to win.

Military Service

Nick Basca
B 1941

Nick Basca

Phoenixville's Mike "Nick" Basca starred in high school, prep school and at Villanova as a halfback on the gridiron and a pitcher on the baseball diamond. Undersized at 5 feet 8 inches and 170 pounds, he went undrafted, but became a hot free agent pursued by five NFL teams after a big performance in the North-South All-Star Game. Greasy Neale signed the swift and shifty back, who could run, pass, catch, punt and kick the ball, in 1941. Used primarily as a kicker and punter in his rookie season, Nick saw the gathering danger in the world and enlisted in the Army that November. His last game as an Eagle was the season finale in Washington on December 7, 1941 — Pearl Harbor Day. Three days later Basca was in the Army.

In the summer of 1942, Nick got married and played on the Army All-Star football team that played several games against NFL teams, including the Giants, Bears and Dodgers, to raise money for the war effort. Nick was sent overseas in December 1943 to join General George S. Patton's 3rd Army in its 4th Armored Division, the tank corps. They landed at Normandy, France in July and first swept south and then pivoted 250 miles east in one of Patton's patented quick and deadly maneuvers. In the French town of Obreck, Basca's tank was hit by a German mortar round and destroyed on November 11, 1944, Armistice Day. Nick's brother Steven, who won three Purple Hearts, was recovering then in an Army hospital 60 miles away, and according to the hospital charts, sat up screaming at the time the mortar hit his brother's tank.

Like major league baseball, the NFL continued operating throughout the war, utilizing all available semi-able bodies. Eagle general manager Harry Thayer wrote to NFL commissioner Elmer Layden in 1945 as to how the league could continue: "For the past two years virtually all of our players have been employed during the week in war plants. Our practices have been held in the evening and our games of course on Sundays. Using men discharged from or rejected by the services, we still conformed with the government idea of having every man in a war job — and still managed to make progress in football."

Close to the anniversary of Nick Basca's death, the Eagles held a special tribute to him before the Giants game on November 9, 1945. Soon after, Villanova began calling its football homecoming "Nick Basca Weekend" in his honor. Nick was survived by his parents, his widowed bride and by his brothers Steven and Paul, who also served in the military. Unfortunately, Basca was not the only Eagle to die in World War II. End Len Supulski also died in France in 1944, and three players who were under contract, but never appeared in an Eagles uniform, died in olive green: Alonzo Hearne, John O'Keefe and Alex Santelli. Some Eagles like Jack Sanders, who lost part of his left arm on Iwo Jima, were maimed, and some like Buddy Elrod ended up as prisoners of war.

These 104 Eagles served in the military during World War II: Ben Agajanian, Al Baisi, Jack Banta, Walter Barnes, Len Barnum, Nick Basca, Chuck Bednarik, John Binotto, Bob Bjorklund, Tony Bova, Leo Brennan, Larry Cabrelli, Rocco Canale, Jim Castiglia, Tony Cemore, Chuck Cherundolo, Gus Cifelli, Gerry Cowhig, Bob Davis, Dan

DeSantis, Dave DiFilippo, Otis Douglas, Woody Dow, Harry Dowda, John Eibner, Drew Ellis, Frank Emmons, Dick Erdlitz, Terry Fox, Joe Frank, Ralph Fritz, Ray George, Elwood Gerber, Lou Ghecas, Mario Giannelli, Fred Gloden, Lyle Graham, Bud Grant, Irv Hall, Bill Halverson, Ray Hamilton, Roger Harding, Maurice Harper, Granville Harrison, Ken Hayden, Kirk Hershey, Jack Hinkle, Frank Hrabetin, Dick Humbert, Mike Jarmoluk, Ed Kasky, Bucko Kilroy, Ben Kish, Bob Krieger, Bert Kuczynski, Mort Landsberg, James Lankas, Steve Levanitis, Don Looney, Jay MacDowell, Art Macioszczyk, Bill Mackrides, John Magee, Eggs Manske, Basilio Marchi, Wes McAfee, Bob McChesney, Hugh McCullough, Fred Meyer, Joe Muha, Rupert Pate, Pete Pihos, Henry Pirro, Robert Priestly, Bosh Pritchard, George Rado, Phil Ragazzo, Frank Reagan, Hank Reese, Dick Riffle, Jack Sanders, John Shonk, Jack Smith, Dave Smukler, Jack Stackpool, Gil Steinke, Cecil Sturgeon, Bob Sufferidge, Len Supulski, Joe Sutton, Tommy Thompson, Bob Thurbon, Lou Tomasetti, Norm Van Brocklin, Foster Watkins, Don Weedon, Izzy Weinstock, Burr West, Boyd Williams, Jerry Williams, Frank Wydo, John Wyhonic, Frank Ziegler and John Zilly. Owner Lex Thompson and future coaches Wayne Milner, Joe Kuharich and Jerry Williams also served. Future owner Jerry Wolman served in the Merchant Marines as a teenager. Owner/coach Bert Bell had served with a hospital unit in World War I.

During the Korean War, the roll call of Eagles includes: Bibbles Bawel, Ed Bell, Hal Bradley, Marion Campbell, Stan Campbell, Russ Carroccio, Tom Catlin, Al Dorow, Hal Giancanelli, Rob Goode, Roscoe Hansen, Bill Horrell, Ken Huxhold, John Huzvar, Don King, Toy Ledbetter, Ken McAfee, Ollie Matson, Don Owens, Volney Peters, Ray Romero, Bob Schnelker, Ed Sharkey, Leo Sugar, Len Szafaryn, Jim Weatherall, Chuck Weber and Ted Wegert. Future coaches Mike McCormack, Marion Campbell, Fred Bruney and Buddy Ryan also served.

Since that time, several more Eagles have fulfilled a military obligation: Sam Baker, Tom Brookshier, Don Burroughs, Ralph Guglielmi, Gerry Huth, Ken Keller, Menil Mavraidies, Jerry Mazzanti, Mike McClellan, John Mellekas, Maurice Nipp, Pete Retzlaff, Tom Saidock, Lum Snyder, Harold Wells and Neil Worden.

These Eagles soared the highest, and we owe them our thanks and respect.

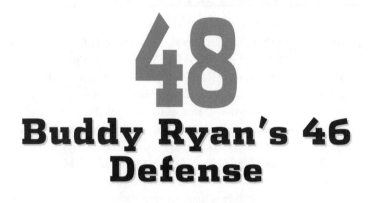

48

Buddy Ryan's 46 Defense

Wes Hopkins
S 1983-93

Wes Hopkins

Success often is fleeting in the harried life of a defensive back; he is always just one slip away from being the goat. Popular, hard-hitting, veteran safety Wes Hopkins discovered that off the field in September 1992. While Hopkins and his teammates were shutting out John Elway and the Broncos 30-0, his wife Erica struck a blow for all the betrayed Eagle wives cheering her on by knocking her husband's shameless girlfriend down nine rows of steps at the Vet. Each time the girlfriend tried to run away, someone would grab her for Erica until security stepped in. It was a sad, wild, embarrassing spectacle, and entirely Wes' doing. However, the difficulties he faced earlier in his career were simply a combination of bad timing and bad luck.

Hopkins received no scholarship offers in high school; his grades weren't good, and coaches thought he was too small and too slow. He enrolled in a summer program at Southern Methodist to bring up his grades and showed enough in practice to earn a football scholarship there as a walk-on. As a sophomore, he was starting at safety, and as a senior, he led the Southwest Conference in interceptions. For Marion Campbell's first Eagles draft in 1983, he picked Hopkins in the second round, and Wes turned out to be the best pick Campbell would ever make.

Wes was an immediate star as a rookie. He was a heavy hitter and tough tackler who was very sturdy in run support. Although he was not extremely fast, he was smart and quick enough for free safety. He was fifth on the team in tackles in 1983, third in 1984 and first with 136 in 1985 — a year he received All-Pro and Pro Bowl recognition. However, the team was a loser each year, and new owner Norman Braman made a change in 1986 by hiring Buddy Ryan, the defensive coordinator of the champion Bears, as the new head coach.

Wes did not endear himself to Ryan by holding out during the Eagles' first mini-camp, and then made it worse by pulling his hamstring early in training camp. Buddy referred to him as "Wallets" and suggested that maybe Wes was injured because his wallet was too heavy. The final blow came in the fourth game of the year when Hopkins tore up his knee while trying to tackle his old SMU teammate Eric Dickerson. He would miss the rest of 1986 and all of 1987 rehabilitating his knee, while Buddy bonded with the team he was building. When Wes returned in 1988, Buddy treated him coldly and platooned him with Terry Hoage on passing downs, although Hopkins remained the starter and finished second on the team in tackles in both 1988 and 1989. Ryan rewarded that performance by drafting Ben Smith, a slightly built college safety projected to be a pro corner, and anointing him the new starting free safety on draft day. After the first month, though, Smith was at corner and Hopkins was back on the field. When Buddy was fired, Hopkins was one player who did not lash out angrily at management in response. He had another good year under new coordinator Bud Carson in 1991, but 1992 and 1993 were injury-plagued years in which Hopkins' speed and range deteriorated so much that he was forced to retire after 10 seasons and 30 interceptions as an Eagle.

The puzzling thing about Wes Hopkins is that on the surface he appeared to be Buddy's type of player, a powerful, aggressive headhunter. However, Ryan never warmed to Hopkins and criticized him regularly. Partly, the two got off to a bad start with the holdout and injuries, but it was also the case that Hopkins was not Ryan's player; he was a holdover from the Campbell era, and Buddy was establishing a new tone. Above all, Buddy inspired loyalty from his boys by being loyal and generous to them both during and after their careers. Former Bear safety Doug Plank, whose number 46 became the name for Buddy's famous defensive scheme, even sat on the Eagles sideline during the first Eagles-Bears game in 1986. Buddy stuck up for his players: he encouraged them all to stay on strike together in 1987 and welcomed contract holdout Keith Jackson back to town with limosine service in 1990. Meanwhile, he was surly to the men who held the purse strings; he referred to Norman Braman contemptuously as "that guy in France" and called the general manager the "illegitimate son" of the owner.

Ryan was big on bluster. He could be crude, tasteless, mean, obnoxious and a braggart, but it all only made him more popular with his team and a large proportion of the fans, who loved the unbridled fury the Eagles exhibited in such games as the Bounty Bowl against the Cowboys and the Body Bag Game against the Redskins. He insulted legendary coaches Don Shula, Tom Landry, Mike Ditka and Jimmy Johnson and bad-mouthed respected defensive coordinators Bud Carson and Fritz Shurmur. Ryan made definitive snap judgments about players and dismissed those who didn't measure up with cutting remarks that could be quite cruel. He called fullback Michael Haddix "a reject guard from the USFL" and said of 1,000-yard rusher Earnest Jackson, "I'd trade him for a six-pack, and it wouldn't even have to be cold." However, Buddy imbued his boys with the feeling that they were the meanest, toughest, renegade SOBs in the league.

And they were. That was Buddy's style. In contrast to the "bend-but-don't-break" scheme of Marion Campbell, Ryan's defenses attacked the quarterback and tried to force the ball free on every play. They aimed not only at stopping the other team, but at getting turnovers and even at scoring. The 46 is heavy on blitzes from linebackers and safeties and strong against the run. The weakness is that the cornerbacks are on their own, which gives the offense a chance for big plays. The actual 46 scheme, some claim, has its roots in Greasy Neale's Eagle defense from the 1940s, which also bunched a lot of bodies close to the line of scrimmage and went all-out in rushing the passer. Neill Armstrong played for Neale in Philadelphia and later coached a short, fat defensive lineman named Buddy Ryan at Oklahoma State. After Armstrong became the defensive coordinator of the Minnesota Vikings under former Eagle player Bud Grant, he hired Ryan as his defensive line coach, and they began to develop the 46. When Armstrong was hired as the Bears' head coach in 1978, he brought Ryan in as his defensive coordinator, and the Bears accumulated the talent to unleash the most ferocious attacking defense yet seen in 1985. How much credit should go to Armstrong is unclear, but it is undeniable that Ryan took all of the applause.

Ryan assembled a lot of talent in Philadelphia as well, and the 46 was a fearsome defense to watch on most occasions, but it could be had by the better teams. Joe

Montana threw four fourth-quarter TD passes to beat the Eagles in 1989, and Buddy never did win a playoff game. Ryan might get a pass for the flukey Fog Bowl in 1988, but in the first-round defeats of 1989 and 1990, the Birds were badly outplayed and out-coached. Ryan had no interest or clue in building or coaching an offense, and his defense lacked discipline, so the coulda-shoulda-wouldas about Super Bowl wins were never more than fantasies. Rival coach Bill Parcells said of Buddy's Eagles that they tried to win wholly on power and intimidation, but neglected strategy. When Buddy was fired, there was a great outcry from players and fans, but the defense actually got better under new coordinator Bud Carson. If Braman had hired defensive coordinator Jeff Fisher to run the team rather than offensive coordinator Rich Kotite, maybe the 1990s would have been a happier decade. As for Ryan, he hired on as the coordinator for the underachieving Oilers in 1993, but his tenure there was noteworthy chiefly for his punching offensive coach Kevin Gilbride during a game and for Joe Montana leading the Chiefs in another comeback victory over Houston in the playoffs. Buddy got another shot when he took the head coaching job in Arizona, but the magic was gone. He brought in a number of his former stars, but still went 12-20 in two seasons and retired to his horse farm.

Coaching Legacies

Jerry Williams
B 1953-54

Originator: Niagara halfback Dan DeSantis averaged 2.8 yards per carry in 1941 for the Eagles and then went into the service. After the war, in 1947, Dan joined the Hamilton (Ontario) Tiger Cats and became the first former NFL player to play in the CFL.

Longest Tenure: Five years, Pat McHugh.

Number Changes: Todd Bell wore 52 in 1988; Luther Broughton wore 86 in 1997, 88 in 1999 and 84 in 2000.

Just Visiting: Todd Bell was a hard-hitting safety for Buddy Ryan in Chicago; Andrew Jordan was the second tight end for the Vikings.

Highs: Pat McHugh starred as a speedy safety in the defensive backfield for Greasy Neale's Eagles. His teammates called him "Spider."

Lows: John Tarver came over from the Patriots in 1975 and gained 20 yards on seven carries for a 2.9 average while catching five passes for 14 yards, a 2.8 average. It's a rare and dubious achievement for someone to have a lower average gain receiving than rushing.

Jerry Williams

1969 seemed like a bright new day in Eagles history after the off-the-field soap opera of owner Jerry Wolman's financial collapse and the on-the-field farce of Joe Kuharich's coaching. The Birds were under the new ownership of Leonard Tose and were bringing home two winners from the past to reroute the franchise: former All-Pro and noted hard-worker Pete Retzlaff as general manager and Jerry Williams, the defensive architect of the 1960 champions, as coach. It just goes to show that you can never predict the weather in Eagleville.

Jerry Williams was a combat pilot in the Pacific during World War II before starring on the football field for the Washington State Cougars in the late 1940s. He was only 5 feet 10 inches and 175 pounds but very fast, and was picked in the seventh round by the Rams in 1949. "Jittery Jerry," as the local papers dubbed him, was a starting safety as a 26-year-old rookie and picked off 15 passes in four years in LA. On occasion, he was used on offense and as a return man as well to utilize his speed. In fact, after Lou Groza kicked a field goal to give Cleveland the lead in the final minute of the 1950 title game, Williams came within one man of breaking the ensuing kickoff return. In his third year with the Rams, Jerry gave a strong indication of his future direction by working part-time as an assistant coach for the University of Idaho. When the Idaho head coaching job became available in 1953, Williams was considered for the position. Instead, the Rams traded him to the Eagles for a draft pick.

The Eagles shifted Jerry to the other side of the ball, and he led the team in total offense in both 1953 and 1954. His strength was his versatility. He was a change-of-pace runner, an able return man and an excellent receiver out of the backfield, who had very small feet and ran in a short, choppy style. After two seasons in Philadelphia, Jerry was offered the head coach's position at the University of Montana and retired from playing. Three years later, new Eagles coach Buck Shaw brought Williams back to the Eagles as the defensive coach and to attend to "off-season detail work," since Shaw only worked six months a year as coach. Jerry improved the standing of the Birds' pass defense to second in the league by 1960, and was credited for creating the five-defensive-back "nickel" defense that George Allen later developed. When everything went south for the Eagles under Nick Skorich, the coaching staff was fired, and Williams went north to Canada.

Jerry worked as an assistant coach for the Calgary Stampeders in 1964, was promoted to head coach in 1965 and was named Coach of the Year in 1967, when he led Calgary to the title game. He was Pete Retzlaff's first choice to rebuild the Eagles when Pete took over the general manager's job in 1969. At the press conference, Retzlaff noted that Williams had been associated with winning teams in 14 of the 17 years he had played or coached professional football. What he didn't specify was that the three losing seasons had all occurred in Philadelphia, and what followed was a slow-motion train wreck. Not only were the Eagles players substandard, as demonstrated by their 2-12 record in 1968, but Retzlaff's drafts were weak and his trade record was abysmal. Williams was a very smart man with a law degree from Temple, but was not much of a motivator and lost control of the team over his three-year tenure. After finishing last with 4-9-1 and 3-10-1 records in his first two seasons, there was a lot of talk that Tose was getting ready to fire Williams. After the Birds began 1971 by losing to the Bengals 37-14, the Cowboys 42-7 and the 49ers 31-3, Tose pulled the plug on Williams, and it was an ugly scene. Just that week, Williams had fined several players for lack of effort, yet he claimed that he was dismissed just as the players and coaches were looking forward to upsetting the Vikings to turn their season around. Williams added, "Unfortunately, I was working for a man who is without courage or character. I was offered a sizeable sum of money to resign, but to accept a bribe of that nature is to lower myself to his depths."

The Eagles did turn their season around later under Ed Khayat to finish 6-7-1, but stunk again in 1972. Williams hooked on as Nick Skorich's end coach in Cleveland for the rest of the season before returning to Canada where he won the Grey Cup with the Hamilton Tiger Cats in 1972. Jerry is one of three former Eagle players, along with Ed Khayat and Marion Campbell, to later serve as the team's head coach. All three were associated with the 1960 championship team and give an indication of what made that team special — its brains. As proof, 12 of the 39 members of that team later went into coaching or front office work in the NFL (Billy Ray Barnes, Maxie Baughan, Marion Campbell, Jim Carr, Ed Khayat, Bob Pellegrini, Jerry Reichow, Pete Retzlaff, Jess Richardson, Norm Van Brocklin, Bobby Walston and Chuck Weber) and two others (Bobby Freeman and John Wittenborn) became successful college assistant coaches.

Altogether, five players or assistant coaches from the 1960 squad (Williams, Skorich, Khayat, Campbell and Norm Van Brocklin) became NFL coaches, but none did particularly well. The combined NFL record of Buck Shaw's protégés was 160-265-17, for a .381 percentage. The record of the two Shaw coaches (Williams and Skorich) and players (Campbell and Khayat) in Philadelphia is even worse — 47-90-8, for a .352 percentage. By contrast, none of Greasy Neale's former players or coaches ever coached the Eagles, but assistant coach Charley Ewart and players Neill Armstrong and Allie Sherman coached in the NFL and compiled an 88-95-5 record for a mediocre .481 percentage. The former Eagles who had the greatest success as NFL coaches all limited their playing time in Philadelphia to two years: Bud Grant, 158-96-5; Mike Ditka 121-95; and Bill Cowher, 130-77. Grant played under Bo McMillan, Wayne Milner and Jim Trimble; Ditka played under Joe Kuharich and hated it; Cowher played under Campbell. Current NFL coaches include two former Eagles, Cowher and Herman Edwards. If you add up the won-lost records of every former Eagle who coached in the NFL (including Algy Clark, Abe Gibron, Jim Leonard, John Rauch and Jim Ringo), their overall regular season record at the end of 2004 was 748-751-31.

50

Vermeil Without Tears

Guy Morriss
C 1974-83

WHO'S WORN THE NUMBER:

Alabama Pitts (B) 1935, Don Jackson (B) 1936, Robert Bjorklund (C) 1941, Ken Hayden (C) 1942, Al Wukits (C) 1943, Baptiste Manzini (C) 1944-45, Bob Kelley (C) 1955-56, Darrel Aschbacher (G) 1959, Dave Recher (C) 1966-68, Ron Porter (LB) 1969-72, Guy Morriss (C) 1974-83, Garry Cobb (LB) 1985-87, Dave Rimington (C) 1988-89, Ephesians Bartley (LB) 1992, James Willis (LB) 1995-98, Alonzo Ephraim (C) 2003, Mark Simoneau (LB) 2004.

Originator: Former felon Alabama Pitts was hired to appear in the Eagles' back-field in 1935, mostly as a gate attraction.

Longest Tenure: 10 years, Guy Morriss.

Number Changes: Don Jackson also wore 10 in 1936; Bap Manzini wore 66 in 1948; Dave Recher wore 51 in 1965; Guy Morriss wore 62 in 1973; Mark Simoneau wore 53 in 2003.

Just Visiting: Dave Rimington spent most of his career in Cincinnati.

Highs: Garry Cobb spent six seasons in Detroit before coming to the Eagles for Wilbert Montgomery. He has been a popular broadcaster in the area.

Lows: North Carolina halfback Don Jackson ran the ball 46 times for 76 yards in 1936, a 1.7 average. He also completed seven of 35 passes while throwing 11 interceptions and no TDs for a passer rating of 0.00.

Guy Morriss

Fellow Texan and new teammate Bill Bradley helped soft-spoken rookie Guy Morriss get settled in Philadelphia in 1973, and now 30 years later, Bradley is Morriss' defensive coordinator at Baylor University. Few would have predicted then that the Eagles' quiet man in the middle of their offensive line for over a decade would end up as a head coach.

Morriss was an All-Southwest Conference guard for Texas Christian's Wishbone offense when he was drafted in the second round by the Eagles in 1973. In midseason that year, starting center Mike Evans came down with the flu, so Morriss stepped in one week. From that point on, he started every game but one over the next 11 years in Philadelphia and established a reputation as a well-conditioned hard worker. Although he was not much of a talker, Guy made the line calls on the field, and he also served as the team's long snapper. With Tom Banks and Jeff Van Note in the NFC and Hall of Famers Mike Webster, Jim Langer and Dwight Stephenson in the AFC, it was difficult to receive All-Pro notice at the center position during Morriss' career, but he was All-NFC in 1981 and was first alternate for the Pro Bowl for three years running.

Morriss was a respected team leader and team captain. In 1983, though, a public dispute with the coaching staff would lead to Guy's departure from Philadelphia. On behalf of his fellow linemen, he complained that offensive line coach Jerry Wampfler was trying to coach the whole offense while the rushing attack had fallen off drastically and was ineffective. In the off-season, the Eagles traded for Mark Dennard, a center four years younger than Morriss, and waived Guy. They also fired Wampfler and offensive coordinator Dick Wood. Guy was signed by the Patriots and got to play in a second Super Bowl in 1985, again on the losing side. A Bears team led by Buddy Ryan's 46 Defense mauled New England. After breaking his hand in 1987, Morriss became an assistant coach for the Patriots and began the nomadic life of a coaching gypsy, making eight stops in 15 years before landing the top job at Baylor in 2003. He spent a season in Arizona with Buddy Ryan and coached in the NFL, CFL and Professional Spring Football League, as well as high school and college.

Morriss is one of three of Dick Vermeil's Eagles, in addition to Herman Edwards and John Bunting, who have become head coaches at the pro or college level. Like their mentor, they all stress dedication, discipline and hard work above all else. Morriss has noted that he most remembers Vermeil for his work ethic and his relentless preparation. Vermeil was so focused and driven that he even had a sign on his desk stating "The Best Way to Kill Time Is to Work It to Death."

Vermeil worked his way up from coaching high school to junior college, to becoming the first special teams coach in NFL history under George Allen, to winning the Rose Bowl at UCLA. He was happy at UCLA and, partly out of loyalty to his staff, resisted the initial overtures from Leonard Tose and Eagle GM Jim Murray to come to Philadelphia. With his staff encouraging him, though, he met with Tose and took the job. What he inherited in Philadelphia was a mess. The team was riddled with drug problems and dissension. They had just finished 4-10, had not had a winning record in nine years and had not been to the postseason in 15. As for reinforcements, he had no draft choice higher than a third-rounder for his first four years because his predecessor had traded them away. Dick just rolled up his sleeves and went to work.

Dick ruthlessly weeded out any suspected drug users. When Mike Hogan and James Betterson were charged with drug possession, he cut them immediately without discussion. It did not matter that the two were later exonerated of the charges — Vermeil was sending a message. He built a tough, new Eagles team through trades (Ron Jaworski and Claude Humphrey), free agents (Herman Edwards and Woody Peoples), low draft picks (Wilbert Montgomery, Carl Hairston, Dennis Harrison and Charlie Johnson) and the core players who remained (Bill Bergey, Guy Morriss, Jerry Sisemore, Stan Walters, John Bunting, Harold Carmichael, Randy Logan and Frank Lemaster).

Vermeil worked 20-hour days and slept on a cot in his office three nights a week. During his first training camp, he complained that a fireworks extravaganza celebrating the nation's Bicentennial was a disruption and wanted it stopped. Vermeil pushed his players as hard as he pushed himself. Bergey told a reporter, "That first week of training camp was the worst week I ever went through in my life." Year by year, the team steadily improved: a winning record and the playoffs in 1978, beating Dallas in 1979 and reaching the Super Bowl in 1980. After that, however, the team declined just as steadily. By 1982, some players had had enough of the intensity. All-Pro defensive tackle Charlie Johnson complained about the endless practice sessions and was traded. The 1982 strike disturbed the team chemistry, and Tose made it worse by blasting the players after a loss when they came back.

Vermeil was also an extremely emotional man. Often, he would be fighting back tears with his voice cracking before games, after games and at press conferences. Finally, it got too much, and Vermeil quit coaching, citing "burnout." He became a college football analyst on TV for several years while occasionally flirting with NFL coaching openings. The most serious flirtation was with the Eagles in 1995 after Jeff Lurie had purchased the team, but the negotiations fell apart at the last minute over control issues — not a surprise with Vermeil. He finally took the coaching job with the downtrodden Rams in 1997, but had trouble winning over the players to his heavy workload. By 1999, he was under a threat of win or else when the Rams' full-throttle offense won the Super Bowl. However, with offensive coach Mike Martz a hot commodity, the Rams pressured Vermeil to step aside and retire. He did, but quickly regretted it. Chiefs general manager Carl Peterson, Dick's old assistant with UCLA and the Eagles, had no trouble luring him to KC the next year.

With Vermeil, his strengths are also his weaknesses. He not only worked time to death, but his team as well. After the Super Bowl debacle with the Eagles, where his overworked team was too tired and tight to perform, Vermeil loosened up just a little with the Rams. His offense evolved from the conservative play selection in Philadelphia to the aggressive attack of the Rams. That much has continued in Kansas City, but what has gotten him into trouble there is his extreme loyalty to players and coaches who aren't performing, particularly on defense. When Vermeil is in your corner, he will not give up on you, even when it is time to move on. Dick Vermeil worked harder than any coach the Eagles have ever had and was successful in turning around a moribund franchise, but he had limitations. Ultimately, it was a good thing that he did not return to the Eagles in 1995.

51

1995 Playoffs

Willie Thomas
LB 1991-99

WHO'S WORN THE NUMBER:

Lyle Graham (C) 1941, Al Milling (G) 1942, Robert Wear (C) 1942, Enio Conti (G) 1944-45, Ray Graves (C) 1946, Boyd Williams (C) 1947, Frank Szymanski (C) 1948, Chuck Weber (LB) 1959-61, Jim Schrader (C) 1962-64, Dave Recher (C) 1965, Dwight Kelley (LB) 1966-72, Dick Cunningham (LB) 1973, Ron Lou (C) 1975, Reggie Wilkes (LB) 1978-85, Chuck Gorecki (LB) 1987r, Ricky Shaw (LB) 1989-90, *William Thomas* (LB) 1991-99, Carlos Emmons (LB) 2000-03.

Originator: Richmond center Lyle Graham enlisted in the Army Air Corps in October 1941, but appeared in every game that year for the Eagles.

Longest Tenure: Nine years, Willie Thomas.

Number Changes: Enio Conti wore 67 from 1941 to 1943; Ray Graves wore 52 in 1942 and 1943; Ron Lou also wore 30 in 1975; Dave Recher wore 50 from 1966 to 1968; Nate Wayne wore 54 in 2003.

Just Visiting: Jim Schrader was the Redskins' center for seven seasons.

Highs: Enio Conti (see 67 top); former Marine Chuck Weber was a tough guy middle linebacker for the 1960 Eagles; in the late 1960s, Philadelphia special teams were known as Kelley's Killers for Ike Kelley; Carlos Emmons was the defensive MVP of the 2003 Eagles.

Lows: Interior linemen Al Milling, Robert Wear, Boyd Williams, Frank Szymanski and Ron Lou appeared in a cumulative 33 games in their one-year stints with Philadelphia.

Willie Thomas

Willie T was the final piece to an awesome defense. With Reggie White, Clyde Simmons, Jerome Brown and Mike Pitts on the front line and Eric Allen, Ben Smith, Wes Hopkins and Andre Waters in the backfield, all the defense needed was a weakside linebacker who could play to the level of middle backer Byron Evans and strongside playmaker Seth Joyner. That was William Thomas, and the Eagles finished first in the NFL in defense in 1991 under new coordinator Bud Carson. Within two years, though, age, injuries and free agency defections would destroy this fearsome force forever.

Thomas played safety in college and was selected in the fourth round as a 215-pound linebacker. By midseason, he had beaten out Jessie Small on the weak side and started to earn attention as a playmaker himself. Willie was a sure tackler with great anticipation in sniffing out where a play was going. As an old safety, his pass coverage skills were excellent for a linebacker. In his nine years in Philadelphia, Thomas intercepted 18 passes, including seven in 1995, and also recorded 33 sacks to show his athletic versatility. Two of those interceptions he returned for touchdowns, and he also scored on two of his nine fumble recoveries. He worked hard to be just as tough against the run as he was against the pass and finished second on the team in tackles in 1994. Four times he finished fourth in tackles.

By the time Ray Rhodes took over the team in 1995, Willie T was the star of the defense. From 1995 through 1997, Thomas was selected the Eagles' defensive MVP each year. He was All-Pro in 1995 and twice was named to the Pro Bowl squad. Rhodes worked hard to transform a team that had lost its last seven games in 1994 by bringing in a slew of free agents and draft picks. Rhodes tried to restructure the Eagles as a very scrappy, hungry team, but was unable to get through to space cadet quarterback Randall Cunningham. So with the team sitting at 1-3, Randall was benched. New starter Rodney Peete did not have the skills that Randall did, but he was a leader with heart who led Philadelphia on a 9-3 stretch that got them into the playoffs for the first time in three years.

In the wild card game, the Eagles would face the Lions, another team that had gotten off to a slow start before getting on track to average 29 points a game over the last 10 games of the year. Veteran Lions tackle Lomas Brown said before the game that it would be over early, but he didn't realize the real meaning of what he was predicting. On December 30, 1995, in the first playoff game at the Vet in five years, the Eagles won at home in the playoffs for the first time since 1980. The final score was 58-37, but it wasn't nearly that close. Defensive coordinator Emmitt Thomas devised a five-defensive-back scheme in which safety Mike Zordich lined up like a linebacker; it completely baffled Lion quarterback Scott Mitchell, who threw four of the six interceptions the Eagles would pick off that day. Willie Thomas and Barry Wilburn returned picks for touchdowns, while altogether the six picks and one fumble recovery led to 34 Eagle points. Rodney Peete completed 17 of 25 passes for 270 yard, including a 43-yard Hail

Mary to Rob Carpenter right before halftime that made the score 38-7 at the break. Bobby Taylor shut down Lions All-Pro receiver Herman Moore aside from a 68-yard touchdown that made the score 51-14 in the third quarter. Randall Cunningham even got in the game to run out the clock in the fourth period.

Cunningham was the underlying story in the next week as the Eagles prepared to meet the Cowboys in a divisional matchup. Randall's wife was due at any time to go into labor with their first child, and Cunningham had permission from Rhodes to attend the birth. The call came on Thursday, and Randall flew off but did not bring his playbook. Rhodes was expecting Cunningham would return the next day, but he didn't come back till Saturday, missing the last two days of practice.

Predictably, Rodney Peete was injured at the end of the first quarter, and the Eagles had to suffer with an unprepared Cunningham, who floundered away any chance the team had against the powerful Cowboys. Deion Sanders scored one Cowboy touchdown on a 21-yard reverse. Their second touchdown was set up by Troy Aikman's passes of 37 yards to Kevin Williams and 26 yards to Moose Johnston and was scored by Emmitt Smith on a one-yard plunge. Philadelphia trailed 17-3 at the half, which was similar to the 17-6 halftime deficit the Birds had overcome when the teams had met a month before in a game famous for the Eagle defense twice stuffing Emmitt Smith on a fourth and one at his own 29 with two minutes left. Philadelphia won that game 20-17, but there would be no comebacks this day with Randall at the controls. This time, Dallas controlled the ball for 35:46, and Ricky Waters gained only 39 yards on 13 carries, while Charley Garner could only manage 13 on five carries. The final score was 30-11 Dallas, and Eagle fans were left with a familiar feeling of depression, especially after the thrilling triumph of the previous week.

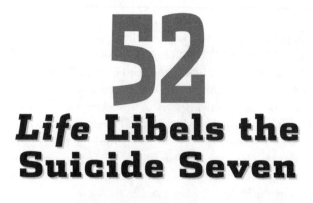

Life Libels the Suicide Seven

Wayne Robinson
LB 1952-56

WHO'S WORN THE NUMBER:

Ray Graves (C) 1942-43, Vic Lindskog (C) 1944-51, *Wayne Robinson* (LB) 1952-56, *Dave Lloyd* (LB) 1963-70, Kevin Reilly (LB) 1973-74, Ray Phillips (LB) 1978-81, Rich Kraynak (LB) 1983-86, Matt Battaglia (LB) 1987r, Todd Bell (LB) 1988, Jessie Small (LB) 1989-91, Louis Cooper (LB) 1993, Vaughan Johnson (LB) 1994, Sylvester Wright (LB) 1995-96, DeShawn Fogle (LB) 1997, Jon Haskins (LB) 1998, Barry Gardner (LB) 1999-02, Jason Short (LB) 2004.

Originator: Center Ray "Parson" Graves captained the Tennessee Volunteers, where he teamed on the line with future Eagles Bob Sufferidge and Burr West. He played for Philadelphia in 1942 and 1943, and then went into the service. Graves later had a Hall of Fame coaching career at Florida, where he mentored Steve Spurrier.

Longest Tenure: Eight years, Vic Lindskog and Dave Lloyd.

Number Changes: Ray Graves wore 51 in 1946; Todd Bell wore 49 in 1989; DeShawn Fogle also wore 54 in 1997.

Just Visiting: Todd Bell (see 49 top); Vaughan Johnson was a tough linebacker for the Saints for eight years.

Highs: Vic Lindskog was an underappreciated center who did not reach the NFL till he was 29 years old and did not achieve All-Pro recognition till he was 37. Dave Lloyd was defensive MVP in 1963 and an able middle linebacker, primarily in the dark days of Joe Kuharich; Ray Phillips was the special teams MVP in 1981.

Lows: Villanova's Kevin Reilly was never more than a special teams performer as an Eagle. After his brief playing career, he had his left shoulder and collarbone removed as well as his left arm amputated due to cancer. He still does Eagle pregames on radio.

Wayne Robinson

The Eagles are one of those teams, like the Bears and the Raiders, who thrive on having a nasty reputation. In the 1950s, the Birds' defensive front seven took on the image of the "Suicide Seven," even posing for a ridiculous picture showing them shirtless with black eye patches, shoulder pads, helmets and pistols. The Suicide Seven were extremely tough against the run and included ends Norm Willey and Tom Scott, tackles Mike Jarmoluk and Jess Richardson, middle guard Bucko Kilroy and linebackers Chuck Bednarik and Wayne Robinson.

In 1952, Robinson, the "Big Swede," was an eighth-round pick out of Minnesota, where he had pushed All-American center Clay Tonnemaker to defense. For the Eagles, Robinson stuck mostly to linebacker himself, although he played center on occasion. He teamed with Chuck Bednarik to give the Eagles the best pair of outside linebackers in the league. Wayne was named All-Pro in 1955 and to the Pro Bowl for the 1954 and 1955 seasons. Bednarik was named All-Pro in each of Robinson's five years in the NFL and to the Pro Bowl in four of them. As with all the members of the Suicide Seven, Bednarik and Robinson were rough customers. Colt Hall of Famer Artie Donovan claimed that Wayne hit even harder than Bednarik. Robinson's specialty was "clotheslining" unsuspecting receivers trying to come over the middle of the field. In 1955, the year Robinson received both All-Pro and Pro Bowl recognition, *Life* magazine came out in its October 24th issue with a photo essay called "Savagery on Sundays" that decried the prevalence of violence in the NFL. In the piece, Robinson was described as punching and kicking Cleveland players, and the alleged crimes were depicted in inconclusive photos. Teammate Bucko Kilroy was described as the "toughest" and "orneriest" of the roughnecks in the league. The pictures appear to show him kneeing tackled Giant quarterback Arnold Galifa in the back in a game in 1953. The text declares that the Giants got Bucko back by wrecking his knee on opening day 1955. By October 28th, Robinson and Kilroy filed a $250,000 libel suit.

For over 60 years now, Bucko Kilroy has worked in the NFL as a player, coach, scout, scouting director, general manager and consultant for the Eagles, Redskins, Cowboys and Patriots. He is one of a kind. Kilroy came into the league as a free agent out of Temple University in 1943 and stuck around for 13 years playing guard and tackle on both sides of the ball and receiving All-Pro recognition seven times as well as going to three Pro Bowls. He lived by the simple credo, "Love your god, respect your elders and fear no son of a bitch that walks," and he played the game fiercely and fearlessly. He was very effective swinging his forearms and elbows freely at opponents, and according to the *Life* article, recommended kicking rather than using your hands because it's too easy to break your hands. Once he was ejected from an exhibition game against the Bears in the 1940s. Rugged Ray Bray deliberately hit Bucko in the nose with his facemask and knocked him down in that game, so Bucko kicked Bray in the groin. Bert Bell fined Kilroy $150 for that, but when Kilroy's wife

Eagle roughneck Bucko Kilroy of the team's Suicide Seven defensive wall tries to break free from two of his sons in 1954.

Dorothy complained, Bert offered to give her the money back at the end of the year if Bucko stayed out of trouble that season. Bucko did, and Bell gave Dorothy the money back.

The libel case did not come to trial until two and a half years later in April 1958. In the meantime, Robinson left the Eagles to become an assistant coach for Winnipeg in the CFL in 1957. The following year, he was named head coach of the British Columbia Lions at the age of 28. Kilroy rehabilitated his injured knee and suited up for the 1955 finale and then retired to become a coach and scout for the Eagles. The trial was a "home game" held in Philadelphia and lasted eight days. Supporting testimony was given that Kilroy was once a choirboy and that Robinson had served as a Big Brother. The defense pointed out that the photos of Robinson could be construed either way and that *Life*'s own reporters realized this beforehand. They also pointed out that Kilroy's knee injury occurred when teammate Frank Wydo fell on Bucko in a pileup, not from the Giants running a "bootsie" play to gang up on Kilroy, as the magazine stated. Because of the story's inaccuracies and because this type of no-holds-barred behavior was the norm at the time, Robinson and Kilroy were exonerated and awarded $11,600 apiece.

There is no denying, though, that the 1950s decade was an especially violent period in pro football. The barely regulated scrum along the line was filled with slugging, kicking and, in a time before facemasks, lots of dental work and broken noses. With ball carriers able to get up and run again after being knocked down, pileups were inevitable and were brutal events with lots of biting, grabbing, squeezing, punching, kneeing and kicking. Players like Ed Sprinkle, Ed Meadows and John Henry Johnson were notorious for their vicious, sadistic play. Undersized linebacker Hardy Brown of the 49ers would launch himself through the air at ball carriers, trying to tackle them by hitting them in the face with his shoulder. Hall of Fame cornerback Night Train Lane preferred the "necktie" tackle in which he knocked down receivers by their necks.

The Eagles fit right into this style. Former Eagle Dick Bielski told Peter Golenbock for his Dallas history, *Cowboys Have Always Been My Heroes,* "Bucko was the sort of guy who would take a swing at you in practice and knock you out cold. He was a nasty human being. We had a few of them. Wayne Robinson was that way, Tom Scott, Norm Willey and damn near the whole Eagle defense. They were nasty, belligerent. They didn't win many games, but you damn sure didn't like a victory over us." So Bucko and the Big Swede weren't really a choirboy and Big Brother on the field after all.

Almost every year from 1950 to 1960, there is at least one fight described in newspaper game accounts of Eagle contests. In the journalistic style of the day, much of the rough play is papered over with vague and brief comment that "passions ran high," but ejections are generally noted. Here's a flavor:

December 10, 1950 — Jack Ferrante is tossed out of a Giants game for fighting.

November 17, 1952 — Kilroy kicks the Cardinals' Charley Trippi and is penalized. After the game, Trippi and a teammate respond by beating Bucko with their helmets.

September 27, 1953 — Toy Ledbetter has his cheek crushed by 49er Hardy Brown and a fight between Eagles Bobby Walston and Al Pollard and 49er Charley Powell escalates into a fourth-quarter free-for-all in which fans and police rush onto the field. Walston and Powell are ejected.

November 9, 1953 — Norm Willey and Giant John Rapacz are ejected for fighting in the game in which Arnold Galifa is injured. Several other fistfights are reported, and Eagle fans pelt the Giants with snowballs.

Ocotber 10, 1954 — "Feelings ran high" in a heavily penalized Steeler game.

November 22, 1954 — Kilroy and Lou Groza have to be separated at the end of an unruly game against Cleveland, noted for flying fists and elbows.

October 1, 1955 — Bobby Walston is ejected for pummeling Redskin Dick Alban on the sidelines.

October 9, 1955 — Mike Jarmoluk and the Browns' Carlton Massey are ejected for a fistfight.

October 30, 1955 — Bednarik and Steelers Leon Campbell and Bob Gaona are ejected for brawling.

November 4, 1956 — Bednarik gets into it with Lindon Crow and Ollie Matson of the Cardinals and both benches empty.

November 18, 1955 — Bednarik and Chuck Noll (yes, that Chuck Noll) have a postgame battle.

December 2, 1956 — Quarterback Bobby Thomason has his nose broken in a rough contest against the Browns.

December 15, 1956 — Don King (no, not that Don King) and Giant Dick Yelvington have a fistfight.

September 22, 1957 — In an exhibition game, Tom Scott punches a 49er and is ejected. Billy Ray Barnes and 49er Val Joe Walker fight, and the Eagle players pour onto the field.

October 13, 1957 — Both benches empty during a donnybrook in the fourth quarter. Eagles Frank Wydo, Bob Gaona, Billy Barnes and Menil Mavraidies and Browns Walt Michaels, Bill Quinlan and Paul Wiggin are all ejected.

November 17, 1957 — A brutally hard-hitting game against the Giants with many injured players on both sides.

December 14, 1957 — Abe Gibron fights Wayne Bock of the Cardinals and both are ejected; Buck Lansford slugs it out with the Cardinals' Bob Konovsky and both are ejected.

November 15, 1959 — Bobby Walston and Darrell Aschbacker fight with the Cardinals' Carl Brettschneider over who has the most German-sounding name and all are ejected.

August 21, 1960 — In an exhibition game against the 49ers, a fight between Fred "the Hammer" Williamson and Maxie Baughan leads to an 80-player rumble. Two plays after order is restored, Billy Barnes is ejected for fighting. Later still, Jerry Wilson is tossed for the same reason.

December 4, 1960 — After the game, former Lion teammates Stan Campbell and Jimmy Hill, now of the Cardinals, fight over comments that Hill made during the game.

The game has been cleaned up a bit since then, but the rough stuff is in the blood of Eagle fans who wistfully recall the Bounty Bowl and the Body Bag Game. No one is more popular in Philadelphia than the big hitter, whether he is Bill Bergey or Wes Hopkins or Andre Waters or Seth Joyner or Jeremiah Trotter or Brian Dawkins or Michael Lewis. Following in the footsteps of Bednarik, Robinson, Kilroy, Willey, Scott, Richardson and Jarmoluk, they are our most esteemed heroes. World without end, amen.

53

The Eagle Defense

Alex Wojciechowicz
C 1946-50

Alex Wojciechowicz

"Wojie" spent one season in the NFL for each letter in his last name, and that's a long career — 13 years. Only Mel Hein had a longer career among contemporary linemen. Yet Alex's greatest fame came in college when he was the center on a Fordham Rams team that went 12-1-3 during 1936-37 with eight shutouts. In 1936, the Rams finished third in the nation, and in 1937, they did not allow a touchdown all season. Their line was called the Seven Blocks of Granite, although they were the second Fordham team with that moniker; it was originally applied to the 1929 team. Today that line is most remembered for an injury-prone guard named Vince Lombardi, who later went into coaching at Saint Cecilia's High School and beyond. Wojie was the leader of the line, however, and finished fourth in the Heisman Trophy balloting in 1937.

The Lions made Wojie their first draft pick in 1938, and he immediately moved into the lineup as the center on offense and a linebacker on defense. The Detroit team he joined had finished 7-4 in 1937, and repeated that record in Alex's rookie year, but started slipping from there. Over the next five years, the Lions went 6-5, 5-5-1, 4-6-1, 0-11 and 3-6-1 before experiencing two winning seasons behind tailback Frank Sinkwich in 1944 and 1945. Wojie injured his shoulder making a tackle in his first season and suffered for three years before having surgery to remove 18 bone fragments and a blood clot from his shoulder. That bad shoulder kept him out of the Army, but not out of the NFL. He received some second-team All-Pro recognition in 1939 and also in 1944 when he intercepted a career-high seven passes. However, Alex, Green Bay's Charley Brock and Pittsburgh's Chuck Cherundolo always were listed just behind future Hall of Famers Mel Hein of the Giants and Bulldog Turner of the Bears in the voting for the league's All-Pro center. Wojie was noted for his wide stance and claimed to be the first center to long-snap the ball on punts with both hands on the front of the ball. On defense, he was a solid tackling linebacker with good pass coverage range.

In 1946, the Lions were en route to a 1-10 record when the 31-year-old Wojie went to the Lion ownership and said that his refrigeration business in New Jersey was suffering and costing him money, so he needed to leave. The Lions waived the veteran, and Alex next got a call from Greasy Neale in Philadelphia, who claimed his rights. Wojie resisted at first, but Neale told him he would only have to show up for games, so he joined the Eagles. In Philadelphia, Wojie played linebacker almost exclusively with Vic Lindskog at center and got to contribute to the Eagles' glory years of the late 1940s.

Greasy Neale had the first NFL team to adopt the Bears' Spread T Formation, and Greasy developed the best defense to counteract the way the T was played in the 1940s. Greasy believed that the best way to stop the pass was at the line of scrimmage — knock down the receivers and get to the passer before he releases the ball. He once commented, "You've got to put the pressure on those passers. You start letting them pinpoint and they destroy the spirit of your defensive line." His alignment has been described alternately as a 7-4, 7-2-2, 5-4-2 and 5-2-4. Along the front line it featured two ends, two tackles and a middle guard. In between the end and the tackle on each side was a linebacker (Wojie on one side and Joe Muha on the other). The new four-man defensive backfield consisted of two defensive halfbacks out on the wings a few yards back and two safeties deep in the middle. The responsibility of the five linemen was to stop the run and rush the passer; the linebackers were lined up over the two offensive ends and were charged with chucking those ends so they could not get into the secondary quickly or easily.

For his part, Wojie was described by one observer as "one thousand elbows without a plan," and his chucking technique was described by teammate Allie Sherman as involving "hands and feet and arms and maybe even fingernails, plus some conversation." Wojie complained to Myron Cope in 1969 that "You see these fast receivers coming off the line without even being touched. Greasy Neale would have hit the ceiling if we were not on top of them and slugging away at them while they were going out." What would he think of the freedom afforded today's receivers? With Alex harassing receivers and blitzing the passer, Neale's Eagle defense ruled the league for five years until the Browns arrived in 1950. Paul Brown showed how to put pressure on the linebackers by sending backs into the flat and splitting receivers out away from the interior line and sending them on sideline and comeback routes. Without a middle linebacker, the defense also could be susceptible to heavy rushes up the gut. The Giants' coach followed on Neale's Eagle Defense with his own Umbrella Defense to counter the Browns in 1950. The Umbrella evolved into the modern 4-3 with athletic linebackers having the varied responsibilities of stopping the run, chucking the tight end, blitzing the passer and dropping into pass coverage.

Wojie retired after the 1950 season at the age of 35 to enter the real estate business, although he did co-coach Newark in the Atlantic Coast Football League with his old Eagle roommate Steve Van Buren for three years. Alex was elected to the College Football Hall of Fame in 1955 and the Pro Football Hall of Fame in 1968 when Neale presented him for induction. Inspired by the desperate straits of his former Eagle teammate Tommy Thompson, Wojie helped form the NFL Players Alumni Association, an organization set up to help destitute retired players, in 1968. He died in 1992.

54
2002 Playoffs

Jeremiah Trotter
LB 1998-01, 2004

WHO'S WORN THE NUMBER:

Gerry Huth (G) 1959, Bill Lapham (C) 1960, **Jim Ringo** (C) 1964-67, Gene Ceppetelli (C) 1968-69, Calvin Hunt (C) 1970, Chuck Allen (LB) 1972, Tom Roussel (LB) 1973, Jim Opperman (LB) 1975, Drew Mahalic (LB) 1976-78, Zack Valentine (LB) 1982-83, Jon Kimmel (LB) 1985, Alonzo Johnson (LB) 1986-87, Kelly Kirchbaum (LB) 1987r, Britt Hager (LB) 1989-94, Kurt Gouveia (LB) 1995, Terry Crews (LB) 1996, DeShawn Fogle (LB) 1997, Jeff Herrod (LB) 1997, *Jeremiah Trotter* (LB) 1998-01 and 2004, Nate Wayne (LB) 2003.

Originator: Guard Gerry Huth was obtained from the Giants for Tom Scott in 1959. He went to Minnesota in the expansion draft after the 1960 title.

Longest Tenure: Six years, Britt Hager.

Number Changes: Gerry Huth wore 65 in 1960; DeShawn Fogle also wore 52 in 1997.

Just Visiting: Jim Ringo was a Hall of Fame center for the Packers for over a decade; Chuck Allen spent nine years in San Diego and Kurt Gouveia spent nine years in Washington, both as linebackers.

Highs: Jim Ringo was still a smart and quick player, ending his career in Philadelphia; long-haired, undersized Britt Hager was the special teams MVP in 1990.

Lows: The Eagles spent a second-round pick on Alonzo Johnson, a linebacker with a history of drug use, Buddy Ryan asserted, because "We believe in giving everybody a chance. This is America, not Russia." Johnson was back in drug rehab less than two years later.

Jeremiah Trotter

Before the 2000 season, Eagles defensive coordinator Jim Johnson told the *Inquirer*, "We have to get better against the run. We were 13th in the league with a 3.9 yards per run average last year, but we have to get that down to 3.5 if we're going to be a championship team." They have not closed that gap fully nor won a championship yet, but the Bird defense has been the toughest against the run when Jeremiah Trotter was in the middle.

Trotter is a 260-pound load out of Texas who is famous for his axe-swinging celebration after a big hit. As an outside linebacker at Stephen F. Austin State College, he was being compared by scouts to Lawrence Taylor before he tore his anterior cruciate ligament as a sophomore. He returned for his junior season and then chose to go into the draft, where the Eagles grabbed him in the third round. He had a rough transition to the pro game, and coach Ray Rhodes even brought in old Giant linebacker Harry Carson to talk to Trotter and give him some tips. The new Andy Reid coaching regime did not know what to expect from Jeremiah in 1999, so they selected middle linebacker Barry Gardner in the second round that year. Trotter beat out Gardner for the starting post and led the team with 202 tackles in 2000. It was the first of three years that he led the Eagles in tackles, and he was named to the Pro Bowl in 2000 and 2001.

Trotter quickly became a fan favorite for his thunderous hits, aggressiveness and spirited leadership on the field. While he could be fooled, particularly on cutbacks and in pass defense, he was a very solid performer for Jim Johnson's attacking defense. The Eagles attempted to tie up Jeremiah with a five-year, $20 million contract extension during the 2001 season. Trotter considered the offer insulting because he wanted to be paid in the Ray Lewis range. In February 2002, the Eagles tagged Trotter as their franchise player, guaranteeing him a one-year, $5.15 million contract, but Jeremiah was furious and would neither sign nor negotiate. As the draft approached, Reid wanted certainty, so he surprised everyone by rescinding the franchise tag in April. Trotter was infuriated further because the free agent market was essentially finished by that time with only the Texans, Packers and Redskins still possibly interested. Jeremiah signed with the division rival Redskins for a seven-year, $35.5 million contract. However, the details of the contract made the last two years of the deal void and reduced it to a five-year, $20 million deal very similar to what the Eagles had offered six months before. The Skins' signing bonus was $7 million as opposed to $5 million, but $6 million of that was deferred to the second year.

To counter the loss, the Birds signed 300-pound, fat, old, slow Levon Kirkland to team with Barry Gardner in the middle. This tandem worked well enough in the regular season as the Eagles went 12-4 and won home field advantage throughout the playoffs despite losing Donovan McNabb to a broken ankle for the last six games of the year. Meanwhile, Trotter tore knee ligaments late in the season and underwent surgery. Reid called him in the hospital and began to repair the strained relationship between the two.

After the bye week, the Eagles took on the Atlanta Falcons in the divisional round of the playoffs. The young Falcons had just become the first team ever to beat the

Packers in Green Bay in the postseason. Donovan McNabb was playing in his first game since the injury, and he played adequately, but the game was won by the defense that hounded Atlanta quarterback Michael Vick. The first score of the game came on a 39-yard interception return by Bobby Taylor, and the Eagles never trailed. They took a 13-6 lead into halftime, and scored the clinching touchdown on a fourth and one gamble when McNabb faked to Duce Staley, then rolled out and found James Thrash for a 35-yard touchdown and the 20-6 win.

This brought Eagle fans just what they were hoping for — a cold-weather show-down with Tampa in the last football game to be played at Veterans Stadium. Not only were the Bucs historically 1-21 in games played at temperatures below 40 degrees, but the Eagles had beaten them handily in the last two postseasons and in the last two regular seasons. Super Bowl, here we come. It got even better when Brian Mitchell returned the opening kickoff 70 yards and Duce Staley followed that with a 20-yard touchdown gallop. Tampa fought back, though, with a field goal and then launched a 96-yard touchdown drive highlighted by Joe Jurevicious catching a little crossing pattern across the middle in front of Barry Gardner and taking off for a 71-yard gain to the Eagles' 5. Eagle fans still wonder whether Trotter would have disrupted that play. Two plays later, Mike Alstott bulled over to give the Bucs a 10-7 first-quarter lead. The Eagles tied the game in the second quarter only to have Brad Johnson hit Keyshawn Johnson with a nine-yard TD in the closing minutes of the first half to go up 17-10.

Philadelphia did not run the ball much, and McNabb struggled throughout the game, completing 26 of 49 passes for 243 yards. He was sacked twice and fumbled twice. Still, they were only down 20-10 with a first and goal at the Bucs' 10 with 3:27 left when McNabb was picked off by Ronde Barber, who went 92 yards the other way for the clinching touchdown in the crushing 27-10 defeat. The Eagles did not blitz much and were unable to get any pressure on Buc QB Johnson all day. Tampa coach Jon Gruden devised a game plan for which Andy Reid had no answer, and Philadelphia lost its second consecutive conference championship.

After a third consecutive conference championship loss, Eagle fans were heartened when Jeremiah Trotter signed a one-year deal at close to the veteran's minimum salary of $600,000 in June 2004. Trotter stayed low-key and upbeat as he started out again as a backup and special teams player. He even made the special teams hit of the year when he blindsided Giant punter Jeff Feagles and sent him flying. But after the Eagles' defense surrendered 252 yards rushing in the Steelers game at midseason, Trotter was inserted back in the starting lineup. The run defense immediately improved from averaging 130 yards per game to 105 for the rest of the season. Despite starting only seven games, Trotter was named to his third Pro Bowl, and the Eagles made their best postseason showing since he left in 2001, even though they still did not win the championship. They are clearly a better team with Trotter in the middle.

Rookies

Maxie Baughan
LB 1960-65

Maxie Baughan

You never know which rookies will work out. In the 1960 draft, the Eagles selected Northeastern halfback Ron Burton with their first pick and Georgia Tech center/linebacker Maxie Baughan in the second round. Burton had a mediocre career in the AFL, while Maxie became a nine-time Pro Bowler and six-time All-Pro at outside linebacker. He was smart and tough, and a good case can be made that he belongs in the Pro Football Hall of Fame. He set a school record for tackles as an undergraduate and is already in the College Football Hall of Fame.

Despite reporting late to training camp after playing in the 1960 College All-Star Game, Maxie started at outside linebacker right from the opening game and had an immediate impact on the team. He won his first game ball in the fourth game of the year against the Lions when he made 15 tackles, 10 unassisted. Later, in the second of two back-to-back wins against the Giants, Baughan came up with a key interception that led to the Eagles' first touchdown as they overcame a 17-0 deficit. He had another interception in the final game against the Redskins, along with 12 unassisted tackles, and was named to the Pro Bowl after his rookie season.

Baughan did not realize it at the time, but 1960 would be the only championship team for whom he would ever play. The team was still a contender in 1961, but everything came apart the next year and would not come together again for more than a decade. Although the team was in serious decline over the next several years, Baughan was named to the Pro Bowl every year as an Eagle except in 1962 when he struggled with a bad ankle. The defensive captain was quick, durable and able to play all three linebacker positions. His biggest strengths were his intelligence at reading defensive keys and his tenacious pursuit on every play. He was named the team's defensive MVP in 1963, even though he played with a broken hand, and did not miss a game for Philadelphia until 1965.

By 1966, Maxie was tired of losing and unhappy with Joe Kuharich and defensive coach Dick Evans, particularly over their use of the blitz. He asked to be traded to the expansion Falcons, closer to his home. Kuharich sent him off to the Rams for Frank Molden, Fred Brown and a third-round draft choice. It was a steal for the Rams, and George Allen later called it the best trade he ever made. In Los Angeles, Baughan became the signal caller for George Allen's complex defense of over 250 plays and went to four more Pro Bowls while enduring ankle and knee surgeries. After Allen moved on to Washington, he traded for Maxie once again, but the battered linebacker retired and became a coach under Allen in 1971. He played in one more game as a Redskin in 1974, but spent roughly the next 25 years coaching in both the pros and in college.

Maxie was not the only Eagle to make a positive impression as a rookie. Here's the Eagles' All-Rookie team:

OFFENSE

Wide Receiver — Don Looney (1940) All-Pro, league-leading 58 catches and 707 yards; Dick Humbert (1941) All-Pro, second in league with 29 catches; Pete Pihos (1947) All-Pro, 23 catches and seven TDs; Bobby Walston (1951) All-Pro and Rookie of the Year, 31 catches for eight TDs and 94 total points.

Tight End — Charlie Young (1973) All-Pro, 55 catches for six TDs; Keith Jackson (1988) All-Pro and Rookie of the Year, 81 catches and six TDs.

Tackle — Lum Snyder (1952) All-Pro; Jim Weatherall (1955) Pro Bowl; Bob Brown (1964) All-Pro.

Guard — Bob Suffridge (1941) All-Pro; Bucko Kilroy (1943), tough right from the start; Bruno Banducci (1944) made All-Pro in his second season.

Center — Guy Morriss (1973) became a starter in the second half of the season.

Quarterback — Davey O'Brien (1939) was actually a tailback, but he completed 49.3 percent of his passes for six TDs and his 1,324 yards led the league. Passer rating was 45.3. Donovan McNabb (1999) completed 49.2 percent of his passes for 948 yards and eight TDs. Passer rating was 60.1.

Halfback — Steve Van Buren (1944) All-Pro, gained 444 yards on 5.6 yards per carry; also scored TDs on punt and kickoff returns. Billy Ray Barnes (1957) gained 529 yards on 3.7 yards per carry; Keith Byars (1986) gained 577 yards on 3.3 yards per carry; Correll Buckhalter (2001) gained 586 yards on 4.5 yards per carry.

Fullback – Joe Muha (1946) gained only 41 yards rushing but was a devastating lead blocker; Clarence Peaks (1957) gained 495 yards on 4.0 yards per carry; Mike Hogan (1976) gained 561 yards on 4.6 yards per carry.

DEFENSE

Defensive End — Norm Willey (1950) became a starter; Reggie White (1986) All-Pro, 18 sacks.

Defensive Tackle — Jess Richardson (1953) became a starter in the second half of the season; Carl Hairston (1976) started in the second half of the season; Jerome Brown (1987) four sacks and 50 tackles; Corey Simon (2000), 9.5 sacks and 74 tackles.

Linebacker — Chuck Bednarik (1949) started on a defending championship team; Bob Pelegrini (1956) starter; Maxie Baughan (1960) Pro Bowl; Jerry Robinson (1979) showed promise, but didn't become a starter till his second season.

Cornerback — Tom Brookshier (1953), eight interceptions; Herman Edwards (1977), six interceptions; Roynell Young (1980), four interceptions for a Super Bowl team; Eric Allen (1988), five interceptions.

Safety — Bibbles Bawel (1952), eight interceptions; Jerry Norton (1954), five interceptions; Randy Logan (1973), five interceptions and voted the team's defensive MVP.

Kicker — Paul McFadden (1984), 116 points on 30 of 37 field goals.

Punter — Mike Horan (1984), 42.2 average.

56
The Hall of Fame

Bill Hewitt
E 1936-39

Originator: Hall of Fame end Bill Hewitt.

Longest Tenure: Eight years, Byron Evans.

Number Changes: Bill Hewitt wore 82 in 1943; Fred Whittingham wore 53 in 1971.

Just Visiting: Small and fast Darrin Smith was more effective in Dallas' defense; Shawn Barber stopped in Philadelphia for one season between Washington and Kansas City.

Highs: Jerry Robinson was a play-making linebacker for Dick Vermeil; Byron Evans was the under-appreciated middle linebacker for the fierce 46 Defense built by Buddy Ryan; 1998 special teams MVP Mike Caldwell capably filled a role in Jim Johnson's defensive scheme.

Lows: Middle linebacker Fred Whittingham played for five teams in seven years in the league, including two tours in Philadelphia. In New Orleans, he decked 57-year-old Sid Gillman during a Saints-Chargers scrimmage in 1968. He later coached for the Raiders.

Bill Hewitt

Bareheaded Bill "Stinky" Hewitt had a flair for making the big play. In 1933, when he was with the Bears, Chicago trailed Green Bay 7-0 with under five minutes to play and the Packers lining up for a field goal. Hewitt blocked the field goal, and the Bears took over. On a third-down end around option play, Stinky threw a 56-yard touchdown pass to Luke Johnsos to tie the score. Green Bay threw three incompletions and dropped back to punt with two minutes to go. Hewitt blocked the punt, scooped it up at the five and ran it in for the winning score in an unbelievable finish.

In 1932, Bears owner George Halas signed Hewitt out of the University of Michigan where he was a teammate of Al Wistert's older brother Francis. In the middle of the Depression, the $100 per game for which Hewitt signed was pretty good money, and he earned it. He was an All-Pro in his second year and capped that season by catching a pass in the last minute of the title game against the Giants and cleverly lateraling the ball to Bill Karr, who carried it the last 19 yards for the game-winning score. Hewitt was named All-Pro again in 1934 and 1936. A two-way star on both sides of the ball, he was already being called an all-time great in 1937. Hewitt was a hard tackler with long, powerful arms who was once described as "three parts gorilla and one part Englishman." He was a tough guy who played without a helmet and who was known to reset his own broken fingers on the sideline. Above all, he was noted for his quickness; some called him the "Offsides Kid" for his ability to get a running start and time the snap of the ball to charge into the opposing backfield. Others jokingly referred to him as "those three guys Halas uses at left end."

Bill was obsessed with not being a tramp athlete; he once exclaimed that the pro football player is the "peon of big league sports." After five years in Chicago, he was earning $130 a game and was offered a good job with the railroad, so he retired. Halas traded him to the Eagles for a number one draft pick, and Bill came out of retirement for Bert Bell's offer of $200 per game. Bell also got him a $24 a week job as a mechanic. Hewitt captained the Birds and made All-Pro again in 1937 and 1938, the first player to be named All-Pro for two different teams. Despite earning $250 a game in 1939, Bill again announced his retirement because "I found myself flinching from physical contact, wincing at shocks I wouldn't have felt a few years earlier…I could remember when I laughed at the veterans lined up in the trainer's room after a game. Now I was first in line, and when I'd had one rubdown, I would go to the tail of the queue and start all over." In his final home game on Thanksgiving, Hewitt gave the fans one more thrill against Pittsburgh by catching a Davey O'Brien pass in the final minute and lateraling the ball to a trailing Jay Arnold, who completed the 66-yard, game-winning touchdown play.

Facing a wartime manpower shortage in 1943, Bert Bell lured Hewitt out of retirement for $400 a game to play for the Steagles. He was forced by league rules to wear a helmet for the first time and also wore a new number — 82. Bill appeared in six games and then quit in November without saying why. Financially, it was his most

Hall of Famer Bill Hewitt is flanked by tackle Jim MacMurdo on the left and coach Bert Bell on the right. Hewitt was the last Eagle to play without a helmet and was sometimes called the "Bareheaded Berserker." The way he and MacMurdo are smiling makes you wonder whether they spiked the water bucket.

lucrative season, but he was nowhere near the same player he had been. He worked for an oil firm and then a milk company and was trying to obtain his own car dealership when he was killed in a winter auto accident on Bethlehem Pike in 1947. He ended up with 51 catches as a Bear and 51 as an Eagle and had his number 56 retired by Chicago in 1949.

Bill Hewitt is one of 15 former Eagles who have been inducted into the Pro Football Hall of Fame in Canton, Ohio. With 15 inductees, the Eagles are tied with the Cardinals for 10th in number of Hall of Famers. Of those 15, eight are considered primarily Eagles, and in this category, the Birds are tied for 13th with the Dolphins. Bert Bell was a charter member, inducted posthumously in 1963, while Bob Brown was the most recent inductee in 2004. These 15 inductees chose a wide range of people to present them for induction:

YEAR	INDUCTEE	PRESENTER
1963	Bert Bell*	David McDonald, President of the Steelworkers' Union
1965	Steve Van Buren	Clarke Hinkle, NFL all-time rush leader before Steve
1967	Chuck Bednarik	Greasy Neale
1968	Alex Wojciechowicz	Greasy Neale
1969	Greasy Neale	Chuck Bednarik
1970	Pete Pihos	Howard Brown, Indiana teammate
1971	Bill Hewitt*	Upton Bell, Bert's son
1971	Norm Van Brocklin	Rankin Smith, Atlanta Falcons owner
1972	Ollie Matson	Joe Kuharich
1981	Jim Ringo	Willard "Whiz" Rinehart, high school coach
1983	Sonny Jurgensen	Edward Bennett Williams
1988	Mike Ditka	Ed O'Bradovich, Bear teammate
1998	Tommy McDonald	Ray Diddinger, sportswriter
2003	James Lofton	His son David
2004	Bob Brown	His son Robert

*Posthumous inductees Bert Bell and Bill Hewitt were represented by Art Rooney and daughter Mary Ellen Cocozza, respectively.

Bell, Bednarik, Van Buren, McDonald and Pihos also have been selected for the new, yet to be built, Philadelphia Sports Hall of Fame.

Several Eagles are also members of the College Football Hall of Fame, including: centers Maxie Baughan, Chuck Bednarik, Bob Pellegrini, Dave Rimington and Alex Wojciechowicz; guards Bob Brown, Augie Lio, John Michels and Bob Sufferidge; ends Mike Ditka, Eggs Manske, Pete Pihos and Tom Scott; quarterbacks Roman Gabriel, Ralph Guglielmi, Jim McMahon, Davey O'Brien, Ken O'Brien, John Rauch and Norm Van Brocklin; running backs Howard Cassady, Leroy Keyes, Ollie Matson, Tommy McDonald, Wilbert Montgomery, Clyde Scott, George Taliaferro and Herschel Walker; defenders Rich Glover, Jerry Robinson and Reggie White; and coaches Sid Gillman, Ray Graves, Greasy Neale, Buck Shaw and Gil Steinke.

Hewitt is also one of a number of Eagles who have been picked for a variety of all-time teams selected by the NFL. For the league's 50th anniversary in 1969, a 16-man all-time team was named, and Chuck Bednarik was the center. For the 75th anniversary all-time team, Steve Van Buren, Reggie White and Mike Ditka were chosen. The 75th anniversary all-time two-way team included Bill Hewitt, Bednarik, Van Buren and Pete Pihos. Each all-decade team includes at least one Eagle as well: 1930s — Hewitt; 1940s — Jack Ferrante, Pete Pihos, Vic Sears, Al Wistert, Bucko Kilroy, Alex Wojciechowicz and Steve Van Buren; 1950s — Chuck Bednarik; 1960s, Bob Brown, Jim Ringo and Sonny Jurgensen; 1970s — Harold Carmichael; 1980s — Reggie White and Sean Landeta; and 1990s — White, Landeta and Cris Carter.

Undrafted
Free Agents

Bill Cowher
LB 1983-84

WHO'S WORN THE NUMBER:

Ernie Calloway (DT) 1969, James Reed (LB) 1977, Mike Osborn (LB) 1978, Mike Curcio (LB) 1981-82, Bill Cowher (LB) 1983-84, Tom Polley (LB) 1985, Scott Kowalkowski (LB) 1991-93, Marc Woodard (LB) 1994-96, James Darling (LB) 1997-00, Keith Adams (LB) 2002-04.

Originator: Spindly defensive tackle Ernie Calloway in 1969.

Longest Tenure: Four years, James Darling.

Number Changes: Ernie Calloway wore 77 from 1970 to 1972.

Just Visiting: None.

Highs: Linebacker Keith Adams has been a hard-working special teams player who earned a starting slot in Super Bowl XXXIX.

Lows: Tom Polley was Randall Cunningham's teammate at the University of Nevada, Las Vegas and was selected in the eighth round of the same draft as Randall. He only appeared in two games for Philly and two for Cleveland in the NFL before being rejected by the CFL due to a neck injury.

Bill Cowher

Bill Cowher is in good Philadelphia company. Like Hall of Fame coach John Madden who spent a season on injured reserve for the Eagles, and All-Pro Dolphin guard Bob Kuechenberg who was cut by the Birds as a rookie, Cowher did not make the team on his first try but became more famous elsewhere. However, like John Rauch, Bud Grant, Mike Ditka and Allie Sherman, he did play briefly for the Eagles before going on to more fame as the coach of a team in an NFL championship game.

Cowher was a lowly free agent out of North Carolina State, who was the last linebacker cut in 1979 by Dick Vermeil. The following year, he hooked on with Cleveland and became the captain of the Browns' special teams. He injured his knee and missed the entire 1981 season, but returned frothing at the mouth in 1982. The next season, the Eagles spent a ninth-round draft pick to reacquire Cowher for depth at inside linebacker. On the Eagles, Bill was called "Face" for his long jaw and intensity. He was not very quick or fast, but was a very physical player who was tough, hard-nosed and disciplined. He also had an attitude that was evidenced within weeks of his arrival in Philadelphia by his taunting of the All-Pro Lawrence Taylor in a game against the Giants. Bill got to play some at linebacker and was voted the MVP of the special teams in 1983. Named the special teams captain in 1984, he went down to a knee injury after four games and never played again. Marty Schottenheimer hired him to coach the Browns' special teams in 1985, promoted him to secondary coach in 1987 and brought him to Kansas City as defensive coordinator in 1989. Three years later, Bill was the head coach of his hometown Pittsburgh Steelers and was still there over a decade later.

Cowher was a young man in a hurry who went far for an undrafted free agent, but these players have to be highly motivated or they find a new line of work. While an all-time Eagles team of free agents might not beat the all-time Eagles team of draft treasures (see 86), they would surely beat the all-time draft bust team (see 77). This free agent team does not include Bill Cowher, Tommy Thompson or David Akers because they did not play first with the Eagles.

OFFENSE

Wide Receiver — Jack Ferrante (no college) 1941, 1944-50; Greg Lewis (Illinois) 2003-04.
Tight End — Chad Lewis (Brigham Young) 1997-04
Tackle — Bucko Kilroy (Temple) 1943-55; Piggy Barnes (Louisiana State) 1948-51.
Guard — Cliff Patton (Texas Christian) 1946-50; Duke Maronic (no college) 1944-50;
    Dick Hart (no college) 1967-71; Artis Hicks (Memphis State) 2002-04.
Center — Hank Fraley (Robert Morris) 2000-04; Bubba Miller (Tennessee) 1996-01.
Quarterback — Allie Sherman (Brooklyn) 1943-47.
Halfback — Dave Smukler (Temple) 1936-39; Vaughn Hebron (Indiana) 1993-95.
Fullback — Josh Parry (San Jose State) 2004.

DEFENSE

Defensive End — Greg Brown (Kansas State) 1981-86; Larry Cabrelli (Colgate) 1941-47.

Defensive Tackle — Ken Clarke (Syracuse) 1978-87; Hollis Thomas (Northern Illinois) 1996-04; Sam Rayburn (Tulsa) 2003-04.

Linebacker — Mike Reichenbach (East Stroudsburg) 1984-89; Harold Wells (Purdue) 1965-68; Wayne Colman (Temple) 1968-69.

Cornerback — Herman Edwards (San Diego State) 1977-85; Jim Nettles (Wisconsin) 1965-68; Rod Hood (Auburn) 2003-04.

Safety — Andre Waters (Cheney) 1984-93; Joe Scarpati (North Carolina State) 1964-69, 1971; Bibbles Bawel (Evansville) 1952, 1955-56; Brenard Wilson (Vanderbilt) 1979-86.

Kicker — Mike Clark (Texas A&M) 1963.

Punter — Tommy Hutton (Tennessee) 1995-98.

Return Man — Wally Henry (UCLA) 1977-82.

Special Teams — Vince Papale (St. Joseph's) 1976-78.

Coach — Charley Gauer (Colgate) 1943-45.

Kamikazes

Ike Reese
LB 1998-04

Ike Reese

Partly because they understand the game so well and partly because they enjoy loud, splattering hits, Eagle fans have long appreciated the work of the kamikaze stars on the Birds' special teams. Ike Kelley was a backup linebacker in the mid-1960s, but he had his own following who called the kick coverage units Kelley's Killers for their ferocious pursuit. Under Dick Vermeil — who after all had been the first special teams coach in the NFL with the Rams in 1969 — Vince Papale, Louie Giammona and Dennis Franks were celebrated for giving up their bodies to make crashing tackles on returns. Franks was voted the Eagles' first special teams MVP in 1978. In the 1980s, Bill Cowher and William Frizzell continued the tradition, and Frizzell was the first to win the special teams MVP award twice. He was followed in that distinction by Ken Rose and Otis Smith in the 1990s.

Under Ray Rhodes, though, the performance of special teams fell off drastically and hurt the team. The inability of Rhodes to fix the special teams problems was a leading indicator of his inability to fix any problem. Finally, with the whole team in disarray in 1998, John Harbaugh came aboard to turn around special teams. Harbaugh brought in the idea that special teams players are starters, too, and he got his players to buy into the concept as well. Seven years later he is still there, and one of the main reasons has been the enthusiastic play of special teams captain Ike Reese.

It is unusual for a special teams player to stay in one city for seven years as Reese has. Although he has never been named the team's special teams MVP, he was honored in 2004 when he was named to the Pro Bowl for his special teams play. Ike was not always so highly regarded. There were some doubts about his character after his involvement in a bar fight as a freshman at Michigan State, but after being given an ultimatum by MSU coach Nick Saban, he became more focused and turned his life around. As proof, he earned the unique honor of being named a team captain in both his junior and senior seasons and was the Spartans' MVP as a senior. Drafted in the fifth round, he was no sure thing to make the Eagles as a 24-year-old rookie in 1998, but fellow linebacker/special teams player Mike Caldwell took Reese under his wing. Ike had some tough times as a rookie when his overly aggressive play would cost the Eagles yardage in penalties, but he learned how to temper his intensity just enough to make a difference.

Reese is too small at 222 pounds to take on blockers as a regular starter, but he is smart, quick, energetic and so persistent in pursuit that he is valuable as the top fill-in at all three linebacker positions. The Eagles recognized his special contribution to the team's success in 2001 by signing Ike to a four-year, $3.2 million deal. He was not able to beat out Caldwell in 2001, Shawn Barber in 2002 or Nate Wayne in 2003 for a starting linebacking position, but did replace the injured Carlos Emmons capably in the 2003 playoffs. In 2004, fellow special teams player Keith Adams surpassed Ike in the rotation at linebacker and started at outside linebacker in the Super Bowl. Reese moved on and signed with Atlanta as a 31-year-old in 2005, but Ike will always hold a special place in the hearts of Eagle fans for his seven years of dedicated leadership on the easily neglected third unit of Eagle starters.

59
Chasing the Ring

Seth Joyner
LB 1986-93

WHO'S WORN THE NUMBER:

Joseph Wendlick (B) 1940, Mike Evans (C) 1968-73, Tom Ehlers (LB) 1975-77, Al Chesley (LB) 1979-82, Joel Williams (LB) 1983-85, *Seth Joyner* (LB) 1986-93, Carlos Bradley (LB) 1987r, Mike Mamula (DE) 1995-00, Derrick Burgess (DE) 2001-02, Tyreo Harrison (LB) 2002, Justin Ena (LB) 2003, Mike Labinjo (LB) 2004.

Originator: Oregon State halfback Joe Wendlick was obtained along with Ray George from the Lions for Dave Smukler in 1940. The next year, Wendlick went to Pittsburgh in the franchise exchange.

Longest Tenure: Eight years, Seth Joyner.

Number Changes: Tyreo Harrison wore 55 in 2003.

Just Visiting: Linebacker Joel Williams sandwiched his three Eagle years between two four-year stints in Atlanta.

Highs: Mike Evans was a decent center who replaced Hall of Famer Jim Ringo and in 1971 was offensive MVP.

Lows: The Eagles traded up to grab workout wonder Mike Mamula with the seventh overall pick in the 1995 draft. It almost paid off each time Mike almost reached the quarterback, but not quite.

Seth Joyner

After 11 years in the NFL without even getting to a Super Bowl, it was bittersweet for former All-Pro linebacker Seth Joyner to watch his former Eagle teammates Reggie White, Keith Jackson and Keith Byars meet in Super Bowl XXXI with White and Jackson winning it all as members of the Green Bay Packers. Joyner said of that experience, "I love all those guys like they're my brothers, so I was happy for them. I was also very envious."

Nobody embodied the dark side of Buddy Ryan's intimidating Eagle teams better than Seth Joyner. Seth was hard-working, competitive and intense, but was also a sullen, moody, mouthy, glowering warrior. He was not someone you could ignore on the field. Buddy drafted him in the eighth round of the 1986 draft and then released him in the team's final cuts. The team told him to stay close to the phone, however, and re-signed Joyner after they dropped Earnest Jackson two weeks later. By the second half of his rookie season, Seth replaced second-round pick Alonzo Johnson in the starting lineup, and that was where he would stay. He was mostly solid at first and played on both running and passing downs, but through film study and dedication he evolved into a playmaker on defense. By his third year, Buddy was calling him the best strongside linebacker in the league, and by his fifth year, Seth led the team in tackles. However, 1990 would be Ryan's last year as coach after the Eagles failed in the first round of the playoffs for the third year in a row.

Joyner did not take Ryan's firing well and publicly blamed his quarterback for lobbying for offensive coordinator Rich Kotite to be named coach. Seth had no respect for Kotite — or for the offense for that matter — and over the next few years he brutally criticized Richie's decisions, questioned his guts and called the coach a puppet. That 1991 season, though, was probably the best year the defense ever had, and Seth was undeniably a team leader. In a memorable Monday night game against the Oilers known as the "House of Pain" game, Joyner forced one fumble, recovered two, and had two sacks and innumerable explosive hits. For the season, Seth was named *Sports Illustrated*'s Player of the Year and the Eagles' defensive MVP. But when boisterous defensive tackle Jerome Brown died in an off-season car crash, Seth took it especially hard. He shaved Brown's number 99 in the back of his head and dedicated the 1992 season to him. Again he was team defensive MVP that year, but those acidic judgments of coaches and teammates began to wear on his team. Attempts to explain it away as "Seth being Seth" seemed less and less acceptable.

When his contract expired in 1994, the three-time All-Pro and Pro Bowl linebacker ran with teammate Clyde Simmons and Andre Waters to the Arizona Cardinals with their newly hired coach, Buddy Ryan. Ryan only spent two years in the desert, though, before being fired again. Joyner lasted one year beyond that and then was released in a salary cap move. This time, he followed Super Bowl champion Reggie White to Green Bay. Seth underwent arthroscopic knee surgery and missed the first five games, but started the last 10 games of the year. He was nowhere near the same player as he was in Philadelphia, but he finally made it to the Super Bowl. Of course, the heavily favored Packers lost to the Broncos, so Seth still did not have his ring. The Packers cut him in 1998, and he hooked on with the champion Broncos as a backup and special teams player. Joyner thought he could still start, but he was happy to get to another Super Bowl. This time, Seth got his ring. However, it wasn't All-Pro #59 Seth Joyner winning a Super Bowl, it was special teams blocker #99 Seth Joyner.

There are seven levels of ringdom in the NFL. The top level is winning a ring as a major contributor on the team you started with. No Eagles have reached this level since Bednarik, McDonald and Brookshier in 1960. Just below that, level two is for those who change teams in mid-career and win the ring with their second team, as Reggie White did in Green Bay. The third level is for players who hook on with another team as a starter near the end of their career, as Keith Jackson did in Green Bay or punter Max Runager did in San Francisco in 1984. A bit further down, level four is for players who win a ring early in their career, as inexperienced, rarely used backups like Sonny Jurgensen and Tim Brown did in 1960. After a steep slide, we arrive at level five for players who hook on as backups at the end of their career, like Seth Joyner in Denver. Similarly, Terry Hoage was on the roster of the 1991 Redskins and Britt Hager was on the same Bronco team as Joyner. As we drop off the side of the mountain and grab madly for a stray tree branch to save us before tumbling into the abyss, we experience level six. This level is for those who don't win a ring but at least get to a Super Bowl, like Keith Byars with the Patriots, like the 1980 and 2004 Eagle teams, and like 1980 veterans Guy Morriss and Tony Franklin who lost a second Super Bowl with New England. The seventh level is the abyss — no ring, not even close — an unfinished career.

Just think of all those Buddy Ryan-era stars who ended up on level seven: Eric Allen, Fred Barnett, Cris Carter, Randall Cunningham, Byron Evans, Wes Hopkins, Mike Pitts, Mike Quick, Clyde Simmons and Andre Waters. Not to mention ringless Eagles before or since: Bill Bradley, Bob Brown, Joe Carter, Irv Cross, Swede Hanson, Ben Hawkins, Jack Hinkle, Harold Jackson, Davey O'Brien, Tom Scott, Norm Willey, Tom Woodeshick and many more. While Seth must be glad he's not in that group, there is much to be said for winning a championship as a full-fledged member of a team. The team that Seth Joyner identified with was the Eagles, and in May of 2000, he and Keith Byars officially retired as Eagles. As Seth put it, "They were the most memorable years of my career."

What If?

Chuck Bednarik
C/LB 1949-62

Originator: Guard Bob Suffridge in 1941.

Longest Tenure: 14 years, Chuck Bednarik.

Number Changes: Bob Suffridge wore 75 in 1945.

Just Visiting: None.

Highs: Bob Suffridge was an All-Pro in the one season he played before the war. The Tennessee Volunteer was named to the Half-Century All-American Team in 1950 and to the College Football Hall of Fame.

Lows: Alvin Thacker, a 5-foot 10-inch guard from Charleston College, played in one NFL game in 1942.

Chuck Bednarik

Before the season finale against the Browns on December 13, 1959, the Eagles said farewell to retiring center Chuck Bednarik by presenting him with a color TV set and a check for $1,000. Philadelphia went on to lose to Cleveland 28-21 that afternoon to finish in a tie for second place in the East, their best finish in five years. Bednarik had been a star on both sides of the ball for 11 years and now, not surprisingly, was stepping aside at the age of 34.

Chuck Bednarik's parents were Slovak immigrants who worked in the steel mills in Bethlehem, Pennsylvania. As a kid he learned the game by playing with a homemade football made out an old nylon stocking stuffed with leaves. He starred on the gridiron at Bethlehem High and then entered the service as a waist gunner on a B-24 that flew 30 missions over Germany in World War II. When Chuck returned after the war, his high school coach contacted University of Pennsylvania coach George Munger, who got him into Penn on the GI Bill. On the football field, he was a man among boys as a Single Wing center on offense and a linebacker on defense. At Penn, he was a two-time All-American who intercepted 13 passes during his junior and senior seasons. One interception he returned for a touchdown and earned an unsportsmanlike conduct penalty for tossing the ball into the stands afterwards. As a senior, Chuck became the first lineman ever to win the Maxwell Award and finished third in the Heisman balloting in 1948.

The champion Eagles won the drawing for the bonus overall first pick in the 1949 draft and selected the hometown hero. Chuck was represented by Father Donnelly from Penn and rejected offers from the All-America Conference's Brooklyn Dodgers to sign with the Eagles for a $3,000 bonus and a salary that has been variously reported as being from $7000 to $10,000. He did not play in either of Philadelphia's first two games in 1949 and went to coach Greasy Neale to complain about playing time. Neale started to work him into a rotation with center Vic Lindskog and linebacker Alex Wojciechowicz, two skilled but aging veterans. Bednarik pushed past Wojie as starting outside linebacker in 1950 and would not miss a game there until the 1957 season finale. In those eight years, Chuck went to seven Pro Bowls and received All-Pro recognition every year. He had decent speed, solid pass coverage ability, great anticipation and was a deadly tackler. Early 1950s Eagles coach Jim Trimble described Chuck's play: "He has an almost superhuman diagnostic ability. He's at the right place at the right time…He's a great tackler, both on power plays and in the open field. He has loose, powerful arms and hands. He's at his best when they have a partial block on him and he reaches over and makes the tackle. He'll knock the head off an end when he catches the ball, and on a sweep, he knows when to close and turn the runner." Bednarik used a high-tackling style in which he would slam into the ball carrier's chest and wrap him tightly in his arms like a python while savagely wrestling him to the ground. Hall of Fame coach George Allen once said admiringly of Chuck, "If not actually dirty, Bednarik was mean."

An action photo of Concrete Charlie Bednarik stopping former Eagle fullback Merrill Douglas at the goal line in 1961. Other Eagles pictured include Don Burroughs (45), Bobby Freeman (41), Jimmy Carr (21), Maxie Baughan (55), Leo Sugar (84), Jess Richardson (72), Ed Khayat (73) and Will Renfro (66). The Cowboy quarterback is Eddie LeBaron (14).

Chuck was also very durable and kept in shape with daily four-hour workouts. In the off-season, he sold concrete, earning him the very apt nickname of Concrete Charlie. Due to injuries, he had played center on occasion and had offered to play both ways for Trimble in 1955, but was asked by the team to switch to offense full time in 1958 because the team had an abundance of linebackers, but a weak offensive line. Although Colt defensive tackle Artie Donovan said in his book *Fatso* that Bednarik, "couldn't block my grandmother," and teammate Tom Brookshier claimed that Chuck often held instead of blocked, he was an able center. It was just that he was so much better on defense where he instinctually could react to a play. After two seasons at center, Chuck announced his retirement and had his "Day" prior to the Browns' finale. If he had actually quit at that time, he would have had an 11-year career in which he went to seven Pro Bowls, received All-Pro recognition eight times and played for one championship team.

That wonderful career can best be judged in comparison to a number of other highly respected outside linebackers who roughly could be called Chuck's contemporaries. Chuck Howley of the Cowboys played for 15 years, received All-Pro notice six times and went to six Pro Bowls while playing on one champion team; Andy Russell of the Steelers played for 12 years, received All-Pro recognition six times and went to seven Pro Bowls while playing for two champion teams; Chris Hanburger of the Redskins played for 14 years, received All-Pro recognition eight times and went to nine Pro Bowls while never playing for a champion. For good measure, let's add middle linebacker Les Richter of the Rams who played for nine years, received All-Pro notice five times and went to eight Pro Bowls while never playing for a champion. One other thing these four stars have in common is that none of them is in the Hall of Fame. Or consider 49ers outside linebacker Dave Wilcox, the brother of John Wilcox from the 1960 Eagles, who played for 11 years, received All-Pro notice seven times and went to seven Pro Bowls while never playing for a champion. Wilcox is in the Hall of Fame, yet had to wait 26 years to be elected. But Chuck Bednarik was inducted into the Hall in his first year of eligibility. What happened?

1960 happened. Bednarik did not retire in 1959, but instead became the 60-minute man, wearing the number 60 on the 1960 championship team. Chuck did have a remarkable run in leading the Eagles to the championship that year, but some of his exploits have been exaggerated. First of all, he was not a two-way player throughout his career; he spent the majority of his career as an outside linebacker. Even in 1960, he did not play both ways for most of the season. He played 394.5 minutes that year in 12 games, an average of just under 33 minutes per game. He began the season as the starting center, but when linebacker Bob Pellegrini was injured in the fifth game of the season against the Browns, he switched over to linebacker. Rookie Bill Lapham played center for the next couple games, until the eighth game of the year, a vital match against the division rival Giants. Lapham started at center, but had so much trouble reacting to the Giants' blitz schemes that Chuck relieved him in the second half, announcing to New York linebacker Sam Huff that "The party's over; the veterans are taking over."

Bednarik played both ways that day and forever made his reputation with perhaps the most famous tackle in NFL history. The Eagles took the lead in the fourth quarter when Bednarik popped Giant fullback Mel Triplett, causing a fumble that defensive back Jimmy Carr grabbed in mid-air and returned 36 yards for a touchdown. When New York got the ball back, quarterback George Shaw tried to drive them for the tying score. He threw a pass to Frank Gifford coming across the middle, and Frank tried to weave his way for more yards. Gifford did not see Bednarik in Frederick Exley's phrase, "bearing down like a tractor trailer on a blind man," and Chuck hit Gifford high in the chest and knocked him backwards onto his head. The ball rolled free and Eagle middle linebacker Chuck Weber fell on it, causing the famous shot of Bednarik celebrating over the fallen Gifford. All Chuck knew was that the Eagles had the ball and "This game is f***ing over!" He did not know that Gifford had such a severe concussion that he would not play again till 1962. There were surprises all around. Gifford's wife did not know that the dead body carried into the Giants' locker room when she rushed down to see Frank was not her husband, but a fan who had suffered a heart attack in the stands that afternoon. Some complain that the only reason the tackle is so famous is that it was two Hall of Famers in a crucial game in New York, but it was a career-defining tackle and is justly celebrated.

The next week the Eagles and Giants had the rematch in Philadelphia, and the Eagles came back to win again with Bednarik playing both ways. When the Eagles clinched the Eastern Division the week after that in St. Louis, though, Bob Pellegrini was back on defense and Chuck played center. In the championship game against the Packers, Bednarik played 58 minutes and, in legendary fashion, made the game-clinching tackle on the last play of the game. But this is often exaggerated in the retelling as well. Trailing by four with nine seconds left, the Packers snapped the ball for one last play from the Eagles' 22. With his deep receivers covered, Bart Starr hit check down receiver Jim Taylor at the 17. Taylor brushed past a couple of Eagle defenders until corner Bobby Jackson hit him low and grabbed his leg at the 9, while Bednarik hit him high and knocked him down with one to two seconds left and defensive back Bobby Freeman came in from the goal line. Bednarik did not make the tackle all by himself; he was not the last line of defense and he did not pin Taylor to the ground for several seconds while the clock ran out, as the story is often told. Still, it was a good, solid, timely tackle.

It was a great season, and Chuck came back as center in 1961, but shifted in mid-year to middle linebacker to shore up the defense. He had never played the position before, but was a quick study and played one final season as a middle linebacker at 37 in 1962 before really retiring. In retirement, his fame only grew. With his flat-nose face, gnarled and oddly bent fingers and no-nonsense candor, he was always a colorful interview for various NFL Films productions. He was elected to the Pro Football Hall of Fame in 1967 and the College Football Hall of Fame in 1969. Also in 1969, Chuck was named to the NFL's 50th Anniversary Team as the center; 25 years later he was named to the NFL's 75th Anniversary Two-Way Team.

While he relished the role of Concrete Charlie, a fan favorite in Philadelphia, he became increasingly bitter along the way. He feuded with old teammate Pete Retzlaff over a job in the organization. He despised contemporary players for the money they make and the way they act on and off the field. He reserved special antipathy for Deion Sanders because flashy Deion played some offense to go with his work at cornerback and boasted of being a two-way player. Saddest of all, he got so resentful of Eagles owner Jeff Lurie, because Lurie would not buy 100 copies of Chuck's 20-year-old autobiography to give to the Eagles as presents, that Bednarik publicly rooted against the Eagles in Super Bowl XXXIX. It seems that his heart has become as twisted as his fingers, but Eagle fans should remember how much he gave to their team and how big a winner he was.

61

Free Agency

Steve Everitt
C 1997-99

Originator: Creighton guard Tony Cemore was voted the outstanding Italian-American Athlete of 1940 and played 10 games for the Eagles in 1941. He played service ball during the war.

Longest Tenure: Seven years, Duke Maronic.

Number Changes: Joe Frank wore 70 in 1941.

Just Visiting: None.

Highs: Steelton's Dusan "Duke" Maronic never attended college, but joined the Eagles at the age of 23 in 1944 as a 5-foot 9-inch guard. He later coached minor league football and officiated college basketball and high school football.

Lows: Wide-body guard Eric "Pink" Floyd showed some promise, but tore his anterior cruciate ligament on the Vet turf.

Steve Everitt

When the Eagles signed pony-tailed center Steve Everitt to a five-year, $11.4 million contract in 1997, owner Jeff Lurie told the *Inquirer* that the team treated free agency like the draft by trying to sign the best player on the board at a weak position. He added, "We're going after young, ascending, Pro Bowl-type players. We've been one of the most aggressive teams, and hopefully one of the smartest in the NFL." What Steve Everitt demonstrated was that free agency, like the draft, is a crap shoot, and best intentions do not always translate into success.

Everitt went to the University of Michigan as a 215-pound long snapper and left as a 290-pound first-round draft pick of the Cleveland Browns. He loved playing in the Dawg Pound in front of Cleveland's rabid fans and was unhappy when the team moved to Baltimore as the Ravens in his fourth season. In his first game as a Raven, he was fined $5,000 by the league for wearing a Browns bandana under his helmet as a salute to Cleveland. During that season, his last under his contract, he tore his pectoral muscle and missed half the year. Although Raleigh McKenzie, the Eagles' veteran center, was still effective, the team decided to try to get younger at the position and signed Steve. For his part, Everitt looked forward to playing in front of the blue-collar Eagle fans that he compared to Cleveland fans.

Things did not work the way Everitt or coach Ray Rhodes envisioned. The two-time playoff team went into a tailspin — particularly on offense where the oft-penalized offensive line performed inconsistently. In November, things got worse when Everitt was heckled as he sat ringside at a professional wrestling spectacle at the Spectrum the night after a loss to the Cardinals. Later that night he was arrested for drunk driving, and this proved to be a persistent distraction for the team, although the conviction would be overturned two years later. Steve's second season in Philadelphia was delayed after he broke his foot in July. He claimed the injury occurred while jogging, but the rumors were that he had gotten hurt in a scuffle at a Metallica concert. After two years in Philly, Everitt was not building the type of reputation that new coach Andy Reid respected. Reid challenged Steve to be a leader on the line in 1999, and he responded reasonably well. He was the third alternate at center for the Pro Bowl in both 1998 and 1999, but Reid made the judgment that Everitt was overpaid for what he delivered and made him a salary cap casualty in the spring of 2000. Undrafted free agent Bubba Miller capably replaced Everitt that year, and undrafted free agent Hank Fraley took over the following year after Miller broke his ankle. Meanwhile, Everitt signed with the champion Rams in 2000, but only appeared in four games as the backup center. He was responsible for breaking Kurt Warner's finger the first time on a bad snap and was cut again in a salary cap move in 2001.

Free agency is an imperfect science, no matter who is running it, but the Eagles have done much better under the Lurie ownership than under the pennywise-pound-foolish Norman Braman regime. The NFL's first attempt to head off calls for full free agency was Plan B Free Agency, in which each team could protect 37 players on its roster with the unprotected players being free to seek a better deal elsewhere. This "free agency for mediocrities" plan lasted from 1989 through 1992, when it was struck down in court. As part of the judge's ruling, the half dozen or so players who were holding out and unsigned at the time were given a brief window to sign with the highest bidder. One of these pioneer free agents was Eagle tight end Keith Jackson, who quickly jumped to Miami, starting the dismantling of the team that Buddy built.

If we grade the three coaches who have dealt with true free agency, we see three very different results. Rich Kotite took over from Buddy Ryan in 1991 and had a very uninteresting first year, gaining John Booty and Dennis McKnight and losing William Frizzell, Terry Hoage and Harper LeBel. Call that a C. Still under Plan B, 1992 saw the departure of Keith Jackson plus Ron Solt and Jessie Small and the arrival of Vai Sikahema and Eric Floyd. That's a D. The Birds also signed Herschel Walker, but he had been cut by the Vikings and was not part of any structured free agency program. In 1993, Reggie White won his landmark case against the NFL and the current system of true free agency for all players was established. It was a disaster for the Eagles; in 1993 alone, they lost White, Keith Byars, Mike Golic, Mike Pitts, Jim McMahon and several others. As replacements they signed a host of broken-down veterans like Tim Harris, Michael Carter, Keith Millard, Erik McMillan, Ken O'Brien, as well as two guys who had a little left in the tank — Bubby Brister and Mark Bavarro. 1993 was a complete failure, an F. In Kotite's last season, Seth Joyner, Clyde Simmons and Andre Waters all fled Philadelphia while Braman still owned the team. In April, Jeff Lurie bought the Birds and the atmosphere changed immediately. The Eagles managed to upgrade each of the lost positions with William Fuller and Burt Grossman at defensive end, Bill Romanowski at linebacker and Greg Jackson and Mike Zordich at safety, giving Kotite his one good free agency grade with a B+ and an overall grade point average of 1.5.

Ray Rhodes was hired in 1995 and continued the good streak. While Eric Allen, Herschel Walker, Bubby Brister and Britt Hager left, Rhodes signed Ricky Watters, Kevin Turner, Guy McIntyre, Raleigh McKenzie, Rodney Peete, Kurt Gouveia, Rhett Hall, Gary Anderson, James Willis and Reggie Johnson. It was an A performance, but the next year ownership let some key players escape that Rhodes wanted to keep, including Romanowski, Gouveia, Dan Stubbs and Jackson. Fred Barnett, Mark McMillan and Vaughn Hebron also left, and Randall Cunningham retired. The Eagles signed Irving Fryar and Troy Vincent as well as Richard Cooper and Mark Seay, but the overall grade is a C+. In Rhodes' third year, he signed linemen Steve Everitt, Ian Beckles and Mike Zandofsky, linebacker Darrin Smith and kicker Chris Boniol, but none of them worked out very well in Philly. Meanwhile, the Eagles let Fuller, McKenzie, McIntyre and Gary Anderson all leave. The net result was a poor season and a grade of D. In his final year, Rhodes signed a few mostly ineffective role players like Bill Johnson, Keith Sims, George Hegamin and Mike Caldwell and let Watters, Darrin Smith and Ty Detmer leave. Another D performance in his final year gives Ray a 2.25 GPA.

Andy Reid took over the team in 1999 and has generally been adept at managing free agency despite upsetting fans by releasing their favorites just as they are about to decline. In 1999, Fryar, Beckles, Cooper, Charlie Garner, Tommy Hutton and Jeff Graham left while Reid signed Charles Johnson, Torrance Small, Doug Pederson, Sean Landeta, Norm Johnson, David Akers, Tim Hauck, Jamie Asher and Eric Bieniemy. A solid B+. In 2000, Everitt, Norm Johnson, Willie Thomas and Kevin Turner were shown the door while Jon Runyan, Carlos Emmons, Brian Mitchell and Stanley Pritchett came aboard for an A performance. There was a lull in 2001 with only James Thrash and N.D. Kalu being added and Mike Mamula, Charles Johnson and Torrance Small being released. That earns a gentleman's C. 2002 was a bad year for free agency. Reid signed the able Sean Barber, the aging Blaine Bishop and the slowing Levon Kirkland while losing Jeremiah Trotter, Landeta, Caldwell and the injured Damon Moore and Bubba Miller. A clear D that held the team back that year. 2003 was a controversial year with the release of Brian Mitchell, Hugh Douglass and Shawn Barber as well as the bloated Kirkland. The only signings were Nate Wayne and Jon Ritchie, but this earns a B for having replacements ready to make the team younger. The Super Bowl season of 2004 can only be given an A for the signings of Jevon Kearse, Trotter, Douglass, Dhani Jones and Jeff Blake — not to mention the signing of Terrell Owens that evolved into a one-sided trade. Once again, Reid had young reinforcements ready so that the departure of Duce Staley, Bobby Taylor, Troy Vincent and Carlos Emmons was unfelt. The team of Andy Reid, Jeff Lurie and salary cap manager Joe Banner has proven to be unbeatable in recent years, and Andy Reid has earned a 2.84 free agency GPA.

Comebacks

Augie Lio
G 1946

Originator: Alabama's Elwood "Woody" Gerber played 16 games at guard for Philadelphia in 1941 and 1942 before going in the service. In the war, he captained the Bainbridge Naval Training Center Commodores.

Longest Tenure: Six years, Pete Perot.

Number Changes: Guy Morriss wore 50 from 1974 to 1983.

Just Visiting: This is the rent-a-guard number. All of these veteran guards stopped in Philadelphia after playing most of their careers elsewhere — Knox Ramsey (Cardinals and Dons), Bill Lueck (Packers), Brian Baldinger (Cowboys and Colts), Guy McIntyre (49ers), Ian Beckles (Bucs).

Highs: Injury-plagued Petey Perot was a battler for Dick Vermeil.

Lows: Tackle Don Talcott jumped to the CFL after one season. He was killed in a truck yard accident at the age of 34.

Augie Lio

For several years, the *Philadelphia Inquirer* beat writer for the Eagles was former Philadelphia Phillies and A's pitcher Stan Baumgartner. In 1946, the Eagles employed a 234-pound guard/kicker named Augie Lio who would go on to a 37-year career as a sportswriter for the *Passaic Herald-News,* covering the New York Giants.

Lio was an All-American at Georgetown University during a period when the Hoyas compiled a 23-game winning streak and played in the 1941 Orange Bowl. The highlight of his college years was when he booted a 24-yard field goal with 33 seconds left to beat Temple 3-2 in 1939. Lio was so well known for his outstanding line play and timely kicking that he finished second to Heisman Trophy winner Tommy Harmon in the balloting for the 1941 College All-Star Game with over a million votes. He would later be inducted into the College Football Hall of Fame.

In the meantime, though, Lio was drafted by the Detroit Lions in 1941 and earned a reputation as a tough guy right from the start. As a rookie, he was fined $25 for slugging Green Bay lineman Charlie Schultz in a game. The fine was rescinded the next week when game footage showed that there was "persistent face blocking" between the two, but no slugging. Lio was named to the league's All-Star team in both 1941 and 1942, but he hit on only two of 20 field goal attempts in his three years in the Motor City. Strangely, they were both in the same game against the Dodgers in 1943. The Lions sold Augie to the Boston Yanks in 1944, and his kicking improved to the extent that he hit six of 13 field goals in his two years in Beantown. As a two-way guard, he received All-Pro recognition three times in his first five years in the league.

The Eagles obtained Lio in a trade for lineman Rocco Canale in 1946, and he stepped in as the team's place kicker for one year. He had his best year, hitting six of 11 field goals and all 27 extra points for 45 total points, fifth in the league in scoring. In the season finale in Boston, Yank fans honored him before the game, and Augie kicked five extra points and a field goal. In 1947, Lio jumped to the rival All-America Conference for a season before serving as a player/coach of the minor league Paterson Panthers while he began his New Jersey sportswriting career. But as the Eagle place kicker, Augie had a hand in the largest comeback in Eagle history. Here's a top 10 of Eagle regular season comebacks:

1. October 27, 1946. The Eagles fell behind 24-0 to the Redskins at halftime in Washington. In the second half, Tommy Thompson threw three TD passes, the last one 30 yards to Jack Ferrante with 90 seconds left in the game, and led the Birds to four second-half touchdowns capped by four Augie Lio extra points. Eagles 28, Redskins 24.

2. October 25, 1959. Almost 13 years later, the Eagles again fell behind 24-0. This time they were playing the Cardinals in the first NFL game played in Minneapolis. Norm Van Brocklin threw two TD passes to Tommy McDonald, while Billy Ray Barnes scored twice on short runs — one after a 71-yard pass play to McDonald. Eagles 28, Cardinals 24.

3. October 23, 1960. In the third quarter, Philadelphia trailed the Browns 22-7 in Cleveland when Van Brocklin led the team to three touchdowns — two on passes to McDonald and Barnes — to take a 28-22 lead. Then, Bobby Mitchell caught a fourth-quarter TD pass to put the Browns back in front. From his own 10, Van Brocklin led the Eagles back down the field in the final minute, and Bobby Walston booted a 38-yard field goal with 10 seconds left for the win. Eagles 31, Browns 29.

4. November 27, 1960. One week after beating the Giants in New York, the Eagles fell behind 17-0 in the first quarter at Franklin Field. They erased that deficit before halftime, but then trailed 23-17 in the fourth quarter. Van Brocklin fired touchdown passes to backs Ted Dean and Billy Ray Barnes in the final period. Eagles 31, Giants 23.

5. October 14, 1973. In St. Louis, the Cardinals took a 24-13 lead in the fourth quarter. In the final two minutes, Roman Gabriel hit Harold Carmichael with a 27-yard score. The Cardinals recovered the onside kick, but the Eagles' defense forced a punt. Gabriel then passed the Birds 56 yards in seven plays — the last being a 23-yard TD to Don Zimmerman with no time remaining. Eagles 27, Cardinals 24.

6. October 23, 1988. The Cowboys built a 20-0 lead late in the first half before Randall Cunningham could get the Eagle offense going. Randall led the Birds on a 99-yard drive that cut the Dallas lead to 23-17 with 6:32 left in the game. The next time he got the ball, he led the team 85 yards on 16 plays and capped the drive with a two-yard TD pass to Anthony Toney with four seconds left. Eagles 24, Cowboys 23.

7. October 15, 1990. The Vikings led 21-9 at the half and 24-15 with five minutes to play on two Cris Carter TD catches. Randall then threw a 40-yard touchdown to Fred Barnett that first bounced off a Viking and then Calvin Williams. Viking QB Rich Gannon fumbled at his 6, and the Birds converted that to a touchdown on an Anthony Toney run with four minutes to go. A William Frizzell interception that led to a Roger Ruzek field goal clinched the win. Eagles 32, Vikings 24.

8. November 10, 1991. The Browns took a 23-0 lead in the second quarter, but after Jim McMahon touchdown passes of 16 yards to Keith Jackson and 70 yards to Fred Barnett, the score narrowed to 30-17 at halftime. The Eagles closed the gap to 30-26 with 10 minutes left, and then Webster Slaughter fumbled on a punt return inside his own 10. As part of his 341 yards passing, McMahon tossed a five-yard touchdown strike to Calvin Williams. Eagles 32, Browns 30.

9. December 22, 1991. With Jeff Kemp completing only eight of 24 passes in the first three quarters, the Eagles fell behind the Redskins 19-7. Kemp caught fire in the final period and hit tight ends Keith Jackson and Maurice Johnson for touchdowns to give the Birds a 21-19 lead. Washington kicked another field goal, and

Kemp got the ball back with less than a minute to play and drove the team 58 yards to set up a 38-yard game-winning field goal. Eagles 24, Redskins 22.

10. October 22, 2001. The Eagles held the ball for only 5:25 of the first half and fell behind 9-0 to the Giants, who had beaten the Birds the last nine times they played. The Eagles kicked a field goal of their own late in the third quarter, and then with 1:52 left, Donovan McNabb hit James Thrash with an 18-yard bullet for the winning score. Eagles 10, Giants 9.

Out of Their Leagues

Bruno Banducci
G 1944-45

Originator: In 1941, Michigan guard Ralph Fritz was a 10th-round pick who played one season before going into the service. After the war, he tried out for the New York Yankees of the All-America Conference, but was cut.

Longest Tenure: Nine years, Ron Baker.

Number Changes: Norm Willey wore 44 from 1950 to 1952 and 86 from 1953 to 1957; Daryle Smith wore 75 in 1990; Joe Panos wore 72 from 1995 to 1997.

Just Visiting: Raleigh McKenzie was a Hog from Washington and the twin brother of the Raiders' Reggie.

Highs: Leo Skladany only played in three games for the Eagles, but blocked a punt and recovered it for a touchdown in the 1949 title game against the Rams; Norm Willey (see 86); Ron Baker was a consistent guard throughout the 1980s; Hank Fraley has anchored the offensive line during the Andy Reid years.

Lows: Mike Woulfe was being groomed to replace Chuck Bednarik as middle linebacker in 1963 when he tore up his knee in an exhibition game. He was cut in training camp in 1964 and became a fireman.

Bruno Banducci

The Eagles had two sons of Italy starting at guard in 1944. Enio Conti was born in Naples and graduated from Bucknell. Bruno Banducci hailed from Tasignano, grew up in California and received a degree in engineering from Stanford. He was one of four members of Stanford's 1941 "Wow Boys" to play for the Eagles along with end Fred Meyer, halfback Pete Kmetovic and center Vic Lindskog. With his engineering degree, Banducci got a job as a production engineer for an oil company that gave him a deferment from the draft and made him very attractive to Philadelphia in the manpower-depleted era of World War II.

As a rookie, Banducci switched from tackle to guard but learned quickly. He was called the best guard in the league that year by Eagle general manager Harry Thayer and received All-Pro recognition in his second season. In 1946, the war had ended and a pro football war began with the formation of the All-America Conference. Bruno took advantage of the opportunity to return to his home by signing with the new San Francisco 49ers, who also signed his old Stanford teammates, quarterback Frankie Albert and fullback Norm Standlee, as well as former Eagle All-Pro guard Dick Bassi.

With the 49ers, Banducci played guard on offense and linebacker on defense, where he was known for being equally tough against the run and pass. Twice the 49er captain was named All-AAC and twice All-NFL, and he played in a Pro Bowl. When he was cut in 1955 over a salary dispute, Bruno was the last original 49er. He played a year in Canada and made news by admitting that American players in Canada were using pep pills to give them the stamina to play both ways. When his old 49er coach Buck Shaw came to Philadelphia in 1958, Bruno successfully sought the job of line coach, but he left before the championship year of 1960 and became a car dealer in California.

Banducci and Bassi were not the first Eagles to jump to a rival league. Red Grange had formed the first American Football League seven years before the Eagles were formed, and that league lasted one season. The second AFL was established in 1936 and featured former Eagles Swede Ellstrom, Dick Frahm, George Kenneally, Ed Matesic, George Mulligan, Harry Obst, Harry Shaub, Clyde Williams, Vince Zizak and Jim Zyntell. The league lasted only two years and was succeeded by a third AFL in 1940 in which former Birds Steve Banas, Max Padlow, Hank Reese and Milt Trost as well as future Eagle Jack Hinkle played.

As for the All-America Conference, 16 former Eagles jumped to the AAC. In addition to Banducci and Bassi, these players included Ben Agajanian, Alf Bauman, Jim Castiglia, Noble Doss, Terry Fox, Fred Gloden, Frank Hrabetin, Mort Landsberg, Augie Lio, Bob Thurbon, Lou Tomasetti, Tex Williams, Al Wukits and John Wyhonic. The AAC also affected the NFL draft: 32 Eagle draft picks in the 1940s ended up signing with an AAC team; six of those picks were in the first five rounds, including the top pick in 1945, John Yonaker. When the AAC was absorbed into the NFL in 1950, a disbursement draft was held and the Eagles claimed seven players under contract to AAC teams, including Lindell Pearson and Joe Sutton. Pearson was traded to the Lions for their first pick in the 1951 draft, and the Eagles used that to select Chet Mutryn from the dis-banded Baltimore Colts who had joined the NFL from the AAC in 1950. Mutryn was a 30-year-old former AAC star who had first been picked by the Eagles in the 20th round of the 1943 NFL draft. He didn't sign with the Eagles this time either. On the other hand, Sutton was one of seven former AAC players to play in Philadelphia in the 1950s, along with Bill Boedeker, Abe Gibron, Bob Oristaglio, Knox Ramsey, Ed Sharkey and George Taliaferro. Sutton was the only one to perform particularly well as an Eagle. Joe was a product of Northeast Catholic High and Temple University; he intercepted a team-high eight passes in 1950 and was supplanted by Tom Brookshier in 1953.

In the 1950s, the Canadian Football League served as a potential destination for disgruntled NFL players. Actually, the first NFL player to head north was former Eagle fullback Dan DeSantis in 1947. Former Eagle starters who went north include Neill Armstrong, Bruno Banducci, Bibbles Bawel, Eddie Bell, Hal Giancanelli, Ralph Goldston, Bud Grant and Jim Weatherall. The biggest loss, though, was Johnny Bright, the Eagles' number one draft pick in 1952, who instead went north for racial reasons and became the CFL's all-time leading ball carrier. Grant and Armstrong also coached in the CFL along with other former Eagles Larry Cabrelli, Wayne Robinson, Allie Sherman, Jim Trimble and Jerry Williams. Other one-time Eagles who also played in Canada are too numerous to list, but quarterbacks who had some success in the CFL, though not in Philadelphia, include Frank Tripucka, Bill Mackrides, Al Dorow, Don Jonas, George Mira, Pete Liske, Joe Pisarcik and David Archer.

The NFL encountered a second serious competitor in the 1960s when Lamar Hunt formed the fourth American Football League. Hunt tried to persuade Phillies owner Bob Carpenter to put a team in Connie Mack Stadium, but Carpenter was hesitant. In all, 27 former Eagles ended up in the AFL, but the only serious loss was wide receiver Art Powell, one of 14 former Birds who played for the AFL's New York franchise. Powell was a speedy deep threat who caught 81 TD passes in the AFL after spending 1959 returning punts and kicks for Philadelphia. Of more importance were the 22 Eagle draft picks who signed with the other league from 1959 through 1966. This group included three number ones (Ron Burton, Art Baker and Ed Budde) and one number two (Wray Carlton). Among the later draft selections who scorned the Birds were wide receivers Otis Taylor, Gary Garrison and Al Denson, linebacker Rick Redman and end Curt Merz. In 1966, Joe Robbie wanted to put an expansion team in Philadelphia, but was per-suaded to choose Miami instead, and in 1967 the two leagues merged.

Since the merger, challengers to the NFL have not been very successful. The World Football League started in 1974 and only lasted two seasons. Onetime Eagles who ended up in the WFL include Tom Bailey, Lee Bougess, Don Brumm, Joe Carollo, Bob Creech, Larry Estes, Rich Glover, Ben Hawkins, Bill Hobbs, John Huarte, John Mallory, George Mira, Cyril Pinder, Ron Porter, Joe Robb, Tim Rossovich, John Sodaski, Billy Walik and Adrian Young. WFL players who joined the Eagles after the league folded include tight end Keith Krepfle and backup quarterback John Walton as well as James McAlister and Don Ratliff. The greatest local significance of the WFL was that when Cincinnati Bengal middle linebacker Bill Bergey signed with a WFL team, Paul Brown traded him to the Eagles. Once Bergey's contract was invalidated, he came to Philadelphia and took over the Eagle defense.

The United States Football League began as a spring league in 1983 and collapsed when it tried to switch to the fall in 1985. Several former Eagles played in the USFL, including John Bunting, Don Calhoun, Dennis DeVaughn, Ken Dunek, Mickey Fitzgerald, Scott Fitzkee, Louie Giammona, Jo Jo Heath, Zac Henderson, Wally Henry, Alvin Hooks, Mitch Hoopes, Eric Johnson, Von Mansfield, Nick Mike-Mayer, Calvin Murray, Richard Osborne, Dave Pacella, Rodney Parker, Ray Phillips, John Reaves, Booker Russell, Charlie Smith and John Walton. The most significant former Eagles were Bunting, Fitzkee, Giammona, Henry and Smith, but they were all spent by the time they reached the USFL. The biggest prizes from the supplemental draft of USFL players in 1985 were Steve Young and Reggie White, and the Eagles landed the future Hall of Famer White. Several other USFL players eventually became Eagles, including Reggie Brown, Joe Conwell, William Fuller, Dave Jacobs, Ron Johnson, Jon Kimmel, Kelly Kirchbaum, Keith Millard, Mike Nease, Jairo Penaranda, Alan Reid, Jay Repko, Roger Ruzek, Broderick Thompson, Mike Ulner, Herschel Walker, Troy West, Gizmo Williams and Luis Zendejas. Aside from Reggie White, the best of the group was a member of the Philadelphia/Baltimore Stars, defensive end William Fuller, who went to three Pro Bowls in three years as an Eagle.

Finally, the marriage of network television money and the World Wrestling Foundation produced the brutally ugly bastard child of the XFL that lasted one excruciating season and employed former Eagles James Willis, James Bostic, Russell Copeland and Casey Weldon in addition to future Bird Rod "He Hate Me" Smart. Other leagues such as the CFL and the Arena Football League still exist, but none is intended as a serious competitor to the NFL. However, if history is any indicator, some bored billionaires are bound to give it another try at some point in the future.

64

College All-Star Game

Mario Giannelli
G 1948-51

Originator: Guard Robert McDonough in 1942.

Longest Tenure: Four years, Mario "Yo Yo" Giannelli.

Number Changes: Randy Beisler wore 80 from 1966 to 1968; Menil Mavraidies wore 65 in 1957; George Savitsky also wore 75 in 1948 and 1949; John Simerson wore 53 in 1957.

Just Visiting: Turkey Joe Jones was a rangy, talented pass rusher with the Browns.

Highs: Former Packer Ed Blaine was a solid guard in the early 1960s, who quit to become a medical researcher.

Lows: Tackle Dean Miraldi had dehydration problems and was a major disappointment as a second-round pick. Ron Jaworski remembered a game against the Cardinals in which he was sacked 11 times. After one sack by Miraldi's man Bubba Baker, Jaws looked over to see Dean Miraldi helping Baker up. Jaws told Coach Marion Campbell, "Get him the [bleep] out of there. He's getting me killed, then he's helping the guy who nailed me." Galen Laack died in a car accident in 1959.

Mario Giannelli

Mario Giannelli was known as "Yo Yo" since childhood when friends shortened his name to something they found easier to say. Throughout his life, this genial giant displayed a remarkable ability to bounce back from adversity.

In 1942, Yo Yo was a star guard on the undefeated and top-ranked Boston College Eagles team led by fullback Mike Holovak. Before their final game against local rival Holy Cross with their 4-4-1 record, BC expected that with their victory would come an invitation to play undefeated Tulsa in the Sugar Bowl for a shot at a national title. After Holy Cross crushed BC 55-12, the planned post-game celebration at the Coconut Grove nightclub was cancelled, and Giannelli and other players headed to a private party elsewhere. From that party, they could hear the sirens fill the night as the Coconut Grove burned down in a horrible fire that killed nearly 500 people.

BC went to the Orange Bowl that year to face Alabama. In the rush to the field from the locker room, Giannelli knocked over the water cooler, which fell on his foot and broke a toe. Mario watched from the sidelines as BC lost to Alabama 37-21. In March 1943, he joined the Army and took part in the horrific invasion of Okinawa on April 1, 1945. During the next few months, over 12,000 American troops would be killed on that Pacific island. Once again, Mario survived, and when he returned to the States, now weighing 265 pounds, he was courted by the Boston Yanks who had drafted him in the NFL draft. Yo Yo was not impressed by their offer, though, and returned to BC. His fellow linemen there included Hall of Famers Ernie Stautner and Art Donovan as well as future pros Art Spinney, John Kissell and Ed King. King later would become governor of Massachusetts. Amazingly, with all these great players, there were no more bowl appearances in Mario's junior and senior seasons.

Boston still owned Giannelli's NFL rights, while Cleveland had drafted him for the All-America Conference. At this point, Mario's coach Denny Myers got involved and talked to his old friend Greasy Neale about Giannelli's talents. Mario was a massive player for his time, but with speed, agility and quickness. Moreover, he was described as a hard-working player who was always at the bottom of the pile with his shirttail hanging out. He was just what the Eagles needed to fill the middle of their line, which had proven to be a weakness in the 1947 championship game loss to the Cardinals. Neale sent a sixth-round pick to Boston for Mario's draft right and signed him for $6,000 — roughly twice what the Yanks and Browns had been offering.

Before reporting to the Eagles, though, Giannelli was invited to play in the 1948 College All-Star Game in Chicago. The College All-Star Game was created in 1934 as a charity benefit by Arch Ward, the same Chicago sportswriter/promoter who conceived baseball's All-Star Game in 1933. College football was king at that time, and this game matched the current NFL champion against a team of just-graduated college all-stars. As Mario prepared to face the Cardinals in 1948, the pros barely led the series by the slim margin of 8-5-1. In the ensuing years, of course, professional football would firmly establish itself as the top level of gridiron competition, and the game was discarded after 1976, due to waning fan interest, with a final tally of 32-9-2.

Mario actually appeared in the game three consecutive years, the first as an All-Star losing to the Cardinals in 1948, and then in 1949 and 1950 as part of the defending champion Eagles. He was on the winning side in 1949 when the Birds won 38-0, but lost again 17-7 to the 1950 All-Stars. From that 1949 game, Chuck Bednarik and Clyde Scott went directly to Eagles training camp, while John Rauch, George Taliaferro, Jerry Williams and Norm Van Brocklin would turn up in Philadelphia in future years. From the 1950 All-Stars, Bob McChesney went directly to the Eagles, while Adrian Burk would later end up there, too.

Eagle teammate Vic Lindskog also played in three consecutive games from 1942 to 1944 as a member of the All-Stars but won only in 1943. The first future Eagle to appear in the game was Ed Manske, who played in the first game in 1934; the first Eagle draft pick to play in the game was Jay Berwanger, who in 1936 had never played professional football, while Clem Woltman was the first Eagle draft pick to play in the game and then play for the Eagles in 1938. The last Eagles to appear in the game were Artimus Parker and Mitch Sutton, who both played in the 1974 game. In 1975 and 1976, Philadelphia had no high draft picks, so no future Eagles took part. Several future Eagle coaches first played in the game as All-Stars, including Sid Gillman in 1934, Wayne Milner in 1936, Joe Kuharich in 1938, Jerry Williams in 1949, Marion Campbell in 1952 and Fred Bruney in 1953. The most representatives from Philadelphia to the All-Star team came in 1956 when Willie Berzinski, Hank Burnine, Frank D'Agostino, Dick Murley and Bob Pellegrini all were on the team that lost to the Browns 26-0. The Eagles last met the All-Stars in 1961, following their 1960 championship, and beat the college boys 28-14. There were no Eagles on the All-Stars that year because their top pick, Art Baker, signed with the AFL instead of Philadelphia.

When Mario Giannelli finally reported to Eagles training camp, he was a 27-year-old veteran and quickly earned a starting guard position. At first he played both offense and defense, but when free substitution was adopted in 1949, he became primarily a defensive middle guard and shored up the center of their defense. In one game against the Bears, the Eagles were having trouble defending the fullback catching passes over the middle. So at halftime, Greasy Neale told Mario to drop back and cover the fullback. Yo Yo said to the coach, "You think a guy as big as me can cover a fullback? You're crazy." But he did it anyway in a precursor to the zone blitz schemes of today. Another personal highlight came in the second game of the 1949 season when Mario blocked a punt out of the end zone for a safety in a 22-14 win over the Lions. His career ended after only four years in 1951 when a chop block by the Redskins ruined his knee. Mario retired rather than undergo surgery.

After football, Giannelli worked in the liquor business and for the Massachusetts State Racing Commission. In 1991, he was inducted into the Boston College Hall of Fame, and he passed away in 2003. Going from BC to Philadelphia, Giannelli was a "double eagle" who is remembered as a big guy in more ways than one.

Fouling the Nest

John Mellekas
DT 1963

John Mellekas

Football is such an emotionally intense game that it is not surprising that in the heat of training camp or practice field competition two teammates will get in a fight. Generally, these fights amount to a punch or two being thrown before the whole thing blows over. Chuck Bednarik told the story of an altercation between him and defensive tackle Jess Richardson one day in training camp. Bednarik walked over to tell Richardson to stop complaining about the exercise program when Jess kicked Chuck in the knee. Bednarik answered with three punches before they were separated. Bednarik expected retaliation from Richardson that night, but instead Jess apologized and said the whole thing was his fault. More recently, Jerome Brown had a showdown on the practice field with offensive tackle Ron Heller that threatened to escalate when the two squared off again in the locker room. Brown diffused the situation with a joke that enabled the two beefy antagonists to develop the basis for a friendship.

In the wake of the John F. Kennedy assassination in 1963, two Eagles got into a fight so ugly that it went way beyond the bounds of normal teammate conflicts. The President was gunned down on Friday, November 22nd, and after talking with Kennedy's press secretary Pierre Salinger, NFL commissioner Pete Rozelle decided that Sunday's games would be played. The rival American Football League cancelled its games for Sunday. However, several major college football games were played on Saturday as well as two NBA games and one NHL contest. Nevertheless, Rozelle's decision was not popular with the press or the players, and he regretted it in retrospect. The Eagles that year were a dissension-ridden club that had instituted team harmony meetings on the Saturday evenings before home games. At the meeting before the Redskin game, there was some sentiment for not playing the game at all, despite the commissioner's ruling, but the major topic of discussion was a plan for the players to donate part of their Sunday paychecks to a fund benefiting the family of Dallas policeman J.D. Tippit, who was killed trying to capture Lee Harvey Oswald. During the meeting, a fight erupted between John Mellekas and Ben Scotti that was instigated by Bill Quinlan. After the meeting, the unsettled conflict would get out of hand.

John Mellekas was a 30-year-old defensive tackle/center who was new to the team. Hailing from Rhode Island, Mellekas had attended the University of Arizona on a basketball scholarship, but ended up playing four years of football there and being drafted by the Chicago Bears in 1956. He was with the Bears for the next six years, missing only the 1957 season due to military service. From 1959 through 1961, John was the Bears' starting center. With the development of rookie Mike Pyle, Mellekas became expendable and was traded for a draft pick to the 49ers in 1962. In San Francisco, Mellekas moved back to defensive tackle and spent one year by the Bay before differences with head coach Red Hickey caused Mellekas to be cut early in 1963. The Eagles signed him after the second game of the year due to injuries to guards Jim Skaggs and Howard Keys. When defensive tackle Frank Fuller broke his leg three weeks later, John moved into the starting lineup for the 2-2-1 Birds. His roommate was Bill Quinlan, a talented but belligerent and unpopular defensive end that both Paul Brown and Vince Lombardi had dumped as soon as they could replace him.

Ben Scotti was an emotional, mouthy cornerback who was originally signed as a free agent by the Redskins in 1959. For three seasons, he carried on a trash-talking feud with Eagle hero Tommy McDonald until Philadelphia obtained Scotti in a trade along with center Jim Schrader for Billy Ray Barnes and Bobby Freeman. Scotti was excited to be getting away from Washington and joining the Eagles at first, but had a tough year in 1962 and was even benched against his old team, the Redskins. By the next season, he was unhappy and tried to play out his option before finally signing a contract in November.

At the meeting, Bill Quinlan groused that they wouldn't be playing the game if it weren't for that "guinea bastard" Rozelle. Although Pete Rozelle was not Italian, Scotti was and took immediate offense to the ethnic slur. He and Quinlan continued back and forth for a minute, before Quinlan backed off. At this point, John Mellekas got involved by saying, "So he said guinea, so what?" Scotti told him to stop. Mellekas added, "You're not so tough, Scotti, and I've had about as much of you as I'm going to take." Teammates interceded and separated the two. The meeting ended, and Mellekas left. However, as he was putting money in a vending machine in the hall, the 180-pound Scotti approached and knocked out the 250-pound lineman with a sucker punch. Scotti continued pounding on Mellekas until he was pulled off. Ironically, the two ended up in adjoining rooms in the hospital for three days. Mellekas needed several stitches to close facial cuts and lost a tooth; Scotti severed a tendon in his finger on Mellekas' teeth while punching him. Each later claimed that the other came into his hospital room and apologized.

The next day the shocked and unmotivated Eagles and Redskins played a flat, lifeless game in front of an extremely subdued sellout crowd at Franklin Field. A bugler played "Taps" before all seven NFL games that day, and none of the games was carried on television as CBS stuck to its news coverage. The Redskins built a first-half lead, then the Eagles came back, but blew a chance to tie the game at 13 in the closing minutes when Mike Clark missed a 16-yard field goal and they lost 13-10. In sorting out the brawl, the Eagles decided that the hot-headed Scotti was the aggressor and waived him, but since his hand was in a cast, he was done for the year. Mellekas was fined $500 and played the following week; nothing happened to Quinlan. It should be pointed out that ethnic sensitivities were different in those days. Hugh Brown introduced the Greek Mellekas to his Philadelphia *Evening Bulletin* readers in an October column with this politically incorrect lead: "Breathes there a Greek with soul so dead who never to a customer has said, 'the homberger she ees deeleeshus…the stromberry pie eet ees out of these wawrld.'"

The next season Scotti signed with the Rams, but broke his wrist and was waived. The 49ers picked him up for one year and then cut him. On the record, he was happy to get out of Washington, happy to get out of Philadelphia, and happy to get out of LA. Mellekas was cut by the Eagles and out of football in 1964, while Quinlan was waived to Detroit for a season and then went to Washington in 1965. In years to come, Scotti spoke of the fight on occasion, but Mellekas always was reticent to say anything except that it was a misunderstanding and was in the past. In August 1997, a similar incident occurred in the Redskins' training camp when troubled receiver Michael Westbrook reacted to something said by runner Stephen Davis by cold-cocking him and pummel-ing him bloody on the ground. Westbrook was fined $50,000 and suspended for a week, but the two remained teammates, surprisingly for five more seasons. Although in DC, it is not out of the ordinary to work across the aisle from someone you despise.

As for the 1963 Eagles, they came into that Redskins game having lost five games in a row and that streak would stretch to eight losses by season's end. The Birds' situa-tion was so bad that the sale of the team to Jerry Wolman was greeted with optimism. That good feeling would not last long.

66

The Future Is Not Now

Bill Bergey
LB 1974-80

WHO'S WORN THE NUMBER:

John Wyhonic (G) 1946-47, Baptiste Manzini (C) 1948, Ed Sharkey (T) 1954-55, Frank D'Agostino (G) 1956, Ed Meadows (E) 1958, Joe Robb (DE) 1959-60, Will Renfro (E) 1961, Bill Byrne (G) 1963, Bruce Van Dyke (G) 1966, Gordon Wright (G) 1967, Don Chuy (G) 1969, Bill Cody (LB) 1972, Roy Kirksey (G) 1973, *Bill Bergey* (LB) 1974-80, Ken Reeves (T) 1985-89, John Hudson (G) 1991-95, Mike Zandofsky (G) 1997, Jerry Crafts (T/G) 1998, Jeff Dellenbach (G/C) 1999, Bobbie Williams (G) 2000 and 2003, Trey Darelik (G/T) 2004.

Originator: Guard John Wyhonic in 1946. He later jumped to the All-America Conference.

Longest Tenure: Seven years, Bill Bergey.

Number Changes: Bap Manzini wore 50 in 1944 and 1945; Roy Kirksey wore 65 in 1974; Jerry Crafts wore 73 in 1997.

Just Visiting: Ed Sharkey played for five other teams; as a Bear, Ed Meadows was notorious for a cheap shot he took at Bobby Layne; he later committed suicide. Joe Robb became an able pass rusher for the Cardinals; Bruce Van Dyke just missed out on the Steeler Super Bowl teams in his seven years in Pittsburgh; Jeff Dellenbach protected Dan Marino for many years in Miami.

Highs: None.

Lows: Guard Don Chuy came to the Eagles from the Rams with Joe Carollo in the 1969 Bob Brown trade. Chuy injured his shoulder that year, and that led to complications. The Eagles claimed he had a rare blood condition and should give up football. Chuy sued for his remaining two years salary because he held the condition was due to his playing injury. A jury awarded Chuy $60,000 in back pay and $70,000 in damages in 1976.

Bill Bergey

Bill "Bubba" Bergey's national reputation was unfairly lessened by the quality of the teams on which he played. In both Cincinnati and Philadelphia, Bergey joined a weak team that slowly evolved into a Super Bowl contender only to be forced to leave just as the team got good. In both cases, Bergey's sterling play at middle linebacker, was a keystone in the team's development. Bergey was a vocal, aggressive leader on the field. He was big, strong and an enthusiastic hitter. He was fast enough to drop into pass coverage and quick enough to fill the running lanes. He was intelligent and could see plays develop. Above all, Bergey was so intense on the field that it was palpable in the stands. He was the greatest middle linebacker the Eagles have ever had.

When Bergey started at Arkansas State, he was a fullback. Over his first couple of years, he was also tried on the offensive and defensive lines before he finally was moved to linebacker as a junior, and found a home. In 1976, he was voted Arkansas State's all-time greatest player and had his number 66 retired there in 1997. Paul Brown drafted him for the Bengals, a second year expansion team, in 1969. The Bengals improved from 4-9-1 in Bill's rookie year to a 10-4 division winner in 1973 and had an overall 34-35-1 record for that five-year period. Bergey made the AFL All-Star Game in 1969 and got along well with Cincinnati's owner/coach Paul Brown until Bill signed a future contract in 1974 with a team in the fledgling World Football League. Brown did not want a lame duck middle linebacker so he traded Bergey to the Eagles. In the meantime, the WFL team Bergey signed with moved from Washington to Virginia to Florida and reneged on Bergey's bonus payments before they ever took the field, which made Bill an Eagle.

The Eagles in 1974 were run by Mike McCormack, who had played under Paul Brown for a decade and had served as an assistant coach under Vince Lombardi and George Allen afterwards. McCormack took his governing principles from Allen, who was fond of saying the "future is now" and trading draft choices for veteran players. McCormack tried the same approach with the Eagles but could not duplicate his mentor's success. McCormack had traded two players and three high draft choices for Roman Gabriel the year before, and that had improved the offense, albeit at a high cost. For Bergey, the Birds surrendered two number one picks and a number two. That deal and a later one with Cincinnati giving up another number two for Stan Walters (along with an exchange of backup quarterbacks) could be justified. Bergey became a fan favorite who inspired "Bergey's Brawlers" banners by leading a defensive resurgence in 1974 with the team giving up 176 fewer points than in 1973 despite having a very weak front four. However, Gabriel only lasted two full seasons before his body began to give out, so that the Eagles clearly overpaid for him. Moreover, McCormack also gave up high draft picks for the likes of Norm Bulaich, Mike Boryla, Jerry Patton, Wes Chesson, Tom Roussel, John Tarver, Randy Jackson, aged John Niland, James McAlister and Horst Muhlmann. These guys did not exactly form the foundation of a Super Bowl team. The result was that the Eagles' highest draft choices from 1974 through 1978 were: 1974, third round; 1975, seventh round; 1976, fifth round; 1977, fifth round;

The Eagles' tough, bearded linebacking corps were known as The Bergey Bunch and posed for this shot in the 1975 preseason. From right to left: Tom Ehlers, Frank LeMaster, John Bunting, Bill Bergey, Kevin Reilly, Dean Halverson and Jim Opperman.

1978, third round. McCormack had not only failed to deliver a winning team, but had destroyed the Eagles' immediate future in the process.

Dick Vermeil faced this untenable situation when he arrived and slowly transformed the team into a winner. Bergey led the team in tackles six times and began to get recognition for his play by being named All-Pro each year from 1974 to 1978 and going to four Pro Bowls. Vermeil switched the defensive alignment to a 3-4 in 1977 with Bergey as one of two inside linebackers, and the Eagles became one of the best defenses in the league by 1979, when Bill went down to a knee injury in the third game of the year. Bergey worked hard to rehabilitate the knee and returned to the field in a diminished capacity in 1980 for the Super Bowl run. Actually, his last game as an Eagle was the Super Bowl loss to the Raiders in January 1981.

Bergey spent 1981 on injured reserve before finally announcing his retirement after that season at a press conference where Dick Vermeil predictably was choked by tears. Bill summed up how he wanted to be remembered by telling the *Inquirer*, "As a linebacker who lined up on every single play and gave it everything I had. That's all." He was that and more. Bergey has remained visible on television in the area and has been successful in various business interests. His sons Jake and Josh play indoor lacrosse professionally; Jake is with the Philadelphia Wings, keeping the revered Bergey name active in Philadelphia sports.

Buck Shaw – Going Out On Top

Stan Campbell
G 1959-61

Originator: Guard Enio Conti in 1941.

Longest Tenure: Eight years, guard John Magee.

Number Changes: Enio Conti wore 51 in 1944 and 1945.

Just Visiting: None.

Highs: Bucknell's Enio Conti was born in Naples, Italy, and joined the Eagles from the Giants' Jersey City minor league team; he had to retire in 1945 due to high blood pressure. Jack Sanders played guard for the Steelers before going into the Marines; despite losing part of his left arm on Iwo Jima, Jack appeared in three games for the Eagles in 1945. At 5 feet 10 inches and 220 pounds, guard John "Tank" Magee has an unusual statistical legacy — 0 catches and seven yards receiving; the yards came off a lateral.

Lows: Rough and tough tackle Proverb Jacobs was a second-round draft pick, but only lasted a year in Philadelphia. In his senior year of college, he was ejected from four football games and two track meets.

Stan Campbell

For an ordinary guard, Stan Campbell lived a fortunate football life. He was drafted out of Iowa State in the 18th round by the Detroit Lions in 1952 and made the team through hard work and dedication. Led by brash quarterback Bobby Layne, the Lions won their first of three 1950s championships in Campbell's rookie season. Stan was called into military service for the next two years, but returned to Detroit in 1955. By 1957, he was a starter and the Lions won their final title that year, beating up Cleveland 59-14 in the championship match. Campbell started one more season at guard in Detroit before future All-Pro John Gordy was drafted to replace him in 1959.

Meanwhile in Philadelphia, a transformation was underway. After two losing seasons, former Notre Dame coach Hugh Devore was let go as the Eagles' coach in 1958. General manager Vince McNally, another Notre Dame man, offered the job to the impressive offensive coach of the division rival Giants, Vince Lombardi. Lombardi shook hands on a deal with McNally, but after discussing it with New York owner Wellington Mara, Vince backed out of the job because the Philadelphia ownership situation seemed unstable. So McNally turned to another Notre Dame man, Buck Shaw. Shaw had been a 178-pound tackle and a teammate of George Gipp under coach Knute Rockne. He then worked as an assistant for 15 years before becoming head coach at Santa Clara University in 1936. Over the next seven years, his Santa Clara teams went 47-10-2 with two Sugar Bowl wins. After World War II, Buck was hired as the first coach of the San Francisco 49ers in the All-America Conference and coached them through the 1954 season, finishing second six times and third twice. He was a part-timer in San Francisco, spending half the year as football coach and half as an executive with a corrugated box company. After the 49ers fired him, Shaw became the athletic director and first football coach at the newly created Air Force Academy, where McNally tracked him down.

Shaw told McNally he wouldn't take the job without an established quarterback on the team; he was not interested in training Sonny Jurgensen. McNally swung the deal for Norm Van Brocklin, and Buck, known as the "Silver Fox" for his shock of gray hair, came aboard. Again, he served in a six-month-a-year capacity, continuing in the business world in the off-season. Since Van Brocklin asserted so much control over the offense and was such a forceful leader for the whole team, much has been made of the notion that Van Brocklin and not Shaw was the real coach of the team. However, Shaw's style was that of a delegator and very much the model of the contemporary head coach. Van Brocklin and offensive coach Charlie Gauer took care of the offense, and defensive coach Jerry Williams handled the defense. Ultimately though, Buck was in control. Shaw was moving bodies in and out of Philadelphia through trades and signings at a record pace as he tried to improve the quality of the team as fast as possible.

At the outset, the team seemed to go backwards. After Devore's 4-8 record in 1957, Shaw's 2-9-1 mark in 1958 was a disappointment. Buck kept the steady stream of players coming and going as he tried to piece together a championship team. His moves paid off quickly. The Birds jumped to a 7-5 second-place finish in 1959 and then to 10-

2 and the championship in 1960. Shaw retired from football immediately, a champion at last. He was inducted into the College Football Hall of Fame in 1972 and died in 1977 from cancer.

Stan Campbell was one of those pieces assembled by Shaw. The Eagles acquired him from the Lions in 1959 for a 10th-round draft pick. One of the weaknesses on the team Shaw inherited in 1958 was a bad offensive line that was further weakened when his best lineman, Buck Lansford, was included in the deal for Norm Van Brocklin. The only 1957 starter to return in 1958 was guard Ken Huxhold, and he was gone by the end of the year. In 1958, Shaw moved Chuck Bednarik over from defense to man the center position. Concrete Charlie was the only carryover to 1959, but that year brought tackle J.D. Smith in the draft, tackle Jim McCusker from the Cardinals and Campbell from Detroit. In 1960, guard John Wittenborn was acquired from the 49ers, and the makeshift championship line was complete. It was adequate at best opening holes for a rushing attack that had the lowest yards per carry average in the NFL at 3.2, but Van Brocklin had time to pass. The Eagles won it all, and Stan had a third title.

As with Detroit, Campbell lasted one more year with Philadelphia after the championship. Stan was a leader on the line, but experienced knee and shoulder problems and was released by the Eagles in 1962. He hooked up with Oakland for one final season before retiring. Neither the Lions nor Eagles have won a championship since they let go of Stan Campbell. Could it be the Campbell curse from which Detroit and Philadelphia have suffered all these years? Is this payback for the secret devilment experienced by a grinder who made a total of $110,000 in his decade in the NFL while playing in front of two of the loudest and most demanding quarterbacks in history, Bobby Layne and Norm Van Brocklin? In the words of Eagle sage Rich Kotite, "Absolutely, without question."

Big Guys

Dennis Harrison
DE 1978-84

Originator: Kansas State guard Ray Romero, who started seven games as a rookie in 1951 before being drafted into the Army, was the first Latino Eagle.

Longest Tenure: Seven years, Mark Nordquist and Dennis Harrison.

Number Changes: Reggie Singletary wore 97 in 1986.

Just Visiting: Bill Koman was a hard-hitting linebacker for the Cardinals for several seasons.

Highs: None.

Lows: Mediocre defensive end Blenda Gay was murdered by his wife with a kitchen knife two days before Christmas in 1976. She claimed her action was in response to a history of physical abuse, and she was acquitted of the crime by reason of insanity in 1978.

Dennis Harrison

Size is one thing you can't teach, but when the 76ers selected 7-foot 6-inch Sean Bradley as the second overall pick in the 1993 NBA draft, they sadly discovered that skills and focus are important for success as well. Football is a different game, but the principle remains the same. A big reason Dick Vermeil was fond of Dennis Harrison was his 6-foot 8-inch size, an Eagle height record. Vermeil told the *Philadelphia Inquirer* that this gave Dennis an innate advantage, "He doesn't have to get as close to the quarterback to cause problems because he's like throwing over a telephone pole." At the same time, Harrison was not drafted until the fourth round in 1978 because many scouts doubted his aggressiveness.

Eagle opponents came to understand that there was more to Bigfoot, as Dennis was called for his size 15 feet, than just size. He ran the 40-yard dash in 4.8 seconds and used his wide wingspan to gain leverage on offensive tackles. He could be dominating in run defense and mobile in pursuit. In Philadelphia, Harrison fit into a very effective defensive line rotation as part of defensive coordinator Marion Campbell's scheme. Generally, Bigfoot would line up at left end with Big Daddy Hairston at right end and Charley Johnson at nose tackle. On passing downs, Harrison would move to the right end, Hairston would move inside and Claude Humphrey would take the left end to boost the ferocity of the pass rush. Dennis became a starter in his third year, 1980, and accumulated nine sacks that year. He tore ligaments in his hand in the Super Bowl, though, and could not lift weights in the off-season. With his strength diminished, he fell off to only four sacks in 1981 before rebounding to 10.5 sacks in only nine games in the strike-shortened 1982 season.

Harrison was honored that year by being selected to the Pro Bowl and as a second-team All-Pro. Dennis followed that with seasons of 11.5 and 12 sacks and was one of several veterans who held out for a better contract in 1985. New owner Norman Braman played hardball and traded Harrison to the Rams for a draft pick, choosing to buy out Reggie White's USFL contract and bring the future Hall of Famer to Philadelphia instead. It was a good choice. Harrison was never close to being the same player. In one season with the Rams, part of another with the 49ers and two final seasons reunited with Marion Campbell in Atlanta, he totaled 5.5 sacks. He was a very tall man, but had a short time at the top, probably because he could not maintain the aggressive intensity necessary to play defensive end effectively in the NFL.

Among the tallest Eagles, the first 6-foot 6-inch player for Philadelphia was center Tom Dimmick in 1956. The first to reach 6 feet 7 inches was Dave Lince in 1966; he was a tight end who caught four passes in two seasons. At 6 feet 7 inches, Harold Carmichael came along in 1971 and is sometimes listed as 6 feet 8 inches. Officially, though, the first 6-foot 8-inch Eagle was tight end Clark Hoss, who appeared in four games in 1972, but caught no passes. At the record height for the tallest Eagle, Hoss was joined in 1978 by Harrison, in 1983 by tackle Jim Fritzsche and by tackle Bernard Williams in 1994. Tra Thomas is sometimes listed as 6 feet 8 inches as well, but his official height is 6 feet 7 inches. Altogether, there have been 33 Eagles who stretched to six and a half feet: 14 tackles, nine defensive ends, four tight ends, three defensive tackles, two centers, one guard and one wide receiver. Leonard Mitchell counts as both a tackle and defensive end in the breakdown.

The crown for the heaviest Eagle has changed hands many times. Tackle Tex Leyendecker was the biggest player on the first team in 1933 at 235 pounds. Guard Forrest "Aimee" McPherson weighed in at 240 for the 1937 season. The following year, tackle Ray Keeling reported at 263 pounds, although some press reports listed him as the heaviest player in the league at 275 pounds. The first official 275-pounder was tackle Jim Kekeris in 1947, and that mark was equaled in 1956 by defensive tackle Jess Richardson. In 1962, angry defensive end John Baker came to Philly from Los Angeles weighing 290 pounds. Bob Brown topped that in 1967 with an official weight of 295, although he is thought to have reached 315 pounds in that season. The first official 300-pounder didn't come until tackle Frank Giddins joined the team in 1981 at 300 pounds exactly, 325-pound tackle Antone Davis blew that mark away in 1991, and 300-pound linemen became commonplace in the 1990s. Davis was exceeded by William "Refrigerator" Perry who waddled into town in 1993 claiming to be 335 pounds. Perry was easily 400 pounds and could barely move. He is probably the fattest Eagle ever, although the heaviest Bird by official weights is Tra Thomas at 349 pounds. It's amazing how Tra manages to keep his weight just under 350 pounds year after year; it must be Jenny Craig.

69

2000 Playoffs

Jon Runyan
T 2000-4

WHO'S WORN THE NUMBER:

Dave DiFilippo (G) 1941, Joe Tyrell (G) 1952, Carl Gersbach (LB) 1970, Rich Glover (DT) 1975, Woody Peoples (G) 1978-80, Dwaine Morris (DT) 1985, Jeff Tupper (DE) 1986, Jim Angelo (G) 1987r, Bruce Collie (G) 1990-91, Burt Grossman (DE) 1994, Harry Boatswain (G/T) 1995, 1997, George Hegamin (G/T) 1998, *John Runyan* (T) 2000-04.

Originator: Villanova's Dave DiFilippo played guard for five games in 1941. Dave was the colorful head coach of the minor league Pottstown Firebirds, the subject of a popular NFL Films production in the 1960s. Later, he was inducted into the Pennsylvania Sports Hall of Fame.

Longest Tenure: Five years, Jon Runyan.

Number Changes: Dave DiFilippo also wore 26 in 1941.

Just Visiting: Woody Peoples started at guard for a decade in San Francisco before wrapping up his career with Philadelphia's Super Bowl run under Dick Vermeil; Bruce Collie spent five years as a 49er; speed rusher Burt Grossman played for five years in San Diego, but was a product of Archbishop Carroll High School in Radnor.

Highs: None.

Lows: Camden's own George Hegamin was the first 6-foot 7-inch tackle to wear 69. When he was demoted from the first team during training camp in 1999, he left the practice field. New coach Andy Reid disciplined Hegamin the next day by having George push Andy 100 yards on the blocking sled. He was cut 10 days later.

Jon Runyan

Former tackle Andy Reid understands the importance of a solid offensive line so it was not surprising that his first major free agent signing after taking over the floundering Eagles was the best lineman on the market in 2000. Reid called Jon Runyan the "best right tackle in football," at the time and signed him to a six-year, $30 million contract to protect franchise quarterback Donovan McNabb. In contrast, when Buddy Ryan rebuilt the Birds in the late 1980s, he left offensive line till last and never got it right. He didn't go for a stud O-lineman till his third year when he traded draft picks for Ron Solt who turned out to be overly-enhanced and injury-riddled. The lack of a good offensive line has been a fatal flaw to many Eagle teams, and they have wasted many high draft picks over the years on tackles in particular who did not pan out.

Reid knew what he doing when he signed Runyan to team with fellow 6-foot 7-inch tackle Tra Thomas to give Philadelphia the biggest and one of the best tackle tandems in the NFL. Beyond size, Runyan is a tough guy with a nasty attitude on the field. The Eagles found that out in his first training camp with the team. Runyan and linebacker Jeremiah Trotter got into a fight when Runyan came to the aid of tackle Tra Thomas. Tempers flared and punches were thrown, but all was forgotten the next day. Runyan does not give an inch on the field; he admits that one time with the Oilers he punched an aggressive opponent in the crotch during a pileup. He described his approach to the *Philadelphia Inquirer,* "I think you get them worried about you getting physical with them. Not that you're going to try to hurt them, but you're trying to rough them up like a bully would do." Not surprisingly, the assertive Runyan has been vocal with his coaches as well continually advocating a more balanced run-oriented attack.

One of the reasons they Eagles signed Runyan was to block New York Giants All Pro defensive end Michael Strahan. The gap-toothed Strahan had tormented the Eagles for years with his often-spectacular play against them. The two antagonists met for the first time in the second game of the 2000 season that the Giants won 33-18 for their seventh straight win in the series. Strahan was quoted after the game as saying "Jon Runyan who?" The Giants won again 24-7 when the teams met in October to drop the Eagles to 5-4 for the season. Afterwards, the dominant Strahan complained that Runyan cut-blocked him near the end of the mismatch. It was a turning point in Philadelphia's season; the only game they would lose after that was five weeks later 15-13 to the Titans on an Al Del Greco 50-yard field goal at the final gun. In Reid's second season, the surprising Eagles made the playoffs as a wild card.

In their first playoff game in four years, the Eagles hosted the Tampa Bay Bucs in a game that was no contest. The Eagles dominated from the start with their big offensive line opening holes this allowed retread running back Chris Warren to run for 85 yards on 22 carries while Donovan McNabb kept making plays to move the chains. Their first touchdown was set up by Tampa QB Shaun King's fumble and came on a McNabb run. The second score was a five-yard pass from McNabb to Na Brown and came off a 69-yard drive in the last two minutes of the half. In the third quarter,

McNabb threw another touchdown to Jeff Thomason, and the Birds won easily 21-3.

Awaiting the Eagles in the Meadowlands the next week were their nemesis the Giants. The Giants were ready; the Eagles were not. Ron Dixon started the game by returning the opening kickoff 97 yards for a touchdown. The Giants got their second touchdown on an amazing interception by Jason Sehorn who dove in front of a pass for Torrance Small, knocked it up in the air, rolled to his knees, caught the ball as he was getting to his feet and raced 32 yards for the score to put New York up 17-0. McNabb was sacked six times and was constantly under pressure in the 20-10 loss. Strahan abused Runyan to an embarrassing degree. If he wasn't running around Runyan, Strahan was knocking over the towering tackle who outweighed him by 50 pounds. It was a humbling experience both for the team and Runyan.

Since that ninth straight loss to New York, the Eagles have beaten the Giants seven of eight times, and Runyan has more than held his own in his personal battles with Strahan. Runyan has not missed a game as a durable and dependable tackle who has fit in well with the Eagles and Philadelphia. His mean, unrelenting style is a good match for Philly fans. Ironically, when Runyan was first visiting the Eagles as a free agent he was having dinner with Reid when Temple basketball coach John Chaney came to their table and warned Jon about how bad Philadelphia fans were. Jon's coach in Tennessee, Jeff Fisher, said at the time, "I've been in Philadelphia, and Jon is going to miss us." As it turned out, both Reid and Runyan made the right choice in 2000.

Eagle Honors

Al Wistert
T 1943-51

Al Wistert

For a player as accomplished as Albert Wistert, it is surprising that he never played high school football. His father, a Chicago police captain, was shot and killed when Al was only five years old, and his widowed mother struggled to raise six children on her own. When Al came to her with the permission slip for him to play high school football, his mother refused to sign because she was worried about potential medical bills should Al get injured. So Al played ball secretly for a local athletic club that did not require parental permission.

In 1938, Al enrolled at the University of Michigan where he followed in his brother Francis' footsteps on the football field. Francis had been an All-American tackle for the Wolverines in 1932-33, and Al was an All-American tackle as a senior in 1942. Both were known as "Whitey," although Al was also called "Ox." Francis later played baseball for the Cincinnati Reds and went to law school before going into the service during the war. A third brother, Alvin, dropped out of high school and went to work as a salesman until joining the Marines during World War II. After the war, Alvin used the G.I. Bill to make his way to the University of Michigan at the age of 31 and become the third Wistert brother to make All-American at tackle in 1948. All three brothers played for Fritz Chrisler, and Francis and Alvin played on National Championship teams. Alvin was team captain; Albert was team MVP. All three brothers wore number 11, and the number is retired in their names.

The Eagles' Al – Albert — was drafted in the fifth round by Philadelphia in 1943. After playing in the College All-Star Game, Al reported to what he thought was Eagles training camp, but this was the season that the Steelers and Eagles merged to form the Steagles. Wistert approached fellow Michigan alumnus Bill Hewitt who was returning to wartime pro football after a four-year absence and introduced himself, but Hewitt simply turned away. Wistert was shocked at the different atmosphere in pro ball, especially since Hewitt had played with his brother Francis. Since this team was a Pennsylvania amalgamation, Al did not even start as a rookie but deferred to Steeler veteran Ted Doyle who did not practice with the team because of his work in a defense plant.

When the teams separated the following year, Wistert took over as a starter and became a star on both sides of the ball. Al only weighed 215 pounds, and that was not particularly big even for the era in which he played. However, Wistert was a master technician. On offense, he was celebrated for his intelligence, quickness, balance and footwork. He was noted for making all his blocks while staying on his feet as opposed to the leaping cross-body blocking that was popular at the time. He out-positioned the defenders and was a master at downfield blocking. On defense, Al utilized his speed, smarts and great pursuit. He was equally talented at pass rushing and stopping the run and was a sure tackler. He also played on the punt and kickoff return teams, usually leading the charge down the field.

Moreover, he was a team leader who served as team captain from 1947 till the end of his career. He took those responsibilities seriously and often took it upon himself to

Two of the Eagles' greatest tackles ever, Al Wistert on the left and Vic Sears on the right, demonstrate the "rough stuff" in 1946. Wistert's number 70 was retired with him in February 1952; only Chuck Bednarik's 14-year tenure is longer than Sears' 13 seasons as an Eagle.

inspire his teammates with pep talks on the night before an important game. Coach Greasy Neale relied on him to do this. Contrary to his own experience with Bill Hewitt, Wistert went out of his way to welcome rookies to the team. Chuck Bednarik remembered how Wistert welcomed him in 1949 when other Eagles wanted nothing to do with Concrete Charlie and resolved to act the same way himself as a veteran.

Wistert received annual honors while with the Eagles. He was named All-Pro from 1944 to 1949 and was named second-team All-Pro in 1950 and 1951. Al also played in the first Pro Bowl in 1951 as a guard. Fans held "Al Wistert Day" at Shibe Park on November 18, 1951 before a loss to Detroit, and Al was given a new car. He, along with his two brothers, was inducted into the College Football Hall of Fame, and in a rare honor, his number is one of six officially retired by the Eagles. The others being 15 for Steve Van Buren, 40 for Tom Brookshier, 44 for Pete Retzlaff, 60 for Chuck Bednarik and 99 for Jerome Brown. With Reggie White's untimely death, it is likely that 92 will become the seventh retired number very soon. Al was also named to the Eagles All-Time Team selected in 1965, which included receivers Tommy McDonald, Pete Pihos and Pete Retzlaff; offensive linemen Wistert, Lum Snyder, Bucko Kilroy, Cliff Patton and Vic Lindskog; quarterback Norm Van Brocklin; runners Steve Van Buren, Tim Brown and Bosh Pritchard; defensive linemen Norm Willey, John Green, Mike Jarmoluk and Vic Sears; linebackers Chuck Bednarik, Maxie Baughan and Wayne Robinson; defensive backs Tom Brookshier, Russ Craft, Don Burroughs and Jerry Norton; and punter Joe Muha and kicker Bobby Walston.

It's stunning that Wistert is not part of the Eagles' Honor Roll as an individual. The Eagles Honor Roll was established in 1987 to pay tribute to outstanding members of the organization. 13 men were inducted in 1987: Chuck Bednarik, Bert Bell, Harold Carmichael, Bill Hewitt, Sonny Jurgensen, Ollie Matson, Wilbert Montgomery, Greasy Neale, Pete Pihos, Jim Ringo, Norm Van Brocklin, Steve Van Buren, Alex Wojciechowicz. Since then, 14 men and two teams have followed: Bill Bergey (1988), Tommy McDonald (1988), Tom Brookshier (1989), Pete Retzlaff (1989), Timmy Brown (1990), Jerry Sisemore (1991), Stan Walters (1991), Ron Jaworski (1992), Bill Bradley (1993), Dick Vermeil (1994), Mike Quick (1995), executive Jim Gallagher (1995), trainer Otho Davis (1999) and the 1948 and 1949 Championship teams collectively (1999). Wistert of course was part of those great championship teams, but it seems that the Eagles could do a better job of celebrating their history by making their Honor Roll a more regular occurrence and having a formal dinner for which fans could buy tickets to commemorate great Eagles of the past. The Packers do this with their team Hall of Fame, and it seems to be a very popular event and attraction.

Even more striking is that the much-honored Wistert, the best tackle of his era, is not a member of the Pro Football Hall of Fame in Canton. He is probably the unheralded Eagle with the best case for enshrinement although he would have to make it as a Veterans Committee nomination at this point. As a whole, the Eagles have not done well at Canton. Only 15 onetime Eagles have been inducted — of the nine teams that date back to the 1930s, only the awful Cardinals franchise has that small a number.

Furthermore, only eight of those 15 are listed as having been primarily Eagles — none of the other eight original franchises have fewer than 10 primary players. There are worthy candidates from Philly, though. In addition to Wistert, there's Maxie Baughan who was All-Pro or Pro Bowl every year he was an Eagle; there's seven-time All-Pro Bucko Kilroy; there's star receiver Harold Carmichael; prototype tight end Pete Retzlaff; and perennial All-Pro Bill Bergey. Of all of them, Wistert is the most deserving.

Although Al had successfully coached Riverside High School in New Jersey for a couple of years before his responsibilities as team captain forced him to give it up, he left football entirely when he retired. He became a successful insurance agent and moved to the West Coast where he still lives today as an octogenarian fitness buff who hopes to live to 105. It would be fitting and well deserved if Canton recognized this great tackle before that time.

71

The Pittsburgh Connection

Eberle Schultz
T 1943

Originator: North Dakota State tackle Cecil Sturgeon in 1941. Four years later, he played on the winning side in the Spaghetti Bowl in Florence, Italy when the 5th Army beat the 12th Air Force 20-6 before 20,000 of their fellow troops.

Longest Tenure: Nine years, Ken Clarke and Jermane Mayberry.

Number Changes: Eberle Schultz wore 48 in 1940.

Just Visiting: Jim Ricca was a large fixture in the Redskin defensive line.

Highs: Ken Clarke was a free agent nose tackle, adept at rushing the passer, who was voted defensive MVP in 1984; Jermane Mayberry slowly developed into a quality guard.

Lows: Well-traveled defensive tackle Don King appeared in only three games as an Eagle, but managed to get into a fist fight with New York Giant Dick Yelvington in one of them.

Eberle Schultz

At 6 feet 4½ inches and over 250 pounds, Elbie Schultz was a huge player for his time. He was a force as either a guard or tackle on offense and was selected twice to All-Pro teams in his eight-year, five-city career. Popular with his teammates, he was team captain on the 1945 NFL champion Cleveland Rams. However, he was not as popular with management after he twice sued teams and won. First in 1948, he sued the Rams for reneging on the details of his contract and won a $5,000 judgment. Then in 1950, he brought to court the defunct Los Angeles Dons from the All-America Conference, with whom he had signed in 1948, and sued them for breach of contract because they cut him after he was injured, and he won a $7,500 judgment. On or off the field, Elbie was not to be trifled with.

Schultz hailed from Oregon and was a second-team All-American at Oregon State in 1939. In the NFL draft, he was picked in the fourth round by Philadelphia. Elbie spent his rookie year with the 1-10 Eagles, blocking for quarterback Davey O'Brien, who was 10 inches shorter than he was. The next year, Schultz's Oregon State teammate Vic Sears was drafted in the fifth round by Pittsburgh. As it turned out, though, Sears would spend the season in Philadelphia while Schultz played in Pittsburgh. The players were not traded, but the franchises were in a very unusual transaction.

Philadelphia and Pittsburgh came into the league together in 1933 as new franchises owned by Bert Bell and Art Rooney, respectively. Neither owner was very successful in assembling a winning team — in the 1930s, the Eagles were 18-55-3, and the Pirates, as Pittsburgh was known until 1940, were 22-55-3 — but Bell and Rooney became good friends while commiserating over all the money they each were losing. In need of relief, Rooney and Bell tried a radical solution in 1940. The initial newspaper reports of the NFL draft meeting in December quoted Bell saying that the two teams were proposing to merge as the only way to improve the quality of the respective clubs. Instead, the next day it was announced that 26-year-old millionaire Lex Thompson had purchased the Pittsburgh franchise from Rooney, and Rooney had bought 50 percent of the Eagles from Bell. In a transaction that had been worked out over months of negotiations, existing players were shifted between the two teams. Thompson was to receive from Bell's Eagles Red Ramsey, Joe Carter, Phil Ragazzo, Clem Woltman, Ted Schmitt, Foster Watkins and Joe Bukant. From Rooney's Steelers, he was to get Bill Sortet, San Boyd, Armand Niccolai, John Woudenberg, Don Campbell, Stan Pavko, John Perko, Ted Grabinski, Joe Maras, Billy Patterson, Merlin Condit, Lou Tomasetti, Swede Johnston, Hank Bruder, Coley McDonough and Tommy Thompson.

From Pittsburgh, Bell and Rooney were to keep George Platukas, Walt Kichefski, John Klumb, Clark Goff, Ted Doyle, Carl Nery, Jack Sanders, Boy Brumbaugh, John Noppenberg, George Kiick and Rocco Pirro. From Philadelphia, they kept Don Looney, Joe Wendlick, George Somers, Ross Thompson, Elbie Schultz, Dick Bassi, Chuck Cherundolo, Moose Harper, Elmer Hackney, Frank Emmons, Elmer Kolberg, Chuck Newton, Fran Murray, Don Jones, Dick Riffle and Jay Arnold.

The original plan was for Thompson to keep his team in Pittsburgh for a season — he announced that they would be renamed the Ironmen under new coach Greasy Neale — and then move them to Boston so he could be closer to his New York business headquarters. Rooney and Bell planned to rename their team the Pennsylvania Keystoners who would operate out of both Philadelphia and Pittsburgh after Thompson moved. But by spring 1941, Rooney was homesick for Pittsburgh and proposed that the two entities swap cities. In April's annual NFL meeting, the swap was approved and announced. Lex Thompson now owned the new Philadelphia Eagles, and Art Rooney, along with Bert Bell, was back in Pittsburgh with the new Steelers. The new Steelers went from two wins in 1940 to a single win in 1941, while the new Eagles went from one win in 1940 to two wins in 1941. Eagles coach Greasy Neale went about completely rebuilding the team. Of the 23 players allocated him from the arrangement, only four (Phil Ragazzo, Foster Watkins, Lou Tomasetti and Tommy Thompson) ever played for Philadelphia. Meanwhile, 20 of the 27 that Rooney and Bell kept played for Pittsburgh along with three original Steelers first allocated to Thompson.

While the Eagles continued to struggle with rebuilding in 1942, the Steelers posted their first winning season that year. By 1943, though, the war was creating a real manpower shortage for the NFL. Bell noted at the time that of the 146 players Pittsburgh had on its active or draft lists, 132 were in the military. At this point, the merger that had been floated three years before became a reality: the Phil-Pitt Eagles-Steelers were born. Known as the Steagles, the team was co-coached by Neale and Steelers coach Walt Kiesling — the only time two Hall of Famers would co-coach a team. The two did not get along at all, however, so Neale was put in charge of the offense while Kiesling handled the defense. Even so, Kiesling once pulled his Steeler players off the practice field after Neale had called one of them a "statue of shit." Behind the hard running of Eagle halfback Jack Hinkle, who finished second in the league in rushing, the Steagles managed a 5-4-1 record, just one game behind the Redskins and Giants in the Eastern Division. They could have been part of a three-way tie for the title if they had been able to knock off Green Bay in the season finale. It was the first winning season of which Philadelphia had taken part.

The Eagles opted out of this arrangement in 1944 and posted a winning record on their own, while the Steelers merged with the Cardinals in a failed 0-10 enterprise known as the Card-Pitts. Neale regularly beat the Steelers, going 12-4-1 against them, but in 1947 the two teams tied for the Eastern crown with 8-4 records, although the Steelers had been outscored by their opponents for the season. In the first postseason game for either franchise, the Eagles won the 1947 Eastern title by beating the Steelers 21-0 in Pittsburgh.

The Eagles continued to dominate the series in the 1950s, winning 13 of 20 for the decade, and in the 1960s, going 10-5-2 for that period. Neither team had an overall winning record in either decade, but the biannual cross-state contests were usually hard-fought, bloody, grudge matches. Both teams were noted for their tough guys, especially in the line, and it was not unusual for fights to break out. Rugged players on both sides, like Steelers Ernie Stautner, Big Daddy Lipscomb and John Henry Johnson, and Eagles Bucko Kilroy and Chuck Bednarik, were not about to back down when things got rough. In one vicious moment, Norm Willey broke Steeler QB Jim Finks' jaw with his forearm in 1954. Fiery leaders like Bobby Layne and Norm Van Brocklin at the turn of the decade, inflamed the rivalry even more. Sadly, commissioner Bert Bell died of a massive heart attack while watching one of those back and forth battles between his two old teams in 1959 in Philadelphia when a fourth-quarter touchdown pass from Norm Van Brocklin to Tommy McDonald won the game 28-24. Ten years later, the rivalry would begin to fade. The Steelers moved to a different division in 1967 and to the American Conference in 1970. In their first 37 years, the two teams met 69 times, but in the last 35 years, they have met only nine times. The occasional prospect of an all-Pennsylvania Super Bowl still rekindles those fires that once burned so brightly between two very different cities with a shared heritage.

Fashion Statements

Jess Richardson
DT 1954-61

Originator: Free agent tackle Burr West came from Tennessee with All-American Bob Suffridge in 1941.

Longest Tenure: 11 years, Wade Key.

Number Changes: Jess Richardson wore 65 in 1953; Joe Panos wore 63 in 1994.

Just Visiting: Frank Fuller played four years each with the Rams and Cardinals.

Highs: Floyd Peters was a crafty defensive tackle and was picked as the best lineman in the 1967 Pro Bowl; Wade Key was a decent lineman for some bad Bird squads in the 1970s; David Alexander was an undersized center in the Ryan-Kotite years; Tra Thomas is the largest Eagle player ever but doesn't always play up to his size.

Lows: Kevin Allen may have been the team's worst draft pick of all time. Not only could he not play, but also he was convicted of sexual assault at the Jersey shore after his first and only season in the NFL.

Jess Richardson

Even though he was the last lineman in the league to play without wearing a facemask, Jess Richardson never lost a tooth. His nose wasn't so lucky. He broke that so many times that he would reset it himself by going in the shower, smearing his nose with Vaseline and rubbing up and down along the sides of his nose till he felt everything was back in place. He claimed that a facemask would ruin his peripheral vision because he had deep-set, narrow eyes. While the rationale seems dubious, Richardson did have special permission from the league to go without the facemask. In an effort to be at his quickest, he didn't wear tape or pads either, and opted for the lightest shoulder pads he could find as well.

In 1949, Jess went from Philadelphia's Roxborough High School to the University of Alabama as a 210-pound defensive guard. Four years later, the Eagles drafted him in the eighth round, and he made the team as a 235-pound defensive tackle. By the end of his rookie season, he was a starter and part of the Suicide Seven, as the Philadelphia linemen and linebackers were known at the time. They were a rugged crew, and Jess fit right in, never afraid to throw an elbow at a distracted opponent. One time he was caught punching Giant quarterback Y.A. Tittle, and a few years later he was ejected from an AFL game for bumping an official. For the latter incident, he was hit with an AFL record $500 fine that he paid with money raised by Boston fans passing the hat at a Patriot game. Although he was big, he was noted for his quickness as well. While he was best at stopping the run, he was an all-around performer who was the Eagles' MVP in 1955, went to the Pro Bowl in 1959 and was a second-team All-Pro in the 1960 title run. By then he was over 270 pounds. Sadly, the week before the championship, Jess' seven-week-old baby died of pneumonia in his crib. Richardson played the game anyway rather than let down his teammates.

When the Eagles went into a late-season slump the year after winning the championship, new coach Nick Skorich tried to shake up things by replacing Chuck Weber at middle linebacker with Chuck Bednarik and benching the popular Richardson. The team still finished second, and in the next training camp, Jess was cut. He caught on with the Boston Patriots for three more seasons despite contracting hepatitis in his first year in New England. He appeared in the 1963 AFL title game, but missed most of it due to knee and hand injuries. Upon retiring, he was hired as the defensive line coach in Boston and stayed through 1970. By 1971, he was back in Philly, coaching the Eagles' defensive line, but was fired along with Eddie Khayat at the end of 1972. Three years later, Jess would be dead from kidney disease at the age of 45. Later that year, the Eagle Alumni Association dedicated the Richardson Memorial Dialysis Section in Mercy Catholic Hospital.

With defensive linemen these days wearing giant, cage-type facemasks and sometimes dark visors, it's hard to imagine a time when players decked out simply like Jess Richardson were common. And not only the equipment has changed, but the fashion as well. The Eagles' first jerseys were yellow with blue numbers on the chest and a blue

Two former Eagle defensive tackles in 1972: head coach Ed Khayat on the left and defensive line coach Jess Richardson on the right. Guess which one never wore a facemask as a player.

vertical stripe from the neck to each wrist. Their leather helmets were unadorned. In the later thirties, Bert Bell dropped the yellow and blue for solid green jerseys with white numerals, white pants and leather helmets. New ownership in 1941 brought a return of the one vertical stripe from the neck to the wrist, but now the color scheme was a white jersey with a green stripe and green pants, or a green jersey with a white stripe and white pants. The Eagles adopted a very unusual helmet design at this time as well. The sides were green, while the front and the top were either silver or white in a rounded design that is said to resemble either a wing or feather, perhaps in a hallucination. No other team has ever worn anything like it.

In 1948, just in time for the back-to-back championships, the Eagles switched to a new, simpler jersey style. Their green jerseys were solid with white numerals and were worn with silver pants; their white jerseys featured green numerals and two horizontal stripes on each sleeve. They would stick with this basic style through the 1962 season, although they switched from silver to white pants around 1953. The feather/wing helmet, now made of plastic, would continue to be used through the 1952 season. A plain green plastic helmet was introduced as an alternative in 1950 and was used through 1953. In 1954, the now-familiar green helmet with two recognizable wings emanating from the front of the helmet was introduced and would continue unchanged for the next 15 seasons.

The 1960s brought some tinkering. Horizontal white stripes were added to the green jerseys and more stripes were added to the white jerseys. In 1967, stripes were added to the shoulder pads, and in 1969, alternate plain green and plain white jerseys without stripes were introduced. The wings on the green helmet were switched to white and an alternate white helmet with green wings was added. From 1970 to 1973, only those alternate jerseys and white helmets were worn, although a black border was added to the green helmet wings in 1973.

Long-lasting changes occurred in 1974. There were now 10 green, silver and white horizontal stripes on the sleeves, numbers were added to the shoulder pads and the home pants were either silver or gray. The green helmet returned, but with silver wings bordered in white, and would last 22 years. The uniform remained stable until another change in ownership in 1985 that brought a return to plain green or plain white jerseys, but now with the team insignia of an Eagle in flight clutching a football in its talons on the sleeves and with numerals on the shoulders.

Jeff Lurie waited a year after he bought the Eagles to remake the uniform again — this time radically. In 1996, bright Eagle kelly green changed to dark Eagle midnight green, and the logo changed to a screaming eagle head. Again, white and green jerseys featured the logo, but there were numerals on the shoulders and no stripes on the sleeves. Green pants were brought back, but not just for the white jerseys. Starting in 2002, the team sometimes went all green as part of a hideous league-wide trend to wear tops and bottoms of the same color and create a look that someday will appear as silly as some "mod" designs from the 1970s do today. The following year saw black jerseys and sometimes even black jerseys with black pants to accentuate the ugliness. The major change on the helmet was that the wings were now a mixture of white, silver and black, making them seem more three-dimensional.

The Eagles have altered their uniform design quite a bit over the years, and that is evident when you go to the Linc to see a game. You'll see fans wearing jerseys of current stars, as well as Cunningham jerseys from the late eighties, Jaworski jerseys from the seventies and expensive throwback jerseys of Chuck Bednarik in the sixties and Steve Van Buren in the forties. Owners come and go and can change the style of uniform all they want, but they can't change the hard-hitting style of Philadelphia football.

73

K2 – Avalanche

Ed Khayat
DT 1958-61, 1964-65

WHO'S WORN THE NUMBER:

Ed Kasky (T) 1942, Rocco Canale (G) 1943-45, Henry Gude (G) 1946, Alfred Bauman (T) 1947, Fred Hartman (T) 1948, Roscoe Hansen (T) 1951, *Lum Snyder* (T) 1952-55, Sid Youngelman (T) 1956-88, Ed Khayat (DT) 1958-61 and 1964-5, Jim Norton (T) 1968, Richard Stevens (T) 1970-74, Pete Lazetich (DT) 1976-77, Steve Kenney (G) 1980-85, Paul Ryczek (C) 1987r, Ron Heller (T) 1988-92, Lester Holmes (G) 1993-96, Jerry Crafts (T/G) 1997, Steve Martin (DT) 1998, Oliver Ross (T) 1999, Jim Pyne (C/G) 2001, Shawn Andrews (G) 2004.

Originator: Tackle Ed Kasky went into the Marines before the 1942 season ended and only played minor league football after the war.

Longest Tenure: Six years, Ed Khayat and guard Steve Kenney.

Number Changes: Lum Snider wore 79 in 1958; Jerry Crafts wore 66 in 1998; Steve Martin wore 91 in 1999.

Just Visiting: Jim Pyne started for the Lions and Browns.

Highs: Lum Snider was a very fast Pro Bowl tackle who retired to go into business in 1956 and returned two years later to become the team's MVP for 1958; the Eagles' offensive MVP for 1990, Ron Heller was a combative overachiever.

Lows: Partly due to a knee injury, Lester Holmes was a major disappointment as a first-round draft pick.

Ed Khayat

The Eagles have employed three head coaches whose names began with the letter K, and all three have been complete disasters. The nicest thing that can be said about former Eagle player Ed Khayat's tenure as coach is that it was over quickly — less than two seasons. He did not hang on for four or five years like Rich Kotite and Joe Kuharich did. As a player, he had a nomadic 10-year professional career in which nothing was ever handed to him.

The Mississippi-bred Khayat was a moderate-sized defensive tackle who joined the Washington Redskins in 1957 as a free agent out of Tulane. In Washington, Ed had the opportunity to absorb some of that special K Coaching Magic from the master himself, Joe Kuharich. Khayat was cut by Kuharich the next season, and Buck Shaw picked him up for the Eagles. Shaw first tried Eddie out as an offensive tackle, and then in 1959, moved him to defensive end, but that didn't take either. Finally, Khayat moved back to defensive tackle as a starter for the 1960 championship Eagles. He wasn't particularly fast, or big or strong, but he was scrappy and motivated.

In 1962, Khayat was let go again and returned to Washington where he spent two seasons with his brother Bob, who was the Redskins' ineffective field goal kicker. During that season, Eddie had a confrontation with New York coach Allie Sherman after the Giants game in DC. Sherman charged at Khayat after the Giants' victory and shook his finger at him while the two had a shouting contest. It was a scene repeated 40 years later when another Coach Sherman, Packers coach Mike Sherman, confronted Buccaneer Warren Sapp after Sapp delivered a cheap shot to Packer tackle Chad Clifton. Giants defensive tackle Dick Modzelewski was quoted in the *Washington Post* the next day saying that Khayat was "dirty. He's no good. He can't play well. He did a lot of punching in New York, and he was punching out there today." Eddie, after all, had been the Novice Division Golden Gloves Heavyweight Champion for Mississippi in 1953 and 1954. Khayat returned to the Eagles in 1964 to spend two more seasons absorbing the brilliant coaching wisdom of Joe Kuharich in Philadelphia, and then concluded his career with a final season with the Patriots in 1966.

Upon retirement, Eddie moved directly into coaching, joining the staff of Tom Fears in New Orleans in 1967 as the defensive line coach. When Fears was fired in 1971, both he and Khayat joined Jerry Williams' staff in Philadelphia. Williams, of course, had coached Khayat on the 1960s team and was in the midst of his third straight losing season in Philadelphia. After losing the first three games of the 1971 season by a combined score of 110-24, Williams was fired by owner Leonard Tose and Ed Khayat was hired as interim coach.

Ed's start as a head coach was not auspicious as the Birds dropped their next two games. Khayat then got the inspired notion that what was holding back the team was its facial hair and ordered the players to shave it off. "Good grooming is one of the many facets of discipline," he said at the time. The Eagles won their next game in the rain against the Giants and went on a 6-2-1 tear for the rest of the season. They concluded the year with a four-game winning streak. Tose was so impressed that he gave Khayat and general manager Pete Retzlaff two-year contract extensions. The key to the team's improvement was the defense led by middle linebacker Tim Rossovich and free safety Bill Bradley, who paced the NFL in interceptions in 1971.

What followed in 1972 was that Ed Khayat became the personification of the Peter Principle and rose to his level of incompetence. As an assistant coach, he was a positive, happy-go-lucky motivator who was big on communication. As an interim head coach of a team that was 0-5, he was under absolutely no pressure to succeed. After the stirring turnaround in 1971, however, increased expectations led to increased pressures, and Khayat seemed to tighten up. Bad things started in training camp when Rossovich and Bradley staged a holdout. Rossovich was traded, and outside linebacker Steve Zabel was asked to move over to the middle where he felt unfamiliar and uncomfortable. With the linebacking corps weakened, the other holes in the defense became more pronounced. As for the offense, the starting quarterbacking was split between rag-armed incumbent Pete Liske and overmatched rookie John Reaves with pretty boy Rick Arrington available as a third unviable option. Because the Eagles were behind and throwing the ball a lot, Harold Jackson provided the one bright spot that year by leading the league in receptions and yardage. The Eagles lost their first five games for the second consecutive year, but this year also lost the last five games to finish 2-11-1. The lowest point came on November 26th when the Birds lost to the Giants 62-10. It was the team's worst loss for the decade, and Khayat accused his team of the ultimate sin — quitting. Three weeks later, Khayat was fired and Retzlaff resigned.

Khayat continued on as a popular defensive line coach in the league for the next 20 years before moving on to the Arena League. In the Arena League, Eddie has been the head coach of three different teams and led the Nashville Kats to back-to-back championship game appearances in 2000 and 2001. He was inducted into the Mississippi Sports Hall of Fame in 2004, joining his brother Robert who was now the chancellor at the University of Mississippi. Eddie Khayat was a decent guy who got in way over his head with a very bad team, but Eagle fans should remember him as a player who would never quit.

Role Players

Walter "Piggy" Barnes
G 1948-51

Originator: Guard Walter Barnes in 1948.

Longest Tenure: Six years, Mike Pitts.

Number Changes: Frank Wydo wore 75 from 1952 to 1956; Len Szafaryn wore 76 in 1957; Steve Smith wore 78 in 1971; Leonard Mitchell wore 99 from 1981 to 1983.

Just Visiting: John Niland was a star guard for the Cowboys.

Highs: Frank Wydo (see 75 top); defensive tackle Riley Gunnels was the team's defensive MVP in 1962; Mike Pitts was an unheralded member of the best Eagles front four in history.

Lows: Number one draft choice Leonard Mitchell failed as a defensive tackle before failing as an offensive tackle. Fellow first-pick Bernard Williams didn't play too badly as a rookie, but failed a drug test and never returned to the NFL.

Walter "Piggy" Barnes

It took Walter Barnes a long time to get started on his career, but he made a name for himself just the same. He was a 30-year-old rookie guard for the Eagles in 1948, but wouldn't get started on his lifelong occupation of acting for five more years.

Piggy was born and raised in Greasy Neale's hometown of Parkersburg, West Virginia. He was a two-time All-State tackle in high school before enrolling at Louisiana State in 1939. As a freshman, Barnes made news by being suspended from the team. Reports differ as to whether he was suspended for criticizing coach Bernie Moore for the food served at the training table or for cutting classes and missing mandatory military drills. After apologizing to the team, he was reinstated a few hours later. Barnes spent two years at LSU and then joined the military where he achieved the rank of sergeant in the Army Air Corps during five years of service. He returned to LSU after the war and played for the Tigers again in 1946 and 1947.

Neale signed Barnes for the Eagles in 1948, just in time to help the Birds to back-to-back NFL championships. In a 1948 win over the Bears, Piggy scored his only two points of his career when he tackled Sid Luckman in the end zone for a safety. Barnes was a big man for the 1940s at 240 pounds and was very strong in the middle of the line. He was an avid weightlifter at a time when coaches discouraged players from lifting so they wouldn't become too muscle bound and inflexible. Piggy was a rough player, but did not consider himself a dirty one. He told the *Chicago Tribune* in 1949 that "A good player doesn't have to slug. The dirty player never is ready for that second try [i.e., effort]." But later that year in a game against Pittsburgh, though, Barnes and teammate Chuck Bednarik were ejected for fighting, along with Steelers Frank Wydo and Charlie Mehelich.

Ironically, Barnes was traded to the Steelers along with quarterback John Rauch for the very same Frank Wydo in 1952. Barnes retired from football and never played for Pittsburgh, but briefly went into coaching under Lou Little at Columbia. In 1953, Walter's fighting skills brought him into a new arena. Local television station WCAU (Channel 10) began producing a live, five-day-a-week, half-hour western called *Action in the Afternoon*. Barnes was originally cast in bad guy roles because he was big and could fight, but when the producers saw that he really could act, he began to get hero parts as well.

Barnes started to draw work in all the top western TV shows of the time — *Gunsmoke, Bonanza, Cheyenne, Have Gun Will Travel* and *Maverick*. His first full-length movie was *Oregon Passage* in 1957, and he would eventually appear in over 50 films, generally as a character actor. He made several spaghetti westerns in Italy in the 1960s and got to know Clint Eastwood. He later appeared with Clint in *High Plains Drifter, Cahill: U.S. Marshall, Every Which Way But Loose* and *Bronco Billy*. He retired from acting in the late 1980s and moved into the Motion Picture and Television Retirement Home where he died in 1998 at the age of 79.

Piggy Barnes was not the only Eagle to act professionally. The first was Reb Russell, who played with the very first Eagles squad in 1933. At that point, he had already appeared in his first movie, *The All-American*, in 1932. He would go on to make several westerns, none memorable, in the 1930s. Timmy Brown, the 1960s star halfback, made close to 20 movies and several TV guest shots in the 1970s and 1980s. His most famous role was his first, as Spearchucker Jones in the 1970 film classic *M*A*S*H*. Tim Rossovich roomed with Tom Selleck at USC and found work as an actor and stunt man in movies and TV throughout the 1970s and 1980s. He even appeared twice on *Magnum P.I.* with his old roommate Selleck. Matt Battaglia was a replacement player during the 1987 strike and has found acting work in action movies, TV soap operas and prime time television since the 1990s.

Some less successful Eagle actors include Reggie White who played himself in *4 Little Girls*, Rev. Reggie Knox in *Reggie's Prayer* and Coach Pruitt on a *Touched By an Angel* episode. His teammate Keith Jackson played an Assistant Coach in *Reggie's Prayer*. Another Jackson receiver, Harold, played a generic football player in *North Dallas Forty* and a piano player in *Swing Shift* to show his range. Don Burroughs played a doctor on the *Donna Reed Show*. Don Chuy appeared in episodes of *Bonanza* and *Perry Mason* but is best remembered for his role in Woody Allen's *Everything You Always Wanted to Know About Sex*, in which he makes out with teammate Tom Mack in a faux commercial. Eternally aspiring actor Darnell Autry has appeared briefly in one movie and one TV show.

And then there's the current Eagles' owner Jeff Lurie, who has not only played himself in *Jerry Maguire* and an episode of *Arli$$*, but also played Barney's friend in the Tony Danza TV movie, *The Garbage Picking Field Goal Kicking Philadelphia Phenomenon*. A born showman, Lurie must be proud of his "gold standard" record as a Hollywood producer: *Sweet Hearts Dance, I Love You to Death, V.I. Warshawski* and several television productions of equal entertainment value.

Finally, several Eagles have played either themselves or a generic football player in a Hollywood production:

PLAYER	ROLE	PRODUCTION	YEAR
Bill Hewitt	himself	*Pro Football*	1934
Jack Banta	generic	*Easy Living*	1949
Jack Zilly	generic	*Easy Living*	1949
Norm Van Brocklin	generic	*The Long Gray Line*	1953
Tom Woodeshick	generic	*M*A*S*H*	1970
Jack Concannon	generic	*M*A*S*H*	1970
Jack Concannon	himself	*Brian's Song*	1971
Tom Brookshier	himself	*Black Sunday*	1977
Steve Zabel	generic	*Everybody's All-American*	1988
Richie Kotite	himself	*Jerry Maguire*	1996
Art Monk	himself	*Jerry Maguire*	1996
Terrell Owens	himself	*Any Given Sunday*	1999
Irving Fryar	himself	*Any Given Sunday*	1999
Ricky Watters	himself	*Any Given Sunday*	1999
Ricky Watters	himself	*In the House*	1999

1970s Decade in Review

Stan Walters
T 1975-83

Originator: Tackle Bill Halverson, who went from the Rose Bowl to the Eagles in 1942.

Longest Tenure: Nine years, Stan Walters from 1975-83.

Number Changes: George Savitsky also wore 64 in 1949; Daryle Smith wore 63 in 1991 and 1992; Bob Suffridge wore 60 in 1942; Frank Wydo wore 74 in 1957.

Just Visiting: Houston Antwine was a load at defensive tackle for a decade with the Patriots.

Highs: Bob Suffridge (see 60 top); Cornell's Frank Wydo played more years (11) in the NFL than any other Red Raider aside from kicker Pete Gogolak and never missed a game. While with the Steelers, Wydo hit Chuck Bednarik with a cheap shot to avenge a Bednarik hit from a Penn-Cornell match. The two would room together while with the Birds.

Lows: Tackle John Michels was obtained in a trade with the Packers for Jon Harris so that neither team would have to have the embarrassment of cutting their own former number one draft pick.

Stan Walters

Stan Walters Sr. was a machinist in Jersey City and Stan Jr. more than lived up to his blue-collar roots on the football field. A football scholarship took Junior to Syracuse University where he underwhelmed scouts to the extent that the 6-foot 6-inch, 275-pound Walters lasted until the ninth round of the 1972 draft before Paul Brown selected him for Cincinnati. Stan made the team's taxi squad, but ended up starting the last eight games of the year after Rufus Mayes was injured. Hepatitis sidelined him in 1973, but he returned to full strength the following season.

In 1975, Cincinnati traded Walters and backup quarterback Wayne Clark to Philadelphia for John Reaves and a second-round pick. Dick Vermeil arrived in town the next year and Walters began to emerge as one of the best left tackles in the game. He and Jerry Sisemore teamed up to form perhaps the top set of tackles in Eagle history. The current twin towers of Jon Runyan and Tra Thomas are not as consistent as Walters and Sisemore were. Old-timers could make a strong case for Al Wistert and Vic Sears from the 1940s, but Stan and Jerry take a back seat to no one. The one bad play that Eagle fans remember from Walters, the Bears' Mike Hartenstine's blind side demolition of Ron Jaworski in 1980, was excused by Jaws, who has always maintained that he hung on to the ball too long on that play. Even if that explanation is simply one teammate sticking up for another, it demonstrates the respect that Jaws had for the sound left tackle who had his back for seven years. Stan twice made the Pro Bowl in his nine years in Philadelphia, playing in 127 of the Eagles' 131 games, 122 of them consecutively.

Walters liked to talk when he was on the field, but it was the opposite of trash talk. His comments usually were a steady stream of compliments for the other team's defensive end — "Nice move. Good play." It was his view that the nasty stuff only serves to fire up your opponent. Once he retired in 1984, Stan got to continue to speak, but this time into a microphone, as he moved up to the broadcast booth as Merrill Reese's radio color analyst for the next dozen years. Walters was popular as a broadcaster because fans appreciated his bluntness, good sense and honesty. He left in 1997 to support a career move of his wife, but he will always be remembered as part of the Eagles Honor Roll; where he was inducted along with his old partner Jerry Sisemore in 1991.

Decade Headline: The Long Climb Back.
Where They Played: Franklin Field, 1958-70; Veterans Stadium, 1971-02.
How the Game Was Played: Improving defensive play eventually led to the liberalizing of pass coverage rules in 1978. Situation substitution began in earnest with George Allen's Nickel (five defensive backs) and Dime (six defensive backs) packages. Almost all placekickers were now soccer-style booters.

Decade Won-Lost Record: 56-84-4, .403; 1-2 in the playoffs.
Record Against the Cowboys: 3-17.
Record Against the Giants: 15-4-1.

Record Against the Redskins: 4-15-1.

Record Against the Steelers: 2-1.

Playoff Appearances: 1978, 1979.

Championships: None.

Unsung Hero: Jim Murray, who served as general manager beginning in the mid-1970s and helped the team finally right itself after a 15-year slide.

Head Coaches: Jerry Williams 1969-71, 3-13-1 for the decade; Ed Khayat 1971-72, 8-15-2; Mike McCormack 1973-75, 16-25-1; Dick Vermeil 1976-82, 29-31 for the decade plus 1-2 in the playoffs.

Best Player: Wilbert Montgomery.

Hall of Famers: None.

Eagle Honor Roll: Bill Bergey, Bill Bradley, Harold Carmichael, Ron Jaworski, Wilbert Montgomery, Jerry Sisemore, Dick Vermeil, Stan Walters.

League Leaders: Bill Bradley — interceptions 1971-72; Harold Jackson — receptions 1972, receiving yards 1972; Harold Carmichael — receptions 1973, receiving yards 1973, TD catches 1979; Roman Gabriel — pass attempts 1973, completions 1973, passing yards 1973, TD passes 1973; Charlie Young — receptions 1974.

Award Winners: Roman Gabriel, Comeback Player 1973; Charlie Young, Rookie of the Year 1973; Dick Vermeil, Coach of the Year 1979.

All-Pros: Bill Bradley 1971-73; Harold Jackson 1972; Harold Carmichael 1973, 1979; Charlie Young 1973-74; Bill Bergey 1974-78; Wilbert Montgomery 1978-79; Charlie Johnson 1979; Stan Walters 1979.

Pro Bowl Selections: Bill Bradley 1971-3; Harold Jackson 1972; Harold Carmichael 1973, 1978-79; Roman Gabriel 1973; Charlie Young 1973-75; Bill Bergey 1974, 1976-8; Mike Boryla 1975; Wilbert Montgomery 1978-79; Stan Walters 1978-79; Jerry Sisemore 1979; Wally Henry 1979; Charlie Johnson 1979; Randy Logan 1979.

Best Offensive Backfield: 1979, with quarterback Ron Jaworski, running back Wilbert Montgomery, fullback Leroy Harris, and wideout Harold Carmichael.

Best Draft Choice: Harold Carmichael was chosen in the seventh round in 1971, while Wilbert Montgomery was taken in the sixth round in 1977.

Best Overall Draft: In 1973, nine draftees made the club, including Charlie Young, Jerry Sisemore, Randy Logan, Guy Morris and Joe Lavender.

Worst Draft Choice: John Reaves was selected in the middle of the first round in 1972 and completed less than half his passes for seven touchdowns and 15 interceptions in three years.

Worst Overall Draft: For the 1975 draft, the Eagles didn't have a pick until the seventh round and only two players stuck with the team even briefly.

Best Free Agent: Herman Edwards was a walk-on in 1977 and is second in team history in interceptions. Honorable mention goes to Vince Papale, a special teams demon who made the team in 1976 after impressing Coach Vermeil in a private workout despite being a 30-year-old high school teacher who never played college football.

Best Trade: The Eagles gave up a lot to the Bengals in 1974 for Bill Bergey (two number one draft picks and a number two), but he was worth it. Bengals All-Pro tackle Stan Walters came cheaper in 1975 — failed quarterback John Reaves and a number two pick. The most interesting deal was trading Tim Rossovich to San Diego in 1972 for a number one pick who turned out to be tight end Charlie Young. After three Pro Bowl seasons, Young was then traded to the Rams in 1977 for quarterback Ron Jaworski, who would take the Birds to the Super Bowl.

Worst Trade: Roman Gabriel cost the Eagles Harold Jackson, Tony Baker, two number one picks and a number three in 1973. Gabriel had one great season, but never led the team to a winning record. A bizarre deal in 1971 gave up three draft picks to the Lions for a backup quarterback, Greg Barton, who had at that point thrown one incomplete pass in his career. Barton then burned the Eagles by signing with the Canadian Football League.

Biggest Off-Field Event: Early in 1972, tight end Fred Hill approached owner Len Tose, distraught because his daughter had leukemia. Tose and general manager Jim Murray started a major campaign called the Eagles Fly for Leukemia that goes on to this day. The drive paid for the construction of the oncology unit in Children's Hospital and laboratories in the Hospital's Cancer Research Center.

Biggest On-Field Development: Hope. Dick Vermeil brought hope and that was best exemplified in the Miracle of the Meadowlands victory over the Giants that led to the Eagles making the playoffs in 1978 for the first time in nearly two decades.

Strangest On-Field Event: Eagle fans are not the only fans who boo. On October 27, 1974, Saints fans held up the Saints' 14-10 victory over Philadelphia for 18 minutes by booing the officials so loudly that the Eagles could not get off a play. The officials sent both teams to the sidelines and had the band play music in the interim till the fans quieted down. When the teams returned, the Eagles, who had been in Saint territory, lost their momentum and failed to score.

Worst Failure: For most of the decade, the Eagles were a horrible football team and could not compete with the hated Cowboys. Dallas beat Philadelphia 17 of 20 times in the decade.

Home Attendance: 4,386,648 in 72 games for an average gate of 60,926.

Best Game: The Cowboys had beaten the Eagles nine straight times from 1974 through 1978; the last six of those times were under Coach Dick Vermeil, who was rebuilding a husk of a franchise. Finally, on November 12, 1979 on *Monday Night Football*, the Eagles showed the whole country that they had caught up to the Cowboys, beating them convincingly 31-21 in Dallas. Tony Franklin kicked a 59-yard field goal, backup quarterback John Walton threw a touchdown pass, and Wilbert Montgomery ran for over 100 yards, including a game-clinching 37-yard touchdown scamper.

First Game: On September 20, 1970, the Eagles lost 17-7 to Dallas with Norm Snead throwing three interceptions.

Last Game: December 16, 1979. The Eagles beat the Oilers 26-20 in Houston to end the regular season. The winning score came on a fourth-quarter touchdown pass from John Walton to Scott Fitzkee. Two weeks later, Philadelphia was ousted from the playoffs, losing 24-17 at Tampa Bay.

Largest Margin of Victory: December 2, 1979. The Eagles pounded Detroit 44-7 with Ron Jaworski throwing two touchdowns and Billy Campfield returning a kickoff for another score.

Largest Margin of Defeat: In the worst defeat in team history, the Eagles lost to the Giants in Yankee Stadium 62-10 on November 26, 1972. Coach Ed Khayat accused the team of quitting, and nobody argued with him.

Best Offense: In 1979, Philadelphia scored 339 points, the seventh best total in the league.

Best Defense: In 1977, the Eagles gave up 207 points in 14 games, seventh in the league; in 1978 they gave up 250 points in 16 games, fifth in the league.

Most Games Played: 121, Wade Key.

Most Points: 342, Harold Carmichael.

Most Field Goals: 66, Tom Dempsey.

Most Touchdowns: 57, Harold Carmichael.

Most Touchdown Passes: 52, Ron Jaworski.

Most Passing Yards: 7,339, Ron Jaworski.

Most Receiving Yards: 6,080 Harold Carmichael.

Most Receptions: 407, Harold Carmichael.

Most Rushing Yards: 3,135, Tom Sullivan.

Most Interceptions: 33, Bill Bradley.

Most Sacks: NA

Most Kickoff Return Yards: 2,075, Larry Marshall.

Most Punt Return Yards: 1,086, Larry Marshall.

Book Notes: *Tales from the Eagles Sidelines,* by *USA Today* columnist and onetime Eagle beat writer Gordon Forbes, profiles prominent and not so prominent Eagles throughout the team's history, but features a lot of names from the 1970s. Similarly, *Eagles: Where Have They Gone?* by Fran Zimniuch, tracks down many Eagles from the 1970s and other decades.

Noted Sportswriter: Ray Diddinger was a beat writer and then columnist for the *Evening Bulletin* and then the *Daily News* before moving on to production work for NFL Films.

Best Quotation: The night before the Eagles recorded their first win over the Cowboys in 10 games, Coach Dick Vermeil said to his team, "What's it going to take to beat the Dallas Cowboys? Just 24 hours."

Bubblegum Factoid: Despite averaging only 10.0 yards per catch in his rookie season, the 1974 Topps card number 379 for Don Zimmerman calls him "One of the Eagles' fine deep threat receivers."

Accidents of Birth: Rick Arrington is the father of sideline reporter Jill Arrington; Louie Giammona was the nephew of his coach, Dick Vermeil; Ove Johansson was born in Sweden; Nick Mike-Mayer was born in Italy; Horst Muhlmann was born in Germany; Tuufuli Upersa was born in Samoa.

Famous Names: Spike Jones, not the musician; Richard Harris, not the actor.

Unusual Names: Houston Antwine, John Bunting, Cleveland Franklin, Roman Gabriel, Blenda Gay, Ove Johansson, Keith Krepfle, Joe Lavender, Herb Lusk, Nick Mike-Mayer, Horst Muhlmann, John Outlaw, Max Runager, Jim Thrower, Tuufuli Upersa.

Nicknames: Bill "Bubba" Bergey, "Dollar" or "Super" Bill Bradley, Don "Boomer" Brumm, Bill "Boone" Bryant, Norm "Big Boo" Bulaich, John "Frito Bandito" Bunting, Tommy "Turk" Campbell, Harold "Hoagie" Carmichael, Ken "Air" Clarke, Bill "Popeye" or "House Mover" Dunstan, James "Happy" Feller, Carl "Big Daddy" Hairston, Richard "Panther" Harris, Dennis "Big Foot" Harrison, Ron "Jaws" or "The Polish Rifle" Jaworski, "Turkey" Joe Jones, Wade "Buck" Key, Joe "Big Bird" Lavender, Al "Pete" Nelson, Artimus "T Bone" Parker, Edwin "Pete" Perot, Charles "Tank" or "Home Boy" Smith, Tom "Silky" Sullivan, Charles "Tree" Young.

Fastest Player: Probably Harold Jackson, although Don Zimmerman and Wilbert Montgomery were sprinters in college as well.

Heaviest Player: Dennis Harrison and Stan Walters were both 275 pounds.

Lightest Player: Return man Wally Henry was 5 feet 8 inches and 175 pounds.

Toughest Injury: Bill Bergey went down with a knee injury early in 1979. Although he returned the next season for the Birds' Super Bowl run, he was not the same player and retired the year after.

Local Boys: From the surrounding area came Mike Evans, Scott Fitzkee, Carl Gersbach, Dick Hart, Larry Marshall, Vince Papale, John Spagnola and Tom Woodeschick. Among local colleges: Villanova — Kevin Reilly, John Sodaski and Billy Walik; St. Joseph's — Vince Papale; Temple — Nick Mike-Mayer; West Chester – Merritt Kersey; and Gettysberg — Jim Ward.

Firsts:

Game at Veterans Stadium — On September 19, 1971, the Eagles opened their brand-new, all-purpose stadium with a 37-14 loss to the Bengals.

Playoff Game at Veterans Stadium — On December 23, 1979, Philadelphia celebrated its first postseason home game in 19 years with a convincing 27-17 victory over the Bears.

Overtime Game — The Birds lost their first regular season overtime game 20-17 to the Redskins on September 27, 1976.

Monday Night Football Game — November 23, 1970. The Eagles beat the Giants 23-20 at Franklin Field in the first season of MNF. Broadcaster Howard Cosell got sick and had to leave before the game was over.

Game (Exhibition) Held Outside the U.S. — On August 5, 1978, the Birds were beaten 14-7 by the New Orleans Saints in a preseason game held in Mexico City.

Soccer-Style Kicker — Horst Muhlmann in 1975.

76

Line of Tackles

Bob Brown
T 1964-68

Originator: Former Bear starting end Les McDonald came to the Eagles in a 1940 trade and played most of the year in Philadelphia.

Longest Tenure: 13 years, Bucko Kilroy.

Number Changes: Les McDonald also wore 26 in 1940; John Eibner wore 77 in 1946; Len Szafaryn wore 74 in 1958.

Just Visiting: Len Szafaryn, Volney Peters and Joe Carollo were decent tackles in Green Bay, Washington and Los Angeles, respectively.

Highs: Bucko Kilroy was a seven-time All-Pro; J.D. Smith was selected for one Pro Bowl; Jerry Sisemore was picked twice for the Pro Bowl.

Lows: After having his salary cut in 1994, Broderick Thompson was a disgruntled cancer on the team. During the year, he was the most penalized Eagle and led the team in sacks allowed. Barrett Brooks gave up nearly a sack a game in 1997.

Bob Brown

The Spirit of '76 for the Philadelphia Eagles is the spirit of an offensive lineman. The team has employed a string of Pro Bowl quality tackles who wore that number. The first star to wear 76 was Francis "Bucko" Kilroy, a 1943 free agent from Northeast Catholic High School by way of Temple University. Kilroy put the "offensive" in his play, no matter which side of the ball he was on. He played for 13 rugged and rough years, was named All-Pro seven times and went to three Pro Bowls. He was known to kick, punch and bite opponents and lived by the motto, "Love your god, respect your elders and fear no son of a bitch that walks." In 1959, the Eagles drafted the 6-foot 5-inch 250-pound J.D. Smith out of Rice University and he moved into the starting lineup immediately. Smith was the team's steadiest lineman and was named to the Pro Bowl squad in 1961. He was a fixture for five years before Joe Kuharich traded him to Detroit for Ollie Matson and Floyd Peters and replaced him with the second overall pick in the 1964 draft, Bob Brown. Brown spent five seasons in Philadelphia, and four years after he left town, the Eagles drafted Jerry Sisemore out of Texas with the third overall pick in the 1973 draft. The easygoing Sisemore was a reliable fixture, mostly at right tackle, for a dozen years and was named to two Pro Bowls. Jerry appeared in 127 consecutive games, and during the 1980 Super Bowl season, he did not give up a sack all year.

Out of all these stars, though, Bob Brown shone brightest. Brown went from the worst part of Cleveland to the cornfields of Nebraska on a football scholarship and played guard and linebacker for the Cornhuskers while earning a degree in biology. He was voted lineman of the year by the Washington Touchdown Club in his senior year and was Joe Kuharich's first and best draft choice. Working with line coach Dick Stanfel, Brown switched to tackle and became a devastating force in the Eagle offensive line as a rookie, making second-team All-Pro. He would be named first or second-team All-Pro each of his five Eagles seasons and be named to three Pro Bowls.

Brown was called the Boomer and played at anywhere from 280 to 315 pounds, although his official weight with the Birds was never listed as more than 295. Despite his size, he was timed at 4.4 in the 40-yard dash. To this size and speed, Brown added an aggressive attitude and unsurpassed strength. He once explained that his philosophy was "not to accept the blows but to deliver them. There are some choice areas like the spleen when I can get at it." When Brown was with the Rams, the battles in practice between him and Deacon Jones were at game-level intensity. Jones' signature move was the head slap, and Brown told him to stop it. When Jones just laughed, Brown got even. He replaced the screws in his helmet with longer ones so that the next time Deacon gave Boomer a head slap, his bloody hand stuck to Brown's helmet. When he went to the Raiders, Boomer announced his arrival on the first day of practice by knocking down a wooden goal post with a forearm shiver.

Brown took this same fierce attitude toward management. The only three coaches he ever liked were Joe Kuharich, Dick Stanfel, and John Madden. He felt great loyalty to Kuharich, who had treated him with utmost honesty, and Stanfel who was a mas-

Hmmm…How can we show how big and strong Hall of Fame tackle Bob Brown was? That's him helping safeties Joe Scarpati (21) and Jim Nettles (9) do an Eagles cheer.

terful technician as a line coach. When Kuharich was fired and Pete Retzlaff was named the new general manager, Brown demanded a trade. He did not trust Retzlaff from the time that they were teammates. He claimed that the relationship between the two was the same as between a mongoose and a cobra, that of natural enemies. Retzlaff dealt the Boomer and cornerback Jim Nettles to the Rams for journeyman tackle Joe Carollo, mediocre guard Don Chuy and cornerback Irv Cross, whereupon Rams coach George Allen called him the "finest offensive lineman in football." Brown, though, felt Allen's rah-rah inspirational stunts were phony and insulting to his intelligence.

Allen was succeeded by Tommy Prothro, but Brown did not respect him either. Moreover, Brown had a contract problem. He claimed that he had been the highest paid player when he was in Philadelphia and wanted to be the same in Los Angeles. Management balked at paying him more than star quarterback Roman Gabriel, so Brown told them that maybe he wouldn't block so hard to protect Gabriel if they didn't want to pay him. He was traded the next day to Oakland for journeyman tackle Harry Schuh and cornerback Kent McCloughan. He got along well with coach John Madden, but was quoted as saying that owner Al Davis' "word wasn't worth a rat's rear."

The Boomer retired in 1973 after 10 seasons, seven All-Pro selections, six Pro Bowls, five knee operations, three offensive lineman of the year awards, and too much static with management. He had earned a master's degree in educational administration from the University of Pennsylvania while with the Eagles and he left football for the business world. He had to wait over 30 years, but finally in 2004, Bob Brown was elected to the Pro Football Hall of Fame. Although his career was relatively brief and his prickly personality did not endear him to sportswriters, the Boomer was the best tackle of his era.

77
Draft Busts

Antone Davis
T 1991

Phil Ragazzo (T) 1941, Bennie Kaplan (G) 1942, Tex Williams (G) 1942, Carl Fagioli (G) 1944, John Eibner (T) 1946, Jim Kekeris (T) 1947, Gus Cifelli (T) 1954, *Jim Weatherall* (T) 1955-57, Don Oakes (T) 1961-62, John Kapele (T) 1962, Ray Mansfield (C) 1963, Ray Rissmiller (T) 1966, Ernie Calloway (DT) 1970-72, Gerry Philbin (DE) 1973, Jerry Patton (DT) 1974, Don Ratliff (DE) 1975, Dennis Nelson (T) 1976-77, Rufus Mayes (T) 1979, Tom Jelesky (T) 1985, Michael Black (T/G) 1986, Donald Evans (DE) 1988, Antone Davis (T) 1991, Keith Millard (DT) 1993, Howard Smothers (G) 1995, Richard Cooper (T) 1996-98, Lonnie Palelei (T/G) 1999, Artis Hicks (T) 2002-04.

Originator: Tackle Phil Ragazzo in 1941, when he received second-team All-Pro recognition. Ragazzo came over from the Rams and spent two years in Philly before going into the Army. He played for three service teams during the war and finished his NFL career afterwards with the Giants.

Longest Tenure: Three years, by Jim Weatherall, Ernie Calloway, Richard Cooper and Artis Hicks.

Number Changes: Phil Ragazzo wore 31 in 1940; John Eibner wore 76 in 1941 and 1942; Ernie Calloway wore 57 in 1969; Antone Davis switched to 78 after his first professional game.

Just Visiting: Don Oakes started for the Patriots for several years; Ray Mansfield anchored the Steeler line for a decade; Gerry Philbin was an All-Pro for the Jets; Keith Millard starred at defensive tackle for the Vikings.

Highs: Phil Ragazzo and Outland Trophy winner Jim Weatherall were tackles who received All-Pro and Pro Bowl recognition, respectively.

Lows: Ernie Calloway was a 6-foot 6-inch 250-pound defensive lineman picked in the second round of the draft. Known as "Spiderman," he was a loquacious, undersized underachiever who once left training camp three times in one month.

Antone Davis

Despite the voluminous data produced in preparation for the NFL draft, it remains more an art than a science. In 1991, the Eagles decided that they had to have massive Tennessee tackle Antone Davis, but were drafting too late in the first round to get him. Philadelphia then agreed to trade its 19th position in the 1991 draft along with its first-round pick for 1992 to Green Bay for its number eight slot in the first round. The Eagles moved up and got their man-mountain Davis, but would later find out that he was more of a candy mountain. At the time, Rich Kotite was ecstatic : "I think that, going into this, if we would have said in the first two rounds we would have got Davis and Jesse [Campbell], we would have said, 'No way.'" As one would expect with Kotite's talent evaluation skills, Campbell was a bust as well.

Antone Davis was the youngest of eight kids and did not play football till he was a junior in high school. The 325-pounder starred as a Tennessee Volunteer and even managed to get his degree before the draft. However, some scouts questioned his work habits and potential for weight problems. They would prove to be accurate. He was a gentle giant who claimed he did not try to get up for a game, but instead tried to calm himself down. As an Eagle rookie, Davis was OK as a run blocker, but a nightmare as a pass blocker. Sacks and penalty flags followed him wherever he went. He was benched for a game in October, and that was a pattern that would recur in later years.

For his part, Davis felt he was the scapegoat for the Eagle's season and stopped talking to the media in his second season so he could get his confidence back. His line coach Bill Muir reported that Antone's biggest problem was that he would lose focus from time to time and would not play a consistent game. In 1994, the Eagles moved him to guard and by the end of the year benched him for Kotite's last two games. New coach Ray Rhodes moved Davis back to tackle but tried desperately to find someone to replace him. After an embarrassing loss to the Raiders, Rhodes remarked angrily that "From a pass-rush standpoint, a 335-pound guy [Davis] is pass-blocking against a 255-pound guy [Aundray Bruce] and gets pushed back to the quarterback. I mean, if you've got the bulk and the weight to stone this guy, then you stone him."

The Falcons signed Davis as a free agent the next season and he was out of the league in two years. While the Packers picked cornerback stiff Vinnie Clark with the Eagles' 1991 pick, Green Bay still came out the winner on the trade because they were able to pass on that extra Eagle 1992 draft pick to the Falcons for rookie flop Brett Favre. The Falcons traded the pick on to Dallas and the Cowboys used it to grab the forgettable Kevin Martin. At the time of the trade, Buddy Ryan wrote a *New York Times* piece criticizing the move up as unnecessary because there would be other equally talented tackles available later in the draft. He cited Pat Harlow, who turned out to be a little better than Davis; Stan Thomas, who was an injury-prone flop, and Philadelphia-bred Erik Williams, whom the Cowboys would grab in the third round and turned into a star. Eagles owner Norman Braman commented at the time, "This was the only impact player left in the draft when we picked him. It will be the worst deal in the world if Davis is not a performer, but it should be no gamble with him." The draft is always a gamble, though, and the Birds have crapped out often. Here's the all-time Eagles draft bust team. Sadly, Davis would be no better than a bench warmer for this squad:

OFFENSE

Wide Receiver — Kenny Jackson (1984, rd. 1, no. 4), the fourth overall pick, never caught more than 40 balls in any season and reached the end zone 11 times in seven seasons; Freddie Mitchell (2001, rd. 1, no. 25), the "people's champ", is not fast enough to get separation from defenders or microphones; Mike Bellamy (1990, rd. 2, no. 50) handled the ball three times as a return man and fumbled once.

Tight End — Jason Dunn (1996, rd. 2, no. 54) caught 40 passes in three years; and went to same college as Jesse Small (below); Lawrence Sampleton (1982, rd. 2, no. 47) caught three passes in three years.

Tackle — Kevin Allen (1985, rd. 1, no 9) topped his rookie year as a swinging door for pass rushers by being sent to prison for sexual assault at the Jersey shore; Bernard Williams (1994, rd. 1, no. 14) decided after one season that smoking dope was more interesting than playing tackle for the Birds; Antone Davis (1991, rd. 1, no. 8); Dan Yochum (1972, rd. 2, no. 37) went to Canada instead and had a 10-year CFL Hall of Fame career.

Guard — Lester Holmes (1993, rd. 1, no. 19): that he started for the Eagles for parts of four seasons says all you need to know about the quality of those Philadelphia lines; Bobby Williams (2000, rd. 2, no. 61): it took this fat tub three seasons to even get activated for a game; Dean Miraldi (1981, rd. 2, no. 55): his poor pass blocking nearly got Jaworski killed on numerous occasions; Henry Allison (1971, rd. 2, no. 50) lasted for a season and a half in Philly; John Brooks (1967, rd. 2, no. 44) was cut for being overweight and never played in the NFL.

Center — Bo Strange (1961, rd. 2, no. 28) never played pro ball. Strange indeed.

Quarterback — John Reaves (1972, rd. 1, no. 14) had the classic deer-in-the-headlights style that Bobby Hoying later perfected; Frank Tripucka (1949, rd. 1, no. 9) was traded in his rookie year without ever appearing in a game; Jack Concannon (1964, rd. 2, no. 16) was a better runner than passer.

Running Back — Jay Berwanger (1936, rd. 1, no. 1), the number one draft pick of all time, decided that he was not interested in pro ball; Harry Jones (1967, rd. 1, no. 19): 44 carries for 85 yards spread over four seasons will not get you to Canton; Michael Haddix (1983, rd. 1, no. 8) was as soft and slow as he was fat; Art Baker (1961, rd. 1, no. 14) signed with the Bills of the AFL and was gone after little more than one season; Neil Worden (1954, rd. 1, no. 9) averaged 2.6 yards per carry over two seasons (if the Eagles gave him the ball on four straight carries, he could eke out a first down on average); Walt Kowalczyk (1958, rd. 1, no. 6) replaced Worden and gained 80 yards on 43 carries over two years.

DEFENSE

Defensive End — Jon Harris (1997, rd. 1, no. 25) had to be traded straight up for the Packers' first-round mistake John Michels so that neither team would have to cut their own number one pick (It was a trade that helped both teams); Mike Mamula (1995, rd. 1, no. 7), the king of the all-important category of "getting close to a sack," was seen as the expressway for the opposing team's running game; Leonard Mitchell (1981, rd. 1, no. 27) failed first as a defensive end and then as an offensive tackle before he was picked up by his old coach Marion Campbell in Atlanta so he could fail for Marion a third time; Randy Beisler (1966, rd. 1, no. 4) switched ineffectively between defensive end and offensive tackle for the Birds, but after being traded to the 49ers for that stiff George Mira, he settled in as a decent guard in San Francisco.

Defensive Tackle — Leonard Renfro (1993, rd. 1, no. 24) was cut after two seasons of lackluster play; Bruce Walker (1994, rd. 2, no. 37) had character issues and was cut in training camp; Ernie Calloway (1969, rd. 2, no. 28) was an undersized defensive lineman with a large wingspan; Proverb Jacobs (1958, rd. 2, no. 17) lasted only one year in Philadelphia.

Linebacker — Barry Gardner (1999, rd. 2, no. 35) will always be somewhat unfairly remembered for letting Joe Jurevicious jet across his area for a 71-yard gain in the 2002 conference championship loss to Tampa; Jessie Small (1989, rd. 2, no. 49): the highlight of his career was knocking out 170-pound kicker Luis Zendejas in the Bounty Bowl; Alonzo Johnson (1986, rd. 2, no. 48) was dropped in his second year after he returned to using drugs; Quinton Caver (2001, rd. 2, no. 55) known as "Range Rover" in college, but he's been more like a Yugo in the pros.

Defensive Back — Leroy Keyes (1969, rd. 1, no. 3) the consolation prize for winning two of Joe Kuharich's last three games in town to finish out of the money in the O.J. Simpson sweepstakes; Jesse Campbell (1991, rd. 2, no. 48) after a season on the practice squad, he was cut in training camp but caught on with the Giants for five years; Ray Jones (1970, rd. 2, no. 34) burned for three 40+ yard touchdowns in a loss to Dallas during his one season as an Eagle; Frank Burns (1949, rd. 2, no. 19) from Rutgers, he never played pro ball, but was rumored to have worked in a MASH unit with Hawkeye, Trapper John and Hot Lips.

Kicker – Happy Feller (1971, rd. 4) connected on only 6 of 20 field goals in little more than half of a season in Philadelphia.

Punter – Ray Criswell (1986, rd. 5) failed to make the Eagles but turned up in Tampa briefly.

78

1980s Decade in Review

Carl Hairston
DE 1976-83

Originator: Big Mike Jarmoluk, a veteran of the Battle of the Bulge, was hard to move in the middle of the Eagles' defensive line from 1949 to 1955. He joked that he was traded from the Bears to the Yanks for George Connor and from the Lions to the Eagles for Frank Tripucka — two Notre Dame All-Americans for one Temple grad. Actually, he came over from Detroit for a number two draft pick.

Longest Tenure: Nine years, defensive tackle Hollis Thomas from 1996 to 2004.

Number Changes: Antone Davis first wore 77 in 1991; Steve Smith wore 74 from 1972 to 1974.

Just Visiting: John Baker was a talented but moody defensive lineman with the Rams and Steelers.

Highs: Several talented defensive tackles have worn 78, including Mike Jarmoluk, Swamp Fox Marion Campbell, who later coached the team and undrafted free agent Hollis Thomas.

Lows: The Eagles traded an extra number one pick to move up and select Antone Davis in 1991, but the unmotivated Davis never lived up to that billing.

Carl Hairston

Carl Hairston graduated from high school in Virginia and took a delivery job with a furniture company. Two years later, a recruiter from Maryland State spotted his size-able, 275-pound frame in a pool hall in Martinsville, Virginia, and asked Carl if he played football. Two weeks later, he was accepted for admission at the small black col-lege, now known as Maryland Eastern Shore. Hairston starred on the field for four years and was spotted by an Eagles scout. In his first season as coach, Dick Vermeil drafted Carl in the ninth round of the 1976 draft. Coming from a small school with little expe-rience, Hairston was very rough around the edges, but he worked hard, demonstrated he was coachable, and made the team.

Along with the Eagles themselves, Hairston made steady progress and improved from year to year. He learned hand moves from Manny Sistrunk and spin moves from Claude Humphrey. Vermeil later said of him, "He had a strong pop. He just exploded into a guy. He disengaged instantly. He was great in pursuit." Carl became an anchor on one side of the defensive line for eight seasons in Philadelphia and three times was the team's defensive MVP, but by 1984 the whole team was aging, Carl had some knee prob-lems and Vermeil's replacement, Marion Campbell, dumped his fellow number 78 onto Cleveland for a ninth-round pick. Under Marty Schottenheimer, Carl took on the per-sona of "Big Daddy," not only playing his position well but serving as a team captain and leader for the younger players. Big Daddy spent six years in Cleveland, popular with teammates and fans alike, before finishing his career with a final season in Arizona at the age of 38.

Hairston racked up 94 sacks in his improbable 15-year NFL career, including 15 in 1979, and then went into coaching. A few years later, when Vermeil returned to coaching in St. Louis, Carl was one of a core of former players he added to his staff. In fact, when Vermeil later moved on to Kansas City, Carl came with him again. He and front office executive Lynn Stiles are the two men who have been with Vermeil for every one of his NFL victories. Carl Hairston was the ultimate underdog and he relished the role: "I liked that. It meant you had something to prove. Then you've got to work hard-er than anybody else." And work harder he did.

Decade Headline: Buddy Brawl
Where They Played: Veterans Stadium, 1971-02.
How the Game Was Played: Due to the crackdown on contact allowed by defensive backs on receivers and the liberalization of pass blocking rules, the passing game returned with a vengeance in the 1980s. San Diego's Air Coryell, the long ball attack of Miami's Dan Marino, and the West Coast short passing attack of San Francisco were three prominent approaches. In the NFC East, though, a "smash mouth" ground game was the key to winning football. On defense, sacks finally became an official statistic, and the top defenses (Chicago's famed 46, the Giants led by Lawrence Taylor and the Eagles with Reggie White) lived by the blitz and

quarterback pressure. By the end of the decade, coaches began to take over the game by making wholesale substitutions on almost every play and not letting any quarterbacks call their own plays.

Decade Won Lost Record: 76-74-2, .507; 2-4 in the playoffs.
Record Against the Cowboys: 9-10; 1-0 in the playoffs.
Record Against the Giants: 9-11; 0-1 in the playoffs.
Record Against the Redskins: 7-13.
Record Against the Steelers: 1-0.

Playoff Appearances: 1980, 1981, 1988 and 1989.
Championships: None.
Unsung Hero: Offensive mastermind Sid Gillman was brought in by Dick Vermeil to coach the quarterbacks in 1979. Gillman, although past retirement age, helped Ron Jaworski have his two greatest years in 1979 and 1980.
Head Coaches: Dick Vermeil 1976-82, 25-16 for the decade plus 2-2 in the playoffs; Marion Campbell 1983-85, 17-29-1; Fred Bruney 1985, 0-1; Buddy Ryan 1986-90, 33-29-1 for the decade plus 0-2 in the playoffs.
Best Player: Reggie White.
Hall of Famers: None yet.
Eagle Honor Roll: Bill Bergey, Jerome Brown, Harold Carmichael, Ron Jaworski, Wilbert Montgomery, Mike Quick, Jerry Sisemore, Dick Vermeil, and Stan Walters.
League Leaders: Mike Quick — receiving yards 1983 and 1985; Reggie White — sacks 1987-88; Paul McFadden — field goals 1985; Randall Cunningham — rushing average 1989.
Award Winners: Ron Jaworski, MVP 1980; Randall Cunningham MVP 1988; Reggie White Defensive MVP 1987; Keith Jackson Rookie of the Year 1988; Paul McFadden NFC Rookie of the Year 1984.
All-Pros: Harold Carmichael 1980; Charlie Johnson 1980-81; Randy Logan 1980; Jerry Robinson 1980-81, 1983; Mike Quick 1983, 1985, 1987; Wes Hopkins 1984-85; Reggie White 1986-89; Randall Cunningham 1988; Keith Jackson 1988-89; Jerome Brown 1989.
Pro Bowl Selections: Harold Carmichael 1980; Ron Jaworski 1980; Charlie Johnson 1980-81; Randy Logan 1980; Frank Lemaster 1981; Jerry Robinson 1981; Jerry Sisemore 1981; Roynell Young 1981; Dennis Harrison 1982; Mike Quick 1983-87; Wes Hopkins 1985; Reggie White 1986-89; Randall Cunningham 1988-89; Keith Jackson 1988-89; Eric Allen 1989.
Best Offensive Backfield: 1981, with quarterback Ron Jaworski, running back Wilbert Montgomery, fullback Hubie Oliver, and wideout Harold Carmichael.
Best Draft Choice: For meeting expectations, Reggie White, 1984 Supplemental Draft, first round. The best sleepers were Seth Joyner from the eighth round in 1986 and

Clyde Simmons from the ninth round of the same year.

Best Overall Draft: 1986 for the two sleepers noted above plus top picks Keith Byars and Anthony Toney.

Worst Draft Choice: Kevin Allen, 1985, first round. Despite such terrible first-rounders during the 1980s as Leonard Mitchell (1981), Michael Haddix (1983) and Kenny Jackson (1984), Allen wins this competition by virtue of being a disaster on the field and off. He played one terrible year in the league and then had legal problems that landed him in jail.

Worst Overall Draft: 1981. Late-round picks Hubie Oliver and Ray Ellis were useful additions, but the top picks — Leonard Mitchell, Dean Miraldi and Greg LaFleur — were nonentities.

Best Free Agent: Former construction worker Greg Brown joined the Eagles in 1981 and was a sack master for a few years; Andre Waters made the team in 1984 and blossomed as a hard-hitting safety on Buddy Ryan's defense.

Best Trade: Picking up nine-year starting guard Ron Baker from the Colts for an eighth-round draft pick.

Worst Trade: Obtaining injury-riddled guard Ron Solt from the Colts for a first-round pick who turned to be Andre Rison and a fourth-rounder.

Biggest Off-Field Event: First, two labor strikes in 1982 and 1987 disrupt the team and the league. Second, owner Len Tose gets in over his head gambling in nearby Atlantic City, and considers moving the team to Phoenix before selling it to Norman Braman.

Biggest On-Field Development: Dick Vermeil flames out emotionally and quits after seven years.

Strangest On-Field Event: The three replacement player games in 1987. The one held in Philadelphia on October 4 drew the lowest attendance of any game throughout the league, 4,074. The real Eagles, fully supported by their coach Buddy Ryan, stuck together for their strike and were stronger for it once they returned. Buddy also felt that Tom Landry's replacement Cowboys ran up the score against his rag-tag replacement Eagles, so he evened the score on October 25 when he had Randall Cunningham pass for a meaningless last second touchdown to beat the real Cowboys 37-20.

Worst Failure: Buddy Ryan assembled a squad of tremendous talent, but failed to harness and fully coach that talent so that those teams never reached their full potential.

Home Attendance: 4,695,237 in 77 games for an average gate of 60, 977.

Best Game: On September 17, 1989, the Eagles twice trailed the Redskins in Washington by 20 points in the first half before pulling the game out at the end. Randall Cunningham threw five touchdown passes, the last came after Gerald Riggs of the Redskins fumbled at the Eagles' 19 with 1:16 left and the Birds trailing 37-35. The fumble was recovered by Al Harris, who gave the ball to Wes

Hopkins as he was being tackled, and Hopkins took it 77 yards to the Redskins' 4 yard line. Randall then hit Keith Jackson for the winning points, 42-37.

First Game: September 7, 1980. The Eagles dominated the Broncos 27-6 at the Vet.

Last Game: December 24, 1989. The Eagles easily beat the Cardinals 31-14 to ensure a winning record for the 1990s, the first winning decade since the 1940s.

Largest Margin of Victory: November 18, 1981. The Eagles smoked the St. Louis Cardinals 52-10 in a game highlighted by five Eagle TD passes, four by Ron Jaworski and one by Joe Pisarcik.

Largest Margin of Defeat: October 16, 1983 — Dallas 37, Philadelphia 7. Ron Jaworski threw an 83-yard touchdown to Mike Quick on the Birds' first play and it was all downhill from there.

Best Offense: In 1980, the Eagles scored 384 points, sixth in the league, en route to their Super Bowl appearance.

Best Defense: In 1980, the Eagles gave up 222 points the lowest total in the NFL, and were second in yards allowed; the following season they gave up 221 points, again first, and were also first in yards allowed.

Most Games Played: 123, Ron Baker.

Most Points: 390, Paul McFadden.

Most Field Goals: 91, Paul McFadden.

Most Touchdowns: 60, Mike Quick.

Most Touchdown Passes: 123, Ron Jaworski.

Most Passing Yards: 19,524, Ron Jaworski.

Most Receiving Yards: 6,329, Mike Quick.

Most Receptions: 354, Mike Quick.

Most Rushing Yards: 3,623, Wilbert Montgomery.

Most Interceptions: 23, Roynell Young.

Most Sacks: 81, Reggie White.

Most Kickoff Return Yards: 1,047, Wally Henry.

Most Punt Return Yards: 753, Evan Cooper.

Book Notes: The two greatest players of the 1980s published autobiographies in the 1990s. Reggie White published *Reggie White: Minister of Defense* in 1991, while still an Eagle, and *In the Trenches: An Autobiography,* five years later when he was a Packer. Randall Cunningham put out *I'm Still Scrambling* in 1993. Cunningham's book is more stylish, but none of the three is all that great.

Noted Sportswriter: Angelo Cataldi covered the team for the *Philadelphia Inquirer* and would go on to greater success in the morning drive slot on WIP sports talk radio.

Best Quotation: After beating Dallas, Buddy Ryan remarked, "Who in the hell are the Cowboys? We beat them every time we play them."

Bubblegum Factoid: 1982 Topps card number 149 for John Spagnola tells us he "was MVP for the Yale Bulldogs in 1978 and in the 1978 Blue-Gray Game."

Accidents of Birth: Steve Kaufusi was born in Tonga; Jairo Penaranda was born in Colombia; Luis Zendejas was born in Mexico.

Famous Names: Anthony Edwards, not the actor; Keith Jackson, not the sportscaster.

Unusual Names: Luther Blue, Elbert Foules, Izell Jenkins, Vyto Kab, Guido Merkens, Jairo Penaranda, Mike Quick, Heath Sherman, Taivale Tautalatasi, Roynell Young.

Nicknames: David "Pillsbury Doughboy" Alexander, Eric "The Flea" Allen, Todd "Taco" Bell, Bill "Bubba" Bergey, Gary "The Mule" Bolden, Aaron "Chunky" Brown, Jerome "Freight Train" Brown, John "Frito Bandito" Bunting, Keith "Tank" Byars, Harold "Hoagie" Carmichael, Cris "Groucho" Carter, Ken "Air" Clarke, Bill "Face" Cowher, Byron "B&E" Evans, Gregg "Trash" Garrity, Carl "Big Daddy" Hairston, Al "Cheeseburger" Harris, Dennis "Big Foot" Harrison, Keith "KJax" Jackson, Ron "Jaws" or "The Polish Rifle" Jaworski, Seth "Zeth" Joyner, Steve "Red Man" Kenney, Rich "Conan" Kraynak, Edwin "Petey" Perot, Mike "Silk" Quick, Mike "Rock 'em Back" Reichenbach, David "Buddy" Ryan, Heath "Wolfman" Sherman, Fred "Boom Boom" Smalls, Charles "Tank" or "Home Boy" Smith, Taivale "Junior" Tautalatasi, Rick "Bootin'" Tuten, Stan "Mule" Walters, Andre "Muddy" or "Dirty" Waters, Reggie "The Minister of Defense" or "Big Dog" White, and Henry "Gizmo" Williams.

Fastest Player: Mike Quick, of whom it was said, "If he's even, he's leavin.'" Other fast Eagles included wide out Kenny Jackson and Fred Barnett as well as ultimate weapon Randall Cunningham.

Heaviest Player: Frank Giddens was the Eagles' first official 300-pounder in 1981.

Lightest Player: Not counting replacement kicker Dave Jacobs who was 5 feet 7 inches and 151 pounds, the lightest Eagle of the decade was defensive back Eric Everett who was 5 feet 10 inches and 165 pounds in 1988 and 1989.

Toughest Injury: Mike Quick may have been the greatest receiver in team history, but his career was shortened by a knee injury in his sixth season of 1988. Wes Hopkins was a hard-hitting Pro Bowl player until he tore up his knee in 1986. Although he played on for several more years, he was never the same.

Local Boys: Gerry Feehery, Jim Gilmore and Mike McCloskey all hailed from Philadelphia. From the surrounding area came Joe Conwell, Jim Culbreath, Mike Curcio, Scott Fitzkee, Anthony Griggs, Rich Kraynak, Calvin Murray, Dave Pacella, Joe Pisarcik, Mike Reichenbach, Ron Solt and John Spagnola. Among local colleges: Temple — Mike Curcio and Zack Dixon; Princeton — Bob Holly; East Stroudsburg — Mike Reichenbach; and Cheney — Andre Waters. 1987 replacement players of local origin included Jim Auer, Victor Bellamy, Carlos Bradley, Tom Catterbone, Topper Clemons, Chris Conlin, Ron Fazio, Chris Gerhard, Chuck Gorecki, Marty Horn, Dave Jacobs, Chris Johnson, Mike Kullman, Jay Repko and Mike Siano.

Firsts:

Quarterback to Lead the Eagles in Rushing — Randall Cunningham from 1987 to 1990.

79

1948 Championship

Vic Sears
T 1941-43, 1945-53

Vic Sears

Vic Sears attended a one-room schoolhouse in Eugene, Oregon and never even saw the game of football played until he was in high school. The 6-foot 3-inch, 210-pounder caught on quickly, though, and won a scholarship to Oregon State University where he would miss only 14 minutes of game time in his whole collegiate career. He was an All-American as a senior and was selected in the fifth round of the NFL draft by the Steelers. By the time he reported, however, Steelers owner Lex Thompson had traded cities with Eagles owners Bert Bell and Art Rooney, so that Vic was now an Eagle.

1941 was Greasy Neale's first year as coach, and he had a lot of work to do. The Eagles won only two games in each of Sears' first two seasons. Things improved when the Eagles and Steelers merged as the Steagles for the 1943 season, and Vic was named All-Pro for the first of five times that season. A broken leg suffered in a preseason game sidelined him for all of 1944, but Sears returned in 1945 like new, teaming with Al Wistert as Philadelphia's tandem of All-Pro, two-way tackles. During the decade of the 1940s, Vic played roughly 50 minutes per game, aside from 1947 when he missed several games due to ulcers. He was a steady player on both sides of the ball and was known as "Smoothie." Neale thought very highly of Sears and called him the greatest defensive tackle he had ever seen because he couldn't be budged if you ran at him and couldn't be eluded if you ran away from him. The superstitious Neale also was in the habit of borrowing Sears' overcoat whenever they played in the rain because the first time he had done so, the team had won.

After finishing second in the East for three consecutive years, the Eagles took the next step in 1947 by reaching the title game against the Cardinals, but lost on an icy field in Comiskey Stadium. By 1948, the great Eagles team that Neale had assembled was ready to kick the door down, but the season started slowly. The Eagles lost the first game to the champion Cardinals 21-14 at Chicago, after which star Cardinal tackle Stan Mauldin died of a heart attack. Philadelphia followed that by tying the Rams in Los Angeles. The Eagles then caught fire, beating the Giants and the Redskins by identical 45-0 scores and then beating the Bears for the first time in franchise history 12-7 behind backup quarterback Bill Mackrides. Philadelphia went on to win eight straight games, including a third 45-0 win, this time over the Boston Yanks. The Yanks would end the winning streak in the next to last game of the season, but the Eagles won their finale 45-21 over the Lions.

This set up a much-anticipated rematch in the championship game between the Cardinals and Eagles, but the weather did not cooperate. A blizzard hit Philadelphia on game day, December 19. The snowfall was so heavy that Steve Van Buren almost missed the game because he figured it would be postponed. Greasy Neale wanted it postponed. He was still mad about losing in bad field conditions the year before and felt it was foolish to strive so hard for three months only to have the title decided on a flukey break. Commissioner Bert Bell insisted the game proceed however due to the lucrative broadcast rights paid by radio, television and newsreel companies. The first obstacle was removing the snow-covered tarp that blanketed the field. It took 90 men, including many players from both teams to slowly roll the heavy tarp off the field, but once that was done snow immediately obliterated all markings on the field. Because of this, it was agreed that there would be no measurements for first downs — they would be awarded at the referee's discretion. Over 28,000 fans showed up at Shibe Park for the game despite the extreme elements, but owner Lex Thompson was not one of them since he was in the hospital with appendicitis.

The Eagles received the opening kickoff and started at their own 35. They opened with a scripted long pass to end Jack Ferrante that worked almost perfectly. Ferrante caught the ball at the Cardinals' 20 between two defenders who knocked him down, but he popped up and raced to the end zone with an apparent touchdown. However, line judge Charley Berry ruled that Ferrante was offsides on the play, which Jack always has denied vehemently. From there, the game settled into a rushing contest that the Eagles won decisively 225 yards to 96. Van Buren alone gained 98 yards on the ground. The Cardinals only scoring opportunity came in the first quarter when they moved the ball to the Eagles' 30 where Pat Harder missed a 37-yard field goal. They would not penetrate that deep into Eagle territory again.

In the second quarter, the Eagles missed two chances to score. Elmer Angsman fumbled for the first time on his own 21 and Cliff Patton and Johnny Green recovered for Philadelphia. Unfortunately, Tommy Thompson was picked off by Johnny Cochran at this point. Later in the quarter, the Eagles were halted inside the Cardinals' 10 and Cliff Patton shanked a 12-yard field goal. In the third quarter, Patton missed another field goal from 39 yards, but the game's big break came late in the period when Angsman fumbled again. Bucko Kilroy recovered the ball at the Cardinals' 17. Bosh Pritchard carried the ball to the 11 on first down to end the third quarter, and fullback Joe Muha got to the 8 on second down to open the fourth quarter. On third and one, Tommy Thompson carried the ball on a keeper to the 5 for a first and goal. Finally, Steve Van Buren got the ball and plowed through a huge hole on the right side for the only score of the game. Cliff Patton would miss a third field goal try from the 30 and the game would end with the Birds running out the clock at the Cardinal two-yard line. It was as convincing a win as a 7-0 victory can be.

After the game, Neale sang the praises of quarterback Tommy Thompson saying he played a smarter game than the previous year. He also noted that only one other player was greatly improved and that was Vic Sears since, "he'd gotten rid of that ulcer trouble." Sears underwent surgery for his ulcers in 1947. Line coach John Kellison added that, "I doubt the Cards could have done much better even on a clear day what with the way Vic Sears and Walter Barnes were rushing their passers — riding them right out into the snow banks beyond the sidelines."

Sears ran a hotel and tavern near Flourtown for several years — he even was raided and shut down once in 1952 for serving liquor after hours — and that is where the team held its postgame celebration. The Eagles repeated as champions in 1949, but under new ownership since Thompson sold the team to the "100 Brothers." Vic continued on with the team through the 1953 season, specializing on the defensive side of the ball as two-platoon football took hold in his later years. Although Vic Sears' name is not heard much anymore, only Chuck Bednarik, Harold Carmichael and Bucko Kilroy spent more seasons playing for the Eagles. After retiring, Vic bought a farm in Bucks County, did some coaching and worked as a sales representative in the area before eventually moving back to a farm in Oregon in 1980.

80
1996 Playoffs

Irving Fryar
WR 1996-98

Originator: End Gran "Rock" Harrison appeared in one game at the beginning of 1941 and then was traded to the minor league Paterson Panthers for guard Jack Anderson, who never played for the Eagles.

Longest Tenure: Five years, Neill Armstrong.

Number Changes: Fred Meyer wore 89 in 1942; Randy Beisler wore 64 in 1968; Billy McMullen wore 81 in 2003.

Just Visiting: John Tracey was a starting linebacker for the Bills' tough 1960s defense; Art Thoms was a large defensive end for the Raiders; Don Brumm was a veteran defensive end for the Cardinals; Cris Carter became an All-Pro in Minnesota; James Lofton was a Hall of Famer in Green Bay and Buffalo.

Highs: End Len Supulski played one season in the NFL before going into the military. He was killed, at age 23, serving his country in France in 1944.

Lows: One of only a handful of players to play major league baseball and NFL football in the same year, Bert Kuczynski was captain of the Penn football team and appeared in six games as a pitcher for the A's and two games as an end with the Lions in 1943. In 1946, he got to play in three games as an Eagle and caught one nine-yard pass.

Irving Fryar

As of 2005, the top two seasons for receptions in Eagle history were 88 by the 34-year-old Irving Fryar in 1996 and 86 by the 35-year-old Irving Fryar in 1997. While it is unexpected that these performances were turned in by a veteran of relatively advanced years, it is even more astounding that the veteran was Irving Fryar. With the indiscretions of his youth, no one was betting on Irving to last that long in the NFL.

Coming out of the University of Nebraska, the Mount Holly, New Jersey native was the first overall selection of the 1984 draft by the New England Patriots. His first several years in New England were filled with off-the-field headlines: allegations of drug and alcohol abuse; allegations of gambling; arrests on assault and weapons charges; and a curious mugging incident. Most famous was a knife incident involving his wife that left Fryar unable to play in the AFC title game due to lacerations to his hand, although he did appear in the Super Bowl loss to the Bears. The result was that Fryar caught only 186 passes in his first six seasons in New England compared to the 174 he caught in his first two years in Philly.

In 1989, Fryar was born again as a Christian and began to turn his life around. The off-field incidents ceased, and his production on the field shot up. After nine seasons as a Patriot, Fryar moved on to Miami where he teamed with Dan Marino for three excellent years as a prime time receiver. In 1996, Ray Rhodes signed the by-now Reverend Fryar to the Eagles and he lit up the Vet for the next two years. Coming off a 10-6 renaissance in Rhodes' first season of 1995 when the Eagles even won a playoff game, Philadelphia was looking to move up. Fryar lived up to billing by setting career highs in catches and TDs and being voted the team's offensive MVP while becoming a prominent voice for the team on television. He also provided the play of the year against the Giants with a leaping, one-handed backhand snag of a wayward pass in an Eagle victory. Starting quarterback Rodney Peete went down early in the year, but his replacement Ty Detmer caught fire and won his first four games as a starter, driving the team to a 7-2 record. At that point, both Detmer and the team went south and stumbled into the playoff with another 10-6 record.

Their opponents in the wild card game were the 49ers, and the sloppy game was played on a muddy field in San Francisco. For the first half, the Eagles dominated the 49ers everywhere but on the scoreboard. On their opening possession, they missed a field goal. In the second quarter, Steve Young dashed into the end zone from the 9 to give San Francisco the lead. The Eagles drove to the 49ers' 7, but when Ty Detmer was rushed on a third-and-one, he threw an interception to Marquez Pope. Philadelphia got the ball back late in the quarter and this time drove to the Niners' 5 where Detmer fired another interception to Roy Barker. In the second half, Detmer was sacked and knocked out of the game, and the 49ers added a second touchdown on a pass from Young to Jerry Rice. The game ended 14-0, but the Eagles had let the 49ers get away by giving up a potential 17 points in the first half.

That loss was more than a simple defeat. It was seen as a clear indication that the Rhodes program was not going to succeed, and that Ty Detmer was not a championship quarterback. Playing for a sagging team that went through three starting quarterbacks in 1997, Fryar caught only two fewer passes in 1997 and upped his average gain by nearly two yards. In 1998, the team went into full crash mode with primary starting quarterback Bobby Hoying throwing zero touchdown passes. Between the quarterback deficiencies and Fryar dropping passes and looking slower, whispers started that Irving could no longer get separation from defenders. He finished with fewer than 50 catches for the first time since 1989 and began to hear boos from the stands. He announced his intention to retire at the end of the year, and the Eagles gave him a going-away present of a Harley-Davidson motorcycle in their last home game.

Within a month, there were reports that Fryar was willing to return to play for the Patriots in 1999. He eventually signed on with the Redskins as their third receiver and spent two more seasons as strictly a possession guy before being released and retiring for good. In his career Irving Fryar accumulated 851 catches, 84 for touchdowns, and will be considered seriously for the Hall of Fame.

81
2004

Terrell Owens
WR 2004

Terrell Owens

One of the top two or three receivers in the game, Terrell Owens has long had a talent for attracting attention, but coming to Philadelphia, he has raised that talent to an art: his Eagle jersey was the top seller in the league for some time; his web site features its own line of T.O. merchandise; his ghosted autobiography, which he called "the most exciting thing I've done since I've been in the NFL," was a best seller. The funny thing is that Owens has repeatedly said that he doesn't even like football — it's not his game and he's not very passionate about it although he is competitive by nature and plays hard on the field.

Owens came from humble beginnings and was raised primarily by his grandmother in Alabama. He earned a scholarship to the University of Tennessee-Chattanooga where he unsurprisingly majored in merchandising. Drafted in the third round by San Francisco in 1996, Terrell got to train under the greatest receiver in NFL history, Jerry Rice. He caught a 25-yard game-winning touchdown pass from Steve Young in a 1998 playoff game against the Packers, and set a league record with 20 catches in one game in Rice's last home game as a 49er in 1999.

To augment his football performance, T.O. took up gridiron choreography and began to take touchdown celebrations to a whole new level of self-absorption. Some were clever and seemed spontaneous, like when he took a cheerleader's pom-poms and did a dance with them. Other times were clearly preconceived, like when he smuggled a Sharpie pen in his sock to autograph the football immediately after scoring. And the time he ran out to the Cowboys' 50-yard line to spike the ball in the Dallas star got him fined by the league. Owens' relationship with his coaches deteriorated from there. He claimed Steve Mariucci did not "go for the jugular" in a game against the Bears because he was friends with Chicago coach Dick Jauron. He ostentatiously berated offensive coach Greg Knapp on the sidelines in 2003 and feuded openly with 49er quarterback Jeff Garcia. It is true that Terrell has never had any legal or drug problems, but his ego grew larger than the team.

Desperate to get out of San Francisco, Owens campaigned for Philadelphia to sign him so he could team up with strong-armed Donovan McNabb. To the surprise of most Eagle fans, Andy Reid did just that. There was a hangup of course, because Terrell's agent had not filed the proper paperwork with the league, and for a time it looked like Owens was the property of the Baltimore Ravens. After much wrangling, T.O. became an Eagle but had made a new enemy in Ravens linebacker Ray Lewis who felt personally betrayed by Owens. The fun started right in mini-camp when Terrell could not believe that Reid insisted on Eagle players wearing shorts and not tights to practice. Owens complied, but not without a lot of noise and a deal with Reid that if T.O. scored 15 TDs, not only could Owens wear his beloved tights, but Andy would don a pair as well. Then there were some comments made by Terrell to *Playboy* magazine in which he insinuated that his former quarterback Jeff Garcia was gay. The ironic thing was that Garcia was dating the current *Playboy* Playmate of the Year at the time this came out. At last, the season began.

While T.O. was grabbing touchdowns and the Eagles were piling up wins, the constant media attention on Owens continued. There were the many and varied end zone celebrations including: flapping his arms like Eagle wings, doing situps, ripping down fans' negative signs in Cleveland, mocking Ray Lewis' preening dance against the Ravens and posing on the end zone star in Dallas. There was the sideline scene of Owens repeatedly trying to talk to McNabb while Donovan tried to ignore T.O. in the Eagles' first loss against Pittsburgh. The following week the two mocked the incident repeatedly on the sidelines for the same TV cameras. There was the recurring soccer-style chant of "Tee Ohh, T.O., T.O., T.O., Tee Ohh" at the Linc each week. There was the *Monday Night Football* promo in which Nicollette Sheridan of *Desperate Housewives* fame got to show her bare back and Terrell got to show his very limited acting skills. There was the gala 31st birthday party T.O. threw for himself, complete with Hollywood actresses and celebrities. Even with the team winning, it got to be exhausting.

In the 14th game of the year, as the Birds were clinching home field throughout the playoffs, the Cowboys Roy Williams yanked Owens back by the collar and T.O. went down awkwardly. He limped off the field and into the tunnel before allowing a cart to take him for x-rays. The bad news was a broken bone in his leg with a prognosis of at least eight weeks time to heal. Unfortunately, the Super Bowl was only seven weeks away. Through the last two weeks of the season, the bye week, the first two playoff games and the two weeks before the Super Bowl, the big story in Philadelphia was T.O.'s recovery. Meanwhile, Andy Reid rested his main starters in the last two games of the year, and everyone was well rested for the playoffs.

First up were the 8-8 Cinderella Vikings who had defeated the Packers at Lambeau Field the week before, but who promptly turned back into pumpkins in Philadelphia. They were easily smashed by the Eagles 27-14 with Freddie Mitchell having a rare big day with two TDs and Brian Westbrook running free on offense. On defense, Jevon Kearse had two sacks and Jeremiah Trotter and Ike Reese each pulled down an interception. The next week, on the day after a major snowstorm, the Falcons hit the Linc for the conference championship and were blown away. With the temperature at 17 degrees and the wind chill at −5, Michael Vick had trouble throwing the ball and could not get outside to run because of the agile speed of defensive ends Derrick Burgess and Jevon Kearse. McNabb had a good day throwing long despite the wind, and the Birds won easily 27-10 after leading by only 14-10 at the half. The Eagles were flying to Jacksonville for the Super Bowl at last.

The Owens watch hit high gear, and it was reported that T.O.'s doctor would not clear him to play after so short a recuperation. Everyone knew he was playing, though. A competitor like Owens was not going to miss a chance to play on the ultimate football stage because of some pain. In the media hullabaloo in Jacksonville during the lead-up to the game, the national story was Owens. How effective could he be? Some commentators even pursued the absurd question of whether he was being selfish by forcing himself into the lineup when he could not help the team. As it turned out, Owens' courageous play was the best thing Eagle fans would take from Super Bowl XXXIX.

In the game, the Birds found out just why the Patriots won three out of the last four Super Bowls: they are fundamentally sound in all phases of the game, don't make mistakes, and adjust well on the fly. The Eagles could not quite match up. Donovan McNabb had a generally awful game throwing the ball over 50 times and tossing three interceptions, but the offensive line gave him little protection and opened few holes for a running game. The Birds' most consistent weapon was T.O., who caught nine passes for 122 yards. The defense played pretty well; they did not shut down New England, but managed to keep the game close while the Eagle offense struggled. Still, the Eagles had a shot to win the game, being only 10 points down with 5:40 to play. Inexplicably, the Eagles did not go into their hurry-up offense, but slowly ground out a 13-play, 79-yard drive that took up nearly four minutes before scoring on a 30-yard pass to Greg Lewis. With only two timeouts left, Philadelphia tried and failed at an onsides kick, but the defense stopped the Patriots from getting a first down. New England's punt, however, was downed at the Eagles' 4 with 46 seconds to go. McNabb strangely tossed a pass to Brian Westbrook in the middle of the field at the 5 while 30 seconds ran off the clock for a one-yard gain. Two plays later, McNabb was picked off for the final time by Rodney Harrison, and the game was over. It was a great season and a big step forward, but still short of a championship.

For 2004 at least, this was a perfect marriage. T.O. craved the attention both on and off the field, and this haunted Eagle team craved the freedom to go about their business without media scrutiny. Is Terrell Owens a Philly Guy? He's been amazingly popular from the start largely because he was exactly what this team needed to get over the NFC Conference title hurdle. Moreover, Philadelphia loves a big talker who can back it up and rub the opponents' noses in it. This town still reveres Buddy Ryan after all, and he never did back up his braggadocio fully. On the other hand, Philly loves its football and is all about passion. If the team starts slipping and Owens complaints are seen as divisive posturing, will his popularity erode? Not long after the 2004 season ended, T.O. was already taking his egotism to the next level. He fired his longtime agent and announced that he wanted to renegotiate his contract so he could "feed his family." On top of that, he began making thinly veiled negative comments about Donovan McNabb, the quarterback he so desperately wanted to play with just one year before. All signs point to a petulant vocal Terrell Owens for 2005. He's come a long way from Alabama, but how long can he maintain his star power? What happens when he leaves the game? Will he learn to love what he was best at only when it's gone?

82
The Fates

Mike Quick
WR 1982-90

WHO'S WORN THE NUMBER:

Robert Krieger (E) 1941, William Combs (E) 1942, **Bill Hewitt** (E) 1943, Milton Smith (E) 1945, Rudy Smeja (E) 1946, Danny DiRenzo (P) 1948, Joe Restic (E) 1952, *Tom Scott* (DE) 1953-58, George Tarasovic (DE) 1963-65, *Tim Rossovich* (LB) 1968-71, Bob Picard (WR) 1973-76, Ken Payne (WR) 1978, Jerrold McRae (WR) 1979, *Mike Quick* (WR) 1982-90, Mickey Shuler (TE) 1991, Victor Bailey (WR) 1993-94, Chris Jones (WR) 1995-97, Karl Hankton (WR) 1998, Dameane Douglas (WR) 1999-02, L.J. Smith (TE) 2003-04.

Originator: End Bob Krieger showed potential, starting opposite fellow rookie Dick Humbert in 1941. Humbert finished second in the league in receptions, while Krieger finished tenth. Both were in the service soon after.

Longest Tenure: Nine years, Mike Quick.

Number Changes: Bill Hewitt wore 56 from 1937 to 1939; Bob Krieger wore 89 in 1946; Milt Smith also wore 30 in 1945; Mickey Shuler wore 85 in 1990.

Just Visiting: George Tarasovic had his best years as a Steeler; Mickey Shuler was a decent tight end with the Jets.

Highs: Bill Hewitt was a Hall of Famer (see 56); Tom Scott was a speedy pass rusher who ended his career as a Giants linebacker; Tim Rossovich was a talented eccentric who literally chewed glass and set his hair on fire, but was the team's defensive MVP in 1969.

Lows: Jerrold McRae got into five games in 1978 and caught one pass for minus two yards.

Mike Quick

In 1982, both the Eagles and the Buffalo Bills were in need of a wide receiver come draft time. In talking with his friend Chuck Knox, who coached Buffalo, Dick Vermeil mentioned that Philadelphia liked Perry Tuttle from Clemson the most. In a cutthroat move, the Bills made a last minute draft day trade to leap-frog over the Eagles and nab Tuttle with the 19th selection in the first round. Double-crossed, the Eagles then selected Mike Quick, who was the favorite of receivers coach Dick Coury anyway, with the next pick. As it turned out, Tuttle was snared by the karmic undercurrents and only caught 24 passes in two injury-plagued seasons in Buffalo. Mike Quick became a five-time All-Pro and Pro Bowl player especially noted for his graceful fluid style, his skill as a deep threat and his penchant for game-breaking plays. Like Jerry Rice, Quick was not the fastest receiver in the league, but no one ever caught him from behind. It was said of Mike that "If he's even, he's leavin'."

As a rookie, Quick continually heard an earful from Vermeil and only caught 10 passes in the strike-shortened season. In retrospect, Quick says that he learned more about how to play football that year under the intense Vermeil than in any other. Mike blossomed in his second year under new coach Marion Campbell catching 69 passes for 13 touchdowns with an average gain of over 20 yards per catch. Over the next five years, Quick averaged 62 catches and 11 TDs per year, catching passes from the aging Ron Jaworski and the evolving Randall Cunningham. It was one highlight after another. In 1983, he caught an 83-yard touchdown against the Cowboys. He caught a 90-yard touchdown against the Cardinals in 1984. He beat Atlanta on a late 53-yard touchdown in 1983, and in 1985, he beat them on a 99-yard touchdown reception in overtime. After suffering a broken nose, Quick beat the Bills on a 32-yard touchdown catch in 1985. He caught three touchdowns passes against the Raiders' two All-Pro corners, Lester Hayes and Mike Hayes, in 1986.

Quick held out in 1985 and in 1987 and was a team leader during the 1987 players' strike, but was immensely popular with the fans because there was never a lack of effort or production from Mike Quick. Early in the 1988 season, Mike suffered his first serious injury when he broke his ankle against the Oilers in October. He worked hard to rehabilitate the leg and was back on the field in December, so he made his only playoff appearance in the Fog Bowl. The following season, he only got into six games before needing surgery on both knees to relieve tendonitis. In 1990, Quick got into just four games before tearing his left quadriceps muscle. When his knees and legs did not come around, Mike was forced to retire prior to training camp in 1991. In his abbreviated career, he caught 363 passes, 61 for touchdowns, and could have broken all Eagle reception records if he had been able to stay healthy.

Of all the Eagles who have had their careers shortened by injury, no one had more potential greatness unfulfilled than Quick. The only names that come close are two defensive backs, Wes Hopkins and Ben Smith, and defensive tackle Andy Harmon. Here's a team's worth of Eagles who had their careers in the league or with the Eagles shortened due to injury:

Wide receiver — Mike Quick (knees and legs); Ben Hawkins (broken leg); Chris T. Jones (knee); Joe Carter (broken collarbone and shoulder separation).

Tight end – Jamie Asher (broken ankle); Keith Krepfle (general accumulation of bangs and bruises).

Offensive line — Ron Solt (knees); Matt Darwin (knee); Bill Lueck (knees); Wade Key (accumulated injuries); Bubba Miller (broken ankle).

Quarterback — Sonny Jurgensen (shoulder separation); Randall Cunningham (knee and broken leg). Neither QB was directly driven from the team by injury, but these were serious injuries that had a major impact on their careers.

Running back — Steve Van Buren (foot and knee); Clyde Scott (shoulder separation); Bosh Pritchard (knee); Correll Buckhalter (two knee injuries).

Defensive line — Norm Willey (broken leg); Bucko Kilroy (knee); Andy Harmon (knee); Derrick Burgess (foot and knee); Hollis Thomas (feet repeatedly). Both Thomas and Burgess keep coming back.

Linebacker — Bill Bergey (knee); Byron Evans (broken leg); Kevin Reilly (shoulder); Chuck Weber (ankle).

Defensive back — Tom Brookshier (broken leg); Ben Smith (knee); Wes Hopkins (knee); Leroy Keyes (Achilles tendon); Damon Moore (anterior cruciate ligament in knee).

Kicker — Nick Mike-Mayer actually lost his job due to poor kicking, but when he was injured in the Miracle of the Meadowlands game, injured punter Mike Michel took his place and personally lost a playoff game with missed kicks against Atlanta.

Punter — John Teltschick (knee).

The Eagles marked Quick's departure by honoring him at a game in 1991 with a bizarre gift — a golf bag without any clubs. It was an empty gesture that said more about Norman Braman than it did about Mike Quick, and the fans indicated their displeasure by embarrassingly booing the gift. Mike was a perennial fan favorite and maintains that greatest number one thrill as a player came after he broke his leg against the Oilers. When he came back on the field to watch the game, he got a standing ovation from the fans. While Quick has a number of business concerns, he still connects to Eagle fans by serving as the color analyst for Eagle radio and does a good job as an honest, perceptive and amusing commentator.

Putting Points on the Board

Bobby Walston
E/K 1951-62

Originator: End Jack Ferrante (see top 87) in 1941.

Longest Tenure: 12 years, Bobby Walston.

Number Changes: Jack Ferrante wore 87 from 1944 to 1950; Kenny Jackson wore 81 in 1984 and 1985 and 84 from 1986 to 1988; Troy Smith also wore 19 in 1999; Jeff Thomason took a two-week vacation from his construction job to return to the Eagles and wear 85 in Super Bowl XXXIX.

Just Visiting: Bill Quinlan was a rugged defensive end for Vince Lombardi's Packers; Jimmie Giles starred as a tight end for the Bucs; Pat Beach and Ed West were journeymen tight ends who spent a decade with the Colts and Packers respectively; Michael Timpson was a third receiver for the Patriots.

Highs: South Philly's Vince Papale was a 30-year-old schoolteacher who had played receiver in the World Football League. He went to an open tryout, impressed Dick Vermeil and played three years as a special teams demon for the rebuilding Eagles. He was the real Rocky.

Lows: Penn State's Kenny Jackson was the fourth overall selection in the 1984 draft, but never caught more than 40 passes in a season in seven years in Philadelphia.

Bobby Walston

In 1957, Bobby Walston passed Steve Van Buren as the Eagles' all-time leading scorer. If placekicker David Akers maintains his current scoring pace, he stands to pass Walston in points in the 2007 season when the record will be 50 years old. Walston was a sure-handed receiver and a reliable kicker in Philadelphia for a dozen years. His teammates called him "Mumbles" for the way he spoke, the "Sheriff" for his one-time job in Georgia, "Cheewah" for his Indian heritage, as well as "Blackie" and "Sure-Foot." However, not only is Bobby Walston largely forgotten today, he was not much appreciated in his time either.

Walston was a 14th-round selection out of the University of Georgia in 1951 and made an impact right away, catching 31 passes for a 16.5 average and scoring 94 points on eight touchdowns, six field goals and 28 extra points. It was the first of 10 seasons in which he would lead the Eagles in points, and he was named Rookie of the Year for the league. Bobby was the second passing option on the team behind Pete Pihos, who led the NFL in receptions for three consecutive seasons, and Bud Grant, who finished second in catches once. Through 1955, Walston benefited by scoring 30 touchdowns in this five-year period. His 11 touchdowns in 1954 helped him lead the NFL in scoring with 114 points. With Pihos retired, Bobby led the team in receptions in 1956 for the first and only time and was the Eagles' MVP. In 1957, though, the Eagles were grooming converted running back Dick Bielski to take Walston's place as "closed," or tight, end. Admittedly, at only 190 pounds, Walston was undersized at his position, but Buck Shaw found that "He'll bite and scratch and fight at every turn, and he'll get it done." Bobby played through such injuries as a broken jaw and ripped tendons in his hand. While fighting off the challenge by Bielski, Walston was surpassed by young receivers Tommy McDonald and Pete Retzlaff, who joined the team in 1957 and made Bobby the third passing option.

Dick Bielski was also challenging Walston as the team's kicker. Walston scored the fewest points of his career in 1955 when the rookie Bielski did almost all the placekicking. Based on that performance, however, Bielski attempted only eight more field goals in his last four years with the team and made none of them. He was not Walston's equal as a receiver or kicker. Bobby was a very talented, multidimensional player — probably the best double threat the team ever had. In the early days of the franchise, Philadelphia placekicking was handled by a variety of players, most prominently by center Hank Reese in the 1930s and a handful of backs in the early 1940s. The team's first significant multiple-scoring threat was quarterback Roy Zimmerman, who also handled kicking and punting duties from 1943 to 1945. He was followed by two linemen, Augio Lio and then Cliff Patton, from 1946 to 1950. At this time the only kicking specialists were the Giants' Ken Strong from 1944 to 1947 and Ben Agajanian in the All-America Conference (although Ben had played briefly with the Eagles and Steelers in the early 1940s). Philadelphia's first pure kicker was Paige Cothren, who was hired in 1959 to kick field goals; Walston still kicked extra points.

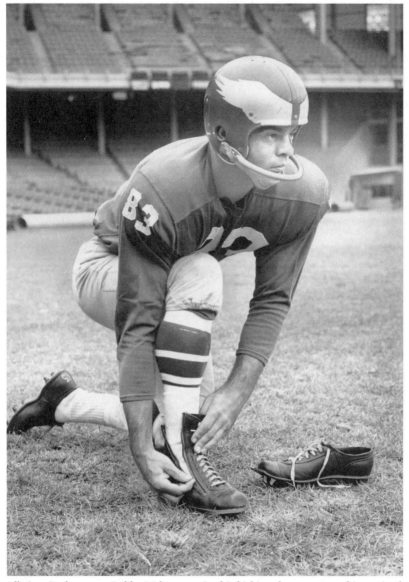

All-time Eagles scorer Bobby Walston unzips his kicking shoe to put on his receiver's cleats.

Bobby won the full kicking job back in the championship season of 1960 and made the Pro Bowl the next two seasons. He was a big part of the success of the team, kicking a number of game-winning field goals. He claimed his biggest thrill was his 38-yard, last-second field goal that beat the Browns 31-29 and boosted the Eagles on their way to the title that year. His second biggest thrill came the following year when he passed Lou Groza in all-time points scored the week after Groza had passed Don Hutson. Groza would take the record back in 1962, but for one year Walston was the NFL's all-time leading scorer.

By 1962, Walston's skills were fading and he retired at the end of the season. He tried out for the Boston Patriots in 1963 on the encouragement of his former Georgia Bulldog and Eagle teammate Marion Campbell, who was an assistant coach in Boston, but did not make the team. He was replaced as kicker and as number 83 on the Eagles by rookie Mike Clark, who was gone by 1964. Bobby worked as a scout for the Eagles, an assistant coach for the Dolphins, and the personnel director for the Bears before going back into scouting for teams in the CFL and USFL. He died of a heart attack at the age of 58 in 1987.

84

1981 Playoffs

Keith Krepfle
TE 1975-81

WHO'S WORN THE NUMBER:

Larry Cabrelli (E) 1941-47, Leslie Palmer (B) 1948, Hank Burnine (E) 1956-57, Leo Sugar (DE) 1961, Mike Clark (K/E) 1963, Don Thompson (E) 1964, Jim Kelly (E) 1965-67, Richard Harris (DE) 1971-73, Keith Krepfle (TE) 1975-81, Vyto Kab (TE) 1982-85, Kenny Jackson (WR) 1986-88, Mike McCloskey (TE) 1987, Anthony Edwards (WR) 1989-90, Floyd Dixon (WR) 1992, Mark Bavaro (TE) 1993-94, Kelvin Martin (WR) 1995, Freddie Solomon (WR) 1996-98, Jamie Asher (TE) 1999, Luther Broughton (TE) 2000, Freddie Mitchell (WR) 2001-04.

Originator: End Larry Cabrelli as a rookie in 1941. Cabrelli was a dependable performer who served as team captain and later became an assistant coach under Greasy Neale.

Longest Tenure: Seven years, Larry Cabrelli and Keith Krepfle.

Number Changes: Les Palmer wore 40 in 1948; Kenny Jackson wore 81 in 1984 and 1985 and 83 in 1990 and 1991; Freddie Solomon wore 17 in 1995; Luther Broughton wore 49 and 86 in 1997 and 88 in 1999.

Just Visiting: Leo Sugar was a good defensive end with the Cardinals; Mark Bavarro had his All-Pro years as a Giant.

Highs: Larry Cabrelli (see above).

Lows: Redskin tight end Jamie Asher signed a $4.1 million contract with Philadelphia in 1999, broke his ankle six plays into the first exhibition game and never played again.

Keith Krepfle

A classic overachiever, Keith Krepfle was a favorite of Dick Vermeil and fans alike. He was drafted out of Iowa State in the fifth round of the 1974 draft by the Eagles, but elected to sign with the Jacksonville Sharks of the World Football League for a better chance at playing time. On the 4-10 Sharks, though, Krepfle caught only six passes backing up the immortal Dennis Hughes, a former Steeler with a career total of 24 NFL receptions.

Krepfle reported to the Eagles in 1975 and made the team as a backup to All-Pro tight end Charlie Young and as a kamikaze special teams player nicknamed Captain Crunch. When Young was traded two years later to the Rams for the rights to Ron Jaworski, Krepfle won the starting job and held it for the next five years. He was undersized for a tight end and took a beating, but he showed up for work every day nonetheless. Longtime trainer Otho Davis said Krepfle was the first player who came to mind when talking about Eagles playing with pain. One time Keith broke his hand and had to have three pins inserted to hold it together, but he didn't miss a day of practice.

Krepfle's best season was 1979 when he finished second on the team with 41 catches. In the 1980 Super Bowl year, Keith had to fight through multiple injuries. He separated his shoulder at the beginning of the year and kept on going. At mid season, he had to undergo arthroscopic surgery on his knee to remove cartilage, but missed only three games. He played in all three playoff games and caught an eight-yard TD pass in the Super Bowl — the first and only Eagle to score a touchdown in that game.

By 1981, the battering was really taking its toll. Krepfle played in every Eagles game but caught only 20 passes and averaged only 10.5 yards per catch, down from his career average of 16. The team started out fast that year, winning its first six games and nine of its first 11. The Eagles then went on a four-game losing streak to lose the divisional race to the Cowboys, who beat them twice. The offense scored the fourth most points in the league with Wilbert Montgomery gaining his second highest total of rushing yards, Harold Carmichael catching his second most passes and Ron Jaworski throwing his second highest total of TD passes. The defense finished first in least yards and points allowed.

The Eagles' opponent in the wild card game at the Vet was the New York Giants, who had started Philadelphia's four-game losing streak the month before with a 20-10 thrashing. The favored Eagles self-destructed in the game's opening quarter. Wally Henry fumbled a punt at his own 26, which the Giants converted into six points when Scott Brunner hit Leon Bright with a nine-yard touchdown toss. The next time New York got the ball, they drove 62 yards and scored on a Brunner 10-yard pass to John Mistler. On the ensuing kickoff, Henry fumbled again, and Mark Haynes recovered the ball in the end zone to give the Giants a 20-0 lead. The Eagles finally got going on a 74-yard drive that culminated with a Carmichael touchdown with 2:16 left in the half. The Giants answered with a five-play, 62-yard drive that ended with a third Brunner TD pass, this time to Tom Mullady.

Trailing 27-7 in the third quarter, Philadelphia put together another drive to pull to 27-14, and then late in the fourth quarter scored again to draw to 27-21 with 2:51 left in the game. But they never got the ball back. Behind Rob Carpenter, who gained 161 yards on 33 carries, the Giants ran out the clock. The aging Eagles' lack of breakaway speed was cited as a factor after the loss, and they would draft Mike Quick the following year to replace the mediocre Charlie Smith, who was released.

That was also Keith Krepfle's last game as an Eagle. The younger, healthier, bigger and stronger John Spagnola was waiting in the wings to take over. Dick Vermeil loved Krepfle. Once, Vermeil went after safety Cliff Harris of the Cowboys because Harris had dropped Keith with a cheap-shot late hit. Vermeil cut Krepfle early in the spring of 1982 to give him the best chance to catch on with another team before training camp. Krepfle signed with the Falcons, but only got into four games for Atlanta. Keith was inducted into the Iowa State Athletic Hall of Fame in 2002. He currently is a businessman who serves on the board of the Otho Davis Foundation, established in 1999 as a scholarship fund when the popular trainer was dying from cancer.

Lifers

Charlie Gauer
E 1945

Originator: End John Shonk in 1941. At the beginning of that season, Greasy Neale instituted a system of $10 bonuses for blocked kicks and turnovers. Shonk won a 10-spot with an interception in the second game against the Steelers.

Longest Tenure: Eight years, Charlie Smith.

Number Changes: Charley Gauer wore 32 in 1943 and 1944; Jay MacDowell wore 88 from 1947 to 1951; Mickey Shuler wore 82 in 1991; Jeff Thomason wore 83 from 2000 to 2002.

Just Visiting: Bob Schnelker turned out to be a skilled receiver for the Giants; Marlin McKeever was a longtime linebacker for the Rams and Redskins; Art Monk caught too many passes against the Eagles as a longtime Redskin All-Pro; Mark Ingram was a mediocre Giants receiver.

Highs: Gary Ballman was too slow to play wide receiver and too small to play tight end, but he was a gamer who did both; Charlie "Homeboy" Smith started opposite Harold Carmichael for seven years, but never caught more than 47 passes in a season.

Lows: By showing the best hands on the team in practice, Na Brown won a job as the Eagles' third receiver. By continually dropping balls in the games, he was cut.

Charlie Gauer

Charlie Gauer Sr. was a Chicago oil man who was also the owner of the original Chicago Bulls — a football team in Red Grange's ill-fated 1927 American Football League that challenged the NFL. Charlie Jr. was born in Chicago but went to high school in Upper Darby. He attended college at Colgate, where he was a backup end and blocking back on the football team and a reserve on the basketball squad. One of his Colgate teammates, Larry Cabrelli, joined the Eagles as a free agent in 1941.

Junior followed Cabrelli and hooked on with the Philadelphia-Pittsburgh Steagles in 1943 as a free agent, appearing mostly as a substitute for fullback Ben Kish. He rushed for his entire career's total of 69 yards as a rookie. He continued with the Eagles in 1944 and got to start four games at end. Playing both ways, he caught two passes and nabbed one interception for the improving Birds. Gauer lasted one more season as a backup end and then joined the Navy. When he got out, he coached high school football for five years before rejoining the Eagles as an offensive coach under Jim Trimble. It was Charlie who told Trimble that quarterback Adrian Burk was only one touchdown pass from tying the NFL record of seven after Burk had been pulled in the fourth quarter of a rout of the Redskins in 1954. Burk went back in and got his seventh TD with 20 seconds left. Under the Eagles' next coach, Hugh Devore, Gauer brought in Villanova track coach Jumbo Elliot to give the backs some tips on improving their running. He also took special interest in two rookies: Tommy McDonald and Sonny Jurgensen. McDonald was drafted as a 170-pound halfback and came very close to being cut several times in his first training camp. Gauer always stood up for him and was the instigator of Tommy's move to the flanker position. Jurgensen, whom Charlie had worked out at Duke, was his special project and the two formed a tight bond.

Charlie stayed on as Buck Shaw took over the team in 1958, and two years later was given the task of scouting the Packers for the championship game. His tip about a weakness in the Green Bay kickoff coverage led to a long return by Ted Dean that set up Philadelphia's winning score. New coach Nick Skorich retained Charlie in 1961, and Gauer's tutelage of Jurgensen paid big dividends. Sonny threw for over 3,000 yards in his first year as a starter and led the team to a 10-4 record. Charlie left the sidelines in 1962 to attend to his oil distribution business. Sonny Grandelius replaced Gauer and many observers attributed Jurgensen's subpar performance over the next two seasons not only to his shoulder separation, but to the absence of Gauer as well. Jurgensen used to take film over to Charlie's house secretly to get his insight without offending the current coaching staff. The perception that Gauer was Jurgensen's Svengali lingered for years even after the quarterback's success in Washington.

In 1965, Charlie joined the Eagle radio broadcasting team as the color man with Andy Musser and had the difficult job of analyzing the last four years of the Kuharich era. Charlie also had a call-in radio show about the Eagles at the time and continued to scout for the team part-time. When Kuharich was let go, former Eagle Pete Retzlaff was brought in as general manager in 1969. Pete wanted to hire former Eagle defensive coach Jerry Williams, who was coaching in Canada, but the Calgary Stampeders would not allow it. It was widely speculated that Gauer was the leading contender for the head coaching position at that point, but Williams became free after all. Williams then hired Gauer as offensive coach, and Charlie spent two years with the incompetent coach before going back into scouting.

In two coaching terms, Charlie spent 12 years as an Eagle assistant under five head coaches. Only Fred Bruney spent a longer time as an assistant with 14 seasons in two terms under three head coaches — Kuharich, Vermeil and Campbell. Ken Iman spent 11 seasons as an assistant under three head coaches — Vermeil, Campbell and Ryan. Five men have spent a decade coaching in Philadelphia: John Kellison under Greasy Neale, Chuck Clausen under Vermeil and Campbell, and three current coaches since 1995 — Juan Castillo, Ted Williams and Mike Wolf.

Charlie was always outspoken and gruff, and always good for an honest opinion. He was an innovative coach and perceptive scout who gave close to 30 years service to the Eagles before he died at the age of 54 in 1973. It's interesting that one of his first teammates as an Eagle in 1943, fellow free agent Bucko Kilroy, is still going strong, working part-time in the Patriots' front office after 62 years in the NFL with the Eagles, Redskins, Cowboys and New England as a player, scout and executive. Two wartime free agents; two lifers.

Draft Treasures

Norm Willey
DE 1953-57

Originator:	End Hal Prescott in 1947.
Longest Tenure:	Seven years, Fred Hill.
Number Changes:	Norm Willey wore 44 in 1950 and 1951 and 63 in 1952; Dialleo Burks also wore 42 and 89 in 1996; Luther Broughton wore 49 in 1997, 84 in 2000 and 88 in 1999; Gari Scott also wore 16 in 2000.
Just Visiting:	Antonio Freeman was Brett Favre's favorite target in Green Bay.
Highs:	Bud Grant left for Canada after finishing second in the NFL in receptions in his second season; Fred Hill was not a great receiver, but his daughter was the instigator for the long-running, successful Eagles Flight for Leukemia charity; Charles Young had a couple of spectacular seasons as a tight end in Philly before being traded for Ron Jaworski's rights; Arkansas' Fred Barnett was an able deep threat and showman.
Lows:	Brian Finneran was the Division I-AA player of the year with Villavova in 1997 and caught on as free agent with the Eagles in 1999. In Andy Reid's first game as coach, he called Finneran's number in the fourth quarter against the Cardinals, but Doug Pederson's pass bounced out of Finneran's hands and was intercepted. Brian got into only two more games in Philadelphia.

Norm Willey

Statistics often fail to tell the story in football, and that was even truer in the past. One example is that sacks were not officially counted by the league until 1982, so that great pass rushers like Deacon Jones, Gino Marchetti and Willie Davis are nowhere to be found in the listings of the all-time sack leaders. At least those players got to play in the television era, so there is ample visual evidence of their excellence. The exploits of Philadelphia's pass rush master in the early 1950s, Norm Willey, are largely lost forever.

Willey went to a West Virginia high school of 43 students where he played six-man football before going into the Navy. After World War II, he enrolled at Marshall University and starred as an end and fullback in football as well as playing on the basketball team. Drafted in the 13th round by the Eagles as a fullback, Norm was almost cut by Greasy Neale in his first training camp until he mentioned that he also had played end in college. At the defensive end position, Willey quickly earned the nickname "Wild Man" by continually knocking down quarterback Tommy Thompson, who started groaning, "There goes that wild man again."

Willey was named to All-Pro teams three times and twice to the Pro Bowl as one of the fiercest members of the rugged Philadelphia defense. He broke the jaw of Pittsburgh quarterback Jim Finks with one hard forearm shot he applied in 1954. Norm's greatest day came on October 26, 1952 when he put on a legendary pass rush performance in a 14-10 victory over the Giants in the Polo Grounds. He asserts that he sacked the Giant quarterbacks 17 times that dreary autumn afternoon. Some have claimed that this number was verified in New York press accounts of the game, but I have not been able to confirm that. What is verifiable is that the game was extremely hard-hitting, as was normal for an Eagle-Giant match, and that the Eagles hit Giant quarterback Charlie Conerly so hard and so often that he was forced out of the game battered and bleeding. Backup quarterback Fred Benners received a similar reception from Philadelphia. The Giant quarterbacks threw for 182 yards that day, but lost 127 yards from being sacked when attempting to pass so the team netted a total of 55 yards passing. How many times Conerly and Benners were dropped and by whom is not a matter of record. Years later, when NFL Films did a piece on this game, venerable *Sports Illustrated* football writer Paul Zimmerman commented that he was at that game and had charted it. His normally thorough and reliable charts show that the Giant QBs were sacked 14 times that day — eight by Willey and six by Pete Pihos who switched to defense for one All-Pro season in 1952.

So maybe 17 sacks is an exaggeration, but eight sacks in one day is more than the modern one-game record of seven and still constitutes an amazing day. Willey was a rangy, instinctual speed rusher who usually lined up far to the outside. His coach, Jim Trimble, remembers trying to give him advice during one game on whether to rush inside or out, depending on the width of the split taken by the offensive tackle. Trimble realized at halftime that Willey was spending so much time figuring out how wide the tackle was split that he was completely ineffectual. Trimble told him to forget about the splits and turned him loose to be the Wild Man again. Norm's feeling was that the best way to stop the pass was to get to the quarterback before he threw the ball.

Wild Man Willey played for Philadelphia for eight years and claimed he averaged two sacks a game for his career. As with the 17-sack game, that number cannot be confirmed and probably is inflated, but he was a consistent threat on the Eagle defensive line for close to a decade. Norm broke his leg against San Francisco in 1956, but came back for a final season in 1957. He found he could not get any speed on the healed leg and also was disenchanted when the Eagles shifted to a four-man line that left him more as a linebacker. So he retired and became a high school teacher and coach for the next 30 years. Norm also worked for several years at the Vet on Eagle game days, directing opposing players onto the field, still part of the organization. But Norm Willey was not the only treasure the Eagles uncovered late in the draft. Here's the All-Time Eagles Draft Treasures Team:

OFFENSE

Wide Receivers — Bobby Walston (14th rd. 1951), a star receiver and kicker for 12 years who is still the leading scorer in team history. Harold Carmichael (7th rd. 1971) the team's all-time leading receiver.

Tight End — Pete Pihos (5th rd. 1945), actually just an end, but a perennial All-Pro and a Hall of Famer. Keith Krepfle (5th rd. 1974), an actual tight end; not great, but an overachiever.

Tackles — Al Wistert (5th rd. 1943), a perennial All-Pro and a member of the Eagles Honor Roll. Wade Key (13th rd. 1969), a 10-year starter.

Guards — Bruno Banducci (6th rd. 1943), an All-Pro who had his greatest success later with the 49ers. Jim Skaggs (10th rd. 1962), a solid pro for nine years.

Center — Ken Farragut (6th rd. 1951), tall Pro Bowler with a short career.

Quarterback — Sonny Jurgensen (4th rd. 1957), Hall of Famer although mostly with Washington.

Running Backs — Wilbert Montgomery (6th rd. 1977), the Eagles' all-time leading rusher. Tom Woodeshick (8th rd. 1963), a tough runner for some bad teams. Tom Sullivan (15th rd. 1972), a decent runner and pass catcher on some more bad teams.

DEFENSE

Defensive Ends — Norm Willey (13th rd. 1950) see above. Clyde Simmons (9th rd. 1986), Reggie White's sacking mate. Carl Hairston (7th rd. 1976), pass rushing leader for Vermeil. Johnny Green (16th rd. 1944), a 200-pound Pro Bowl pass rushing star.

Defensive Tackles — Charlie Johnson (7th rd. 1977), a Pro Bowl run stuffer for Vermeil. Jess Richardson (8th rd. 1953), the last player to play without a face mask. Andy Harmon (6th rd. 1991), a light but active defensive tackle.

Linebackers — Seth Joyner (8th rd. 1986) Buddy's playmaker. John Bunting (10th rd. 1972), a longtime signal caller. Frank LeMaster (4th rd. 1974), a force inside for Vermeil. William Thomas (4th rd. 1991), light and fast; always around the ball in pass coverage.

Defensive Backs — Tom Brookshier (10th rd. 1953), a star corner who became a local institution. Russ Craft (15th rd. 1943), an All-Pro corner for Greasy Neale. Irv Cross (7th rd. 1961), a solid all-around cornerback. Nate Ramsey (14th rd. 1963), hard-hitting safety. Joe Lavender (12th rd. 1973), a big, gangly cornerback.

Kicker — Paul McFadden (12th rd. 1984), a barefooted lefty who was very accurate for a few years.

Punter — Max Runager (8th rd. 1979), limited by a barely adequate leg.

2003 Playoffs

Todd Pinkston
WR 2000-04

WHO'S WORN THE NUMBER:

Jack Ferrante (E) 1944-50, Andy Nacelli (E) 1958, Art Powell (WR) 1959, Dick Lucas (E) 1960-63, Bill Cronin (E) 1965, Dave Lince (E) 1966-67, Fred Brown (LB) 1969, Kent Kramer (TE) 1971-74, Claude Humphrey (DE) 1979-81, Lawrence Sampleton (TE) 1982-84, John Goode (TE) 1985, Eric Bailey (TE) 1987r, Ron Fazio (TE) 1987r, Carlos Carson (WR) 1989, Harper LeBel (TE) 1990, Maurice Johnson (TE) 1991-94, Frank Wainwright (TE) 1995, Jason Dunn (TE) 1996-98, Jed Weaver (TE) 1999, Todd Pinkston (WR) 2000-04.

Originator: Camden, New Jersey's own Jack Ferrante in 1944. Ferrante dropped out of high school to support his family and never attended college, but played semi-pro and minor league ball for many years before sticking with the Eagles where he was a starter for seven years. He coached Monsignor Bonner High School throughout the 1950s.

Longest Tenure: Seven years, Jack Ferrante.

Number Changes: Jack Ferrante wore 83 in 1941; Fred Brown wore 55 in 1967 and 1968.

Just Visiting: Carlos Carson was a good receiver for the Chiefs; Harper LeBel was a long snapper for five different teams.

Highs: Jack Ferrante was an underrated end for the back-to-back championship teams; Claude Humphrey still had sacks left in him when Dick Vermeil brought the veteran All-Pro in from Atlanta.

Lows: A 6-foot 6-inch 270-pound tight end, Jason Dunn was a second-round pick who never came close to living up to his immense potential, catching 40 passes in three seasons. He hooked on as a backup in Kansas City under Dick Vermeil.

Todd Pinkston

The Eagles surprised their fans in 2003 when they gave Todd Pinkston a five-year contract extension complete with a $4 million signing bonus. Pinkston is hardly the prototypical wide receiver with his slight build and the skinniest legs this side of the Miss Teen USA Pageant. His repertoire generally boils down to two plays: a quick toss to the sideline for a few yards or a deep fly pattern down the field. Rarely does he wander into the middle of the field. The second round pick from 2000 has gotten better over time, but is far from a star. He went from 10 catches as a rookie to 42 as a starter in 2001 and then 60 in 2002. In 2003, Pinky slipped back to 36 catches but upped his average from 13.3 yards per catch to 16, and the following year he increased that to 18.8 yards per catch, again on 36 catches.

The limitations of Pinkston were illustrated best in the 2003 playoffs. In the first game against the weak secondary of the Packers, Pinkston had his best day as a pro, catching seven passes for 95 yards; the next week in the NFC title game against a better Carolina defense, he was shut out. The Packer game, of course, will be long remembered for Donovan McNabb's 27-yard completion on fourth and 26 in the closing minute. For most of the game, the Packers' punishing ground attack ran all over the Eagles' defense. Green Bay went up 14-0 on two passes from Brett Favre to Robert Ferguson. The Eagles answered with a touchdown to close the gap, but the Packers drove the field again. On fourth and goal from the 1, Ahman Green got the call, but could not get to the hole without tripping over pulling guard Mike Wahle, so the score remained 14-7 at the half. In the fourth quarter, McNabb took the Eagles 89 yards for the tying touchdown, a 12-second scramble culminating in a 12-yard strike to Pinkston. Green Bay went back up on a field goal, and then stopped the Eagles on defense. Driving again, the Packers were faced with fourth and inches at midfield, having accumulated over 200 yards on the ground for the day. With two minutes to play and the Eagles having no timeouts, the Packers punted. A minute later, McNabb completed that fourth and 26 pass to Freddie Mitchell and moved on to kick a field goal and send the game to overtime. Overtime was brief as Favre quickly threw an ill-advised lob at midfield that Brian Dawkins intercepted. A few plays later David Akers kicked the winning field goal.

Things were different one week later against the Carolina Panthers. Panther rookie cornerback Ricky Manning Jr. called out the Eagle receivers in the week before the game, saying he was not impressed at all with Pinkston and James Thrash. Todd responded coolly by saying, "I'll let him do all the talking." Unfortunately, at game time, he let Manning do all the playing as well. The Panthers beat up the Eagles in the NFC championship. They knocked McNabb out of the game in the second half and never gave him a chance in the first half by being so physical with the Eagle wideouts that they disappeared. With three interceptions, Manning caught more passes than Thrash and Pinkston combined. One of those interceptions came in the third quarter when Pinkston broke off his slant route rather than go over the middle, and Manning came up with the ball inside the Carolina 20 to thwart a rare Eagle drive. The Panthers scored their second touchdown a few plays after Manning's third interception, which first bounced off Thrash's hands.

Even more aggravating to passionate Eagle fans was Pinkston's comment on his play after the 14-3 body slam defeat that "I think it was a lack of focus." He was roasted on talk radio for that remark. He even inspired a cruel but funny Internet game called "Pass to Pinky" in which McNabb throws passes while Pinkston falls down, breaks off his route, misses the ball or drops it and then makes comments like, "I lacked focus on that one" or "We lacked urgency on that play" or "I thought I heard a whistle." With the signing of Terrell Owens in 2004, much of the focus was taken off Pinkston, and that helped him catch an occasional deep ball, but there were several disheartening incidents of Todd backing away from potential catches to avoid contact. Todd had a good first half in the Super Bowl with four catches for 82 yards, but he left the game early in the third quarter because of cramps. The contrast with T.O. playing on a broken leg could not be starker. Pinkston will never be popular in Philadelphia.

1988 Playoffs

Keith Jackson
TE 1988-91

Originator: End John Durko caught two passes in four games in 1944. Durko had starred in basketball and football at Albright College in Reading.

Longest Tenure: Nine years, tight end John Spagnola.

Number Changes: Red Ramsey wore 12 from 1938 to 1940; Jay McDowell wore 85 in 1946; Bob Hudson wore 42 in 1954 and 1955; Luther Broughton wore 49 in 1997, 84 in 2000 and 86 in 1997.

Just Visiting: None.

Highs: Jay MacDowell played offensive tackle and defensive end for back-to-back Eagle champions; Bob Hudson (see 42 top); Gary Pettigrew was the Eagles' defensive MVP in 1970; John Spagnola, a diligent, hard-working tight end in the 1980s, was the offensive MVP in 1984.

Lows: Tight end Bill Larson played for six teams in four years. He appeared in five games for the Eagles but never caught a pass.

Keith Jackson

Like Sonny Jurgensen at run-oriented Duke University, Keith Jackson did not play in a college offense that fully exploited his talents. The 6-foot 4-inch, 250-pound Jackson got to block quite a bit in Oklahoma's vaunted Wishbone Offense, but caught only 62 passes in four years as a Sooner. On those few receptions, though, he averaged 23.7 yards per catch.

Buddy Ryan made Jackson his first-round pick in 1988, and Keith paid immediate benefits by catching 81 passes as a rookie and being named Rookie of the Year. He quickly became Randall Cunningham's security blanket whenever the pocket broke down — which was frequent with the Eagles' weak offensive line. Cunningham could always pick out the big target of Jackson breaking free, and that season the Eagles won the Eastern Division and made the playoffs for the first time under Buddy Ryan. Even better, their opponents would be the Chicago Bears, coached by Buddy's nemesis, Mike Ditka. The Eagles literally roared into Chicago the day before the game by circling Soldier's Field three times in their team buses with the horns blaring.

The game turned out to be one of the strangest playoff games in league history. The Bears got off to a fast start with a 64-yard touchdown pass from Mike Tomczak to Dennis McKinnon at 3:02 into the first quarter. After a Seth Joyner interception gave Philadelphia the ball deep in Chicago territory, bizarre things began to happen. A nine-yard touchdown pass from Cunningham to Cric Carter was nullified by a motion penalty on Anthony Toney. On the very next play, a 14-yard touchdown toss to Mike Quick was nullified by a holding penalty on Toney, and the Eagles settled for a field goal. In the second quarter, Wes Hopkins recovered a fumble in Bear territory, leading to another field goal. Neal Anderson capped a Bear drive with a four-yard touchdown run. Meanwhile, the normally solid Keith Jackson, who would catch seven passes for 142 yards, dropped a touchdown pass in the end zone. With 1:58 in the half, Kevin Butler kicked a 46-yard field goal to put Chicago up 17-6 just as the fog began to roll in. Philadelphia would add another field goal set up by a 65-yard completion to Keith Jackson before the half ended.

In the second half, the field was completely shrouded by an eerie, dense fog, and the Eagles continued to self-destruct. Coaches could not see to the other sideline, officials could not see down the field, and quarterbacks had trouble making out receivers. The coaches in the booth upstairs came down to the field because they could not see anything, and TV camera crews shot the second half entirely from ground level. Ryan stopped sending out punt returners since it was too difficult to find the ball. For the game, Philadelphia was inside the Bears' 20 nine times, but never got into the end zone. They outgained the Bears 430 yards to 341, and Cunningham completed 27 of 55 passes for 407 of those yards with three interceptions. The Eagles added a third quarter field goal set up by Terry Hoage's interception at the Bears' 17, and the Bears countered with a fourth-quarter field goal to make the final score 20-12. Ditka pointed out that his team was clever enough to score while the sun was shining. Years later, Ryan still was haunted by his big tight end dropping a sure touchdown pass in the second quarter, convinced that it would have won the game.

Although Keith's catches declined in his second year, he demanded a contract renegotiation before his third season and held out for the first two games of the 1990 season. When the Eagles lost both those games, Jackson called off his holdout partly because he feared for his coach's job. Buddy sent a white stretch limo to the airport to pick up Keith and then the two of them held a very weird joint press conference. Jackson claimed that there was a front office conspiracy to let the team lose so it would be easier to fire Ryan. As Jackson spun out his theory with his arm around Ryan, Buddy just smiled. Owner Norman Braman was furious that once again his coach and players were upstaging him. He would not forget or forgive this episode.

Jackson's catches continued to slip in 1990 and in 1991 under new coach Rich Kotite. In 1992, Keith was a holdout again, but this time the timing was advantageous. During his holdout, an antitrust lawsuit by the Jets' Freeman McNeil was being heard and the jury struck down the NFL's existing Plan B free agency program. Jackson and three other NFL holdouts at the time (Webster Slaughter, D.J. Dozier and Garin Veris) were given a five-day window by the judge to sign as free agents with any team they chose.

Miami's Don Shula bested the Eagles' offer, and Jackson became a Dolphin. Jackson put up decent numbers for three years in Miami, but in 1995 was traded to the Packers. Keith refused to report; once again he was a holdout. He was reluctant to play in the cold Green Bay weather despite the fact that his old friend and teammate Reggie White was the leader of the Pack's defense. After two months, Jackson realized that Mike Holmgren and Ron Wolf were serious that they would play in Wisconsin or nowhere, and he reported for the second half of the season. As the second tight end behind Mark Chmura, Jackson did not do much in 1995, but he had a big playoff game against the 49ers and then followed that with a 10-touchdown season in 1996 when he and Reggie got to celebrate the Super Bowl victory Buddy's Boys were so convinced that Ryan could have brought to Philadelphia. It seems that all of Buddy's stars harbor the belief that they were just one good draft away from a run of two or three Super Bowls. They are deluding themselves; Ryan's Eagles had a lot of stars, but ultimately they weren't good enough.

The Return Game

Wally Henry
KR 1977-82

Originator: End Henry "Whitey" Piro showed promise as a rookie in 1941 before joining the Army. He went into college coaching after the war.

Longest Tenure: Eight years, Chad Lewis.

Number Changes: Fred Meyer wore 80 in 1943; Robert Krieger wore 82 in 1941; Mike Ditka wore 98 in 1967 when he couldn't pry 89 loose from the immortal Mike Morgan; Dialleo Burks also wore 42 and 86 in 1996.

Just Visiting: Ben Agajanian was still kicking in the league when he was 45; tight end Mike Ditka made the Hall of Fame as a Bear.

Highs: John Green was a fleet, lightweight pass rusher for Greasy Neale; Calvin Williams was a solid but unspectacular possession receiver for a few years.

Lows: Dialleo Burks went through three uniform numbers in 1996, but never actually got into a game.

Wally Henry

In Dick Vermeil's last game as a college coach, his 8-2-1 UCLA Bruins upset the unde-feated, number-one-ranked Ohio State Buckeyes 23-10 in the 1976 Rose Bowl. For the Bruins, quarterback John Sciarra threw second-half touchdown passes of 16 and 67 yards to wide receiver Wally Henry to spur the victory. The undersized Sciarra was drafted in the fourth round by the Bears, but did not make the team; the undersized Henry was not even drafted.

Hollywood Henry made Vermeil's Eagles as a free agent receiver in 1977, but his status with the team was always precarious — he would be waived five times by Philadelphia over the next six years. Although he was too small to be a receiver and only caught 15 passes as a Bird, he returned more punts than any other Eagle before or since. But even his hold on the punt returner position was tenuous. In 1978, Sciarra signed on with Philadelphia as a defensive back and punt returner, and he and his old teammate from UCLA tossed the job back and forth for the next few seasons. In that season, Henry scored on a 57-yard return in the opener against the Rams, but broke his leg in the third game of the year, so Sciarra took over. The following season, Sciarra returned 16 punts for a league-best 11.4 average, while Henry handled 35 punts for a 9.1 aver-age. Wally made the Pro Bowl that year and returned a punt 88 yards for a touchdown in the game. Against the Bears in 1980, Henry was tackled so hard that his spleen was ruptured. He was done for the season and could have died. Sciarra again took over punt return duties in that Super Bowl season.

Wally came back in 1981 and returned a team record 54 punts as well as 25 kick-offs, but fumbled four times in the regular season and twice in a devastating playoff loss to the Giants. Vermeil commented after the loss that, "Maybe some of our guys have been on special teams too long." He added specifically of Henry, "It's tough to be a real-ly good punt-returner two years in a row." Sciarra opened 1982 with the punt return job again, but broke a bone in his leg in the opener, so Henry was hired back by the Eagles for the fifth time. In that final, strike-shortened season, Henry would return 20 punts and 24 kickoffs, but would fumble four more times, including twice more against the Giants. The next season he would turn up on the Arizona Wranglers of the USFL on his way out of football.

From the time of his becoming a regular punt return man in 1978, Wally's statis-tics assumed a perfect downward slope. His return average declined every year from a high of 15.0 in 1978 to a low of 5.2 in 1982. His figures as a kickoff returner were more stable, but still his best return average was in his first season as a regular returner. In addition, his propensity to fumble increased as time went on. While he holds the team record with 148 punt returns, he is not among the leaders in total yardage because his average was only 8.3. In comparison, his friend Sciarra's was 7.8.

It is probably surprising that the best return man in Eagle history is Hall of Fame runner Steve Van Buren, but he holds the highest kickoff return average with 26.7 and the highest punt return average at 13.9. (Brian Westbrook pulled ahead of Steve's PR average in 2003, but his status is in flux.) Steve scored on three kickoffs and two punts as well. In this, he was bested by Timmy Brown, who scored on five kickoffs, one punt and one missed field goal that Brown brought back 105 yards. Two of those kickoff returns came in the same game against Dallas in 1966. The only other Eagle to score more than twice on returns has been Brian Mitchell, one of the greatest return men in league history, who returned two kicks and two punts for touchdowns in his three seasons in Philly.

The first Eagle to return a kick for a touchdown was Dave Smukler, who returned a Brooklyn Dodger kickoff 101 yards in 1938. Ernie Steele was the first Bird to score on a punt. In George Halas' last game before entering the military in 1942, the Bears walloped Philadelphia 45-14. The one Eagle highlight came when Tommy Thompson caught a Chicago punt at his 20 and handed the ball to Steele coming the other way, and Ernie raced 80 yards for the score. Bosh Pritchard, who scored on one punt and one kickoff during regular season action, is the only Eagle to score on a return in the postseason. In the 1947 Eastern Division playoff game against Pittsburgh, Bosh returned a punt 79 yards to help Philadelphia win 21-0. The top team-wide punt return performance came in 1942 when the Eagles averaged 14.2 yards per return, led by Ernie Steele's 26.4 average on 10 returns. The top team-wide kickoff return performance was an average return of 25.0, achieved in 1952 with Don Stevens and Al Pollard, and in 1963 with Timmy Brown and Ted Dean.

The most memorable game for the Eagle return teams was against the Cowboys in 1966 when Timmy Brown scored on 90- and 93-yard kickoff returns and Aaron Martin scored on a 67-yard punt return to slip past Dallas 24-23. The most memorable debut as a returner was by defensive back Bobby Shann, who returned his first punt 63 yards for a touchdown in the last game of the 1965 season. Shann was out for the 1966 season, and only returned three punts for 17 yards in 1967, dropping his career average to an even 20 yards per return. The most memorable return might be Vai Sikahema's 87-yard punt return for a touchdown in the Meadowlands against the Giants, which Vai punctuated by treating the goal post like a punching bag in a spontaneous end zone celebration.

There have been 22 kickoffs returned for touchdowns by the Eagles:

1938	Dave Smukler	1968	Alvin Haymond
1942	Bosh Pritchard	1977	Wilbert Montgomery
1944	Steve Van Buren	1979	Billy Campfield
1945	Steve Van Buren	1994	Herschel Walker
1947	Steve Van Buren	1995	Derrick Witherspoon
1950	Russ Craft	1996	Derrick Witherspoon
1955	Jerry Norton	1997	Willie Clark
1961	Timmy Brown	1999	Allen Rossum
1962	Timmy Brown	2000	Brian Mitchell
1963	Timmy Brown	2001	Brian Mitchell
1967	Timmy Brown (2)		

There have been 23 punts returned for touchdowns by the Eagles:

1942	Ernie Steele	1959	Tommy McDonald
1944	Steve Van Buren	1961	Timmy Brown
1946	Steve Van Buren	1965	Bobby Shann
1947	Pete Pihos	1966	Aaron Martin
1947	Pat McHugh	1968	Alvin Haymond
1948	Bosh Pritchard	1978	Wally Henry
1949	Clyde Scott	1986	Gregg Garrity
1949	Frank Reagan	1992	Vai Sikahema
1952	Don Stevens	2000	Brian Mitchell
1952	Bibbles Bawel	2002	Brian Mitchell
1959	Art Powell	2003	Brian Westbrook (2)

90

1990 Playoffs

Mike Golic
DT 1987-92

Mike Golic

Lewis Golic, who spent seven seasons in the Canadian Football League, sent three large sons to Notre Dame, where they all shone on the football field. Bob starred as a defensive tackle for the Browns and the Raiders, while offensive tackle Greg did not make the pros. The youngest son was Mike, who captained the Fighting Irish in his senior year before being drafted in the 10th round by the Oilers in 1985. After a season on injured reserve, Mike made the Oilers as a sometime starter in 1986. However, in the 1987 strike season, he fell out of favor with Houston coach Jerry Glanville and was waived. Buddy Ryan signed him two days later as a backup to the Eagles' fearsome foursome defensive line just taking wing at the time.

Golic fit into the Eagles' plans as a fifth lineman who regularly rotated onto the field to give Jerome Brown or Mike Pitts or Clyde Simmons or Reggie White a breather. Mike's primary skill was stopping the run; he only recorded 11.5 sacks in his eight years in the league. Mike had other skills as well. He was good at anticipating plays and was known to read the opposing quarterback's lips in the huddle on occasion. He was personable and popular with teammates, reporters and fans.

In 1990, Mike Pitts went down with an injury early in the year, and Golic got his chance to be a starter. The defense slipped a bit, going from eighth in points allowed to 11th, but was still tough and fierce — they also set a team record for penalties. In Buddy Ryan's last year of his contract, Philadelphia finished second in the East and was assigned to play the third-place Redskins at the Vet in the wild card game. There were two undertones to this game. First, the team knew that they would have to win at least one playoff game or Ryan would be fired by owner Norman Braman. Ryan had never curried favor with his boss who he referred to sneeringly as "that guy in France." Second, just eight weeks prior, the Redskins had been beaten up by the Eagles in what came to be known as the Body Bag Game because Ryan had exhorted his team to play so ferociously that they would have to carry the Skins out in body bags. Philadelphia knocked nearly a dozen Redskins out of the game that Monday night, and Washington had to finish the game with kick returner Brian Mitchell at quarterback.

Washington coach Joe Gibbs told his team simply to "win with class" before they took the field on January 6, 1991 for the wild card matchup, but the Eagles dominated the early going. Randall Cunningham completed a pass to tight end Keith Jackson with which he rumbled 66 yards to the Redskins' 11 and the Eagles kicked a field goal. Then early in the second quarter, Philadelphia recovered a fumble at the Redskins' 26, and this was converted into another three points. Washington answered with a drive that ended with a 16-yard touchdown pass to Art Monk to go up 7-6. After intercepting a Cunningham pass at midfield with two minutes remaining in the half, Washington moved the ball through the air again. Mark Rypien passed three times to runner Earnest Bynar, but on the third completion, Ben Smith tackled Bynar, who coughed up the ball. Smith scooped it up and raced 88 yards for an apparent touchdown. The play was reviewed by instant replay officials, however, and was overturned. It was ruled that the ground had caused the fumble so that Washington kept the ball and kicked a field goal to extend their lead to 10-6 at the half.

In the third quarter, Washington scored 10 points on a field goal and a touchdown pass to Gary Clark to go up by 14 points. In between those two scores, Ryan put the final nail in his own coffin by pulling Randall Cunningham for Jim McMahon to try to jump-start the stalled offense. Ryan put Randall back in after one three-and-out series, but the damage was done. The sensitive Randall was insulted, and Braman was furious. Randall did not play a very good game, but the real key was the line play. The Eagles' offensive line could not thwart a Washington pass rush that netted five sacks and frequent hurries, while the Eagles could not sack the immobile Rypien even once. In addition, Cunningham completed only one pass to a wide receiver and only two to his favorite target, Keith Byars. Two days later, Braman fired Ryan and hired offensive coordinator Rich Kotite as coach.

Under Kotite in 1991, Golic went back to assuming a reduced role in the defensive line rotation. His public exposure was not reduced, however. The popularity of his amusing "Golic Got It" spots on the local news led to increased speaking engagements, personal appearances and commercial endorsements for Mike. This caused resentment from some less recognized but more talented teammates who felt Golic's recognition was out of proportion to his status on the team. While that is understandable, it is also understandable why Mike was so much in demand — he was funny in a charming, goofy, self-deprecating way.

In the following year, Jerome Brown died. While Golic was a close friend and served as a pallbearer at the funeral, he was also put in the awkward position of trying to replace Brown on the field. Mike was a starter for most of the 1992 season until some lighthearted comments of his after a loss to the Vikings late in the year led to his being benched and to his refusing to talk to the media. The 1992 Eagles only gave up one more point than the 1991 team. At the end of the year he signed with the Dolphins, where he joined former teammates Keith Jackson, Ron Heller and Keith Byars. All returned to the Vet in November to help coach Don Shula set the record for most coaching wins by beating the Eagles. Golic only spent one year in Miami before moving on to ESPN as a ubiquitous broadcaster and analyst with a sunny personality and a sharp wit.

91
1990s Decade in Review

Andy Harmon
DT 1991-97

Originator: Linebacker Tim Golden played two games for the Eagles in 1985.

Longest Tenure: Seven years, Andy Harmon, from 1991 to 1997.

Number Changes: Reggie White more famously wore 92 from 1985 to 1992; Steve Martin wore 73 in 1998.

Just Visiting: George Cumby was an undersized linebacker for the Packers.

Highs: Future Hall of Famer Reggie White started out wearing 91 in deference to the immortal Smiley Creswell.

Lows: Cherry Hill's Greg Mark only lasted two games as an Eagle in a sterling six-game NFL career at defensive end.

Andy Harmon

In 1991, Andy Harmon was a long-shot, sixth-round pick out of Kent State, a school more known for its antiwar protests than its football prowess. Originally a defensive end backing up Reggie White, Harmon was moved into the starting lineup as a defensive tackle in 1992 by coordinator Bud Carson. Despite being somewhat undersized for the middle of the line, Harmon was quick and strong and blossomed in a hurry, providing a strong push up the middle for the Eagle defense. From 1992 through 1995, Harmon recorded 7.5, 11.5, nine and 11 sacks while also playing stoutly against the run. Carson said of him, "Without him, I see our defense falling apart. He may be the most important guy we have." TV analyst Matt Millen added, "What he does best is never stop. He just keeps going; he's got a great motor." Carson agreed: "That's why he gets more late sacks than anyone I've seen, because he's always working. He never, never thinks a play is over."

Despite this record and high praise, Harmon never was selected for a Pro Bowl, although he did make an All-Pro team in 1995. Another honor came in October 1995 when he was named NFC Defensive Player of the Week after getting three sacks in a 37-34 victory over the Redskins. The Eagles rewarded his work with a $7.5 million contract extension late in 1995. Unfortunately, Andy injured his knee in the 1996 preseason and underwent surgery that August. He would only appear in two more games in his NFL career as he struggled to rehab the knee for two years, but sadly could never get back to anything approaching normal and retired in 1997. Harmon was a quiet, modest and self-effacing hard worker who made those around him better. His quick exit was one reason for the team's steep decline in the late 1990s.

Decade Headline: Bird Brains.
Where They Played: Veterans Stadium, 1971-02.
How the Game Was Played: Endless variations of the West Coast (ball control short passing) Offense were countered by a plethora of complicated defensive schemes. In the 1990s, players were plugged into situations on each play by coaches attempting to script a game that is still ruled by the bounce of an oblong sphere.

Decade Won-Lost Record: 80-79-1, .503; 2-4 in the playoffs.
Record Against the Cowboys: 8-12; 0-2 in the playoffs.
Record Against the Giants: 9-11.
Record Against the Redskins: 13-7; 0-1 in the playoffs.
Record Against the Steelers: 2-1.

Playoff Appearances: 1990, 1992, 1995, 1996.
Championships: None.
Unsung Hero: Bud Carson took over Buddy Ryan's fiery and talented but undisciplined defense and made it even more dominant.

Head Coaches: Buddy Ryan 1986-90, 10-6 for the decade plus 0-1 in the playoffs; Rich Kotite 1991-94, 36-28 and 1-1 in the playoffs; Ray Rhodes 1995-98, 29-34-1 and 1-2 in the playoffs; Andy Reid 1999; 5-11 for the decade.

Best Player: Runner Ricky Waters.

Hall of Famers: None yet.

Eagle Honor Roll: Jerome Brown and Mike Quick.

League Leaders: Randall Cunningham — TD passes 1990, rushing average. 1990; Heath Sherman — rushing average 1992; Charley Garner — rushing average. 1995; Clyde Simmons — sacks 1992; Irving Fryar — TD catches 1996; Roger Ruzek — points after touchdown 1990.

Award Winners: Randall Cunningham, MVP 1990, Offensive MVP 1990; Comeback Player of the Year 1992; Reggie White Defensive MVP 1991; Eric Allen, NFC Defensive MVP; Jim McMahon, Comeback Player of the Year 1991; Ray Rhodes, Coach of the Year 1995.

All-Pros: Jerome Brown 1990-91; Randall Cunningham 1990, 1992; Byron Evans 1990, 1992; Keith Jackson 1990; Reggie White 1990-92; Eric Allen 1991, 1993; Seth Joyner 1991-93; Clyde Simmons 1991-92; Vai Sikahema 1992; William Fuller 1995; Andy Harmon 1995; William Thomas 1995.

Pro Bowl Selections: Jerome Brown 1990-91; Randall Cunningham 1990; Keith Jackson 1990; Reggie White 1990-92; Eric Allen 1991-94; Seth Joyner 1991, 1993; Clyde Simmons 1991-92; Fred Barnett 1992; William Fuller 1994-96; William Thomas 1995-96; Ricky Waters 1995-96; Irving Fryar 1996-97; Brian Dawkins 1999; Troy Vincent 1999.

Best Offensive Backfield: 1990, with quarterback Randall Cunningham, running back Heath Sherman, H-back Keith Byars and slot receiver Fred Barnett.

Best Draft Choice: Donovan McNabb 1999, first round. The best sleeper was William Thomas 1991, fourth round.

Best Overall Draft: 1999. In addition to McNabb, almost every other pick was useful to the Eagles before moving on to another team.

Worst Draft Choice: There were several first-round lineman flops in the 1990s, including Antone Davis in 1991, Bernard Williams in 1994 and Mike Mamula in 1995, but defensive end Jonathan Harris in 1997 was a ridiculous reach that no one expected to go anywhere near this high. He was later traded to Green Bay for fellow first-round flop John Michels so each team would not have to have the humiliation of cutting a former first-round pick.

Worst Overall Draft: 1994. First-rounder Bernard Williams had drug problems and Charlie Garner, Joe Panos and Mitch Berger all had greater success elsewhere.

Best Free Agent: Huge Hollis Thomas went undrafted in 1996 but has served as a decent run stuffer when he's been healthy.

Best Trade: Bill Parcells felt that Hugh Douglas would not fit into his Jet defense, so he traded him to Philadelphia for two draft picks. Douglas was not only an All-Pro for the Eagles, but a team leader as well.

Worst Trade: The Eagles had such a burning need for Antone Davis in 1991 that they gave up a second number one pick to move up in the draft and nab the overweight underachiever.

Biggest Off-Field Event: The inception of true free agency in the NFL hit the Eagles hard in 1993 when the biggest free agent, Reggie White, left Philadelphia for Green Bay. Several other stars from that great defense would leave via the same route in the next few years.

Biggest On-Field Development: Ray Rhodes brought the West Coast Offense to Philadelphia in 1995, and it's still here 10 years later.

Strangest On-Field Event: Philadelphia fans cheering when flamboyant Cowboy receiver Michael Irvin was laid out on the turf in 1997.

Worst Failure: After firing Buddy Ryan in 1990, Norman Braman picked offensive coordinator Rich Kotite over defensive coordinator Jeff Fisher as the new Eagles coach. Kotite would drive the team into the ground, while Fisher has had consistent success in Tennessee.

Home Attendance: 5,170,694 in 80 games for an average gate of 64,634.

Best Game: On November 22, 1992, the Eagles fell behind the Giants 20-6 in the second quarter before going on a 34-0 scoring spurt that put the game away, final score 47-34. For those who go in for heavy hitting, there was the "Body Bag" game on Monday night, November 12, 1990 when the Eagles knocked several Redskins out of the game including both the first and second string quarterbacks in a 28-14 win. Finally, there's the "fourth and one" game against Dallas on December 10, 1995, when the Cowboys decided to go for a fourth and one at their own 29 with 2:00 remaining and the score tied. They ran Emmitt Smith to the left and he was stuffed for no gain, but the officials ruled that the two minute warning had come before the ball was snapped. With the benefit of a do-over, Dallas ran the very same play again and were stuffed again. Eagles' ball. Eagles kick a field goal and win 20-17.

First Game: September 9, 1990. The Eagles were beaten 27-20 by the New York Giants in a game that was not as close as the score would indicate. The Eagles scored 10 points late in the fourth quarter.

Last Game: December 19, 1999. The Eagles beat the New England Patriots 24-9 behind third-string quarterback Koy Detmer's three TD passes, each followed by Detmer's strange whip-cracking gesture. Two weeks later, the Eagles finished the 1999 season on January 2, 2000 by beating the eventual Super Bowl champion Rams 38-31 behind Donovan McNabb's three TD passes without any whip-cracking.

Largest Margin of Victory: October 2, 1994. The Eagles demolished the 49ers 40-8 in San Francisco. The 49ers would lose only one more game the rest of the year on their way to winning the Super Bowl; the Eagles were en route to a 7-2 start before losing the last seven games of the season.

Largest Margin of Defeat: On opening day of the 1998 season, Ray Rhodes' Eagles were overwhelmed 38-0 by the Seahawks led by Warren Moon.

Best Offense: In 1990, the Eagles scored 396 points, third in the league and were also third in yards gained behind Randall Cunningham at his peak.

Best Defense: In 1991, the Eagles gave up only 244 points the fifth best figure in the league and finished first in yards allowed.

Most Games Played: 140, William Thomas.

Most Points: 344, Roger Ruzek.

Most Field Goals: 73, Roger Ruzek.

Most Touchdowns: 32, Ricky Waters.

Most Touchdown Passes: 73, Randall Cunningham.

Most Passing Yards: 10,944, Randall Cunningham.

Most Receiving Yards: 4,634, Fred Barnett.

Most Receptions: 308, Fred Barnett.

Most Rushing Yards: 3,794, Ricky Waters.

Most Interceptions: 21, Eric Allen.

Most Sacks: 40, Andy Harmon.

Most Kickoff Return Yards: 2,427, Allen Rossum.

Must Punt Return Yards: 778, Vai Sikahema.

Book Notes: Two Philadelphia Eagle beat writers wrote accounts of the failure of the Buddy Ryan-era team to reach their potential based on the 1992 season. Phil Anastasia of the *Courier-Post* wrote *Broken Wing, Broken Promise: A Season Inside the Philadelphia Eagles* in 1993, while Mark Bowden from the *Philadelphia Inquirer* published *Bringing the Heat* in 1994. Both books are very good reads, but Bowden's is more in-depth and lively.

Noted Sportswriter: Both Mark Bowden and Sal Paolantonio covered the team for the *Philadelphia Inquirer,* and both achieved greater fame beyond that — Bowden with his book on Somalia, *Black Hawk Down,* and Paolantonio by becoming an ESPN reporter.

Best Quotations: When the Eagles beat up Houston 13-6 on *Monday Night Football* in what the Oilers liked to call the House of Pain, the Astrodome, defensive tackle Jerome Brown remarked, "They brought the house; we brought the pain." After the team lost on opening day to the Buccaneers in 1995, new free agent running back Ricky Watters was asked by reporters why he didn't fully extend to try to catch a pass over the middle. His response did not endear him to Eagle fans, "For who? For what?"

Bubblegum Factoid: The 1999 Upper Deck card for Doug Pederson says of him that "Lambeau Field has also been the home of one of the NFL's premier backup signal callers as well in recent years..." 1993 Fleer card number 176 was more believable, "Reggie White is quite simply the most dominating defensive player in the game today."

Accidents of Birth: Gary Anderson was born in South Africa; Jay Fiedler is related to conductor Arthur Fiedler; Vai Sikahema is the second Eagle born in Tonga.

Famous Names: Jimmie Johnson, not the coach; Steve Martin, not the comedian.

Unusual Names: John Booty, Harry Boatswain, Bubby Brister, Dialleo Brooks, Smiley
  Creswell, Moe Elewanibi, DeShaun Fogle, Kurt Gouveia, Vaughn Hebron, Dietrich
  Jells, Izell Jenkins, Ndukwe Kalu, Harper LeBel, Sean Love, Jermayne Mayberry,
  Mike Quick, Heath Sherman, Vai Sikahema, Kaseem Sinceno, Morris Unutoa.

Nicknames: David "Green" Akers, David "Pillsbury Doughboy" Alexander, Eric "The
  Flea" Allen, Gary "Mr. Automatic" Anderson, "Arkansas" Fred Barnett, Jerome
  "Freight Train" Brown, Keith "Tank" Byars, Dick "Tank" Chapura, Richard "The
  Colonel" Dent, Byron "B&E" Evans, Eric "Pinky" or "Sleepy" Floyd, Irving "Rev"
  Fryar, Al "Cheesburger" Harris, Vaughn "Pretty Boy" Hebron, Keith "KJax"
  Jackson, Ed "Troup" Jasper, Izell "Toast" Jenkins, Vaughan "Meat" Johnson, Seth
  "Zeth" Joyner, Scott "Red" Kowalkowski, Kelvin "Kmart" Martin, Guy "Angus"
  McIntyre, Dennis "Conan" McKnight, Mark "Little Mac" McMillian, Keith
  "Moamar" Millard, Stephen "Bubba" Miller, Art "Money" Monk, Eddie "Money"
  Murray, William "Refrigerator" Perry, Mike "Silk" Quick, Heath "Wolfman"
  Sherman, Duce "Buddy Lee" Staley, William "Willie T" Thomas, William "Tra"
  Thomas, Andre "Muddy" or "Dirty" Waters, and Reggie "The Minister of Defense"
  or "Big Dog" White.

Fastest Player: Return man Allen Rossum was also a sprinter.

Heaviest Player: Antone Davis and William Perry were both officially 325 pounds, but
  Perry was certainly much more than that. Officially, Tra Thomas would be the
  heaviest player ever at 349 pounds.

Lightest Player: Receiver Kelvin Martin and defensive back Mark McMillian were both
  162 pounds, a few pounds lighter than return man Mel Gray at 166.

Toughest Injury: Randall Cunningham's season-ending knee injury in the first game of
  1991 and broken leg in the fourth game of 1993 essentially wiped out two Eagle
  seasons.

Local Boys: Burt Grossman hailed from Philadelphia. From the surrounding area came
  Matt Bahr, Irving Fryar, Tom Gerhart, Marvin Hargrove, George Hegamin, Reggie
  Lawrence, Greg Mark, Mickey Shuler, Ron Solt, Troy Vincent, and Ricky Watters.
  Among local colleges: Temple – Maurice Johnson; Villanova – Brian Finneran;
  Cheney – Andre Waters.

Firsts:

  New Uniforms and Logo – Eagles go to midnight green with a fiercer screaming
    Eagle head in 1996.

  NFL Stadium with a Courtroom and a Judge – After a Monday night game against
    the 49ers in which there were over 60 fights in the stands and one fan set off a
    flare gun in the Vet, the Eagles arranged with the city to have Judge Seamus P.
    McCaffrey in session during games to deal with rowdy drunks and miscreants.

  **NFL Player to Score on 90-yard Plays Rushing, Receiving and Returning in One
    Season** – Herschel Walker in 1994.

The Ministry of Defense

Reggie White
DE 1985-92

Originator: Defensive end Smiley Creswell in 1985.

Longest Tenure: Eight years, Reggie White.

Number Changes: Reggie White also wore 91 in 1985.

Just Visiting: None.

Highs: None.

Lows: Smiley Creswell blasted the Patriots when they cut him in training camp and blasted the Eagles when they cut him after three games, but was added to the Patriots' Super Bowl roster before fading from the league.

Reggie White

Reggie White was the "Big Dawg" in many ways for the Philadelphia Eagles. He was a leader on the field and one of the greatest defensive ends ever to play pro football. He was a labor leader who helped bring about player free agency in the NFL. Finally, he was a spiritual leader in the forefront of the muscular Christianity movement on display in football stadiums across the nation in the last 20 years.

Born and raised in Tennessee, Reggie attended the University of Tennessee where he set sack records as a defensive tackle and was named an All-American and the Southeastern Conference Player of the Year in his senior year. He signed a five-year contract with the Memphis Showboats of the rival USFL spring football league before the NFL draft in 1984 and spent two seasons in Memphis, recording 12 and 11.5 sacks as an interior lineman. White was named USFL Defensive Player of the Year in 1985 and was selected by the Eagles in the USFL supplemental draft held by the NFL in 1984, fourth overall after Steve Young, Mike Rozier, and Gary Zimmerman. Philadelphia bought out the remainder of his contract from Memphis and he played in 13 games for the Eagles that fall despite having played 18 USFL games the previous spring. That year he recorded his first 13 NFL sacks and was chosen NFL Rookie of the Year as a defensive end. The next season, on the strength of 18 sacks and 83 solo tackles, Reggie made the Pro Bowl for the first of 13 consecutive times from 1986 to 1998. From 1987 through 1992 as an Eagle, he achieved 21, 18, 11, 14, 15 and 14 sacks. Beyond the sacks, though, Reggie was a 290-pound lineman who could run the 40 in a 4.6 and who was equally adept in shutting down the run. He was a complete and dominating player.

In Buddy Ryan's ferocious pressure defense known as the 46, White moved around in the line so opposing offenses were never sure from which direction he would attack. Opposing coaches regularly devised schemes specifically to block Reggie, and he was consistently double- and even triple-teamed. This extra attention made it possible for a decent defensive end like Clyde Simmons to lead the NFL in sacks one year with 19. Reggie had a handful of moves to get to the passer. He could simply bullrush right through the lineman trying to block him, or use his forearm like a club to beat his way through the line, or swing his arm in a swimming motion to toss the opposing lineman aside like a toy. In eight years in Philadelphia, Reggie accumulated 124 sacks, but the team won only one playoff game in 1992 over the New Orleans Saints.

The team's lack of ultimate success was not the only source of disappointment for White. He was a prominent leader in the players' strike in 1987. In 1989, he was on the brink of suing the league over its restrictive free agency regulations when the Eagles met his demands with a four-year contract. Of greatest significance, White's was the lead name in a class action antitrust suit several players filed against the NFL in 1992. The suit led to a collective bargaining agreement in 1993 that instituted free agency in pro football, and Reggie was the first star to take advantage of it.

Eagles owner Norman Braman made it clear that he had not bought into football to pay large sums of money to free agents. In particular, he felt Reggie's best years were behind him, and he was not going to overpay to retain him. While sports talk radio station WIP attracted over 2,000 fans for a rally to re-sign White, Reggie went on a well-publicized, 37-day free agency tour and shocked the sports world by signing with Green Bay. Reggie said that God told him to go to Green Bay; cynics figured that money had more to do with the decision. In reality, the Packers made a very competitive offer and had an improving team with an impressive young quarterback in Brett Favre and a persuasive head coach in Mike Holmgren. On the surface, Braman was right; the older White was not as good a player in Green Bay as the younger White was in Philadelphia. However, he was still among the best linemen in the game, would still make clutch, game-turning plays that no one else could, and was a revered leader in the clubhouse and on the field. Braman saved some money, but his football team never went to the Super Bowl.

After Reggie signed with Green Bay, the Packer defense improved its rank in points allowed each year from 15th in 1992 to first in the Super Bowl season of 1996 when the victory culminated in the image of Reggie White circling the New Orleans Superdome after the game holding up the Vince Lombardi trophy, a champion at last. The following season the aging White suffered from back troubles all year and struggled throughout the season and a Super Bowl loss to the Broncos. He announced his retirement, but then rescinded it a week later after consultation with the Lord and came back fiercely with 16 sacks in 1998. However, most of the sacks were in the first half of the year. Reggie was clearly wearing down and left football for the second time in 1999. The Packers retired his jersey at halftime of a *Monday Night Football* game that year, but he returned again in 2000 to play one last, uneventful season with the dismal Carolina Panthers before retiring for the third and final time.

It was time to get on with his life's work. The "Minister of Defense" had been ordained as a man of God when he was just 17 and had done pavement preaching in some of the worst neighborhoods in Philadelphia when he was an Eagle. As a player, Reggie had never made any secret of his Christian beliefs, and he played a large role in the visible manifestation of religion in the NFL over the past two decades. White openly proselytized for his beliefs in the locker room and made so many references to God in interviews that CBS was reluctant to talk to him on the air after the 1997 Super Bowl victory. He would lead postgame prayer meetings at the 50-yard line for both teams, a practice that became common and was noted in the press when the Bills and Giants knelt together after the 1991 Super Bowl. Other players began to take this religious expression further, some by kneeling in the end zone after a touchdown, and many others by pointing to the sky after almost any successful play. What may have once seemed sincere has taken on a decidedly ostentatious appearance. Even the clearly appropriate practice of spontaneous prayers given on the field when a player is laid out with a serious injury was desecrated when the flashy shaman-showman Deion Sanders chose to make a spectacle of laying on healing hands for fallen comrades when he was with Dallas.

It's obvious that things are not always as they seem, both throughout the league and even with Reggie. White had a church in Tennessee that burned down in 1996 and

Packer fans raised a quarter of a million dollars to help Reggie rebuild it. However, the church was never rebuilt, and Reggie's partner in the institution went to prison on drug and weapons charges after all the money was spent. White was invited to address a session of the Wisconsin State Assembly in 1998 and made some very politically incorrect statements regarding the special talents of different ethnic groups. In a 2002 broadcast on Fox Sports, Reggie disavowed interest in the Christian church because it does not forcefully address sin. Instead, he claimed to strive to follow the Bible and to explore "what I need to do to be holy." He traveled to the Holy Lands and was studying Hebrew seven hours a day when he died from a heart attack at the age of 43 in 2004. In 2003, White published a book discussing the negative effects of integration on the black community. While his off-field activities often seemed curious, his football performances never were. The 11-time All-Pro will be elected to the Pro Football Hall of Fame in the coming years, and Eagle fans likely will remember Reggie White as the greatest defensive player the team has ever had.

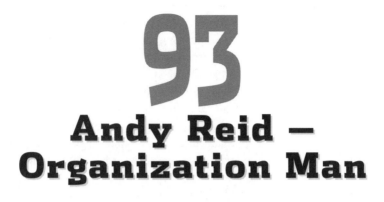

93

Andy Reid — Organization Man

Jevon Kearse
DE 2004

Originator: Defensive end Tom Strauthers in 1983. He would play four years in Philly and four more in Detroit and Minnesota, but would only start seven games total.

Longest Tenure: Four years, Tom Strauthers.

Number Changes: None.

Just Visiting: Levon Kirkland was a powerful middle linebacker for the Steelers.

Highs: Darion Connor was the team's special teams MVP in 1997, as if anyone deserved to be honored from those anything-but-special teams.

Lows: One high-mileage retread after another — Greg Townsend, Dan Stubbs, Darion Connor and Levon Kirkland.

Jevon Kearse

In college, Jevon Kearse's teammates labeled him "The Freak" for the speed, quickness, and power he generated from his odd-shaped physique. At 6 feet 4 inches and 260 pounds with a massive wingspan, Kearse was a terror as an outside linebacker for the Florida Gators. Some scouts were scared off by his lack of bulk, but the Titans picked him with the 15th selection in the first round of the 1999 draft. Jevon made an immediate impact, recording 14.5 sacks and being named Rookie of the Year in 1999. His intensity and pursuit were remarkable, and he had a nonstop motor. His sacks and tackles declined for the next two years and then he started to have serious injury problems — a broken foot in 2002 and a bad ankle sprain in 2003. The Titans were convinced that Kearse's best days were behind him because he couldn't push off his left foot very well any more. One of the reasons Jevon caused such havoc in his first couple of seasons was his ability to line up on either side of the line, distract the quarterback and disrupt the play. If he only could push off from his right foot, he could not slide along the line and line up on either side. The Eagles struck quickly when he became available as a free agent, signing him to an eight-year, $66 million contract with a $16 million signing bonus and two $4 million roster bonuses. Kearse turned in a big play performance in 2004 that justified Andy Reid's judgment.

Coupled with the fact that the Eagles were simultaneously negotiating with Terrell Owens, the signings were surprising to Philly fans. Andy Reid is seen as a cautious organization man, and the Eagles are a very frugal team. Almost every year, Andy would bring in a couple of free agents, but they were usually role players to fit into his system. For his first team, Reid brought in retread wide receivers Torrance Small and Charles Johnson along with veteran backup quarterback Doug Pedersen to throw to them. He added veteran punter Sean Landeta, veteran kicker Norm Johnson and unknown kicker David Akers to shore up special teams in 1999. The following season, Reid signed massive tackle Jon Runyan, a blue chipper, and little known veteran linebacker Carlos Emmons. 2001 saw a downgrade in free agency as James Thrash and N.D. Kalu were signed from Washington. Another former Redskin was signed in 2002, Sean Barber along with Levon Kirkland and Blaine Bishop. All three were gone after one season. Nate Wayne was brought in to replace Barber, and they signed fullback Jon Ritchie in 2003 as well. Clearly, Andy saw 2004 as the time to make the final leap to upgrade the team to championship caliber by picking up the best offensive and defensive players on the board — not to mention signing linebacker Dhani Jones and bringing back Jeremiah Trotter and Hugh Douglass as well as Jeff Blake as low-cost depth pickups later.

Sometimes Philadelphia fans forget what a lousy team Reid inherited in 1999. Ray Rhodes' undisciplined final squad in 1998 finished 3-13 and scored only 161 points while giving up 344. Starting quarterback choices were deer-in-the-headlights Bobby Hoying, weak-armed Koy Detmer or ancient Rodney Peete. In Andy's second season, the Eagles won a playoff game. How did Andy manage this transformation in just two years?

There are five tenets that Reid seems to abide by. First, coach up what you have on hand. Rhodes' offensive line was a sieve, but three of the linemen starting in the playoffs were from the Rhodes era. Nine of Rhodes' defensive players were part of the primary rotation for Reid's wild card team in 2000. Something must have happened to make these losing team players stalwarts on a winner. The answer would be coaching. Andy and his staff get the best out of their players and put them in situations in which they can excel. Second, add regularly through the draft. Reid's drafts aside from Donovan McNabb and Corey Simon are often downplayed, but he picks up a lot of players who fit into his system to some degree, and Reid makes use of his roster. Third, as noted above, judiciously use free agency to supplement your roster without breaking your budget. Fourth, the other side of free agency is holding on to the players you want to keep at a reasonable expenditure to avoid getting anywhere close to salary cap hell. Fifth, don't pay for past performance. Age is a reality that cannot be evaded.

By subscribing to these principles, Reid built a solid squad and has maintained it at a top level for several seasons. The final piece is the game coaching. Andy's teams are always prepared, and he is constantly designing imaginative new plays. While he is sometimes justly criticized for not making in-game adjustments — particularly in championship games, he has proven to be a very clever play caller, always willing to throw in change-ups and gadget plays to keep the offense from getting stale. Although Reid's devotion to the West Coast Offense and his clear propensity toward the forward pass may not be the first choice of smash-mouth Philadelphia fans, no one can argue with the results.

Redskins Rivalry

N.D. Kalu
DE 2001-03

WHO'S WORN THE NUMBER:

Byron Darby (DE/TE) 1983-86, Dan McMillen (DE) 1987r, Steve Kaufusi (DE) 1989-90, Leonard Renfro (DT) 1993-94, Kevin Johnson (DT) 1995-96, Bill Johnson (DT) 1998-99, Kelly Gregg (DT) 1999-00, N.D. Kalu (DE) 2001-03.

Originator: Defensive end and investment counselor Byron Darby from 1983 to 1986. Darby was sued by Howard Cross of the Giants for alleged bad investments.

Longest Tenure: Four years, Byron Darby.

Number Changes: N.D. Kalu wore 53 in 1997.

Just Visiting: Kelly Gregg has made a name for himself in the middle of the Ravens line.

Highs: None.

Lows: Leonard Renfro was a first-round flop of large proportions. Veteran starting defensive tackle Bill Johnson reportedly was abruptly cut after an altercation with special teams coach John Harbaugh.

N.D. Kalu

Nigerian Ndukwe Kalu is the first member of his family to be born in the U.S. His father and mother came to this country to pursue graduate studies at Johns Hopkins University in Baltimore where N.D. was born. N.D.'s father Dike obtained a faculty position at the University of Texas in San Antonio, and that is where N.D. grew up. He graduated from Rice University and was drafted in the fifth round of the 1997 draft by Philadelphia. He got into only three games that season and was cut in training camp the next year. The Redskins picked him up and used him as a pass rusher for three seasons. In 2001, he returned to Philadelphia as a free agent and was signed by Andy Reid.

While defensive coordinator Jim Johnson experimented with converting Kalu into a linebacker in the 2002 training camp, he was back at defensive end by the start of the season and registered a personal high with eight sacks. When Hugh Douglass left via free agency in 2003, Kalu stepped into the starting lineup but clearly wore down as the season wore on. In the off-season, Kalu traveled to his native Nigeria and ran a football camp for kids. He also bulked up to 275 pounds in an effort to build his stamina. Unfortunately, he tore his anterior cruciate ligament in training camp to end his season.

The biggest highlight of Kalu's career came in the Eagles' first victory at their new stadium in 2003. Against his former team, the Redskins, N.D. grabbed a Patrick Ramsey pass that was deflected by Darwin Walker and returned it 15 yards for a touchdown. The Eagles would hold on to win the game 27-25. Kalu came back from the Eagles the same year James Thrash did. A year after that, Shawn Barber would leave Washington for Philly, while Jeremiah Trotter went in the opposite direction. In 2004, Trotter was back in Philadelphia, and Thrash was back in DC. There has been a lot of scuttling between these two division rivals over the years. Most prominent of course, was the 1964 trade of starting quarterbacks — the Eagles getting the mediocre but younger Norm Snead and the Redskins getting Hall of Famer Sonny Jurgensen. Going back further, Washington drafted Texas Christian All-American tailback Sammy Baugh, who would last for 16 seasons, while Philadelphia drafted Baugh's successor at TCU, the 5-foot 7-inch Davey O'Brien, who lasted only two years.

Lud Wray was both the first coach of the Redskins, then called the Boston Braves, in 1932 and of the Eagles a year later. Wray did not achieve terrific success with either team, but he did ignite the rivalry by bringing former Braves George Kennealy, Joe Kresky, Jim MacMurdo and Swede Ellstrom to Philadelphia with him. The first game in the series did not take place until 1934, when the Redskins prevailed 6-0 on October 21st. The Eagles beat the Redskins for the first time the following November 3 with a score of 7-6. The Redskins moved to Washington in 1937, and the Eagles' first trip to DC was also their first encounter with rookie Sammy Baugh and resulted in a 14-0 loss. Davey O'Brien's first and last games as a pro came against the Redskins. He lost his opener 7-0 and lost his finale 13-7 despite completing 33 of 60 passes that December day in 1940. O'Brien's last game culminated the Lud Wray/Bert Bell era and the Eagles were 2-9 against the Redskins in those years. Ray Flaherty coached the Redskins for most of that time, and he would end up 13-1 against Philly and was wholly responsible for the longest Eagle losing streak in the series, 11 games from 1937 to 1942.

Greasy Neale took over the Eagles in 1941 and would compile a 12-6-2 record with an eight-game winning streak from 1947 to 1950 against Washington in the next decade; for the actual decade of the 1940s, the Eagles went 10-8-2. One of the most notable games under Neale was the greatest comeback in Eagle history on October 27, 1946. Trailing 24-0 in the third quarter, the Birds switched to a Single Wing, similar to the shotgun formation and scored four touchdowns in the second half, three on Tommy Thompson passes, to win 28-24. The biggest margin of victory was recorded in 1948 when the Eagles thrashed Washington 45-0, one week after doing the same to the Giants. The wildest game came on opening day 1947 when Philadelphia outlasted Washington 45-42, setting new NFL records for points scored, touchdowns and touchdown passes.

Neale was fired after the 1950 season, and both teams were mediocre and went through several coaches in the decade. The Eagles came out on top in those years 10-9-1. The most memorable game was Adrian Burk's seven-touchdown explosion in October 1954; a month later he threw five more against the Skins. That's 12 of his season total of 23 in those two games. Sammy Baugh's last game came against the Eagles on December 12, 1952. The Redskins won the game 27-21, but Baugh was no longer the starter and threw no passes that day. The Eagles' biggest loss in the entire series came in December 1957 when they lost 42-7 to Joe Kuharich's Redskins.

The 1960s started out well for the champion Eagles, but they managed to swiftly crash. The decade's even 9-9-2 record is a bit deceiving because there was a clear negative trend in place as soon as new Eagles coach Joe Kuharich traded Sonny Jurgensen in 1964. Jurgensen had led a memorable comeback for the Eagles on October 29, 1961 when he directed a three-pass, 80-yard drive in the last minute to beat Washington 27-24 on a 41-yard touchdown pass to Tommy McDonald. In his first game against the Eagles in 1964, Jurgy threw for five touchdowns in a 35-20 Redskin victory. For the rest of his career, Jurgensen would go 12-3-3 in games played against Philadelphia. The Eagles began a winless streak in 1967 that would stretch 15 games through 1974. Joe Kuharich's record against the Redskins was 3-6-1. If you combine that with his record in the series as Redskin coach, you find that the Eagles went 7-12-1 in games coached by Kuharich.

The 1970s were the most one-sided decade in the series. Philadelphia went 4-15-1 in that time. George Allen finished 11-2-1 against the Eagles. Jurgensen had one last hurrah in his final season by coming in relief against Philadelphia and leading a fourth-quarter comeback to beat the Eagles 27-20 on a 30-yard touchdown strike to Charley Taylor. The teams also went to overtime for the first time in 1976, and the Redskins prevailed 20-17. Dick Vermiel did not have great success against Washington, going 5-9 against them.

The 1980s brought Joe Gibbs to Washington and his Redskins beat up on Marion Campbell's and Buddy Ryan's teams to go 16-8 in his tenure. For the decade, the Eagles went 7-13. The two highlights for the Eagles were a couple of Randall Cunningham comebacks: 31-27 on November 8, 1987 and 42-37 on September 17, 1989. The latter was from 20 points behind, and the former concluded on a touchdown pass to Greg Garrity in the last minute.

In the 1990s, the Eagles went 13-7 against the Redskins and ran off an eight-game winning streak from 1992 to 1996. The most notable game of the decade was the "Body Bag Game" on Monday night, November 12, 1990, when the Eagles' defense enacted Buddy Ryan's pregame exhortation to hit the Redskins so hard that they'd need to be carted out in body bags. In all, 11 Redskins were knocked out of the game, and Washington had to finish the game with kick returner Brian Mitchell playing quarterback. The Eagle defense scored two times in the 28-14 win. Payback came two months later when the teams met in the running and the Redskins knocked the Eagles out of the playoffs and Buddy Ryan out of a job. The decade was filled with close games for the Eagles: a 24-22 comeback in 1991, a 34-31 comeback win in 1993, a 31-29 squeaker in 1994, a 37-34 overtime victory in 1995, a 20-17 overtime loss in 1999 and Donovan McNabb's first start later in 1999 — a 35-28 victory. The first decade of the new millennium has continued the trend as the Eagles have won eight of the first 10 games, and Andy Reid's record stands at 9-3 with a seven-game winning streak from 2001 to 2004. While the overall record for the series stands at 59-73-6, the arrow is pointing up for the McNabb era.

95
1979 Playoffs

John Bunting
LB 1972-82

WHO'S WORN THE NUMBER:

John Bunting (LB) 1972-82, Jody Schulz (LB) 1985-87, Doug Bartlett (DT) 1988, Al Harris (LB) 1989-90, Mike Flores (DT) 1991-93, *William Fuller* (DE) 1994-96, Richard Dent (DE) 1997, Henry Slay (DT) 1998, Tyrone Williams (DE) 1999-00, Justin Ena (LB) 2002, Jerome McDougle (DE) 2003-04.

Originator: Linebacker John Bunting in 1972.

Longest Tenure: 11 years, John Bunting.

Number Changes: Jody Schulz wore 53 in 1983 and 1984; Mike Flores wore 96 in 1994.

Just Visiting: Richard Dent was a world-class pass rusher with the Bears.

Highs: William Fuller was a punishing defensive end who went to three Pro Bowls in three Eagle seasons.

Lows: Henry Slay spent his entire three-game NFL career in Philadelphia in 1998 when the Eagles picked him up to replace the injured Hollis Thomas.

John Bunting

When John Bunting arrived at Eagle training camp as a 10th-round pick out of North Carolina in 1972, he was not expected to make the team. A good indication that he was seen as training camp fodder was the number he was assigned, 95. Up to that point, the only Eagles to have worn numbers in the nineties were Mike Ditka in 1967, who wore 98 when his familiar 89 was unavailable, and Mel Tom, who switched from 58 to 99 in 1971. Bunting was relatively small and slow and likely to be an early cut by coach Ed Khayat. However, John was also a smart, tough overachiever who would never quit.

Bunting made the team as a special teams player and backup weakside linebacker and got to start three games as a rookie before suffering a separated shoulder. Under new coach Mike McCormack, the blue-collar Bunting became the starting strongside linebacker, although he missed half of 1973 with a broken left forearm. McCormack called him the team's best linebacker in 1975 and claimed that John screwed up the team's passing game every day in practice with his alert and effective play. When Dick Vermeil became coach in 1976, he brought in Marion Campbell as his defensive coordinator, and Bunting would develop special relationships with both of these coaches. Campbell called him "A total student of the game…probably the smartest player I have coached."

Bunting was the signal caller for the Eagles' steadily improving defense and was seen as a coach on the field for his intelligent reads, play calling and audibles. Not only that, but he was a team leader both on the field and off. He was the team's player representative and an active member of the union. He was a dedicated hard worker who spent hours in film study to make himself the most knowledgeable player on the field. He also was active in the community with charity work and a willing source with the media. Above all, he was tough. In addition to the injuries noted above, Bunting played through broken ribs, a broken hand, concussions, groin injuries and hamstring pulls. In 1978, he had played in 62 straight games when he suffered a devastating knee injury in midseason and had to undergo surgery to remove cartilage and repair torn ligaments. The Eagles made the playoff that year for the first time since John had joined the team, and he missed it. In the off-season, Bunting worked strenuously to rehab the knee and return to the field for the next season. Not surprisingly, he was back in the starting lineup for the 1979 season.

By 1979, Vermeil's Eagles were beginning to get really good. They were not the most talented club, but were a team of smart, scrappy overachievers. Bunting, as the team's defensive MVP in his comeback year, was emblematic of the team. After a 6-1 start, the Eagles went into a three-game tailspin so that when they traveled to Dallas for a Monday night game on November 12th, their season was in danger of slipping away. For the first time in five years, though, Philadelphia beat Dallas 31-21 that night and finished the season winning five of their last six games. With an 11-5 record, they lost the Eastern Division crown to the Cowboys on a tiebreaker, but made the playoffs as a wild card.

Eagle linebackers John Bunting (95) and Reggie Wilkes (56) make a wish before dropping Lions runner Bo Robinson in 1979.

The Eagles began the playoffs at home with the wild card game against the Chicago Bears. After a rocky first half that left the Eagles trailing 17-10, Ron Jaworski threw an interception early in the third quarter that led to the fans booing and chanting "We Want Walton," the backup quarterback. From that point, the team got untracked and outscored the Bears 17-0 in the second half. The winning points came on a flare pass to running back Billy Campfield that he took 63 yards for a touchdown. The Eagles' dominating defense held Walter Payton to 67 yards rushing and QB Mike Phipps to 142 yards passing.

Philadelphia was favored again the following week when they traveled to Tampa to face the Central Division champion Bucs, who were experiencing their first winning season in their fourth year of existence. In the game, the Bucs' ball control offense would hold the ball for 36½ minutes while gaining 186 yards on the ground, 142 by runner Ricky Bell. The Bucs asserted themselves early, taking the opening kickoff and going 80 yards in an 18-play drive that consumed 9:34 of the clock. They added 10 more points in the second quarter to go up 17-0 before linebacker Jerry Robinson intercepted a Doug Williams pass with under two minutes to go and returned it 37 yards to the 11. Jaworski then hit wide out Charlie Smith for a touchdown to put the Eagles back in the game at the half. Philadelphia pulled within a touchdown with a Tony Franklin field goal in the third quarter, but a Doug Williams touchdown pass midway through the fourth quarter extended Tampa's lead to 24-10. The Eagles got one more score on a touchdown pass from Jaworski to Harold Carmichael with three minutes left, but for the game they were simply outplayed. Their normally sturdy defense was dominated.

Dick Vermeil's Eagles were noted for their togetherness and had their greatest season in 1980, going to the Super Bowl. In 1981, Bunting again missed almost half the year, and the Eagles slipped to a 10-6 record. The strike season of 1982 signaled the sad end of Vermeil's run. Bunting was a vocal leader of the players' union and held the veteran Eagles together throughout their eight-week strike. When they returned for a belated third game of the season, Philadelphia lost 18-14 at home to the Bengals and were booed lustily with much vituperation directed at players' rep Bunting. After the game, team owner Leonard Tose put a further chill on team chemistry by berating the team in the locker room and telling them that they should have stayed on strike. The multiple forces of injuries, aging players and a disgruntled team led to Vermeil stepping aside at the end of the season. Marion Campbell assumed the head coaching job, and Bunting looked forward to playing for his defensive mentor. However, John was released in February. The team said he was too old and banged up, and it was giving him a chance to catch on with another team. Bunting felt he was dropped as a recrimination for being the team's labor leader.

A month later, Bunting hooked up with the Philadelphia Stars of the USFL as a player/coach under Jim Mora. He would stick with the Stars for two seasons and played in the first two USFL championship games, finally winning a title in his final year. Bunting parlayed his coaching "internship" to an assistant coaching position with Glassboro State College in New Jersey. A year later, he was head coach and built a strong, winning program in five years. This success led him back to the pros as an assistant, ultimately under Vermeil again with the Rams before he achieved his dream job as head coach at his alma mater, the University of North Carolina. While Bunting has had a bit of a rocky road in Chapel Hill, it's not for lack of effort. If success is possible, John Bunting will find a way to achieve it.

96

1989 Playoffs

Clyde Simmons
DE 1986-93

WHO'S WORN THE NUMBER:

John Sodaski (LB) 1972-73, Harvey Armstrong (DT) 1982-84, *Clyde Simmons* (DE) 1986-93, Marvin Ayers (DE) 1987r, Mike Flores (DT) 1994, Mark Gunn (DL) 1995-96, Keith Rucker (DT) 1996, Al Wallace (DE/LB) 1997-99, Paul Grasmanis (DT) 2000-04.

Originator: Linebacker John Sodaski in 1972. Sodaski played linebacker and quarterback at Villanova, safety with the Steelers, linebacker again with the Eagles and then with the Philadelphia Bell in the WFL.

Longest Tenure: Eight years, Clyde Simmons.

Number Changes: Mike Flores wore 95 from 1991 to 1993.

Just Visiting: None.

Highs: None.

Lows: Nose tackle Harvey Armstrong spent three nondescript seasons in Philadelphia and then five with the Colts. He had problems with the bottle and was charged more than once with alcohol-related incidents involving ill treatment of his girlfriend. He later surfaced as an assistant coach in the XFL.

Clyde Simmons

Clyde Simmons played in the shadow of fellow defensive end Reggie White on the line in Philadelphia. This was not new to Clyde. As a schoolboy on his Babe Ruth League baseball team, he was overshadowed by teammate Michael Jordan. While Jordan went to the University of North Carolina to create a legend, Simmons enrolled at Western Carolina as a 235-pound defensive end.

Simmons, an undersized Division 1A All-American, was selected in the ninth round by Buddy Ryan in his first draft as Eagle coach in 1986. The combination of Simmons with the 234th pick overall and linebacker Seth Joyner from the University of Texas-El Paso in the eighth round established his reputation as someone who knew talent. Although having vastly different personalities, the two future Eagles stars bonded immediately as long shots who worked hard and became stars. Defensive line coach Dale Haupt, who had worked out Clyde at Western Carolina, took a special interest in Simmons and helped him develop his talent. As an Eagle rookie, he appeared primarily on special teams and as a pass rush specialist in Philadelphia's nickel defense.

Simmons showed enough burst and power in his first year that he won the starting right defensive end in training camp the next year. The player he replaced, 30-year-old Greg Brown, was swapped to Atlanta for 27-year-old Mike Pitts in September. Pitts was first seen as a competitor to Simmons at end, but was soon shifted inside where he paired with number one draft pick Jerome Brown at defensive tackle. Along with the aforementioned Reggie White, the greatest defensive line in Eagle history was now assembled. They would wreak havoc with opposing offensive lines over the next half decade in Philly. Simmons went from two sacks as a rookie to six in 12 games in 1987, eight in 16 games in 1988, to 15.5 in 1989 (including 3.5 against John Elway in a victory over Denver in October). He was always around the ball and a master of the big play. In 1988, he blocked a game-winning field goal attempt by Pittsburgh and the next week returned a blocked field goal for the winning touchdown in overtime against the Giants. In a game against the Giants the following year, Clyde intercepted a pass and showed his speed by racing 60 yards for the score.

As Simmons improved under Buddy Ryan, so did the team. They made the playoffs in 1988, but lost to Chicago in the Fog Bowl. In 1989, the Eagles closed fast, winning five of their last six games, to finish 11-5 and enter the playoffs as a wild card. The Eagle defense was second in the league in sacks and in fewest passing yards allowed. They topped the league in takeaways, interceptions, fumble recoveries and turnover ratio. Led by their front four, Philadelphia was a rampaging opportunistic bunch. The other NFC wild card team was the Los Angeles Rams, known mostly for their passing attack with 4,000-yard quarterback Jim Everett. Playing at home against a team with several injuries to its starting defenders, the Eagles were a three-point favorite. Before the game, Ryan remarked, "It will be up to our defensive line to decide how far we go in the playoffs. If they play like they should, they'll take us to the Super Bowl." Reggie White added that "If the Rams' offensive line plays better than we do, they'll win the game." With NFL interception leader Eric Allen bothered by an ankle injury and unable to start, the play of the defensive line was even more critical.

On a cold and drizzly day, the game quickly turned disastrous for Philadelphia. Three minutes into the game, Rams receiver Henry Ellard beat cornerback Izell "Toast" Jenkins on a 39-yard touchdown reception when Jenkins gambled on an interception at the 30. On the next series, Ellard beat Allen's replacement Eric Everett for a 30-yard reception to the Eagles' 16. Jim Everett hit tight end Damone Johnson for a four-yard touchdown four plays later to put LA up 14-0. Still in the first quarter, Rams receiver Flipper Anderson blew past Everett for a 55-yard reception to the Eagles' 5. The Eagles avoided any further score by recovering a fumble to stay in the game. Eric Allen was inserted into the game at that point, and the defense tightened up. On the other side of the ball, Eagle quarterback Randall Cunningham was completely flummoxed by the special defense that clever coordinator Fritz Shurmer had devised for the banged-up Rams. On passing downs, the Rams lined up in a zone defense with five linebackers and six defensive backs, and the Eagles could make no progress against it. Finally, in the fourth quarter Cunningham managed to string together an 11-play, 80-yard drive in which Randall ran for 15 yards and passed for 41 and they scored on a one-yard run by Anthony Toney. The Rams answered that score with one of their own in the final period when Greg Bell put together runs of 54, three and seven yards to put LA up 21-7. That would be the final score in a disappointing Eagle loss in which the celebrated Eagle front four came up small.

Over the next two seasons, Simmons racked up 7.5 and 13 sacks as part of that dominant front four. In 1992, Jerome Brown was killed in an automobile accident, and the Eagles dedicated their season to his memory. The quiet and unassuming Simmons was especially fierce in honoring his fallen friend, recording a personal best 19 sacks that included a team record 4.5 in one game against the Dallas Cowboys. The big plays continued with a fumble recovery for a touchdown in the 1990 "Body Bag" game against the Redskins and another touchdown on a fumble recovery against the Cardinals in 1991. The 1992 season ended in another playoff defeat, however, and Reggie White left the next year in free agency. Without the All-Pro White drawing attention to the other side, Simmons' sacks dropped from 19 to five in 1993. Disappointed in the Eagles management and coaching staff, Simmons and his partner Seth Joyner left together as free agents and signed with Buddy Ryan again in Arizona. Both were two-time Eagle defensive MVPs. The bloom was off the desert rose for all three of them, however, and the Cardinals did not achieve success. Simmons continued on a nomadic experience in the following years with two seasons in Jacksonville, one in Cincinnati, and finally two in Chicago. In his post-Eagle career, he never had more than 11 sacks and generally recorded from five to 8.5 per year. In his 15-season career, Clyde never missed a game, playing in 236 of them and recording 121.5 sacks — 76.5 as an Eagle — and over 1,000 tackles.

Four years later in 2004, Clyde retired officially as an Eagle in a June ceremony in Philadelphia, saying, "This is where I started. It's like a homecoming for me...The majority of guys I played with here, I'm still friends with and still know how to get in touch with...It's time to be here."

2000s Decade in Review

Darwin Walker
DT 2000-04

WHO'S WORN THE NUMBER:

Thomas Brown (DE) 1980, Reggie Singletary (DT/G) 1986, John Klingel (DE) 1987-88, Jim Auer (DE) 1987r, Dick Chapura (DT) 1990, Leon Seals (DT) 1992, Tim Harris (DE) 1993, Rhett Hall (DT) 1995-98, Mark Wheeler (DT) 1999, Darwin Walker (DT) 2000-04.

Originator: Defensive end Thomas Brown in 1980.

Longest Tenure: Five years, Darwin Walker from 2000 to 2004.

Number Changes: Reggie Singletary wore 68 as a guard from 1987 to 1990.

Just Visiting: Tim Harris, see below.

Highs: None.

Lows: Former All-Pro pass rusher Tim Harris was a big bust trying to replace Reggie White in 1993 and only appeared in four games as an Eagle.

Darwin Walker

Drafted in the third round by the lowly Arizona Cardinals in 2000, the strong and sturdy Darwin Walker made the club, but was surprisingly waived in September after appearing in only one game for Arizona. Philadelphia picked him up and started coaching him up. He appeared in no games in 2000, 10 in 2001, and became a starter in 2002. As a starter, he has shown the ability to be a playmaker, recording 7.5 sacks in 2002 and another six in 2003, and that earned him a seven-year contract extension in 2002. He provides a good push up the middle in the pass rush. However, he is not a run stuffer and that has been a problem for the Eagle defense at times.

Walker is an intelligent player who earned a civil engineering degree from the University of Tennessee and is involved in a host of business opportunities. He is very representative of the Andy Reid era in many ways. He's smart, unassuming and dedicated to the community. He's also proven to be coachable and willing to be used to play a role that best fits his skills in coordinator Jim Johnson's defense. At the same time, Walker and the Eagles have a weakness against the run that some teams have been successful in exploiting. Will superior coaching schemes bring Philadelphia a championship?

Decade Headline: Phat City.

Where They Played: Veterans Stadium, 1971-02; Lincoln Financial Field, 2002-04.
How the Game Is Played: Fast and furious. Players grow ever faster and bigger, making for more dangerous and damaging collisions. The NFL continues to tinker with the rules so that scoring is emphasized and quarterbacks are protected.

Decade Won-Lost Record: 59-21, .738; 7-5 in the playoffs.
Record Against the Cowboys: 9-1.
Record Against the Giants: 7-3; 0-1 in the playoffs.
Record Against the Redskins: 8-2.
Record Against the Steelers: 2-0.

Playoff Appearances: 2000, 2001, 2002, 2003, 2004.
Championships: None.
Unsung Hero: Capologist Joe Banner may not receive the affection of the fans, but his astute working of player contracts has kept the most important players in Eagle uniforms without overspending.
Head Coaches: Andy Reid 1999-04, 59-21 for the decade, plus 7-5 in the playoffs.
Best Player: Donovan McNabb.
Hall of Famers: None.
Eagle Honor Roll: None yet.
League Leaders: Donovan McNabb — rush avg. 2000.

Award Winners: Donovan McNabb, NFC MVP 2000; Andy Reid, NFL Coach of the Year 2000, 2002.

All-Pros: Hugh Douglas 2000, 2002; Jeremiah Trotter 2000; David Akers 2001-02; Brian Dawkins 2001-03; Corey Simon 2001; Jermane Mayberry 2002; Bobby Taylor 2002; Tra Thomas 2002; Troy Vincent 2002-03.

Pro Bowl Selections: Hugh Douglas 2000-02; Chad Lewis 2000-02; Donovan McNabb 2000-04; Jeremiah Trotter 2000-01, 2004; Troy Vincent 2000-03; David Akers 2001-02, 2004; Brian Dawkins 2001-02, 2004; Tra Thomas 2001-02, 2004; Jermane Mayberry 2002; Jon Runyan 2002; Bobby Taylor 2002; Corey Simon 2003; Terrell Owens 2004; Ike Reese 2004; Lito Shepard 2004; Michael Lewis 2004; Brian Westbrook 2004.

Best Offensive Backfield: 2004, with quarterback Donovan McNabb, running back Brian Westbrook, fullback Jon Ritchie, and slot receiver Terrell Owens.

Best Draft Choice: Corey Simon 2000, first round, lived up to his billing. The best sleeper has been Brian Westbrook, 2002, third round.

Best Overall Draft: 2002. Three starters for the defensive backfield — Lito Shepard, Michael Lewis and Sheldon Brown — plus Westbrook.

Worst Draft Choice: Freddie Mitchell, 2001, first round. He has very slowly developed into a barely competent third receiver.

Worst Overall Draft: 2001. Besides Mitchell, Derrick Burgess and Correll Buckhalter have had injury problems, and Quinton Caver washed out.

Best Free Agent: Greg Lewis is a speedy receiver who went undrafted in 2003. Clinton Hart was a real long shot. He did not play football in college, but passed an Arena Football League tryout, excelled in that league and made the Eagles as a free agent in 2002.

Best Trade: Getting Terrell Owens for Brandon Whiting and a fifth-round pick in 2004.

Worst Trade: Allen Rossum had his faults, but was a good return man who only netted the Eagles a fifth-round pick in 2000.

Biggest Off-Field Event: The Vet, often considered the worst field in the NFL during its 32-year run as the home of the Eagles, was imploded and turned into a parking lot in 2003.

Biggest On-Field Development: The Eagles as one of the most imaginative teams on both sides of the ball. Jimmy Johnson's ever-changing blitz schemes and Andy Reid's gadget plays and pass-happy play-calling make Philadelphia a fun team to watch.

Strangest On-Field Event: The cancellation of the Eagles-Ravens preseason game in 2002 due to the unplayable condition of the turf.

Worst Failure: Three straight failures in the NFC Championship game, two at home.

Home Attendance: 2,659,378 in 40 games for an average gate of 66,484.

Best Game: December 30, 2001. The Eagles beat the Giants 24-21 in a close contest that was a defensive struggle for three quarters with New York leading 10-7 before a 28-point explosion in the last quarter. Philadelphia began the fourth quarter with a

57-yard TD bomb from McNabb to James Thrash. The Giants answered with a field goal, a touchdown and a two-point conversion to lead 24-14. McNabb tied the game with another TD pass at the two-minute mark. After the Giants were forced to punt, McNabb led another drive that culminated in a 35-yard David Akers field goal with seven seconds left. After the kickoff, the Giants executed a nearly flawless hook and lateral that ended the game when safety Damon Moore shoved Ron Dixon out of bounds on the Eagles' 6 yard line with no time remaining.

First Game: September 3, 2000. Andy Reid signaled a new era in Eagle football by beginning a 41-14 thrashing of the hated Cowboys in Dallas with a successful onside kick. Duce Staley ran for 201 yards in a game also remembered for the pickle juice downed by the Eagles to prevent cramping in the Texas heat.

Last Game: December 2009. To be determined.

Largest Margin of Victory: November 18, 2001. The Eagles slammed the Cowboys 36-3 after having whipped them 40-18 two months before. The two games marked the most lopsided sweep of Dallas by Philadelphia since 1961.

Largest Margin of Defeat: On November 10, 2002, the Indianapolis Colts blew out the Eagles 35-13 behind the running of third-string runner James Mungro and the passing of Peyton Manning to Marvin Harrison.

Best Offense: In 2004, the Eagles scored 386 points, eighth in the league, en route to the Super Bowl.

Best Defense: In 2001, the Eagles gave up only 208 points, the second best figure in the league, and finished seventh in yards allowed.

Most Games Played: 80, Jon Runyan, David Akers and Ike Reese.

Most Points: 605, David Akers.

Most Field Goals: 136, David Akers.

Most Touchdowns: 22, Brian Westbrook.

Most Touchdown Passes: 110, Donovan McNabb.

Most Passing Yards: 15,978, Donovan McNabb.

Most Receiving Yards: 2,816, Todd Pinkston.

Most Receptions: 204, Chad Lewis.

Most Rushing Yards: 2,440, Duce Staley.

Most Interceptions: 13, Troy Vincent and Brian Dawkins.

Most Sacks: 40, Hugh Douglas.

Most Kickoff Return Yards: 3,311, Brian Mitchell.

Most Punt Return Yards: 1,369, Brian Mitchell.

Book Notes: Former sportswriters and current talk radio hosts Glen Macnow and Anthony Gargano co-wrote *The Great Philadelphia Fan Book*, which is very fun to read, although it deals with all Philadelphia sports over the last quarter century and not just the Eagles. Macnow and Angelo Cataldi followed this with *The Great Philadelphia Sports Debate* in 2004.

Noted Sportswriter: Les Bowen covers the team smartly for the *Philadelphia Daily News*.

Best Quotation: Before having won any of the multiple Super Bowls that Jeffrey Lurie once promised the city was his goal, he was quoted as referring to his team as "the Gold Standard" in the league. Lurie's reign has been a positive one, but comments like this emphasize the elitism that often separates him from the fans.

Bubblegum Factoid: The 2001 Topps XFL card for former Eagle James Willis noted, "'Bring it.' " J-Dubb likes to say... 'I know what you are going to do,' he says, 'before the ball is snapped."

Accidents of Birth: Mike Labinjo was born in Canada; Thomas Tapeh was born in Liberia.

Famous Names: Sam Rayburn, not the politician; J.R. Reed, not the basketball player.

Unusual Names: Correll Buckhalter, Justin Ena, Uhuru Hamiter, Tyreo Harrison, Dorsey Levens, Jermane Mayberry, Quintin Mikell, Lito Shepard, Darwin Walker.

Nicknames: David "Green" Akers, Hank "Honey Buns" Fraley, Jevon "The Freak" Kearse, Levon "Captain Kirk" Kirkland, Anthonia "Amp" Lee, Dorsey "Horse" Levens, Stephen "Bubba" Miller, Terrell "T.O." Owens, Rod "He Hate Me" Smart, Duce "Buddy Lee" Staley, William "Tra" Thomas.

Fastest Player: A race between James Thrash and Greg Lewis would be close.

Heaviest Player: Tackle Tra Thomas at 349 pounds is officially the heaviest Eagle in history.

Lightest Player: Todd Pinkston supports 174 pounds on his pipe-cleaner legs.

Toughest Injury: Correll Buckhalter, Hollis Thomas and Derrick Burgess each lost two seasons to knee or foot injuries.

Local Boys: Uhuru Hamiter hailed from Philadelphia. From the surrounding area came Jon Ritchie and Troy Vincent. Among local colleges: Villanova – Brian Finneran and Brian Westbrook.

Firsts:

Game at Lincoln Financial Field — September 8, 2003. The Eagles were shut out 17-0 by the defending champs, Tampa.

Win at the Linc — October 5, 2002. A 27-25 win over the Washington Redskins.

Playoff Game at the Linc — January 11, 2004. The Eagles beat the Green Bay Packers 20-17 in overtime in the "Fourth and 26" game.

Game Cancelled Due to the Condition of the Field — Scheduled for August 13, 2001 against the Baltimore Ravens.

NFL Player to Intercept a Pass, Recover a Fumble, Sack the Quarterback and Catch a TD Pass in One Game — Brain Dawkins, September 29, 2002, against the Houston Texans.

98

Owners – The Good, the Bad and the Ugly

Greg Brown
DE 1981-86

Greg Brown

Greg Brown's path to the NFL was the type of story that chatty play-by-play broadcasters love to tell and retell ad nauseum while they cover a game. Brown dropped out of college in Illinois to support his family. He was working construction for $10.50 an hour in DC when he happened to run into his former defensive line coach at Eastern Illinois, John Teerlink, who promised to get Greg a pro tryout. Teerlink called Eagles defensive line coach Chuck Clausen, who agreed to bring Brown in. Greg came in weighing 220 pounds, 15 under his college weight, but worked hard and ate heartily. He gained 25 pounds by the end of training camp and made the team.

In 1981 and 1982, Brown primarily was a special teams player, but he did manage to score two touchdowns on fumble recoveries. During the 1983 season, he became a starter under new head coach Marion Campbell and recorded 8.5 sacks. He followed that up with 16 sacks in 1984 and parlayed that season into a new three-year, $1.5 million contract. It seems that there were rumors that Brown and safety Ray Ellis were being courted by the USFL's Donald Trump. So in the final days of Leonard Tose's ownership, both players received generous contracts well beyond the going rate for players of their good-but-not-great caliber. When other Eagle veterans read about these deals, they wanted to be rewarded in the same manner. The trouble was that the new owner, Norman Braman, was as stingy with money as Tose was profligate. He made it understood that draft choices would no longer be given large bonuses, requests for contract renegotiation would be summarily refused, and any unwritten promises made by the former regime to current players would not be honored. Consequently 11 veteran starters, including Mike Quick, Wes Hopkins, Jerry Robinson, Wilbert Montgomery and Dennis Harrison, held out of training camp in 1985. All but Quick and Hopkins were released or traded in relatively short order.

As for Greg Brown, he managed 13 sacks in 1985, but with new coach Buddy Ryan in 1986, Greg's playing time was reduced. He was relegated to second string before being traded to the Falcons for Mike Pitts in 1987. In Atlanta he was reunited with former coach Marion Campbell and several former Eagles, but failed to produce in his final two seasons in the league. Still, one can't deny his million-to-one-shot success.

The most relevant part of Greg Brown's story is his interaction with ownership. The Eagles have had seven ownership groups over their more than 70-year history, and these owners have differed greatly in personality, finances and success. Philadelphian Bert Bell purchased the original franchise along with partner Lud Wray for a $2,500 franchise fee and the assumption of $11,000 in debts incurred by the defunct Frankford Yellow Jackets. Bell was a "blue blood" by birth, but a man of the people by choice. He served as owner, general manager, ticket seller, publicity agent and more in trying to keep the struggling Eagles aloft in the early days. In 1936 he bought out Wray for $4,000 and replaced him as coach of the team as well. Bell was a persuasive raconteur whose main success was keeping the team from folding in perilous times. His pluck and opti-

At the 1941 Maxwell Club dinner, 26-year-old new Eagles owner Alexis Thompson is sandwiched by Villanova coach Clipper Smith on the left and Eagles founder Bert Bell on the right. Thompson lived fast and died young of a heart attack at 39; his father also died early of pneumonia at age 49.

mism would serve him well when he became NFL Commissioner in 1946. The team's record under Bell's ownership, though, was a dismal 19-65-3.

In 1940, Art Rooney sold his Steelers to steel magnate Alexis Thompson for $165,000 and bought half the Eagles from his friend Bell. A few months later, the two groups swapped teams and Lex Thompson came to town. Thompson was a fascinating, larger-than-life figure. His father died when Lex was 16 and left his son his entire multimillion-dollar estate. Lex graduated from Yale in 1936, the same year he went to the Olympics as part of the U.S. field hockey team. Three years later, he competed in the world bobsled championships in Italy. When he purchased what would become the Eagles in 1941, he was only 26 years old, but was a man of the world. Thompson hired the backfield coach from Yale, Greasy Neale, to coach and run the team while Lex poured money into it. As the team rose in the standings, their payroll rose much faster than Thompson had planned due to the bidding war with the rival All-America Conference. Thompson was a constant voice for a negotiated settlement with the other league because he was losing money with a championship club. Shortly after that first title, Lex threw in the towel and sold the team to a Philadelphia group of 100 "brothers" in 1949 for $250,000. He had received several bids for the team including one from a group led by singer Frankie Laine, who wanted to move the Eagles to San Francisco. Thompson served in the Army during World War II and was married three times. In 1954, he had to interrupt his honeymoon with his third wife to testify in a paternity suit brought against him. Sadly, he would die a few months later at the young age of 39. In his eight years as owner, the Eagles went 46-36-5 and won their first championship.

The "brothers" were a group of 100 prominent Philadelphians, led by Democratic City Chairman James Clark who each chipped in $3,000 to buy the champion Eagles. When the team repeated its NFL title that year, all looked rosy. However, the team was aging and coach Neale and chairman Clark fought unceasingly. After a so-so 6-6 record in 1950, Clark fired Neale. The team on the field was run by general manager Vince McNally, while Joe Donoghue ran the financial side. The 1950s were mediocre at best and in 1956, a bid from a Louisville group to move the team to Kentucky was entertained. In 1958, McNally offered the coaching position to Giants assistant Vince Lombardi, who was dying for such an opportunity. Lombardi turned down the offer, though, because he had doubts about the stability of the ownership group. McNally then turned to Buck Shaw who produced a title in three years and then retired. By 1963, the "brothers" were interested in selling the team. One prospective group of promise was headed by former Cleveland coach Paul Brown. Instead, the Eagles were sold for $5.05 million to construction millionaire Jerry Wolman in 1964. Each of the remaining "brothers" saw a $60,000 return on their initial investment. The record on the field for the brothers' 15-year reign was 87-91-8 with two championships.

Jerry Wolman was a high school dropout from Shenandoah, Pennsylvania, who after serving in the Navy, moved to Washington DC and made a fortune constructing apartment buildings. As an Eagles fan from childhood, Wolman fulfilled a dream by buying the team. Jerry went looking for a coach who would be his friend, and found two-time NFL failure Joe Kuharich. Wolman rewarded his friend with a 15-year contract and the disaster had begun. Kuharich made lots of trades, but they did not transform the team into a winner. In the meantime, Wolman continued his buying spree by purchasing decrepit Connie Mack Stadium and the Yellow Cab Company while problems arose in his construction business. He was overextended to the max and unable to borrow more money to pay off his debts. Over the course of the next couple of years, Wolman's financial problems dragged out until at last he had to sell his beloved Eagles. In 1969, he found local trucking executive Leonard Tose, who was willing not only to buy the club for $16 million dollars, but also to include a proviso saying that Wolman could buy the club back if he could pay off his debts in the next few months. Wolman later claimed that he had fulfilled the proviso. Tose disagreed and the matter snaked on through the courts for six more seasons before Wolman ultimately was defeated in his bid to regain the team. In five years as owner, Wolman's Eagles went 28-41-1.

Leonard Tose was like a character from Damon Runyon — crude and unrefined in many ways, but with a very big heart. He spent money freely, whether he had it or not, feeling that the aim in life was for your money and your breath to run out at the same time. Tose went through several coaches before finding Dick Vermeil, who would at last rebuild the Eagles into a winning team. Leonard's main problem was gambling, which he made worse by combining it with drinking. With Atlantic City just 60 miles away, Tose went through an immense fortune in just a few years by gambling as much as $100,000 on a single hand of cards. He would later unsuccessfully sue the casinos for taking so much of his money when he was clearly inebriated, but by 1984, he was considering moving the Eagles to Phoenix when Mayor Goode sweetened the local stadium deal. Tose extended the lease on the Vet, but still was running out of money to pay his gambling debts. In 1985, he sold the team to Norman Braman, as noted above, for $65 million. Tose's teams went 96-129-6 in 16 seasons.

Braman had grown up in Philadelphia, but after making a fortune in car dealerships, he split his time between South Florida and the South of France. He was hated by the fans, his players and even his coach (Buddy Ryan) for his perceived cheapness and his elitist behavior. However, he was a major success financially, with his team making a significant profit every year, and in helping the NFL by leading its NFL Properties and Super Bowl committees to more profitable practices. On the field, Ryan brought him success at first, but with the advent of free agency, Braman dismantled the team by refusing to pay his players market value. As the team declined, Braman sold it in 1994 to Jeffrey Lurie for $190 million, nearly triple what he paid for it only nine years before. Braman's won-lost record was 78-64-1.

Lurie's family had made its money in General Cinema theaters, and Jeffrey tried to parlay that into the movie business by producing three motion pictures, but none did much business. At first, the New Englander with a Ph.D. in social policy tried to buy the hometown Patriots, but was rebuffed. Lurie planned to model his team on the 49ers, but had to undergo some fits and starts over the first five years as he went through front office people like toilet tissue until he hired Andy Reid in 1999. Reid stabilized the situation on the field and in the front office, along with Lurie's boyhood friend Joe Banner, to the extent that Lurie was heard crowing that the Eagles were the "gold standard" in the NFL before they had won a single Super Bowl. Comments like that conveyed an elitist attitude that separated Lurie from the blue-collar Eagle fans despite his willingness to spend money on free agents and his skill in getting a beautiful new stadium erected. Even if the team does win a Super Bowl, I don't think Lurie will ever be popular with the fans because he lacks the common touch that Bert Bell and Lex Thompson seemed to possess so many years ago. But Lurie's record on the field is an impressive 100-75-1.

Rating the Drafts

Jerome Brown
DT 1987-91

WHO'S WORN THE NUMBER:

Mel Tom (DE) 1971-73, Leonard Mitchell (DL) 1981-83, Joe Drake (DT) 1985, *Jerome Brown* (DT) 1987-91, Skip Hamilton (DT) 1987r, Greg Liter (DE) 1987r. **RETIRED**

Originator: Defensive end Mel Tom in 1971.

Longest Tenure: Five years, Jerome Brown for whom it is retired, 1987 to 1991.

Number Changes: Mel Tom first wore 58 from 1967 to 1970; Leonard Mitchell wore 74 from 1984 to 1986.

Just Visiting: None.

Highs: Mel Tom was an undersized, active and outspoken defensive end who challenged assistant coach Jerry Wampfler to a fight and quit the team in 1973, forcing a trade to Chicago.

Lows: First-round pick Leonard Mitchell lasted six unproductive years, three as a backup defensive end and three as an ineffective starting offensive tackle.

Jerome Brown

The first impression Jerome Brown made in the Philadelphia area was not favorable. He was the star defensive tackle for the University of Miami, who led his teammates in walking out of the pre-Fiesta Bowl banquet for Miami and Penn State in 1987, adding the overheated and stupid comment that "the Japanese don't sit down and eat with Pearl Harbor before they bombed them." Despite the Hurricanes' unity of purpose, they lost the National Championship on the field. In retrospect, though, what we take from that incident is that Brown was a leader who had the unquestioned respect of his teammates. Miami fullback Alonzo Highsmith was eating when he heard that Brown said the team was leaving, and his reaction was "if Jerome says so, I guess we're all going." There are many instances of Brown exercising that leadership in more positive ways, too. When the KKK tried to hold a demonstration in Brown's hometown of Brooksville, Florida, they were driven away by Brown, who parked his SUV with the oversized speakers next to their rally, pumped up the volume on his car stereo, and drowned out the hate mongers.

Jerome liked to refer to himself as a "big old kid", and his boisterous, profane, and obnoxious personality was well-matched with Buddy Ryan, who drafted him number one in 1987. The Eagles' track record for first-round picks in the 1980s was pretty pitiful, including Leonard Mitchell, Michael Haddix, Kenny Jackson and Kevin Allen. Even Buddy's first pick from 1986, Keith Byars, had not yet shown his versatile array of talents. Jerome, however, fit right in and became a major presence in the locker room, providing a funny, friendly and secular contrast to the Minister of Defense, Reggie White. His personality and playing style were well-matched to Philadelphia as well.

On the field, Brown was a throwback player. In a time of increasing specialization when there were "2 technique" defensive tackles and "3 technique" defensive tackles, depending on how they would line up across from the center, Jerome was a complete player. He was a run stuffer, but he was not a 350-pound fat guy whose primary duty was to take up space in the middle of the field. He could move. He could stuff the run and get upfield to rush the passer. His play was reminiscent of the great tackles of the past, like Mean Joe Greene and Bob Lilly. Adding his talents to those of Reggie White, Clyde Simmons, Seth Joyner, Byron Evans, Eric Allen, Wes Hopkins and Andre Waters made for a truly frightening defense that was among the best in the league. When Buddy Ryan left and Steel Curtain architect Bud Carson was brought in to run the defense in 1991, they got even better — stingier and more disciplined — and led the NFL that year in fewest rushing yards, fewest passing yards and fewest total yards.

A week before training camp in 1992, though, tragedy struck when Brown lost control of the sports car he was driving in Brooksville and crashed. Both he and his passenger, his 12-year old nephew, were killed instantly. The news devastated his Eagle teammates, and most attended the funeral for their fallen teammate and friend later that week. Spokesmen Reggie White and Seth Joyner dedicated the 1992 season to the memory of Brown. On opening day pregame ceremonies to honor Brown at the Vet, White and Clyde Simmons announced that Brown's 99 had been officially retired.

Philadelphia would finish the year 11-5, second in the East to the emerging Dallas Cowboys, whom they met in a divisional playoff game. Without Brown in the middle, though, they could not contain the Cowboy offense, while the Eagles' offense could do nothing against the Cowboy defense. The game ended 34-10. Reggie White had played his last game as an Eagle, and Buddy's boys were done.

Jerome Brown turned out to be one of the Eagles best draft choices, but not all picks turn out so well. The Eagles can really be said to have started the draft since Eagle owner Bert Bell had the original idea for it and persuaded the other owners in the NFL to go along with him in 1936. That 1936 draft turned out to be the worst in team history. None of the Eagles' nine selections ever played in the NFL. Things could only improve from there, although some years were not better by much. The Eagles were also innovators in scouting, as when Greasy Neale and business manager Harry Thayer showed up at the 1942 draft proceedings with a cart filled with 64 notebooks of scouting information. Before this, many teams made their draft selections from what they read in the *Street and Smith's College Annual*. In later years, Philadelphia often did its scouting on the cheap and the results showed.

In order to get an overview of the relative success of the last 70 years of Eagle drafts, I created the following draft rankings table. I used a simple system to rate each draft: one point for anyone who makes the team, two points for someone who becomes a regular starter, three points for a star (indicated by Pro Bowl and All-Pro selections), and four points for Hall of Famers. No points are given to star players selected who had their success elsewhere, like Bob Kuechenberg. I also counted the total number of players who made the team and divided it into the overall draft score to get an average. The number of star players uncovered is also included. Drafts are grouped by the coach or general manager presumed to be in control. This method is a quick and dirty one. The ratings are crude and the raw number of players making the team would be expected to increase over time as rosters expanded, and to be greater for poorer clubs. However, this method does allow us to see the broad patterns and overall quality of those who ran the Eagle drafts.

YEARS	COACH/GM	AVG. # OF PLAYERS	AVG. SCORE	AVG. PLAYER SCORE	TOTAL STARS
1936-40	Bert Bell	4.0	6.6	1.65	3
1941-50	Greasy Neale (a)	4.2	7.6	1.81	10
1951-63	Vince McNally (b)	5.7	10.1	1.77	15
1964-68	Joe Kuharich	5.8	9.6	1.66	2
1969-72	Pete Retzlaff	7.3	11.5	1.59	2
1973-75	Mike McCormack (c)	5.7	10.0	1.76	4
1976-82	Dick Vermeil	5.3	8.7	1.65	6
1983-85	Marion Campbell (d)	7.0	11.0	1.57	3
1986-90	Buddy Ryan (e)	6.4	11.2	1.75	7
1991-94	Rich Kotite (f)	6.3	8.8	1.40	2
1995-98	Ray Rhodes (g)	6.8	11.0	1.63	6
1999-2004	Andy Reid (h)	5.5	8.7	1.58	5

a. Neale picked the players and the GMs signed them. General managers included Harry Thayer, Al Ennis, Charley Ewart and James Clark.

b. Several coaches served under McNally — Bo McMillan, Wayne Milner, Jim Trimble, Hugh Devore, Buck Shaw and Nick Skorich.

c. Jim Murray was given the title of general manager in 1975 and held it through 1982.

d. Campbell worked with scouting director Lynn Stiles. Harry Gamble became GM when Norman Braman bought the team in 1985 and left when Braman sold the team in 1994.

e. Joe Wooley was hired to replace Lynn Stiles in scouting in 1986.

f. Kotite worked with Joe Wooley for the first few years.

g. New owner Jeffrey Lurie went through the following personnel people/scouting directors/GMs during Ray Rhodes' tenure: Bob Wallace, Bob Ackles, Dick Daniels, John Wooten, Chuck Banker, Mike Lombardi and Bryan Broaddus.

h. Reid was assisted by GM Tom Modrak in his first year. Modrak was squeezed out, Reid took over personnel and Joe Banner took over the business side.

Looking at the table, it is not surprising to find that Greasy Neale and Buddy Ryan have been the most successful draft selectors. Neale has the highest Average Player Score at 1.81 and selected 10 stars in 10 years. Ryan's score is a little lower at 1.75, but he has the highest percentage of stars to years with seven in five years. Vince McNally and Mike McCormack scored virtually the same as Ryan, and both found more than one star per year as well. McCormack should be penalized, though, for trading so many draft picks for veterans that he left a tough situation for his successor, Dick Vermeil. At the other end of the spectrum, Rich Kotite achieved the lowest Average Player Score at 1.4. He shares the title for finding the fewest stars with Joe Kuharich and Pete Retzlaff, each having picked only two. Andy Reid's numbers at this point are middling, but they could clearly rise if some of his young players develop into full-fledged stars to join Donovan McNabb and Corey Simon. It is too early to say.

Eagles
All-Time Roster

with uniform numbers

PLAYER	POSITION	YEAR	NUMBER
Abercrombie, Walter	RB	1988	32
Absher, Dick	LB	1972	53
Adams, Gary	DB	1969	6
Adams, Keith	LB	2002-04	57
Adams, Theo	G	1995	61
Agajanian, Ben	G	1945	89
Akers, David	K	1999-04	2
Alexander, David	C	1987-94	72
Alexander, Kermit	DB	1972-73	39
Allen, Chuck	LB	1972	54
Allen, Eric	CB	1988-94	21
Allen, Ian	T	2004	79
Allen, Jackie	DB	1972	21
Allen, Kevin	T	1985	72
Allert, Ty	LB	1987-89	58
Allison, Henry	G	1971-72	65
Amerson, Glen	B	1961	46
Amundson, George	RB	1975	38
Anderson, Gary	K	1995-96	1
Andrews, Shawn	G	2004	73
Angelo, Jim	G	1987r	69
Antwine, Houston	DT	1972	75
Archer, Dave	QB	1991-92	18
Armour, Justin	WR	1997	86
Armstrong, Harvey	DT	1982-84	96

PLAYER	POSITION	YEAR	NUMBER
Armstrong, Neill	E	1947-51	80
Arnold, Jay	B	1937-40	34
Arrington, Rick	QB	1970-73	11
Aschbacher, Darrel	G	1959	50
Asher, Jamie	TE	1999	84
Atkins, Steve	FB	1981	38
Auer, Howard	T	1933	24
Auer, Jim	DE	1987r	97
Autry, Darnell	RB	1998, 2000	24, 26
Ayers, Marvin	DE	1987r	96
Bahr, Matt	K	1993	11
Bailey, David	DE	1990	93
Bailey, Eric	TE	1987r	87
Bailey, Howard	T	1935	20
Bailey, Tom	B	1971-74	31
Bailey, Victor	WR	1993-74	82
Baisi, Albert	G	1947	63
Baker, Jason	P	2002	7
Baker, John	DE	1962	78
Baker, Keith	WR	1985	80
Baker, Ron	G	1980-88	63
Baker, Sam	K	1964-69	38
Baker, Tony	B	1971-72	38
Baldinger, Brian	G	1992-93	62
Ballman, Gary	TE	1967-72	85
Banas, Stephen	B	1935	29
Banducci, Bruno	G	1944-45	63
Banta, Jack	B	1941, 1944-45	33
Barber, Shawn	LB	2002	56
Barker, Bryan	P	1994	4
Barlow, Corey	CB	1992-94	24
Barnes, Billy Ray	RB	1957-61	33
Barnes, Larry	FB	1978-79	38
Barnes, Walter	G	1948-51	74
Barnett, Fred	WR	1990-95	86
Barnhardt, Dan	B	1934	26
Barni, Roy	B	1954-55	33
Barnum, Leonard	B	1940-42	13
Bartholomew, Sam	B	1941	27
Bartlett, Doug	DT	1988	95
Bartley, Ephesians	LB	1992	50
Bartrum, Mike	TE	2000-04	88
Basca, Nick	B	1941	47

PLAYER	POSITION	YEAR	NUMBER
Bassi, Dick	G	1940	35
Bassman, Herman	B	1936	19, 24, 29
Battaglia, Matt	LB	1987r	52
Baughan, Maxie	LB	1960-65	55
Bauman, Alfred	T	1947	73
Bausch, Frank	C	1941	55
Bavaro, Mark	TE	1993-94	84
Bawel, Ed	B	1952, 1955-56	20, 81
Baze, Winford	B	1937	26, 37
Beach, Pat	TE	1992	83
Beals, Shawn	WR	1988	81
Beaver, Jim	G	1962	65
Beckles, Ian	G	1997-98	62
Bednarik, Chuck	C/LB	1949-62	60
Beisler, Randy	DE	1966-68	64, 80
Bell, Eddie	DB	1955-58	81
Bell, Todd	LB	1988-89	49, 52
Bellamy, Mike	WR	1990	81
Bellamy, Victor	CB	1987r	39
Bendross, Jesse	WR	1987r	85
Benson, Henry	G	1935	30, 39
Berger, Mitch	P	1994	17
Bergey, Bill	LB	1974-80	66
Berry, Dan	B	1967	19
Berzinski, Willie	B	1956	33
Betterson, James	RB	1977-78	34
Bielski, Dick	B	1955-59	36
Bieniemy, Eric	RB	1999	33
Binotto, John	B	1942	30
Bishop, Blaine	S	2002	24
Bjorklund, Robert	C	1941	50
Black, Michael	T/G	1986	77
Blackmore, Richard	CB	1979-82	27
Blaine, Ed	G	1963-66	64
Blake, Jeff	QB	2004	11
Bleamer, Jeff	T	1975-76	67
Bleeker, Mel	B	1944-46	49
Blue, Luther	WR	1980	80
Blye, Ron	RB	1969	33
Boatswain, Harry	G/T	1995, 1997	69
Boedeker, William	B	1950	21
Bolden, Gary	DT	1987r	65
Boniol, Chris	K	1997-98	18

PLAYER	POSITION	YEAR	NUMBER
Booty, John	DB	1991-92	42
Boryla, Mike	QB	1974-76	10
Bostic, James	RB	1998-99	27
Bostic, Jason	CB	1999-00	32
Bouggess, Lee	RB	1970-73	46
Bouie, Kevin	RB	1995-76	33, 35
Bova, Tony	E	1943	85
Bowman, Kevin	WR	1987r	83
Boykin, Deral	S	1996	25
Bradley, Bill	S	1969-76	28
Bradley, Carlos	LB	1987r	59
Bradley, Hal	G	1958	65
Bredice, John	E	1956	89
Brennan, Leo	T	1942	70
Brewer, John	B	1952-53	36
Brian, William	T	1935-36	31
Brister, Bubby	QB	1993-94	6
Britt, Rankin	E	1939	18
Brooks, Barrett	T	1995-98	76
Brooks, Clifford	DB	1975-76	23
Brooks, Tony	RB	1992-93	39
Brookshier, Tom	CB	1953, 1956-61	40, 45
Broughton, Luther	TE	1997, 1999-00	49, 84, 86, 88
Brown, Aaron	LB	1985	90
Brown, Bob	T	1964-68	76
Brown, Cedrick	CB	1987	23
Brown, David	LB	1987r	56
Brown, Deauntae	CB	1997	35
Brown, Fred	LB	1967-69	55, 87
Brown, Greg	DE	1981-86	98
Brown, Jerome	DT	1987-91	99
Brown, Na	WR	1999-01	85
Brown, Reggie	RB	1987r	24
Brown, Sheldon	CB	2002-04	24, 39
Brown, Thomas	DE	1980	97
Brown, Tim	RB	1960-67	22
Brown, Willie	WR	1966	23
Brumm, Don	DE	1970-71	80
Brutley, Daryon	CB	2003	31
Bryant, Bill	CB	1978	25
Brzezinski, Doug	G	1999-02	74
Buckhalter, Correll	RB	2001, 2003	28
Budd, Frank	E	1962	20

PLAYER	POSITION	YEAR	NUMBER
Bukant, Joe	B	1938-40	36
Bulaich, Norm	RB	1973-74	36
Bull, Ron	RB	1971	47
Bunting, John	LB	1972-82	95
Burgess, Derrick	DE	2001-04	56, 59
Burk, Adrian	QB	1951-56	10
Burke, Mark	DB	1976	29
Burks, Dialleo	WR	1996	42, 86, 89
Burnette, Tom	B	1938	19
Burnham, Lem	DE	1977-80	67
Burnine, Hank	E	1956-57	84
Burroughs, Don	DB	1960-64	45
Bushby, Thomas	B	1935	45
Buss, Art	T	1936-37	12, 45
Butler, Bob	G	1962	53
Butler, John	B	1943, 1945	27
Byars, Keith	RB	1986-92	41, 42
Byrne, Bill	G	1963	66
Cabrelli, Larry	E	1941-47	84
Caffey, Lee Roy	LB	1963	34
Cagle, Jim	DT	1974	78
Cahill, Dave	DT	1966	58
Caldwell, Mike	LB	1998-01	56
Calhoun, Don	RB	1982	30
Calicchio, Lonny	K	1997	17
Calloway, Ernie	DT	1969-72	57, 72
Campbell, Glenn	E	1935	29
Campbell, Marion	DT	1956-61	78
Campbell, Stan	G	1959-61	64
Campbell, Tommy	DB	1976	37
Campfield, Billy	RB	1978-82	37
Campion, Thomas	T	1947	72
Canale, Rocco	G	1943-45	73
Carmichael, Harold	WR	1971-83	17
Carollo, Joe	T	1969-70	76
Carpe, Joe	T	1933	24
Carpenter, Rob	WR	1995	81
Carr, Earl	RB	1979	32
Carr, Jim	S	1959-63	21
Carroccio, Russ	G	1955	64
Carroll, Terrence	S	2001	33
Carson, Carlos	WR	1989	87
Carter, Cris	WR	1987-89	80

PLAYER	POSITION	YEAR	NUMBER
Carter, Joe	E	1933-40	17, 31
Case, Pete	G	1962-64	67
Cassady, Howard	B	1962	41
Castiglia, Jim	B	1941, 1945-46	31
Caterbone, Tom	CB	1987r	49
Catlin, Tom	LB	1959	63
Cavanaugh, Matt	QB	1986-89	6
Caver, Quinton	LB	2001	55
Cemore, Tony	G	1941	61
Ceppetelli, Gene	C	1968-69	54
Chalenski, Mike	DL	1993-95	71
Chapura, Dick	DT	1990	97
Cheek, Louis	T	1990	75
Cherry, Je'Rod	S	2000	25
Cherundolo, Chuck	C	1940	21
Chesley, Al	LB	1979-82	59
Chesson, Wes	WR	1973-74	21
Christensen, Jeff	QB	1984-85	11
Chuy, Don	G	1969	66
Cifelli, Gus	T	1954	77
Clark, Al	CB	1976	21
Clark, Mike	K/E	1963	84
Clark, Myers	B	1934	28
Clarke, Ken	DT	1978-87	71
Clay, Willie	CB	1997	25
Clemons, Topper	RB	1987r	27
Cobb, Garry	LB	1985-87	50
Cody, Bill	LB	1972	66
Colavito, Steve	LB	1975	58
Cole, John	B	1938, 1940	37
Coleman, Al	DB	1972	8
Collie, Bruce	G	1990-91	69
Colman, Wayne	LB	1968-69	49
Combs, William	E	1942	82
Concannon, Jack	QB	1964-66	3
Conjar, Larry	FB	1968	25
Conlin, Ray	DT	1987r	91
Conner, Darion	DE	1996-97	93
Conti, Enio	G	1941-45	51, 67
Conwell, Joe	T	1986-87	79
Cook, Leon	T	1942	72
Cook, Rashard	S	1999-02	42
Cooke, Ed	E	1958	86

PLAYER	POSITION	YEAR	NUMBER
Cooper, Evan	DB	1984-87	21
Cooper, Louis	LB	1993	52
Cooper, Richard	T	1996-98	77
Copeland, Russell	WR	1998	86
Cornish, Frank	G	1995	68
Coston, Zed	C	1939	23
Cothren, Paige	B/K	1959	45
Cowher, Bill	LB	1983-84	57
Cowhig, Jerry	B	1951	36
Crabb, Claude	DB	1964-65	23
Craft, Russ	B	1946-53	33
Crafts, Jerry	T/G	1997-98	66, 73
Crawford, Charles	RB	1986-87	45
Creech, Bob	LB	1971-72	58
Creswell, Smiley	DE	1985	92
Crews, Terry	LB	1996	54
Cronin, Bill	E	1965	87
Cross, Irv	DB	1961-65, 1969	27
Crowe, Larry	RB	1972	47
Crutchfield, Darrel	CB	2001	29
Cuba, Paul	T	1933-35	21, 23
Culbreath, Jim	FB	1980	32
Cullars, Willie	DE	1974	75
Cumby, George	LB	1987r	91
Cunningham, Dick	LB	1973	51
Cunningham, Randall	QB	1985-95	12
Cuppoletti, Bree	G	1939	37
Curcio, Mike	LB	1981-82	57
Curtis, Scott	LB	1988	91
D'Agostino, Frank	G	1956	66
Darby, Byron	DE/TE	1983-86	94
Darilek, Trey	G	2004	66
Darling, James	LB	1997-00	57
Darwin, Matt	C	1986-90	78
Davis, Al	B	1971-72	43
Davis, Antone	T	1991-95	77, 78
Davis, Bob	B	1942	27
Davis, Norm	G	1970	64
Davis, Pernell	DT	1999-00	93
Davis, Stan	B	1973	81
Davis, Sylvester	B	1933	16
Davis, Vern	DB	1971	16
Dawkins, Brian	S	1996-04	20

PLAYER	POSITION	YEAR	NUMBER
Dawson, Dale	K	1988	4
Dean, Ted	RB	1960-63	35
DeLine, Steve	K	1989	2
Dellenbach, Jeff	G/C	1999	66
Delucca, Gerry	T	1959	74
Dempsey, Jack	T	1934, 1937	27
Dempsey, Tom	K	1971-74	19
Dennard, Mark	C	1984-85	65
Dent, Richard	DE	1997	95
DeSantis, Dan	B	1941	49
Detmer, Koy	QB	1997-04	10
Detmer, Ty	QB	1996-97	14
DeVaughn, Dennis	DB	1982-83	25
Dial, Alan	DB	1989	24
Dial, Benjy	QB	1967	4
Diaz-Infante, David	G	1999	63
Dickerson, Kori	TE	2003	86
DiFilippo, Dave	G	1941	26, 69
Dimmick, Tom	T	1956	65
Dimry, Charles	DB	1997	38
Dingle, Nate	LB	1995	55
DiRenzo, Danny	P	1948	82
Dirks, Mike	G	1968-71	62
Ditka, Mike	E	1967-68	89, 98
Dixon, Al	TE	1983	86
Dixon, Floyd	WR	1992	84
Dixon, Ronnie	DT	1995-96	90
Dixon, Zach	RB	1980	25
Dobbins, Herb	T	1974	67
Dorow, Al	QB	1957	10
Dorsey, Dean	K	1988	2
Doss, Noble	B	1947-48	45
Douglas, Dameane	WR	1999-02	82
Douglas, Hugh	DE	1998-02, 2004	53
Douglas, Merrill	B	1962	33
Douglas, Otis	T	1946-49	71
Dow, Elwood	B	1938-40	14
Dowda, Harry	B	1954-55	44
Doyle, Ted	T	1943	72
Drake, Joe	DT	1985	99
Drake, Troy	T	1995-97	75
Drummond, Robert	RB	1989-91	36
Duckworth, Bobby	WR	1986	80

PLAYER	POSITION	YEAR	NUMBER
Dudley, Paul	B	1963	28
Dumbauld, John	DE	1987-88	93
Duncan, Rick	K	1968	32
Dunek, Ken	TE	1980	86
Dunn, Jason	TE	1996-98	87
Dunstan, Bill	DT	1973-76	61
Durko, John	E	1944	88
Edwards, Anthony	WR	1989-90	84
Edwards, Herman	CB	1977-85	46
Ehlers, Tom	LB	1975-77	59
Eibner, John	T	1941-42, 1946	76, 77
Eiden, Edmund	B	1944	71
Elewonibi, Moe	T	1995	65
Ellis, Drew	T	1938-40	35
Ellis, Ray	S	1981-85	24
Ellstrom, Marv	B	1934	10
Emanuel, Charles	S	1997	47
Emelianchik, Pete	E	1967	39
Emmons, Carlos	LB	2000-03	51
Emmons, Franklin	B	1940	44
Ena, Justin	LB	2002-03	59, 95
Engles, Rick	P	1978	13
Enke, Fred	B	1952	17
Ephraim, Alonzo	C	2003-04	50, 76
Erdlitz, Richard	B	1942, 1945	11, 30
Estes, Larry	DE	1972	81
Evans, Byron	LB	1987-94	56
Evans, Donald	DE	1988	77
Evans, Mike	C	1968-73	59
Everett, Eric	CB	1988-89	42
Everett, Major	FB	1983-85	39
Everitt, Steve	C	1997-99	61
Fagioli, Carl	G	1944	77
Farmer, Ray	LB	1996-98	55
Farragut, Ken	C	1951-54	53
Fazio, Ron	TE	1987r	87
Feagles, Jeff	P	1990-93	5
Feehery, Gerry	C/G	1983-87	67
Feeley, A.J.	QB	2001-02	14
Felber, Fred	E	1933	32
Feller, Happy	K	1971	1
Fenci, Richard	E	1933	29
Ferko, John	G	1937-38	11, 19

PLAYER	POSITION	YEAR	NUMBER
Ferrante, Jack	E	1941, 1944-50	83, 87
Ferris, Neil	B	1952	27
Fiedler, Bill	G	1938	38
Fiedler, Jay	QB	1994-95	11
Finn, Mike	T	1994	79
Finneran, Brian	WR	1999	86
Fitzgerald, Mickey	FB	1981	38
Fitzkee, Scott	WR	1979-80	81
Flores, Mike	DT	1991-94	95, 96
Floyd, Eric	G	1992-93	61
Fogle, DeShawn	LB	1997	52, 54
Folsom, Steve	TE	1981	86
Fontenot, Chris	TE	1998	85
Ford, Charles	DB	1974	32
Ford, Fredric	CB	1997	46
Foules, Elbert	CB	1983-87	29
Fox, Terry	B	1941, 1945	36
Frahm, Herald	B	1935	?
Fraley, Hank	C	2000-04	63
Frank, Joseph	T	1941, 1943	61, 70
Franklin, Cleveland	RB	1977-78	30
Franklin, Tony	K	1979-83	1
Franks, Dennis	C	1976-78	53
Frazier, Derrick	CB	1994-95	23
Freeman, Antonio	WR	2002	86
Freeman, Bob	DB	1960-61	41
Frey, Glenn	B	1936-37	32
Friedlund, Bob	E	1944	85
Friedman, Bob	G	1944	72
Fritts, George	T	1945	71
Fritz, Ralph	G	1941	63
Fritzsche, Jim	T/G	1983	72
Frizzell, William	S	1986-90, 1992-93	33
Fryar, Irving	WR	1996-98	80
Fuller, Frank	T	1963	72
Fuller, James	S	1996	22
Fuller, William	DE	1994-96	95
Gabbard, Steve	T	1989	67
Gabriel, Roman	QB	1973-77	5, 18
Gambold, Bob	B	1953	14
Gaona, Bob	T	1957	64
Gardner, Barry	LB	1999-02	52
Garner, Charlie	RB	1994-98	25, 30

PLAYER	POSITION	YEAR	NUMBER
Garrity, Gregg	WR	1984-89	86
Gary, Russell	DB	1986	24, 38
Gauer, Charley	E	1943-45	32, 85
Gay, Blenda	DE	1975-76	68
George, Ed	T	1976-78	64
George, Raymond	T	1940	23, 42
Gerber, Elwood	G	1941-42	62
Gerhard, Chris	S	1987r	46
Gerhart, Tom	DB	1992	25
Gersbach, Carl	LB	1970	69
Ghecas, Lou	B	1941	11
Giammona, Louie	RB	1978-82	33
Giancanelli, Hal	B	1953-56	27
Giannelli, Mario	G	1948-51	64
Gibbs, Pat	DB	1972	45
Gibron, Abe	G	1956-57	64
Giddens, Frank	T	1981-82	79
Giddens, Herschel	T	1938	26
Gilbert, Lewis	TE	1980	86
Giles, Jimmie	TE	1987-89	83
Gill, Roger	B	1964-65	32
Gilmore, Jim	T	1986	75
Ginney, Jerry	G	1940	31
Glass, Glenn	B	1964-65	49
Gloden, Fred	B	1941	37
Glover, Rich	DT	1975	69
Goebel, Brad	QB	1991	8
Golden, Tim	LB	1985	91
Goldston, Ralph	B	1952, 1954-55	22
Golic, Mike	DT	1987-92	90
Gollomb, Rudy	G	1936	14
Gonya, Robert	T	1933-34	27
Goode, John	TE	1985	87
Goode, Rob	B	1955	38
Goodwin, Marvin	S	1994	22
Goodwin, Ron	E	1963-68	31, 81
Gorecki, Chuck	LB	1987r	51
Gossage, Gene	E	1960-62	79
Gouveia, Kurt	T	1963-69	78
Graham, Jeff	WR	1998	81
Graham, Lyle	C	1941	51
Graham, Tom	G	1935	31
Grant, Bud	E	1951-52	86

PLAYER	POSITION	YEAR	NUMBER
Grant, Otis	WR	1987r	81
Grasmanis, Paul	DT	2000-04	96
Graves, Ray	C	1942-43, 1946	51, 52
Gray, Cecil	G/DT	1990-91	71
Gray, Jim	B	1967	28
Gray, Mel	KR	1997	28
Green, Donnie	T	1977	74
Green, Jamaal	DE	2004	65
Green, John	E	1947-51	89
Green, Roy	DT	1999-00	94
Gregory, Ken	E	1962	80
Griffin, Don	CB	1996	28
Griffin, Jeff	CB	1987r	45
Griggs, Anthony	LB	1982-85	58
Grooms, Elois	DE	1987r	98
Gros, Earl	FB	1964-66	34
Grossman, Burt	DE	1994	69
Gudd, Leonard	E	1934	25
Gude, Henry	G	1946	73
Guglielmi, Ralph	QB	1963	17
Guillory, Tony	LB	1969	61
Gunn, Mark	DL	1995-96	96
Gunnels, Riley	T	1960-64	74
Hackney, Elmer	B	1940-41	20
Haddix, Michael	FB	1983-88	26
Haden, Nick	G	1986	62
Hager, Britt	LB	1989-94	54
Hairston, Carl	DE	1976-83	78
Hajek, Charles	C	1934	8
Hall, Irving	B	1942	32
Hall, Rhett	DT	1995-98	97
Hallstrom, Ron	G	1993	65
Halverson, Bill	T	1942	75
Halverson, Dean	LB	1973-76	56
Hamilton, Ray	E	1940	18
Hamilton, Skip	DT	1987r	99
Hamiter, Uhuru	DE	2000-01	91
Hamner, Thomas	RB	2000	33
Hampton, Dave	RB	1976	34
Hampton, William	CB	2001	41
Hankton, Karl	WR	1998	82
Hansen, Roscoe	T	1951	73
Hanson, Swede	B	1933-37	14, 42

PLAYER	POSITION	YEAR	NUMBER
Harding, Greg	DB	1987r	28
Harding, Roger	C	1947	72
Hardy, Andre	RB	1984	47
Hargrove, Marvin	WR	1990	80
Harmon, Andy	DT	1991-97	91
Harper, Maurice	C	1937-40	10
Harrington, Perry	RB	1980-83	35
Harris, Al	LB	1989-90	95
Harris, Al	CB	1998-02	31
Harris, Jim	B	1957	20
Harris, Jon	DE	1997-88	90
Harris, Leroy	FB	1979-82	20
Harris, Richard	DE	1971-73	84
Harris, Rod	WR	1990-91	80
Harris, Tim	DE	1993	97
Harrison, Bob	LB	1962-63	42
Harrison, Dennis	DE	1978-84	68
Harrison, Granville	E	1941	80
Harrison, Tyreo	LB	2002-03	55, 59
Hart, Clinton	S	2003	33
Hart, Dick	G	1967-71	71
Hartman, Fred	T	1948	73
Harvey, Richard	DB	1970	41
Haskins, Jon	LB	1998	52
Hasselbeck, Tim	QB	2002	11
Hauck, Tim	S	1999-01	45
Hawkins, Ben	WR	1966-73	18
Hayden, Aaron	RB	1998	33
Hayden, Ken	C	1942	50
Hayes, Ed	DB	1970	47
Hayes, Joe	WR	1984	80
Haymond, Alvin	DB	1968	30
Heath, Jo Jo	DB	1981	29
Hebron, Vaughn	RB	1993-95	20, 43
Heck, Ralph	LB	1963-65	43
Hegamin, George	G/T	1998	69
Heller, Ron	T	1988-92	73
Henderson, Jerome	CB	1995	26
Henderson, Zac	S	1980	24
Hendrickson, Steve	LB	1995	48
Henry, Maurice	LB	1990	53
Henry, Wally	WR	1977-82	89
Henson, Gary	E	1963	80

PLAYER	POSITION	YEAR	NUMBER
Herrod, Jeff	LB	1997	54
Hershey, Kirk	E	1941	80
Hertel, Rob	QB	1980	16
Hewitt, Bill	E	1936-39, 1943	56, 82
Hicks, Artis	T	2002-04	77
Higgins, Tom	T	1954-55	71
Higgs, Mark	RB	1989	22
Hill, Fred	E	1965-71	86
Hill, King	QB	1961-68	10
Hinkle, Jack	B	1941-47	43
Hix, Billy	E	1950	85
Hoage, Terry	S	1986-90	34
Hobbs, Bill	LB	1969-71	56
Hogan, Mike	FB	1976-78, 1980	30, 35
Holcomb, William	T	1937	?
Holly, Bob	QB	1984	12
Holmes, Lester	G	1993-96	73
Hood, Roderick	CB	2003-04	29
Hooks, Alvin	WR	1981	80
Hoover, Mel	WR	1982-84	85
Hopkins, Wes	S	1983-93	48
Horan, Mike	P	1984-85	2
Hord, Roy	G	1962	64
Horn, Marty	QB	1987r	14
Horrell, Bill	G	1952	62
Hoss, Clark	TE	1972	80
Howard, Bob	CB	1978-79	23
Howell, Lane	T	1965-69	79
Hoyem, Lynn	G	1964-67	63
Hoying, Bobby	QB	1996-98	7
Hrabetin, Frank	T	1942	71
Huarte, John	QB	1968	7
Hudson, Bob	B	1953-55, 1957-58	42, 88
Hudson, John	G	1991-95	66
Hughes, Chuck	WR	1967-69	13
Hughes, William	C	1937-40	15, 29
Hultz, Don	DT	1964-73	83
Humbert, Dick	E	1941, 1945-49	81
Humphrey, Claude	DE	1979-81	87
Hunt, Calvin	C	1970	54
Hunter, Herman	RB	1985	36
Huth, Gerry	G	1959-60	54, 65
Hutton, Tom	P	1995-98	4

PLAYER	POSITION	YEAR	NUMBER
Huxhold, Ken	G	1954-58	63
Huzvar, John	B	1952	38
Ingram, Mark	WR	1996	85
Irvin, Willie	B	1953	81
Jackson, Al	CB	1994	26
Jackson, Bob	B	1960	28
Jackson, Don	B	1936	10, 50
Jackson, Earnest	RB	1985-86	41
Jackson, Greg	S	1994-95	47
Jackson, Greg	DE	1995-00	79
Jackson, Harold	WR	1969-72	29
Jackson, Johnny	DE	1977	62
Jackson, Keith	TE	1988-91	88
Jackson, Kenny	WR	1984-88, 1990-91	81, 83, 84
Jackson, Randy	RB	1974	33
Jackson, Trent	WR	1966	27
Jacobs, David	K	1987r	4
Jacobs, Proverb	T	1958	67
James, Angelo	CB	1987r	42
James, Po	RB	1972-75	27, 33
Janet, Ernie	T	1975	64
Jarmoluk, Mike	T	1949-55	78
Jarvi, Toimi	B	1944	32
Jasper, Ed	DT	1997-98	74
Jaworski, Ron	QB	1977-86	7
Jefferson, William	B	1942	43
Jelesky, Tom	T	1985	77
Jells, Dietrich	WR	1998-99	83
Jenkins, Izel	CB	1988-92	46
Jeter, Tommy	DT	1992-95	98
Jiles, Dwayne	LB	1985-89	53
Johansson, Ove	K	1977	10
Johnson, Albert	B	1942	44
Johnson, Alonzo	LB	1986-87	54
Johnson, Bill	DT	1998-99	94
Johnson, Charles	WR	1999-00	81
Johnson, Charlie	DT	1977-81	65
Johnson, Chris	DB	1987r	30
Johnson, Dirk	P	2003-04	8
Johnson, Don	B	1953-55	40
Johnson, Dwight	DE	2000	62
Johnson, Eric	DB	1977-78	49
Johnson, Gene	B	1959-60	27

PLAYER	POSITION	YEAR	NUMBER
Johnson, Jay	LB	1969	48
Johnson, Jimmie	TE	1995-98	88
Johnson, Kevin	DT	1995-96	94
Johnson, Lee	P	2002	6
Johnson, Maurice	TE	1991-94	87
Johnson, Norm	K	1999	9
Johnson, Reggie	TE	1995	80
Johnson, Ron	WR	1985-89	85
Johnson, Tom	B	1948	27
Johnson, Vaughan	LB	1994	52
Jonas, Don	B	1962	28
Jones, Chris	WR	1995-97	82
Jones, Dhani	LB	2004	55
Jones, Don	B	1940	22
Jones, Harry	RB	1967-72	23
Jones, Jimmie	DL	1997	98
Jones, Joe	DE	1974-75	64
Jones, Julian	S	2001	27
Jones, Preston	QB	1993	8
Jones, Ray	DB	1970	21
Jones, Spike	P	1975-77	6
Jones, Tyrone	DB	1989	31
Jordan, Andrew	TE	1998	49
Jorgenson, Carl	T	1935	42
Joseph, James	RB	1991-94	32
Joyner, Seth	LB	1986-93	59
Jurgensen, Sonny	QB	1957-63	9
Kab, Vyto	TE	1982-85	84
Kalu, N.D.	DE	1997, 2001-03	53, 94
Kane, Carl	B	1936	36
Kapele, John	T	1962	77
Kaplan, Bennie	G	1942	77
Karnofsky, Sonny	B	1945	40
Kasky, Ed	T	1942	73
Kaufusi, Steve	DE	1989-90	94
Kavel, George	B	1934	10
Kearse, Jevon	DE	2004	93
Keeling, Ray	T	1938-39	28
Keen, Allen	B	1937-38	24
Kekeris, Jim	T	1947	77
Keller, Ken	B	1956-57	23
Kelley, Bob	C	1955-56	50
Kelley, Dwight	LB	1966-72	51

PLAYER	POSITION	YEAR	NUMBER
Kelly, Jim	E	1965-67	84
Kelly, Joe	LB	1996	56
Kemp, Jeff	QB	1991	16
Kenneally, George	E	1933-35	13
Kenney, Steve	G	1980-85	73
Kersey, Merritt	P	1974-75	37
Key, Wade	G/T	1970-80	72
Keyes, Leroy	DB	1969-72	20
Keys, Howard	T/C	1960-64	61
Khayat, Ed	DT	1958-61, 1964-65	73
Kilroy, Bucko	T	1943-55	76
Kimmel, Jon	LB	1985	54
Kinder, Randy	CB	1997	43
King, Don	T	1956	71
Kirchbaum, Kelly	LB	1987r	54
Kirkland, Levon	LB	2002	93
Kirkman, Roger	B	1933-35	3, 19
Kirksey, Roy	G	1973-74	65, 66
Kish, Ben	B	1943-49	44
Klingel, John	DE	1987-88	97
Kmetovic, Pete	B	1946	27
Knapper, Joe	B	1934	11, 24
Knox, Charles	T	1937	29
Koeninger, Art	C	1933	30
Kolberg, Elmer	B	1939-40	16, 22
Koman, Bill	LB	1957-58	68
Konecny, Mark	RB	1988	35
Kopenberg, Harry	T	1936	28
Kowalczyk, Walt	B	1958-59	43
Kowalkowski, Scott	LB	1991-93	57
Kramer, Kent	TE	1971-74	87
Kraynak, Rich	LB	1983-86	52
Krepfle, Keith	TE	1975-81	84
Kresky, Joe	G	1933-35	5, 26
Krieger, Robert	E	1941, 1946	82, 89
Kriel, Emmet	G	1939	25
Kuczynski, Bert	E	1946	80
Kullman, Mike	S	1987r	35
Kupcinet, Irv	B	1935	31, 37
Kusko, John	B	1936-38	16, 21
Laack, Galen	G	1958	64
Labinjo, Mike	LB	2004	59
Lachman, Dick	B	1933-35	15, 24

PLAYER	POSITION	YEAR	NUMBER
Lainhart, Porter	B	1933	18
Landeta, Sean	P	1999-02	7
Landsberg, Mort	B	1941	30
Landsee, Bob	G/C	1986-87	65
Lang, Israel	FB	1964-68	29
Lankas, James	B	1942	43
Lansford, Buck	T	1955-57	79
Lapham, Bill	C	1960	54
Larson, Bill	TE	1978	88
Latimer, Al	CB	1979	29
Laux, Ted	B	1942-44	15, 27
Lavender, Joe	CB	1973-45	30
Lavette, Robert	RB	1987	22
Lawrence, Kent	WR	1969	12
Lawrence, Reggie	WR	1993	80
Lazetich, Pete	DT	1976-77	73
Leathers, Milton	G	1933	27
LeBel, Harper	TE	1990	87
Lechthaler, Roy	G	1933	34
Ledbetter, Toy	B	1950, 1953-55	25
Lee, Amp	RB	2000	28
Lee, Bernie	B	1938	11
Lee, Byron	LB	1986-87	58
Leggett, Scott	G	1987r	75
LeMaster, Frank	LB	1974-83	55
Leonard, Jim	B	1934-37	19
Leshinski, Ron	TE	1999	89
Levanities, Stephen	T	1942	72
Levens, Dorsey	RB	2002, 2004	25
Lewis, Chad	TE	1997-04	89
Lewis, Greg	WR	2003-04	83
Lewis, Joe	T	1962	71
Lewis, Michael	S	2002-04	32
Leyendecker, Charles	T	1933	35
Lilly, Sammy	DB	1989-90	37
Lince, Dave	E	1966-67	87
Lindskog, Vic	C	1944-51	52
Lio, Augie	G	1946	62
Lipski, John	C	1933-34	20
Liske, Pete	QB	1971-72	14
Liter, Greg	DE	1987r	99
Little, Dave	TE	1985-89	89
Lloyd, Dave	LB	1963-70	52

PLAYER	POSITION	YEAR	NUMBER
Lofton, James	WR	1993	80
Logan, Randy	S	1973-83	41
Long, Matt	C	1987r	61
Looney, Don	E	1940	30
Lou, Ron	C	1975	30, 51
Louderback, Tom	LB	1958-59	61
Love, Clarence	CB	1998	28
Love, Sean	G	1997	64
Lucas, Dick	E	1960-63	87
Lueck, Bill	G	1975	62
Luft, Don	E	1954	89
Luken, Tom	G	1972-78	63
Lusk, Herb	RB	1976-78	32
MacAfee, Ken	E	1959	80
MacDowell, Jay	E	1946-51	85, 88
Macioszczyk, Art	B	1944, 1947	31
Mack, Bill	WR	1964	25
Mackey, Kyle	QB	1986	11
Mackrides, Bill	B	1947-51	39
MacMurdo, Jim	T	1934-37	6, 20
Magee, John	G	1948-55	67
Mahalic, Drew	LB	1976-78	54
Mahe, Reno	RB	2003-04	34
Mallory, John	B	1968	47
Malone, Art	RB	1975-76	26
Mamula, Mike	DE	1995-00	59
Mandarino, Mike	G	1944-45	62
Manning, Roosevelt	DT	1975	65
Mansfield, Ray	C	1963	77
Mansfield, Von	DB	1982	45
Manske, Ed	E	1935-36	11, 36
Manton, Taldon	B	1940	33
Manzini, Baptiste	C	1944-45, 1948	50, 66
Marchi, Basilio	C	1942	55
Mark, Greg	DE	1990	91
Maronic, Duke	G	1944-50	61
Marshall, Anthony	S	1998	35
Marshall, Larry	KR	1974-77	22
Marshall, Whit	LB	1996	58
Martin, Aaron	DB	1966-67	42
Martin, Cecil	FB	1999-02	38
Martin, Kelvin	WR	1995	84
Martin, Steve	DT	1998-99	73, 91

PLAYER	POSITION	YEAR	NUMBER
Mass, Wayne	T	1972	78
Masters, Bob	B	1937-38, 1942-43	30, 31, 33
Masters, Walt	B	1936	53
Matesic, Ed	B	1934-35	12
Matson, Ollie	RB	1964-66	33
Mavraides, Menil	G	1954, 1957	64, 65
May, Dean	QB	1984	5
Mayberry, Jermane	G/T	1996-04	71
Mayes, Rufus	T	1979	77
Mazzanti, Jerry	E	1963	62
McAfee, Wesley	B	1941	40
McAlister, James	RB	1975-76	43
McChesney, Bob	E	1950	86
McClellan, Mike	B	1962-63	23
McCloskey, Mike	TE	1987	84
McCoo, Eric	RB	2004	22
McCrary, Fred	FB	1995	41
McCullough, Hugh	B	1943	25
McCusker, Jim	T	1959-62	75
McDonald, Don	E	1944-46	81
McDonald, Lester	E	1940	26, 75
McDonald, Tommy	WR	1957-63	25
McDonough, Robert	G	1942-46	64
McDougle, Jerome	DE	2003-04	95
McFadden, Paul	K	1984-87	8
McHale, Tom	G/T	1993-94	68
McHugh, Pat	B	1947-51	49
McIntyre, Guy	G	1995-96	62
McKeever, Marlin	LB	1973	85
McKenzie, Kevin	WR	1998	88
McKenzie, Raleigh	C	1995-96	63
McKnight, Dennis	G	1991	62
McMahon, Jim	QB	1990-92	9
McMillan, Erik	S	1993	43
McMillen, Dan	DE	1987r	94
McMillian, Mark	CB	1992-95	29
McMullen, Billy	WR	2003-04	80, 81
McNabb, Dexter	FB	1995	38
McNabb, Donovan	QB	1999-04	5
McNeill, Tom	P	1971-73	12, 36
McPherson, Don	QB	1988-90	9
McPherson, Forrest	T	1935-37	26, 35
McRae, Jerrold	WR	1979	82

PLAYER	POSITION	YEAR	NUMBER
McTyer, Tim	CB	1997-98	24
Meadows, Ed	E	1958	66
Medved, Ron	DB	1966-70	45
Mellekas, John	T	1963	65
Mercer, Giradie	DT	2000	61
Merkens, Guido	QB	1987r	19
Meyer, Fred	E	1942-43	80, 89
Meyers, John	T	1964-67	75
Miano, Rich	DB	1991-94	38
Michaels, Ed	G	1943-46	60
Michel, Mike	P/K	1978	2
Michels, John	G	1953	61
Michels, John	T	1999	75
Middlebrook, Oren	WR	1978	81
Mikell, Quintin	S	2003-04	46
Mike-Mayer, Nick	K	1977-78	1
Millard, Keith	DT	1993	77
Miller, Bubba	C/G	1996-01	65
Miller, Don	B	1954	46
Miller, Tom	E	1943-44	89
Milling, Al	G	1942	51
Milon, Barnes	G	1934	30
Milons, Freddie	WR	2002	85
Mira, George	QB	1969	10
Miraldi, Dean	T	1982-84	64
Mitcham, Gene	E	1958	80
Mitchell, Brian	KR	2000-02	30
Mitchell, Freddie	WR	2001-04	84
Mitchell, Leonard	DL	1981-86	74, 99
Mitchell, Martin	DB	1977	48
Mitchell, Randall	NT	1987r	90
Molden, Frank	T	1968	74
Monk, Art	WR	1995	85
Monroe, Henry	CB	1979	24
Montgomery, Monty	CB	2001	25
Montgomery, Wilbert	RB	1977-84	31
Mooney, Tim	DE	1987r	74
Moore, Damon	S	1999-01	43
Morey, Sean	WR	2001, 2003	19, 85
Morgan, Dennis	KR	1975	42
Morgan, Mike	LB	1964-67	89
Morris, Dwaine	DT	1985	69
Morriss, Guy	C	1973-83	50, 62

PLAYER	POSITION	YEAR	NUMBER
Morse, Bobby	RB	1987	36
Mortell, Emmett	B	1937-39	31
Moseley, Mark	K	1970	3
Moselle, Dom	B	1954	24
Mrkonic, George	T	1953	72
Muha, Joe	B	1946-50	36
Muhlmann, Horst	K	1975-77	16
Mulligan, George	E	1936	42
Murley, Dick	T	1956	68
Murray, Calvin	HB	1981-82	42
Murray, Eddie	K	1994	3
Murray, Francis	B	1939-40	11
Myers, Brad	B	1958	46
Myers, Jack	B	1948-50	32
Nacelli, Andy	E	1958	87
Nease, Mike	C/T	1987r	78
Nelson, Al	DB	1965-73	26
Nelson, Dennis	T	1976-77	77
Nettles, Jim	DB	1965-68	9
Newton, Charles	B	1939-40	40
Nichols, Gerald	DT	1993	74
Niland, John	G	1975-76	74
Nipp, Maurice	G	1952-53, 1956	68
Nocera, John	LB	1959-62	29
Norby, Jack	B	1934	26
Nordquist, Mark	G	1968-74	68
Norton, Jerry	DB	1954-58	41
Norton, Jim	T	1968	73
Nowak, Walt	E	1944	81
Oakes, Don	T	1961-62	77
O'Boyle, Henry	B	1933	16
O'Brien, Davey	QB	1939-40	5, 8
O'Brien, Ken	QB	1993	7
Obst, Henry	G	1933	22
Oden, Derrick	LB	1993-95	58
Olds, Bill	RB	1976	38, 39
Oliver, Greg	RB	1973-74	48
Oliver, Hubie	FB	1981-85	34
O'Neal, Brian	FB	1994	31
Opperman, Jim	LB	1975	54
O'Quinn, John	E	1951	81
Oristaglio, Bob	E	1952	89
Ormsbe, Elliott	B	1946	40

PLAYER	POSITION	YEAR	NUMBER
Osborn, Mike	LB	1978	57
Osborne, Richard	TE	1976-78	86, 88
Outlaw, John	DB	1973-78	20
Overmeyer, Bill	LB	1972	56
Owens, Don	T	1958-60	70
Owens, Terrell	WR	2004	81
Pacella, Dave	G/C	1984	72
Padlow, Max	E	1935	28
Pagliei, Joe	B	1959	32
Palelei, Lonnie	T/G	1999	77
Palmer, Leslie	B	1948	40, 84
Panos, Joe	G	1994-97	63, 72
Papale, Vince	WR	1976-78	83
Parker, Artimus	DB	1974-76	24
Parker, Rodney	WR	1980-81	83
Parmer, Jim	B	1948-56	43
Parry, Josh	FB	2004	49
Paschka, Gordon	G	1943	61
Pastorini, Dan	QB	1982-83	6
Pate, Rupert	G	1942	63
Patton, Cliff	G	1946-50	65
Patton, Jerry	DT	1974	77
Payne, Ken	WR	1978	82
Peaks, Clarence	FB	1957-63	26
Pederson, Doug	QB	1999	14
Peete, Rodney	QB	1995-98	9
Pegg, Harold	C	940	19
Pellegrini, Bob	LB	1956, 1958-61	53
Penaranda, Jairo	RB	1985	38
Peoples, Woody	G	1978-80	69
Perot, Pete	G	1979-84	62
Perrino, Mike	T	1987r	64
Perry, William	DT	1993-94	90
Peters, Floyd	DT	1964-69	72
Peters, Scott	OL	2002	62
Peters, Volney	T	1958	76
Pettigrew, Gary	DT	1966-74	88
Philbin, Gerry	DE	1973	77
Phillips, Ray	LB	1978-81	52
Phillips, Ray	DE	1987r	93
Picard, Bob	WR	1973-76	82
Pihos, Pete	E	1947-55	35
Pilconis, Joe	E	1934, 1936-37	2, 18, 24, 28

PLAYER	POSITION	YEAR	NUMBER
Pinder, Cyril	RB	1968-70	22
Pinkston, Todd	WR	2000-04	87
Piro, Henry	E	1941	89
Pisarcik, Joe	QB	1980-84	9
Pitts, Alabama	B	1935	50
Pitts, Mike	DL	1987-92	74
Pivarnick, Joe	G	1936	29
Poage, Ray	E	1964-65	35
Pollard, Al	B	1951-53	21
Polley, Tom	LB	1985	57
Porter, Ron	LB	1969-72	50
Poth, Phil	G	1934	23
Powell, Art	WR	1959	87
Powlus, Ron	QB	2000	11
Preece, Steve	DB	1970-72	33
Prescott, Harold	E	1947-49	86
President, Andre	TE	1997	48
Priestly, Robert	E	1942	81
Prisco, Nick	B	1933	18
Pritchard, Bosh	B	1942, 1946-51	30
Pritchett, Stanley	FB	2000	36
Puetz, Garry	T	1979	64
Pylman, Bob	T	1938-39	39
Pyne, Jim	C/G	2001	73
Quick, Mike	WR	1982-90	82
Quinlan, Bill	DE	1963	83
Rado, George	E	1937-38	27
Ragazzo, Phil	T	1940-41	31, 77
Ramsey, Herschel	E	1938-40, 1945	12, 88
Ramsey, Knox	G	1952	62
Ramsey, Nate	DB	1963-72	24
Rash, Lou	CB	1984	28
Raskowski, Leo	T	1935	45
Ratliff, Don	DE	1975	77
Rauch, John	QB	1951	11
Rayburn, Sam	DT	2003-04	91
Raye, Jim	DB	1969	30
Reader, Jamie	FB	2001	34
Reagan, Frank	B	1949-51	40
Reaves, John	QB	1972-74	6, 7
Recher, Dave	C	1965-68	50, 51
Reed, J.R.	S	2004	30
Reed, James	LB	1977	57

PLAYER	POSITION	YEAR	NUMBER
Reed, Michael	FB	1998	39
Reed, Taft	B	1967	17
Reese, Henry	C/LB	1935-39	20, 25
Reese, Ike	LB	1998-04	58
Reeves, Ken	T	1985-89	66
Reeves, Marion	DB	1974	45
Reichenbach, Mike	LB	1984-89	55
Reichow, Jerry	E	1960	17
Reid, Alan	RB	1987	24
Reid, Mike	S	1993-94	42
Reilly, Kevin	LB	1973-74	52
Renfro, Leonard	DT	1993-94	94
Renfro, Will	E	1961	66
Repko, Jay	TE	1987r	89
Restic, Joe	E	1952	82
Retzlaff, Pete	TE	1956-66	25, 44
Reutt, Ray	E	1943	81
Ricca, Jim	T	1955-56	71
Richards, Bobby	DE	1962-65	68
Richardson, Jess	DT	1953-61	65, 72
Richardson, Paul	WR	1993	81
Riffle, Dick	B	1938-40	45
Riley, Lee	DB	1956, 1958-59	22
Rimington, Dave	C	1988-89	50
Ringo, Jim	C	1964-67	54
Rissmiller, Ray	T	1966	77
Ritchie, Jon	FB	2003-04	48
Robb, Joe	DE	1959-60	66
Roberts, John	B	1933-34	12
Robinson, Burle	E	1935	27
Robinson, Jacque	FB	1987r	22
Robinson, Jerry	LB	1979-84	56
Robinson, Wayne	LB	1952-56	52
Roffler, William	B	1954	23
Rogalla, John	B	1945	32
Rogas, Dan	G	1952	65
Romanowski, Bill	LB	1994-95	53
Romero, Ray	G	1951	68
Roper, John	LB	1993	53
Rose, Ken	LB	1990-94	55
Ross, Alvin	FB	1987r	41
Ross, Oliver	T	1999	73
Rossovich, Tim	LB	1968-71	82

PLAYER	POSITION	YEAR	NUMBER
Rossum, Allen	KR	1998-99	25
Roton, Herbert	E	1937	18, 36
Roussel, Tom	LB	1973	54
Rowan, Everitt	E	1933	32
Rowe, Robert	B	1935	37
Royals, Mark	P	1987r	5
Rucker, Keith	DT	1996	96
Rudolph, Joe	G	1995	64
Runager, Max	P	1979-83, 1989	4
Runyan, John	T	2000-04	69
Russell, Booker	FB	1981	32
Russell, James	T	1936-37	17, 22
Russell, Laf	B	1933	15
Russell, Rusty	T	1984	79
Ruzek, Roger	K	1989-93	7
Ryan, Pat	QB	1991	10
Ryan, Rocky	E	1956-58	45
Ryczek, Paul	C	1987r	73
Rypien, Mark	QB	1996	11
Sader, Steve	B	1943	33
Saidock, Tom	T	1957	75
Sampleton, Lawrence	TE	1982-84	87
Samson, Michael	DT	1996	98
Sanders, John	G	1945	67
Sanders, John	DB	1977-79	26
Sanders, Thomas	RB	1990-91	45
Sandifer, Dan	DB	1950-51	31
Sapp, Theron	B	1959-63	30
Savitsky, George	T	1948-49	64, 75
Saxon, James	FB	1995	22
Scarpati, Joe	S	1964-69, 1971	21
Schad, Mike	G	1989-93	79
Schaefer, Don	B	1956	24
Schau, Ryan	G/T	1999-01	67
Schmitt, Ted	C	1938-40	41
Schnelker, Bob	E	1953	85
Schneller, Bill	B	1940	24
Schrader, Jim	C	1962-64	51
Schreiber, Adam	C/G	1986-88	76
Schuehle, Jake	B	1939	38
Schultz, Eberle	G	1940, 1943	48, 71
Schulz, Jody	LB	1983-7	53, 95
Sciarra, John	DB	1978-83	21

PLAYER	POSITION	YEAR	NUMBER
Sciullo, Steve	G	2004	68
Scott, Clyde	B	1949-52	27
Scott, Gari	WR	2000	16, 86
Scott, Tom	DE	1953-58	82
Scotti, Ben	B	1962-63	48
Seals, Leon	DT	1992	97
Sears, Vic	T	1941-53	79
Seay, Mark	WR	1996-97	81
Sebastian, Mike	B	1935	34
Selby, Rob	G	1991-94	75
Shann, Bob	B	1965, 1967	25
Sharkey, Ed	T	1954-55	66
Shaub, Harry	G	1935	23
Shaw, Ricky	LB	1989-90	51
Sheppard, Lito	CB	2002-04	26
Sherman, Al	B	1943-47	10
Sherman, Heath	RB	1989-93	23
Shires, Marshall	T	1945	72
Shonk, John	E	1941	85
Short, Jason	LB	2004	52
Shuler, Mickey	TE	1990-91	82, 85
Siano, Mike	WR	1987r	86
Sikahema, Vai	KR	1992-93	22
Simerson, John	C	1957-58	53, 64
Simmons, Clyde	DE	1986-93	96
Simon, Corey	DT	2000-04	90
Simoneau, Mark	LB	2003-04	50, 53
Sinceno, Kaseem	TE	1998	89
Singletary, Reggie	DT/G	1986-90	68, 97
Sisemore, Jerry	T	1973-84	76
Sistrunk, Manny	DT	1976-79	79
Skaggs, Jim	G	1963-72	70
Skladany, Leo	E	1949	63
Skladany, Tom	P	1983	5
Slater, Mark	C	1979-83	61
Slay, Henry	DT	1998	95
Slechta, Jeremy	DT	2002	79
Small, Jessie	LB	1989-91	52
Small, Torrance	WR	1999-00	80
Smalls, Fred	LB	1987r	53
Smart, Rod	RB	2001	24
Smeja, Rudy	E	1946	82
Smith, Ben	DB	1990-93	26

PLAYER	POSITION	YEAR	NUMBER
Smith, Charles	WR	1974-81	85
Smith, Darrin	LB	1997	56
Smith, Daryle	T	1990-92	63, 75
Smith, Ed	TE	1999	89
Smith, J.D.	T	1959-63	76
Smith, Jack	E	1942	83
Smith, Jackie	DB	1971	32
Smith, John	T	1945	83
Smith, L.J.	TE	2003-04	82
Smith, Milton	E	1945	30, 82
Smith, Otis	CB	1991-04	30
Smith, Phil	WR	1986	83
Smith, Ralph	E	1962-04	85
Smith, Ray	C	1933	29
Smith, Rich	C	1933	35
Smith, Robert	B	1956	43
Smith, Ron	WR	1981-83	81
Smith, Steve	T	1971-74	74, 78
Smith, Troy	WR	1999	19, 83
Smothers, Howard	G	1995	77
Smukler, Dave	B	1936-39	13
Snead, Norm	QB	1964-70	16
Snyder, Lum	T	1952-55, 1958	73, 79
Sodaski, John	LB	1972-73	96
Solomon, Freddie	WR	1995-98	17, 84
Solt, Ron	G	1988-91	65
Somers, George	T	1939-40	19
Spagnola, John	TE	1979-87	88
Spillers, Ray	T	1937	33
Stackpool, John	B	1942	36
Stacy, Siran	RB	1992	27
Stafford, Dick	E	1962-63	86
Staley, Duce	RB	1997-03	22
Steele, Ernie	B	1942-48	37
Steere, Dick	T	1951	72
Steinbach, Laurence	T	1933	34
Steinke, Gil	B	1945-48	41
Stetz, Bill	G	1967	65
Stevens, Don	B	1952, 1954	20
Stevens, Matt	S	1997-98	45
Stevens, Pete	C	1936	20
Stevens, Richard	T	1970-74	73
Steward, Dean	B	1943	36

PLAYER	POSITION	YEAR	NUMBER
Stewart, Tony	TE	2001	81
Stickel, Walt	T	1950-51	75
Stockton, Herschel	G	1937-38	21
Storm, Edward	B	1934-35	22
Strauthers, Tom	DE	1983-86	93
Stribling, Bill	E	1955-57	80
Striegel, Bill	G	1959	68
Stringer, Bob	B	1952-53	44
Stubbs, Dan	DE	1995	93
Sturgeon, Cecil	T	1941	71
Sturm, Jerry	C	1972	55
Suffridge, Bob	G	1941, 1945	60, 75
Sugar, Leo	DE	1961	84
Sullivan, Tom	RB	1972-77	25
Supluski, Leonard	E	1942	80
Sutton, Joe	B	1950-52	45
Sutton, Mitch	DT	1974-75	79
Swift, Justin	TE	1999	89
Sydner, Jeff	WR	1992-94	85
Szafaryn, Len	T	1957-58	74, 76
Szymanski, Frank	C	1948	51
Talcott, Don	T	1947	62
Taliaferro, George	QB	1955	24
Tamburello, Ben	C/G	1987-90	61
Tapeh, Thomas	FB	2004	41
Tarasovic, George	DE	1963-65	82
Tarver, John	RB	1975	49
Taseff, Carl	DB	1961	23
Tautalatasi, Taivale	RB	1986-88	37
Tautolo, Terry	LB	1976-79	58
Taylor, Bobby	CB	1995-03	21
Teltschik, John	P	1986-90	10
Thacker, Alvin	B	1942	60
Thomas, Hollis	DT	1996-04	78
Thomas, Johnny	CB	1996	41
Thomas, Markus	RB	1993	46
Thomas, Tra	T	1998-04	72
Thomas, William	LB	1991-99	51
Thomason, Bobby	QB	1952-57	11
Thomason, Jeff	TE	2000-02, 2004	83, 85
Thomason, Stumpy	B	1935-36	15, 29
Thompson, Broderick	T	1993-94	76
Thompson, Don	E	1964	84

PLAYER	POSITION	YEAR	NUMBER
Thompson, Russ	T	1940	25
Thompson, Tommy	QB	1941-42, 1945-50	10, 11
Thoms, Art	DE	1977	80
Thornton, Richard	B	1933	28
Thrash, James	WR	2001-03	80
Thrower, Jim	DB	1970-72	49
Thurbon, Robert	B	1943	49
Timpson, Michael	WR	1997	83
Tinsley, Scott	QB	1987r	11
Tom, Mel	DE	1967-73	58, 99
Tomasetti, Lou	B	1940-41	15
Toney, Anthony	FB	1986-90	25
Torrey, Bob	FB	1980	39
Townsend, Greg	DE	1994	93
Tracey, John	DE	1961	80
Tremble, Greg	DB	1995	25
Tripucka, Frank	QB	1949	10
Trost, Milt	T	1940	27
Trotter, Jeremiah	LB	1998-01, 2004	54
Troup, Bill	QB	1975	12
Tupper, Jeff	DE	1986	69
Turnbow, Guy	T	1933-34	28, 33
Turner, Kevin	FB	1995-99	34
Turral, Willie	RB	1987r	23
Tuten, Rick	P	1989	14
Tyrell, Joe	G	1952	69
Ulmer, Michael	DB	1987r	32
Unutoa, Morris	C	1996-98	68
Upersa, Tuufuli	G	1971	75
Valentine, Zack	LB	1982-83	54
Van Brocklin, Norm	QB	1958-60	11
Van Buren, Ebert	B	1951-53	17, 31
Van Buren, Steve	RB	1944-51	15
Van Dyke, Alex	WR	1999-00	86
Van Dyke, Bruce	G	1966	66
Vasys, Arunas	LB	1966-68	61
Vick, Roger	RB	1990	43
Vincent, Troy	CB	1996-03	23
Wagner, Steve	S	1980	42
Wainwright, Frank	TE	1995	87
Walik, Billy	WR	1970-72	9
Walker, Adam	FB	1996	29
Walker, Corey	RB	1997-98	29, 39

PLAYER	POSITION	YEAR	NUMBER
Walker, Darwin	DT	2000-04	97
Walker, Herschel	RB	1992-94	34
Wallace, Al	DE/LB	1997-99	96
Walston, Bobby	E/K	1951-62	83
Walters, Pete	G	1987r	68
Walters, Stan	T	1975-83	75
Walton, John	QB	1976-79	10, 11
Ward, Jim	QB	1971	7
Ware, Matt	CB	2004	21
Warren, Busit	B	1945	41
Warren, Chris	RB	2000	35
Waters, Andre	S/LB	1984-93	20
Waters, Mike	FB	1986	33
Watkins, Foster	B	1940-41	39, 41
Watkins, Larry	B	1970-72	34
Watson, Edwin	RB	1999	35
Watson, Tim	S	1997	33
Watters, Ricky	RB	1995-97	32
Wayne, Nate	LB	2003-04	51, 54
Wear, Robert	C	1942	51
Weatherall, Jim	T	1955-57	77
Weaver, Jed	TE	1999	87
Weber, Chuck	LB	1959-61	51
Weedon, Don	G	1947	60
Wegert, Ted	B	1955-56	46
Weiner, Albert	B	1934	18
Weinstock, Isadore	B	1935	10
Welbourn, John	G/T	1999-03	76
Weldon, Casey	QB	1992	11
Wells, Billy	B	1958	27
Wells, Harold	LB	1965-68	53
Wendlick, Joseph	B	1940	59
Wenzel, Jeff	T	1987r	72
West, Ed	TE	1995-96	83
West, Hodges	T	1941	72
West, Troy	S	1987r	31
Westbrook, Brian	RB	2002-04	36
Whalen, Jim	TE	1971	81
Wheeler, Mark	DT	1999	97
White, Allison	T	1939	21
White, Reggie	DE	1985-92	91, 92
Whiting, Brandon	DL	1998-03	98
Whitmore, David	S	1995	42
Whittingham, Fred	LB	1966, 1971	53, 56

PLAYER	POSITION	YEAR	NUMBER
Wilburn, Barry	S	1995-96	45
Wilcox, John	T	1960	71
Wilkes, Reggie	LB	1978-85	51
Wilkins, Jeff	K	1994	14
Will, Erwin	DT	1965	67
Willey, Norm	DE	1950-57	44, 63, 86
Williams, Ben	DT	1999	90
Williams, Bernard	T	1994	74
Williams, Bobbie	G	2000, 2003	66
Williams, Boyd	C	1947	51
Williams, Byron	WR	1983	80
Williams, Calvin	WR	1990-96	89
Williams, Charlie	CB	1978	47
Williams, Clyde	T	1935	20
Williams, Henry	WR	1989	81
Williams, Jerry	B	1953-54	49
Williams, Joel	LB	1983-85	59
Williams, Michael	RB	1983-84	32
Williams, Roger	DB	1973	23
Williams, Ted	B	1942	31
Williams, Tex	G	1942	77
Williams, Tyrone	DE	1999-00	95
Willis, James	LB	1995-98	50
Wilson, Bill	E	1938	23
Wilson, Brenard	S	1979-86	22
Wilson, Harry	B	1967-70	41
Wilson, Jerry	E	1959-60	88
Willson, Osborne	G	1933-35	15, 25
Winfield, Vern	G	1972-73	67
Wink, Dean	DT	1967-68	64
Wirgowski, Dennis	DE	1973	75
Wistert, Al	T	1943-51	70
Witherspoon, Derrick	RB	1995-97	31
Wittenborn, John	G	1960-62	62
Wojciechowicz, Alex	C	1946-50	53
Wolfe, Hugh	B	1940	32
Woltman, Clem	T	1938-40	15
Woodard, Marc	LB	1994-96	57
Woodeshick, Tom	RB	1963-71	37
Woodruff, Lee	B	1933	11
Woodruff, Tony	WR	1982-84	83
Woodson, Sean	S	1998	37
Worden, Neil	RB	1954, 1957	32

PLAYER	POSITION	YEAR	NUMBER
Woulfe, Mike	LB	1962	63
Wright, Gordon	G	1967	66
Wright, Sylvester	LB	1995-96	52
Wukits, Al	C	1943	50
Wyatt, Antwuan	WR	1997	85
Wydo, Frank	T	1952-57	74, 75
Wyhonic, John	G	1946-47	66
Wynn, Dexter	CB	2004	31
Wynn, William	DE	1973-76	71
Young, Adrian	LB	1968-72	35
Young, Charles	TE	1973-76	86
Young, Glen	WR	1983	89
Young, Michael	WR	1993	83
Young, Roynell	CB	1980-88	43
Youngelman, Sid	T	1956-58	73
Yovicsin, John	E	1944	81
Zabel, Steve	LB	1970-74	89
Zandofsky, Mike	G	1997	66
Zendejas, Luis	K	1988-89	8
Ziegler, Frank	B	1949-53	41
Zilly, John	E	1952	88
Zimmerman, Don	WR	1973-76	80
Zimmerman, Roy	QB	1943-46	7
Zizak, Vince	T	1934-37	23
Zomalt, Eric	S	1994-96	27
Zordich, Mike	S	1994-98	36
Zyntell, James	G	1933-35	9, 16, 21

Bibliography

Books

Allen, George, with Ben Olan. *Pro Football's 100 Greatest Players: Rating the Stars of Past and Present*. Indianapolis: Bobbs-Merrill, 1982.

Anastasia, Phil. *Broken Wing, Broken Promise: A Season Inside the Philadelphia Eagles*. Philadelphia: Camino Books, 1993.

Ashe, Arthur. *A Hard Road to Glory: A History of the African-American Athlete*. New York: Warner Books, 1988.

Barber, Phil. *Football America: Celebrating America's National Passion*. Atlanta : Turner Publishing, 1996.

Benedict, Jeff, and Don Yeager. *Pros and Cons: The Criminals Who Play in the NFL*. New York: Warner Books, 1998.

Bennett, Tom. *The Pro Style*. Englewood Cliffs, NJ: Prentice-Hall, 1976.

Blount, Roy, Jr. *About Three Bricks Shy of a Load: A Highly Irregular Lowdown of the Year the Pittsburgh Steelers Were Super But Missed the Bowl*. Boston: Little, Brown and Company, 1974.

Bowden, Mark. *Bringing the Heat*. New York: Knopf, 1994.

Campbell, Donald. *Sunday's Warriors*. Philadelphia: Quantum Leap, 1994.

Campbell, Jim. *Golden Years of Pro Football*. Avenel, NJ: Crescent Books, 1993.

Carroll, Bob, Pete Palmer and John Thorn. *The Hidden Game of Football: The Next Edition*. New York: Total Sports, 1998.

Carroll, Bob, Michael Gershman, David Neft, and John Thorn. *Total Football: The Official Encyclopedia of the National Football League*. New York: HarperCollins, 1999.

Carroll, Bob. *When the Grass Was Real: Unitas, Brown, Lombardi, Sayers, Butkus, Namath and All the Rest: The Ten Best Years of Pro Football*. New York: Simon and Schuster, 1993.

Chalk, Ocania. *Pioneers of Black Sport: The Early Days of the Black Professional Athlete in Baseball, Basketball, Boxing, and Football*. New York: Dodd, Mead, 1975.

Claassen, Harold (Spike). *The History of Professional Football*. Englewood Cliffs, NJ: Prentice-Hall, 1963.

Clary, Jack. *Pro Football's Great Moments*. New York: Bonanza Books, 1983.

Cohen, David. *Rugged and Enduring: The Eagles, the Browns and 5 Years of Football*. Philadelphia: Xlibris, 2001.

Cohen, Richard M., Jordan A. Deutsch, Roland T. Johnson and David S. Neft. *The Scrapbook History of Pro Football*. Indianapolis: Bobbs-Merrill, 1976.

Cope, Myron. *The Game That Was: An Illustrated Account of the Tumultuous Early Days of Pro Football*. New York: Crowell, 1974.

Cunningham, Randall, and Steve Wartenberg. *I'm Still Scrambling*. New York: Doubleday, 1993.

Curran, Bob. *Pro Football's Rag Days*. Englewood Cliffs, NJ: Prentice-Hall, 1969.

Daley, Arthur. *Pro Football's Hall of Fame*. New York: Grosset and Dunlap, 1968.

Daly, Dan, and Bob O'Donnell. *The Pro Football Chronicle: The Complete (Well Almost) Record of the Best Players, the Greatest Photos, the Hardest Hits, the Biggest Scandals, and the Funniest Stories in Pro Football*. New York: Collier Books, 1990.

Dolson, Frank. *The Philadelphia Story: A City of Losers, Winners*. South Bend, IN: Icarus, 1981.

Eisenberg, John. *Cotton Bowl Days: Growing Up with Dallas and the Cowboys in the 1960s*. New York: Simon and Schuster, 1997.

Exley, Frederick. *A Fan's Notes: A Fictional Memoir*. New York: Random House, 1968.

Forbes, Gordon. *Tales from the Eagles Sidelines*. Champaign, IL: Sports Publishing, 2002.

Garraty, John A., and Mark C. Carnes (eds). *American National Biography*. New York: Oxford University Press, 1999.

Golenbock, Peter. *Cowboys Have Always Been My Heroes: The Definitive Oral History of America's Team*. New York: Warner Books, 1997.

Goodman, Murray, and Leonard Lewin. *My Greatest Day in Football*. New York: Barnes, 1948.

Gordon, Robert. *The 1960 Philadelphia Eagles: The Team That They Said Had Nothing But a Championship*. Champaign, IL: Sports Publishing, 2001.

Green, Jerry. *Super Bowl Chronicles: A Sportswriter Reflects on the First 25 Years of America's Game*. Grand Rapids, MI: Masters Press, 1991.

Harrington, Denis. *The Pro Football Hall of Fame: Players, Coaches, Team Owners and League Officials, 1963-1991*. Jefferson, NC: McFarland, 1991.

Harris, David. *The League: The Rise and Decline of the NFL*. New York: Bantam Books, 1986.

Hersch, Hank. *The Greatest Football Games of All Time*. New York: Sports Illustrated/Time-Life, 1998.

Herskowitz, Mickey. *The Golden Age of Pro Football: NFL Football in the 1950s*. Dallas: Taylor Publishing, 1990.

————. *The Quarterbacks: The Uncensored Truth About the Men in the Pocket*. New York: Morrow, 1990.

Izenberg, Jerry. *Championship: The Complete NFL Title Story*. New York: Four Winds Press, 1966.

Kaine, Elinor. *Pro Football Broadside*. New York: Macmillan, 1969.

King, Joe. *Inside Pro Football*. Englewood Cliffs, NJ: Prentice-Hall, 1958.

King, Peter. *Football: A History of the Professional Game*. New York: Bishop Books/Time, Inc. Home Entertainment, 1997.

Greatest Quarterbacks. New York: Bishop Books Time. Inc. Home Entertainment, 1999.

Kuklick, Bruce. *To Every Thing a Season: Shibe Park and Urban Philadelphia, 1909-76*. Princeton, NJ: Princeton University Press, 1991.

LaBlanc, Michael L., (ed). *Football*. (Professional Sports Team Histories Series.) Detroit: Gale Research, 1994.

Landry, Tom, with Gregg Lewis. *Tom Landry: An Autobiography*. Grand Rapids, MI: Zondervan Publishing, 1990.

Leuthner, Stuart. *Iron Men: Bucko, Crazy Legs, and the Boys Recall the Golden Days of Professional Football*. New York: Doubleday, 1988.

Longoria, Mario. *Athletes Remembered: Mexicano/Latino Professional Football Players, 1929-70*. Tempe, AZ: Bilingual Press, 1997.

Lyon, Bill. *When the Clock Runs Out: 20 NFL Greats Share Their Stories of Hardship and Triumph*. Chicago: Triumph Books, 1999.

MacCambridge, Michael. *America's Game: The Epic Story of How Pro Football Captured a Nation*. New York: Random House, 2004.

Macnow, Glen, and Anthony L. Gargano. *The Great Philadelphia Fan Book*. Moorestown, NJ: Middle Atlantic Press, 2003.

Macnow, Glen, and Angelo Cataldi. *The Great Philadelphia Sports Debate*. Moorestown, NJ: Middle Atlantic Press, 2004.

Maraniss, David. *When Pride Still Mattered: A Life of Vince Lombardi*. New York: Simon and Schuster, 1999.

March, Harry. *Pro Football, Its "Ups" and "Downs": A Lighthearted History of the Post Graduate Game*. Albany, NY: J. B. Lyon, 1934.

Maule, Tex. *The Game: The Official Picture History of the NFL and AFL*. New York: Random House, 1967.

————. *The Players*. New York: New American Library, 1967.

McCallum, Jack, with Chuck Bednarik. *Bednarik: Last of the Sixty Minute Men*. Englewood Cliffs, NJ: Prentice-Hall, 1977.

McClellan, Keith. *The Sunday Game: At the Dawn of Professional Football*. Akron, OH: University of Akron Press, 1998.

McCullough, Bob. *My Greatest Day in Football: The Legends of Football Recount Their Greatest Moments*. New York: Thomas Dunne Books, 2001.

McDonald, Tommy, and Ed Richter. *They Pay Me to Catch Footballs*. Philadelphia: Chilton, 1962.

McGrane, Bill. *Bud: The Other Side of the Glacier*. New York: HarperCollins, 1986.

Merchant, Larry. *...And Every Day You Take Another Bite*. Garden City, NY: Doubleday, 1971.

Michael, Paul. *Professional Football's Greatest Games*. Englewood Cliffs, NJ: Prentice-Hall, 1972.

Neft, David S., Richard M. Cohen and Richard Korch. *The Football Encyclopedia: The Complete History of Professional Football from 1892 to the Present*. New York: St. Martin's, 1994.

Olderman, Murray. *The Pro Quarterback*. Englewood Cliffs, NJ: Prentice-Hall, 1966.

————. *The Running Backs*. Englewood Cliffs, NJ: Prentice-Hall, 1969.

Owens, Terrell, and Stephen Singular. *Catch This: Going Deep with the NFL's Sharpest Weapon*. New York: Simon and Schuster, 2004.

Peterson, Robert. *Pigskin: The Early Years of Pro Football*. New York: Oxford University Press, 1997.

Porter, David L. (ed.). *Biographical Dictionary of American Sports: Football*. New York: Greenwood Press, 1987.

————. *Biographical Dictionary of American Sports, 1989-1992: Supplement for Baseball, Football, Basketball, and Other Sports*. New York: Greenwood Press, 1992.

————. *Biographical Dictionary of American Sports, 1992-1995: Supplement for Baseball, Football, Basketball, and Other Sports*. Westport, CT: Greenwood Press, 1995.

Pruyne, Terry W. *Sports Nicknames: 20,000 Professionals Worldwide*. Jefferson, NC: McFarland, 2002

Rathet, Mike, and Don R. Smith. *Their Deeds and Dogged Faith*. New York: Rutledge Books, 1984.

Reese, Merrill, and Mark Eckel. *Merrill Reese: "It's Gooooood!"* Champaign, IL: Sports Publishing, 1998.

Riffenburgh, Beau. *Great Ones: NFL Quarterbacks from Baugh to Montana*. New York: Viking, 1989.

Riger, Robert. *Best Plays of the Year 1962: A Documentary of Pro Football in the National Football League*. Englewood Cliffs, NJ: Prentice-Hall, 1963.

————. *Best Plays of the Year 1963: A Documentary of Pro Football in the National Football League*. Englewood Cliffs, NJ: Prentice-Hall, 1964.

Ross, Charles K. *Outside the Lines: African-Americans and the Integration of the National Football League*. New York: New York University Press, 1999.

Sahadi, Lou. *Super Sundays I-XVI*. Chicago: Contemporary Books, 1982.

Schaap, Dick. *Quarterbacks Have All the Fun: The Good Life and Hard Times of Bart, Johnny, Joe, Francis, and Other Great Quarterbacks*. Chicago: Playboy Press, 1974.

75 Seasons: The Complete Story of the National Football League, 1920-1995. Atlanta: Turner Publishing, 1994.

Smith, Myron J. *Pro Football: The Official Pro Football Hall of Fame Bibliography*. Westport, CT: Greenwood Press, 1993.

_____ . *The Pro Football Bio-Bibliography*. West Cornwall, CT: Locust Hill Press, 1989.

Smith, Robert. *Illustrated History of Pro Football*. New York: Grossett and Dunlap, 1977.

Smith, Ron. *The Sporting News Selects Football's 100 Greatest Players: A Celebration of the 20th Century's Best*. St. Louis: Sporting News, 1999.

_____ . *Sporting News Books Presents Pro Football's Heroes of the Hall*. St. Louis: Sporting News, 2003.

Strother, Shelby. *NFL Top 40: The Greatest Football Games of All Time*. New York: Viking, 1988.

Sugar, Bert Randolph. *I Hate the Dallas Cowboys: And Who Elected Them America's Team Anyway?* New York: St. Martin's/Griffin, 1997.

Sullivan, George. *Pro Football's All-Time Greatest: The Immortals in Pro Football's Hall of Fame*. New York: Putnam, 1968.

The Super Bowl: Celebrating a Quarter Century of America's Greatest Game. New York: Simon and Schuster, 1990.

Thorn, John. *Pro Football's Ten Greatest Games*. New York: Four Winds Press, 1981.

_____ . *The Armchair Quarterback*. New York: Scribner's, 1982.

Van Brocklin, Norm, and Hugh Brown. *Norm Van Brocklin's Football Book: Passing, Punting, Quarterbacking*. New York: Ronald Press, 1961.

Wagner, Len. *Launching the Glory Years: The 1959 Packers — What They Didn't Tell Us*. Green Bay, WI: Coach's Books Jay Bengtson, 2001.

Westcott, Rich. *Philadelphia's Old Ballparks*. Philadelphia: Temple University Press, 1996.

_____ . *A Century of Philadelphia Sports*. Philadelphia: Temple University Press, 2001.

White, Reggie, with Terry Hill. *Reggie White: Minister of Defense*. Brentwood, TN: Wolgemuth and Hyatt, 1991

White, Reggie, with Jim Denney. *In the Trenches: The Autobiography*. Nashville, TN: Thomas Nelson, 1996.

White, Reggie with Steve Hubbard. *God's Playbook: The Bible's Game Plan for Life*. Nashville, TN: Thomas Nelson, 1998.

Whittingham, Richard. *What a Game They Played*. New York: Harper and Row, 1974.

Wiebusch, John (ed.). *More Than a Game*. Englewood Cliffs, NJ: Prentice-Hall, 1974.

Zimmerman, Paul. *The New Thinking Man's Guide to Pro Football*. New York: Simon and Schuster, 1984.

Zimniuch, Fran. *Eagles: Where Have You Gone?* Champaign, IL: Sports Publishing, 2004.

Newspapers

The following were checked extensively:

Chicago Tribune

Evening Bulletin (Philadelphia)

Los Angeles Times

New York Times

Philadelphia Daily News

Philadelphia Inquirer

Washington Post

Periodicals

The following were the most prolific periodical sources:

Colliers
Football Digest
Life
Newsweek
Philadelphia Eagles Media Guides
Saturday Evening Post
Sport
Sports Illustrated
Time

Videos and DVDs

Highlights of the 1960 Championship Game. NFL Films/Fox Hills Video, 1986.
The Philadelphia Eagles: The Complete History. NFL Films/Warner Home Video, 2004.

Web Sites

College Football Hall of Fame (http://collegefootball.org/)
Concrete Field (http://www.concretefield.com/index.php)
Current Team Histories (http://www.jt-sw.com/football/pro/teams.nsf)
Draft History (http://www.drafthistory.com/index.php)
Ghosts of the Gridiron (http://www.geocities.com/ghostsofthegridiron/)
NFL.com (http://www.nfl.com/)
NFL History Network (http://nflhistory.net/)
Philadelphia Eagles (http://www.philadelphiaeagles.com/default.jsp)
The Pro Football Encyclopedia (http://www.profootballencyclopedia.com/index.htm)
Pro Football Hall of Fame (http://www.profootballhof.com/)
Professional Football Researchers Association (http://www.footballresearch.com/)